Harvard Historical Studies · 127

Published under the auspices
of the Department of History
from the income of the
Paul Revere Frothingham Bequest
Robert Louis Stroock Fund
Henry Warren Torrey Fund

DOROTHEA DIX
New England Reformer

THOMAS J. BROWN

HARVARD UNIVERSITY PRESS
Cambridge, Massachusetts
London, England
1998

Library of Congress Cataloging-in-Publication Data

Brown, Thomas J., 1960–
Dorothea Dix : New England reformer / Thomas J. Brown.
p.   cm. — (Harvard historical studies ; 127)
Includes bibliographical references and index.
ISBN 0-674-21488-9 (alk. paper)
1. Dix, Dorothea Lynde, 1802–1887.
2. Women social reformers—United States—Biography.
3. Unitarians—United States—Biography.
4. Mentally ill—Care—United States—History.   I. Title.
II. Series: Harvard historical studies ; v. 127.
HV28.D6B75   1998
362.2′1′092
[B]—DC21   97-44207

Designed by Gwen Nefsky Frankfeldt

For my mother and father

Contents

Illustrations

Preface

DOROTHEA DIX'S authorized biographer boldly presented his work in 1890 as a direct rebuttal to George Eliot's recent *Middlemarch*. Dix, he argued, embodied precisely the character that the novelist had sought to create, a modern Teresa of Ávila confronted with the clash between her heroic sense of consecration and the prosaic lives open to women in the nineteenth century. Contrary to the tragic fate of Eliot's protagonist, Dix's transformation from a timid, ailing spinster into a humanitarian crusader demonstrated that spiritual grandeur could still find a suitable medium of expression. Much as her saintly prototype had revitalized religion by founding convents, Dix had reformed the moral sensibility of her time by persuading state legislatures, the federal government, the British Parliament, and even the pope to establish mental hospitals for the poor.[1]

While disclaiming such expansive literary and philosophical pretensions, this biography begins from the similar premise that the central interest of Dorothea Dix, like that of Dorothea Brooke, is the story of "a mind struggling towards an ideal life."[2] Both sought by force of will to realize deeply conventional dreams of glorious self-sacrifice. In both cases, the forging of an altruistic personality led to inner conflict, and in both cases, Dix's remarkable achievements notwithstanding, the ardent and arduous quest ended in crushing frustration. These collisions between imagination and experience can be used to illuminate some of the tensions in the cultural and social patterns of an era.

To be sure, Dix escaped spectacularly, if narrowly and unforeseeably, from the buried life that Eliot portrayed. Her struggle to personify conventional ideals involved extraordinary challenges, for more than any other woman of her generation she lived at the center of both the so-called separate spheres of female virtue and public affairs. In August 1852, for example, she read Susan Warner's domestic epic *Wide, Wide World* during the evenings with a sense of religious rapture while she devoted her days to consulting with the president of the United States and issuing instructions to senators for the congressional debate over the legislation known as "Miss Dix's bill." Close examination of her goals and methods as a lobbyist brings a crucial figure into the recent exploration of the political lives of nineteenth-century women. The strategies she developed in pursuit of her cause and the resources she mobilized demonstrate the means by which conservative women worked within prevailing gender norms to exercise policymaking influence without the prospect of voting or holding office. At the same time, the dilemmas she confronted and the limits of her political perceptions reveal some of the contradictions in the ideology she sought to implement.

This approach to Dix contrasts sharply with previous biographies that treat her career primarily as a vehicle for tracing changes in the treatment of insanity.[3] Needless to say, the following pages fully detail Dix's role in the growth and decline of the asylum regimen known as "the moral treatment." But a narrow focus on Dix as the spokeswoman for a therapeutic movement misunderstands her sweeping goals for the regeneration of American society and confuses the background to her efforts with the immediate context in which she worked. The intellectual transformation culminating in the moral treatment had spread widely before Dix took a special interest in insanity, an initiative that owed less to medical theories than to her early aspirations as a schoolteacher to present a broadly applicable model of moral discipline. Her ideas about insanity and education, like her ideas about the social role of women, were for the most part not novel; the burden of her career was to fuse these ideas and seek their fulfillment in specific political settings.

The implications of recognizing Dix as a participant in American politics rather than a humanitarian visionary are illustrated by her most important legislative initiative, the six-year congressional campaign to fund a network of state mental hospitals through a revenue-sharing program similar to the plan later adopted to establish land-grant colleges.

The issue presented by her proposal was not the nature of insanity but the nature of public lands. The proceedings on the bill intersected constantly with the related controversies about the federal domain that defined the major political parties, absorbed vast profit-seeking energies, framed sectional disputes over slavery, and convulsed the nation between the acquisition of the Mexican Cession and the passage of the Kansas-Nebraska Act. As a result, careful examination of Dix's measure not only exposes neglected dimensions of Victorian womanhood but also sheds new light on some of the most thoroughly reviewed questions of American political history.

This study also differs markedly from previous works in its approach to the private life of the subject. Biographers have advanced a series of lurid conjectures to fill the void left by Dix's refusal to elaborate on a few oblique, anguished comments about her upbringing. Evidence of her father's alcoholism has fueled speculation that her personality reflected the effects of child abuse or, alternatively, the experience of witnessing abuse of her mother. Even less substantiated are the claims that she suffered a permanent psychological scar in youth through the supposed murder of her grandfather and that her career sublimated her supposed disappointment in a romance with a cousin. Her decision to commit herself to the cause of the insane after several years without clear direction has been baselessly attributed to the effects of menopause and to her recovery from a supposed depressive condition that had brought her to the brink of madness.[4]

The biographer of Dix must attempt to explain the sources of the personality that has prompted one of the most insightful students of romantic reform to single her out as "the real thing."[5] But in analyzing her motivations and temperament, I have turned to unused evidence and focused on unexplored links between her private and public experience. For example, Dix's most important surviving correspondence is a collection of several hundred letters that she sent over a period of fifty years to her friend Anne Heath. As the first biographer to use the diaries of Heath and her family, and by dating many of the letters that Dix wrote during her youth, I have been able not only to analyze the trajectory of Dix's closest adult relationship but also to clarify the perspective that informs her most detailed record of her activities.

Examination of the dynamics in Dix's personal life and attention to the context of her political efforts converge in the first thorough review of her disastrous tenure as Superintendent of Women Nurses for the Union Army. Dix turned sharply away from her failure, and biographers interested primarily in the treatment of insanity have regarded this period of her life as an anticlimactic departure from her mission. To the contrary, however, her eagerness to lead the women nurses reflected her recognition that the opportunity represented a logical capstone to her career. Her resulting ordeal vividly bears out Robert Penn Warren's observation that in the Civil War "the self-divisions of conflicts within individuals become a series of mirrors in which the plight of the country is reflected, and the self-division of the country a great mirror in which the individual may see imaged his own deep conflicts, not only the conflicts of political loyalties, but those more profoundly personal."[6] The only New England reformer to work extensively in the slave South, Dix had mapped onto her career a deep ambivalence toward her home in Boston and internalized the sectional controversy in a distinctive and powerful way. Her appointment to the most prominent position yet held by an American woman reflected her paradoxical stature as both an exemplar of female benevolence and a political insider in Washington. The attempt to negotiate these conflicts in her Civil War, culminating in the shattering of her antebellum reputation, poignantly measures the transformation of values that accompanied the triumph of the Union.

In exploring Dix's construction of her self-image and her rise and fall as a national heroine I have not hesitated to indicate where her view of events was mistaken or deluded, but I have tried to present her point of view as fairly as possible. A few specific applications of this principle deserve explanation. I have not pretended to any conclusive knowledge about the nature of mental disorders, nor have I presumed to judge the mental condition of any of the institutionalized individuals whom Dix considered "insane." I have followed standard historical practice in using the vocabulary with which she and her contemporaries addressed these topics. Indeed, any discussion of the moral treatment depends on recovering the shifting definitions of certain words, like the lost dual meaning of "moral" as "psychological" as well as "ethical" or the gradual emergence of a distinction between an "asylum" and a "hospital." In addition to using the same terms as Dix, I have quoted her often to convey her distinctive tone. In all quoted passages I have spelled out abbreviated words. I have also applied standard rules of punctuation to Dix's often scribbled handwriting, in which a dash might reasonably be read as a dash, a comma, or a period. I have scrupulously retained the copious underscorings that manifested her emphatic personality.

Dorothea Dix

1

Almost Alone in This Wide World

"WHATEVER IS DONE, must be done solely by myself," insisted seventy-six-year-old Dorothea Dix as she prepared in August 1878 to confront "the mountainous burthen" of writing a memoir. For decades, the celebrated humanitarian had rejected the arguments of journalists and potential biographers that her inspirational example and involvement in public affairs virtually obliged her to publish the story of her life. Only after deteriorating health foreclosed other activities had she finally acceded. But when she began to sift through the letters and other papers she had accumulated since her twenties, she soon worried that her reminiscences would be little more satisfactory than a second-hand account. No narrative could "fully embrace the real *daily* work of half a Century's weeks & months." And difficult as it was merely to record her career, explanation of its significance seemed to her to be impossible. No reader could understand "what *cannot* be *realized* because there is no relative standard of contrast, nor comparison," Dix wrote after she quickly abandoned the projected autobiography. "The whole of my years, from ten years till the present, differ essentially from the experience and pursuits of those around me."[1]

— 1 —

Dix did not haphazardly point to the age of ten as the fundamental dividing line of her life. Most conspicuously, she resisted the temptation to date her uniqueness from the day of her birth, April 4, 1802, in

Hampden, Maine, then a thinly settled village on the Massachusetts frontier. The isolated surroundings in which Dix had spent her first decade belied a family inheritance that tied her directly to the social, economic, and religious heart of New England. Far from alone, she had formed her "relative standard of contrast" as a member of a coalescing Boston elite.

Mary and Joseph Dix indicated the most plausible hopes for their first child by naming her Dorothy Lynde Dix, after her father's mother. Through strategic marriage and skillful promotion of family relations, the only avenues available to her, the grandmother thus honored had impressively renewed and heightened the social prominence that the Lyndes had enjoyed in Charlestown from the Puritan migration until the battle of Bunker Hill. Dorothy Lynde's marriage in 1771 to Elijah Dix of Worcester marked the path that the rest of the family followed after the destruction of the picturesque Lynde's Point estate in the bombardment of Charlestown. In Worcester the Lynde sisters maintained close relationships that shaped their lives and contradicted the legal fiction that their collective identity had ended when they wed. By the early 1790s, Dorothy Lynde Dix, her four sisters, their husbands, and two Lynde brothers formed a substantial network of doctors, lawyers, and municipal officials who lived in neighboring houses near the Worcester courthouse.[2]

Dorothy's husband, Elijah, was the most ambitious and forceful member of this local circle. Born into a line of undistinguished tradesmen, he had served apprenticeships under a Worcester physician and a Boston apothecary before returning to Worcester and building a successful medical practice. Several years after his marriage to Dorothy Lynde, he shrewdly seized the opportunity for economic advancement presented by the Revolutionary War. Although a patriot who sheltered Dr. Joseph Warren's family during the British occupation of Boston, Elijah also maintained friendly relations with the Loyalist refugee Silvester Gardiner, who had been the leading physician in colonial Boston and the dominant wholesale importer of European medicines. At the close of hostilities, Elijah sailed to England to repay debts to Gardiner that wartime legislation had canceled. He returned to Worcester armed with pharmaceutical treatises, chemicals, apparatus, and trade connections that provided the basis for a fortune.[3]

During the next decade, Elijah Dix rose from a prosperous doctor to an influential merchant who in 1789 rated the second largest tax assessment in Worcester. He vigorously promoted his town, helping to fund the Worcester and Boston Turnpike, investing in real estate, and lobbying for the state legislature to move to central Massachusetts after Shays's Rebellion. He played a key role in the establishment of a town academy, a county medical society, a fire company, and other institutions that united the local gentry.[4] Although ordinarily overbearing in manner, he took a conciliatory position in the Worcester religious schism that initiated the separation of orthodox and liberal Congregational churches in New England. Educated by a notoriously tendentious Calvinist minister, Elijah did not break from the standing order to join the voluntary congregation of liberal preacher Aaron Bancroft. But he proposed a compromise with the founders of the new church in the dispute over ownership of the town's religious property, and he worked with other leading merchants in the established church to recruit a minister who largely shared Bancroft's vision of a benign divinity.[5]

After several years of planning, Dorothy and Elijah Dix moved from Worcester to Boston in 1795, following the same course as the Cabots, Appletons, Lawrences, and other families from outlying Massachusetts towns who filled the commercial and social void that the Revolution had left in the capital. The Dixes built a three-story brick mansion on Orange Street—later incorporated into Washington Street when their granddaughter lived in the house—directly across from Harvard Street. The location on the south cove of the Boston peninsula was somewhat distant from the most prestigious neighborhoods of the city but offered a promising investment. Developed only a few decades before the Revolution and now rebuilding from the great fire of 1787, the district had attracted many prosperous West Indies rum merchants. Elijah could easily drive one of his carriages to the store that he opened on State Street in June 1795 and later to his shop on the south side of the Faneuil Hall market, his import firm on the Central Wharf, or his chemical factories in South Boston. Orange Court, as the mansion was called, also boasted a large and spectacular garden featuring trees bearing the Dix pear, the family's own variety of the fruit cultivated most assiduously in a city that regarded horticulture as emblematic of moral culture.[6]

Elijah and Dorothy Dix's move to Boston coincided with other steps they were taking toward creating a new family network comparable to their Worcester alliances. A few months after they settled into Orange Court, their oldest son, William, graduated from Harvard Medical School under the tutelage of Elijah's old acquaintance John Warren, now the foremost physician in Boston, and soon opened a practice in the North End. The marriage of their only daughter, Polly, added the standard son-in-law of a rising Boston family, an impecunious but well-credentialed minister. Thaddeus Mason Harris had distinguished himself as a charity student at Harvard, earning an appointment to serve as George Washington's secretary that an untimely smallpox attack prevented him from accepting. Instead he taught in Worcester for a year, where he met eleven-year-old Polly Dix. They married eight years later, shortly after Harris assumed the pastorate in Dorchester. A respected if pedantic scholar, a stalwart in the liberal clerical fraternity of Boston, and like Elijah an active Freemason, the minister reflected the aspirations of the Dixes as vividly as the gilt mirrors at Orange Court.[7]

But the Dixes' ascent began to sputter with the college career of their second son, Joseph. A forgettable member of the famous Harvard class of 1798, he failed to merit any notice in the exhaustive class chronicles of Sidney Willard, the son of the college president. He earned no commendations, joined no clubs, and formed no friendships with promising classmates like Joseph Story, Stephen Longfellow, Joseph Tuckerman, and Joseph Emerson. He moved in a separate world from the elite circle that surrounded the first scholar and acknowledged leader of the class, William Ellery Channing. The faculty disciplined Dix occasionally for erratic attendance at classes and chapel service, and he once received a more severe punishment for attending a party at which at least one fellow student was drunk. His withdrawal from the college late during his third year was hardly a disgrace, as one-fourth of the sixty-four original class members did not graduate. But unlike Jonathan Phillips and other merchant heirs who dropped out after forming important new personal connections, Dix did not compensate for the tedious Harvard curriculum by otherwise advancing his position in Boston.[8]

The lack of ambition that Joseph Dix displayed at Harvard proved to be his most striking characteristic. The reasons for this breakdown of family momentum are not well documented. Joseph's older brother William once suggested that Elijah Dix's volatile, imperious manner was to blame. According to William, their father's "eccentric mode of Conduct" cowed his sons and broke the heart of "the best & most affectionate of mothers."[9] Later, descendants of estranged relatives reported that the six Dix brothers "were all lively young 'daredevils,' 'roaring *young* blades,' in the language of those days, [who] gambled and diced, and spent their father's large fortune lavishly, ran up betting debts, and denied themselves no pleasures, seemly or unseemly." One of Joseph's nieces indicated that he was an alcoholic.[10] His daughter would almost never talk about him, prompting future biographers to speculate freely about his character and its effect on the future reformer.[11] Certainly, however, her acute sensitivity to her social position suggested that she deeply felt the effects of his status reversal. When she broke her policy of silence on one rare occasion, for example, it was to tell a distinguished acquaintance that her father had been a Harvard classmate of the great Channing.[12]

From the vantage point of his family, Joseph's marriage to Mary Biglow in December 1800 cast aside another important chance to solidify a place in the Boston elite. The Biglows were no less respectable than the ancestors of Elijah Dix, but the union represented a long step backward from Polly's marriage to Thaddeus Mason Harris. As with Joseph Dix, subsequent accounts of Mary deplored her morals as well as her social standing. A writer who collected memories of Dorothea Dix from the Lynde clan in Worcester during the late nineteenth century reported that "of the mother unpleasant stories were told of excesses which would be inexcusable in the eyes of her more than puritanic daughter."[13] Mary left almost no other record of her personality except a miniature portrait that her daughter saved for decades, presenting a lively and attractive young woman on the eve of her wedding to Joseph Dix.[14]

Joseph's parents provided the newlyweds a financially advantageous but suitably distant home in Hampden, Maine. Since the early 1790s, Elijah had joined his model Silvester Gardiner and other wealthy Bostonians in investing in the eastern country. He bought thousands of acres in western Maine and added a sawmill and a gristmill to start a town that he called Dixfield. His chief enterprise was the development of Dixmont, down east near the Penobscot River, where he purchased 20,000 acres of land from Bowdoin College. Located close to the head of the navigable Penobscot tidewaters, Hampden seemed to be emerging as the regional commercial center with about nine hundred residents in

1800, three times the size of neighboring Bangor. The village offered a promising opportunity for Joseph as a Dixmont land agent, in addition to which he maintained a general store on his farm. The tempestuous Elijah retained title to the Hampden farm and store, however, and the young couple may have been trying to propitiate Dorothy Dix by naming the baby born in April 1802 for her. They also started to call their daughter by the same nickname, Dolly.[15]

The Dix family fortunes began to decline sharply within a few years of Dolly's birth. Joseph's older brother, William, had already died, and his next three brothers now ran rapidly through large stakes in business before they too died young. Beginning in 1807, the Jeffersonian embargo devastated the New England sea trade, the cornerstone of the Dixes' wealth. Finally, in June 1809 the family's progress into the upper class halted altogether when Elijah died while on a visit to Dixmont.[16] In the absence of a capable successor among his sons, his business interests were liquidated.

The division of Elijah's estate brought a dangerous economic independence to Joseph and Mary Dix. The merchant's will had recognized the improvidence of his oldest surviving son by leaving him only a modest annuity and providing seven-year-old Dolly with an equivalent independent income until her marriage. The heirs joined to overturn Elijah's will, however, on the ground that recent illness had rendered him mentally incompetent, and Dolly received no money from the provision. Dorothy Dix and her children then jostled for the property in a sometimes rancorous proceeding that pitted the Harrises against the Dix brothers. Joseph ultimately inherited about one-tenth of his father's wealth, a combination of money and real estate valued at approximately $12,000.[17]

Shortly after Joseph took the title to his Hampden farm and several thousand additional acres of Maine land, the prospects of the area around Dixmont darkened dramatically upon the outbreak of war between the United States and England. The Penobscot River offered an open highway for British naval expeditions into Maine; indeed, British forces would eventually occupy the tidewater valley after a brief battle at Hampden. Mary and Joseph Dix did not wait for the shooting to begin before they left. Rather than heading back to Worcester or Boston, they turned from the eastern to the western edge of the New England frontier.

In 1812 they abandoned Maine and set out for Barnard, Vermont, with Dolly, who was now ten years old.

— 2 —

Dolly's parents made their final break from the world of her Dix grand-parents upon settling into Barnard, an idyllic village of about seventeen hundred residents in the upper Connecticut River valley. In a turnabout more shocking than his college failures or his socially downward marriage, Joseph Dix became an active Methodist. He exchanged large tracts of his Dixmont lands for books and opened a store near the denominational meetinghouse, where he began an unsuccessful wholesale and retail business. As the heart of his inventory, he published reprints of well-known Methodist revival narratives, doctrinal pamphlets, and sermons of John Wesley. Dolly's job was to stitch together the pages of these tracts, a task that she bitterly detested.[18]

Dolly's hatred for the bindery work reflected more than a youthful desire to play in the nearby Green Mountain foothills, named the Delectable Mountains by early settlers who saw the countryside through the imagination of John Bunyan. As she approached the age at which Methodism urged young women to look to their salvation, Dolly was not too young to notice that this new faith was the social antithesis of the Dixes' previous religious leanings. Strengthened in Barnard by the New England conference that the town had hosted in the summer of 1811, Methodism in the upper Connecticut River valley mainly attracted farmers and rural artisans rather than the genteel adherents of liberal Congregationalism, now establishing itself independently in New England coastal towns under the banner of Unitarianism. The styles and languages of the sects clashed violently. Methodism promised salvation through the explosive revivals described in Joseph Dix's tracts, Unitarianism through a gradual, self-disciplined cultivation of piety and rectitude. Methodists accused Unitarians of pretentious insensibility to genuine religion; Unitarians regarded Methodist enthusiasm as merely unbridled passion.[19] As an evangelical in the heartland of New England religious radicalism, Joseph not only accepted but celebrated his turn from the family trajectory epitomized by his sister's marriage to a liberal Boston minister. Dolly would in turn recoil from her father's Methodist example during her early adolescence, embracing Unitarianism with the fervor of an ardent evangelical.

These tensions were deepened and complicated by another crisis during Dolly's tenth year, the birth of a younger brother in October 1812. Mary and Joseph named their first son Charles Wesley Dix, underscoring their Methodist model by calling him Wesley. Apart from the intensification of religious friction, the extraordinary gulf in age between the Dix children presented Dolly with an abrupt transition from life as an only child to the role of self-sufficient older sister. She exaggerated both sides of the adjustment, developing a lasting image of herself as an orphan prematurely deprived of parental attention and burdened with the grave responsibilities of adulthood.

Dix best described this emotional transition in an autobiographical fantasy written during her twenties as a children's tale. The first-person narrator of "The Pass of the Green Mountains" looked back to her days as a ten-year-old in Bennington, Vermont (where in fact the Dix family moved shortly after the birth of a third child, Joseph, in January 1815) as the turning point of her life. "I trace many of my governing principles to that one year," she emphasized. Recalling that her parents hardly noticed her prolonged absences in the fields and hills near her home, the narrator reflected that "my situation then has given a character to my more mature years. I acquired an independence and determination which have been invaluable to me." Beneath this self-reliance, however, the narrator revealed a powerful desire to replace her uncaring parents. Crossing a stream to reach for a wildflower, Dix's heroine fell into turbulent water and almost drowned. She regained consciousness to find that she had been saved by the family of a wise, elderly widow, whom she adopted as a substitute mother. The widow combined tenderness and firm judgment, caring affectionately for her young visitor but railing vehemently against the cowardice of men like Joseph Dix who abandoned their homes to flee from the British in the War of 1812. The story ends with the narrator leaving Bennington for adulthood, surviving a perilous journey across the snowy Green Mountain pass in which the widow's husband had died.[20]

"The Pass of the Green Mountains" recorded Dix's private myth of her emotional development. Feeling herself neglected by her parents after the birth of her brothers, she nurtured a resilient pride in the independence and tenacity that she would always consider to be her chief character traits. Less deliberately, she also struck back at her parents by imagining her death as their child and her rebirth as the daughter of an ideal mother.

A unique history of her inner life, Dix's autobiographical sketch also drew upon her overt response to the stresses of early adolescence. Acting much more purposefully than her fictional protagonist, she ran away from her parents while staying temporarily in Worcester when she was twelve years old. She naturally headed toward Boston, and successfully made the forty-mile journey to her grandmother's mansion on Orange Street. Dorothy Dix evidently sent the runaway back to Mary and Joseph at this point, but two years later she arranged for her namesake to live in Worcester with the family of Sarah Fiske, the daughter of a Lynde and the wife of a prominent physician who had often aided Elijah Dix's initiatives. In 1816, fourteen-year-old Dolly joined the Fiske household in the sort of semi-independent arrangement that typically signaled the end of childhood in the early republic.[21]

Like many New England girls hastening toward womanhood in the nineteenth century, Dolly proclaimed her maturity by opening a school. She lengthened her skirts and sleeves to affect an adult appearance before her young pupils, who included Aaron Bancroft's daughter and other children from leading Unitarian families. Already strikingly tall for the era, if not yet at her full adult height of 5 feet 7 inches, she maintained an erect posture that added to her stature. Her rigid manner matched her dress and upright carriage. Although seemingly at odds with her round, innocent face, her stern expression accurately evinced a determination to command obedience. Pupils thought her well-intentioned but dictatorial. Chastised almost daily although he was the grandson of a recent United States Attorney General, William Lincoln later recalled that "it was her nature to use the whip, and use it she did." She spared girls the birch rod but devised other severe punishments for them. With a fine Puritan appreciation for the power of shame, she compelled one girl to walk about during the busy Worcester court week wearing a large placard that branded her "A Very Bad Girl Indeed."[22]

In her old age, Dix would tell inquiring friends that she had been born in Worcester.[23] The inaccuracy was merely factual. In running away from home, searching for a new mother, and straining to assert moral authority over her students, she traced a pattern of behavior that she would continue to demonstrate for much of her life. Unable to forgive or condemn the wrongs she felt as an adolescent and in subsequent crises, she withdrew to higher ground. Living righteously became the best revenge, sanctioned by the friendship of older women mentors.

Otherwise so deeply unsatisfying to Dolly, her parents splendidly fulfilled her desire to be rid of them. Joseph Dix died in April 1821 after exhausting his inheritance. Mary Dix then moved to Fitzwilliam, New Hampshire, to live with Biglow relatives; six-year-old Joseph apparently accompanied her or lived in Worcester. Dolly assumed responsibility for her nine-year-old brother at Orange Court, calling him Charles rather than Wesley. She never entirely severed family ties in the remaining thirteen years that her mother lived, and at times she showed genuine affection toward the Biglows.[24] But although she traveled to Fitzwilliam for emergencies and occasionally even lapsed into private moments of nostalgia about childhood, she mainly sought to drive her parents farther and farther behind her. Later in life, she would claim that her father had died when she was seven years old and her mother when she was twelve.[25] As she settled at the age of nineteen into the family mansion to which she had once fled, however, she expressed her rebellion less directly. To take the first step toward correcting her past, she sought to create a future for herself.

— 3 —

Already a Bostonian in spirit, Dix quickly made herself at home in "this happy part of our country." She arrived at a signal moment in the transformation of the Puritan city upon a hill, now a rapidly growing community of almost 50,000 residents. The Unitarian movement stood at high tide after years of conflict between liberalism and orthodoxy. Calvinist ministers continued to attack "the Boston religion," as one writer had dubbed Unitarianism in pointed contrast to "the Christian religion," but liberal preachers avoided doctrinal confrontation in favor of less controversial moral exhortation and, in some cases, rhetorical brilliance. Dix thrived in this religious atmosphere. In full agreement that salvation depended solely on "purity of Life, and devout affections," she saw little value in "speculative opinions, abstract principles, and creeds." She listened to as much Unitarian preaching as she could, supplementing two Sunday sermons each week by faithfully attending the Great and Thursday Lecture, a Boston religious tradition instituted by John Cotton in 1633.[26]

Magnified by the sacerdotal light of Unitarianism, the Boston clergy became the dominant figures in Dix's view of the city. The similarity of their thinking enabled her to concentrate all the more intently on the appearance and style of each minister. "Could I give you *any* idea of the sermon by writing a few well remembered passages I would," she told a friend after hearing one of her favorite preachers, Charles Lowell of the West Church, "but the *manner,* the impressive energy of the speaker could only be conveyed by himself."[27] She filled her letters with similar observations. Henry Ware, Jr., her other favorite minister, seemed always to be "*piously* and *religiously composed.*" Nathaniel Frothingham was "solemn and impressive." She could listen for hours to "the persuasive tones" of Joseph Tuckerman. Her only reservation about Boston religious life was that "here we are blessed with such *excellent* Teachers that . . . we are prone to criticise too nicely." She managed generous praise for almost every Unitarian clergyman, even revering a nonentity like Eliphalet Porter as "one of our Patriarchs."[28]

Dix's delight in the churches of Boston contrasted starkly with the disappointments of Orange Court. She chafed at the constrained family finances that belied the spacious Dix mansion and its lovely garden. As the former prospect of great wealth dwindled to a single valuable asset, her grandmother no longer lived in the main house but in a small cottage to the rear of the property. A tenant named Mehetable Hathorne looked after Madam Dix and operated a boardinghouse in the mansion. Dolly and Charles joined the transient boarders in a netherworld that mocked her desire for a home.[29]

Dix's unpleasant relationship with her grandmother intensified her loneliness. Seventy-five years old in 1821 but still constantly at work at her sewing, Madam Dix impressed visitors as "the very picture of propriety & politesse, of the 'old regime.' " Almost everyone praised her disposition as "affectionate and benevolent."[30] To her young namesake, however, Madam Dix seemed impossible to please. Her grandmother ridiculed her needlework, and in religious matters as well Dolly complained that she was "never ready to give me credit for *solidity* and seriousness of feeling."[31] The upbringing of Charles furnished a steady ground for bickering between the young woman and her grandmother. Madam Dix objected that she was making the boy too dependent on herself; Dolly retaliated with stubbornness. Despite her admiration for Charles Lowell, she insisted that her brother join her on Sundays at the nearby Hollis Street Church and only reluctantly permitted him to accompany their grandmother to the West Church.[32]

Soon the younger Dorothy Lynde Dix even stopped sharing names with her grandmother. "Do not allow people to designate me as *Dolly* Dix," she instructed friends. "I start when I hear the name now, as one quite foreign to myself."[33] Instead of Dolly or Dorothy, she called herself Dorothea. Unlike so many contemporary New England women who carried their ancestral names as badges of honor, she reduced her association with the Lyndes to a meaningless initial. For the rest of her life, she would almost never write out her full name, "disliking it altogether."[34]

Perhaps more surprising than the friction between generations at Orange Court was the discord in Dix's relations with Thaddeus Mason Harris and his wife. The Dorchester pastor was an important connection for a niece who idolized the Unitarian clergy. Now an overseer of Harvard College, a fellow of the American Academy of Arts and Sciences, and a member of numerous philanthropic and historical societies, Harris eminently represented the pillars of the community; Nathaniel Hawthorne would later swear that his ghost haunted the Boston Athenæum. Although a popular satirist once caricatured him as Dr. Snivelwell because he shed tears so effusively in the pulpit and in the sickrooms of his parishioners, Harris's sentimental piety and mawkish sympathy did nothing to diminish his authority at Orange Court. In a thinly disguised fictional sketch of her uncle, Dix acknowledged that "I must try to imitate him."[35]

But family ties frustrated as well as stimulated her strivings to impress Harris. Beneath the minister's overblown compassion and eagerness to please, his colleagues could easily see his deep bitterness about the dissipation of Elijah Dix's wealth. Shortly after Dorothea moved into the Dix mansion, Harris's financial disappointment intensified when an English publisher pirated the treatise that he had spent years in writing, an explication of all Biblical references to plants and animals. Mortified by his need for the patronage of colleagues like Jared Sparks, for whose biography of George Washington he collated documents and hired out his children as copyists, Harris may well have directed some of his resentment toward Joseph Dix's daughter. Whether he did or she imagined his prejudice, she thought him as unfairly critical as her grandmother was. Nor did she feel more at ease with his wife, a hardhearted and overbearing match for the pastor. As Dix took an increasingly expansive view of the holy office of a Unitarian minister's wife, her revulsion for Polly Harris assumed the proportions of a religious judgment.[36]

At odds with her grandmother and aunt, Dix sought attachments to older women outside of her family. She formed friendships in the neighborhood of Orange Court with Mrs. Joshua Hayward, Mrs. William Worthington, and a Mrs. Hunt. In the spring of 1823, the blossoming of a much deeper friendship with twenty-six-year-old Anne Heath at last satisfied her longings.

Five years older than Dix, Heath was well suited to assume for her the central role so often played by sisters and close female friends in nineteenth-century America in mediating the entry of young women into adulthood.[37] She had learned about such mentoring relationships as the second of six sisters, four of whom now lived with her, their parents, and their two brothers on Heath Hill in rural Brookline, about five miles from Orange Court across the Mill Dam that spanned the back bay of the Charles River. Anne also often visited her married younger sister in Dorchester, where she met Dix in November 1822. Not only a devout Unitarian but a particular admirer of Thaddeus Mason Harris, Anne quickly concluded along with her family that the minister's niece was "a sweet girl & so superior & very much of a lady!"[38]

In addition to Heath's admiration for her young friend, the relationship thrived on Dix's yearning for the domestic bliss of Heath Hill. Ignoring Mary Dix in New Hampshire, she mourned that "you dear Anne, in your admirable mother have one who may always put you right if you are tempted to go astray, but I wander alone, with none to guide me."[39] Heath responded by providing comforts that ranged from mending Dix's blouses to monitoring her finances to satisfying her craving for kind words.

The friendship vividly demonstrated the intensity that characterized intimate female relationships of the era. Dix and Heath sent notes to each other every few days, enclosing flower petals and locks of hair in letters that flowed rapidly from the heart to the page. Heath gave Dix a pet name, reversing Dorothea to Theadora, and Dix lovingly signed her notes Thea. They constantly exchanged bouquets, fruit baskets, and other tokens of affection; when Heath broke a seal given by Dix, her sister Susan recorded that "her lamentations were long and loud about it." Dix tried as often as possible to meet Heath in Dorchester or visit her in Brookline for an afternoon or a few days. "My dreaming and my waking hours are alike given to the idea of mine friend," she declared rapturously. She prayed for Heath every night and laughed that "I so often dream of you that I shall come to identify *facts* with the images fertile fancy is ever producing, and possess a double store of pleasurable recollections having you for their object."[40]

Dix often thought of Heath as the older sister that her own dreary family lacked. "Oh Anne, if you were my sister in very reality as you are in heart how happy we might be!" she exclaimed. "I should not then feel so *homeless.*" The powerful model of affection also brought subtle undercurrents of rivalry and guilt, and Dix tended to exaggerate the sense of competition that her wishes incited among Heath's sisters. Although not entirely wrong in detecting a tinge of jealousy at Brookline about Anne's absorption, Dix protested too vigorously that she had not "purloined from the rights of others." In one of her poems to Heath, she forthrightly asserted that "*more* than a sister's love binds *thee* to me."[41]

In addition to the complexities of sisterhood, Dix's entry into the social circle at Heath Hill also introduced the prospect of new relations with the opposite sex. Friendly with their pastor and with Harvard divinity students who boarded in Brookline, the Heaths regularly entertained aspiring and recently ordained Unitarian ministers. The tenor of this society perfectly suited Dix's disdain for the lighthearted pastimes of young men and women in Boston during the early 1820s. "Happily for me, I have little taste for fashionable dissipation," she told Heath. "Cards, dancing, the theatre and tea-parties are my aversion, and I look with little envy on those who find their enjoyment solely in such transitory delights, if delights they must be called."[42]

Proud of her independence, Dix would not pine for romance or chase a husband. But she evidently had not sworn herself to lifelong celibacy as she approached the peak age of marriage. Several years earlier, Worcester had buzzed with rumors about a Lynde courtship between Dix and her older cousin Edward Bangs. She showed no sign in Boston that the lawyer and state legislator had broken her heart.[43] She often bubbled with news of the latest engagements in her letters to Heath, who at twenty-six was becoming increasingly unlikely to wed. Dix alluded more cryptically to her own marital prospects, at times backhandedly acknowledging the contemporary cliché that an intense female friendship might prove to be an emotional steppingstone toward marriage. The marriage of Heath's younger sister prompted Dix to ponder gravely but expectantly "some things that might in the lapse of time loosen the ties that now unite us." "But let us not think much on so unwelcome a subject," she concluded. "It will be time enough to lament when the *evil is at hand.*"[44]

— 4 —

The Heaths' annual Thanksgiving party in November 1823 afforded Dix an excellent opportunity to survey her new social horizon. Guests crowded into every niche of the old farmhouse on the Friday evening after the traditional New England holiday. The visitors drank gallons of tea and politely admired Anne's arrangement of dried flowers while some of the livelier spirits danced to the thin airs of her brother's flute.

Dix was the belle of this austere ball. At twenty-one, she was ingenuously pretty if not strictly beautiful. Her rich chestnut hair and pleasant complexion softened her prominent nose and nervous, thin-lipped smile. A demurely fashionable collar accentuated her long neck and made her look even taller and more slender than she was. Anne Heath's older sister Susan, a severely understated observer, noted approvingly that their prim friend "looked sweetly and was very much admired."[45]

Dix's manner also perfectly suited the spirit of the occasion. Earnest to the point of awkwardness, she spoke softly, but in a precise, substantial tone. Along with her regal stature, her graceful enunciation would remain throughout her life the personal characteristic that people most often noticed. In part, the compliments for her clear, sweet, and low voice reflected the extent to which she personified traditional ideals of femininity. But attentive listeners recognized that she struck a note that was distinctive as well as representative. One observer commented that

Dix's voice was "so invariably potent in holding her listener at arm's length, it especially impressed me as a feature of her very marked individuality." The suppleness of the modulation belied its power; in an instant, the music might "drop its silvery intonations and come forth sharp enough to turn her sweetness to gall."[46] Usually, however, Dix's formal sense of dignity created a charming impression.

Its measured decorum the very keynote of Unitarianism, the Heaths' Thanksgiving gathering as usual included their pastor, many fellow Brookline parishioners, and an assortment of other Unitarian guests. On this occasion the latter contingent included a somber young schoolmaster preparing to study for the ministry, twenty-year-old Ralph Waldo Emerson. There is no record of this meeting between Dix and Emerson, but the deep reticence they shared probably went far to stifle conversation. They undoubtedly did not talk about the decline that both of their families had suffered since the days when Elijah Dix and Emerson's uncle were business partners and Emerson's mother was an intimate friend of Dix's aunt. Fond of singing, Dix more likely joined the chorus of young ladies who serenaded Emerson and the other young gentlemen after supper. In an ominous overture for two of the most significantly parallel lives in nineteenth-century America, the future reformer may well have added her voice to the tune the future philosopher requested, a requiem.[47]

To Dix, the most interesting young man at the Heaths' party was not Emerson but his college friend Ezra Stiles Gannett. A boarder at Heath Hill during the previous summer, Gannett was now moving into the highest echelon of the Unitarian ministry following his graduation from the Harvard Divinity School. A few weeks earlier, William Ellery Channing had invited him to preach at the Federal Street Church as the first step toward becoming the Olympian pastor's assistant and heir apparent. The pairing presented a curious contrast. Although Gannett was the grandson of a Yale president and had taken first honors in his class at Harvard College, he shared none of Channing's intellectual ambition or flair. While Channing won an international reputation for his literary and political essays as well as his religious discourses, Gannett aspired to deliver solid, practical homilies and to earn the confidence of his parishioners in their personal affairs. Henry James, who later studied Gannett as "strikingly typical" of the provincial New England mind that James's fiction would so often dissect, observed that "in his tastes, in his habits, in his temperament, he was a pure ascetic; his life was altogether a life of the conscience." As James pointed out, the only anomaly in the minister's "extreme simplicity of organization" was his religious liberalism. By temperament, "he ought to have belonged to a Church of the rigid, old-fashioned sort."[48]

Dry and colorless as his character would seem to the novelist, Gannett personified Dix's highest ideals. Susan Heath noted with interest that her sister's friend was "charmed" by the thin young clergyman when they were introduced. Dix did not fail to join the Heaths at the Federal Street Church one week later to hear Gannett preach. Delighted by "the thrilling pathos of his voice, and the impressive tones with which he utters his thoughts and pours forth his whole soul," she soon ranked him with Charles Lowell and Henry Ware, Jr., as a model of Unitarianism.[49]

In the following months, a series of tantalizing incidents also prompted Dix to consider Gannett in a more personal light. She drank Sunday tea with the minister at the house of the Heaths' relatives in Boston, heard that he had teased Anne about their friendship when he called at Brookline, and learned that he had inquired about her over tea with his parishioner Mrs. Hunt and had asked who owned the splendid garden at Orange Court. Dix's letters began to mention Gannett frequently. Repeatedly going to hear him preach, she scrutinized his every inflection and gesture. She listened intently to all talk about the new minister and subjected every comment to review. Writing in the guarded language of sexual attraction, she contentedly echoed the praise she heard. "My friend is delighted with him," she relayed to Heath after Gannett's visit to Mrs. Hunt. "His affability and I know not how many other excellencies quite won her regard: she even thinks him *better looking* than do you Lady Anne." Artlessly inviting correction, Dix doubted effusively that Gannett knew she existed.[50]

Dix's romantic interest in Gannett underscored not only the similarity of their personalities but also the convergence of their success in settling into Boston. Ineligible for the ministry, Dix exemplified the complementary domestic, benevolent, and educational roles available to a Unitarian woman. Her most immediate concern remained the upbringing of her brother, and she moved easily from her duties at Orange Court

17

into community charity, joining Madam Dix in 1824 as a member of the Fragment Society, which furnished clothes to the local poor. But teaching took precedence in her heart. "My happiest hours are spent in school," she declared, "surrounded by those I hope to benefit."[51] Like her zest for Unitarian worship, her dedication to teaching found an especially congenial home in Boston, where schools were commanding more and more of the attention traditionally accorded to churches. And just as Gannett was assuming his position as assistant at Federal Street in May 1824, the twenty-two-year-old Dix was emerging as one of the most prominent young schoolmistresses in the city.

— 5 —

Dix's enthusiasm for teaching did not grow out of her own schooling. She benefited only briefly, if at all, from the expansion of educational opportunities for young women in the decades following the American Revolution. Her fictional memoir emphasized that during the crucial period of her youth in Vermont she did not attend school and almost never opened a book. Upon returning to Massachusetts, she evidently received some formal instruction through an arrangement involving her Harris relatives but found the studies frustratingly difficult.[52] Later in life, she never mentioned any of her schoolteachers or indicated that they had ever influenced her firm ideas about education.

But Dix hardly needed experience as a student to form a lofty conception of teaching. She had grown up in an era of rapidly rising public attention to schools, reminded by countless post-Revolutionary commentators that the future of the republic depended on the education of its citizens. And as more women "kept school," the work was becoming central to conventional ideals of womanhood as well as republican views of America. Virtually the only form of employment available for respectable single young women, teaching was developing into a common phase of female experience. Almost one-fifth of all Massachusetts women in Dix's generation taught at some point in their lives.[53] For some women, moreover, teaching also offered a rare opportunity to achieve public distinction. Dix might have heard of Emma Willard's innovative school in Middlebury, Vermont, thirty-five miles from Barnard, several years before Willard's widely publicized efforts to improve women's education in New York culminated in the establishment of her Troy Female Seminary. At Orange Court, Dix lived only a few blocks from the young ladies' academy run by one of the most famous women in the country, Susanna Haswell Rowson, whose school on Hollis Street added to her earlier celebrity as an actress and best-selling author.

Shortly after moving into Boston, Dix expressed her hopes for a similar career, asking her grandmother for permission to use the Orange Court barn as a schoolroom for "charitable and religious purposes." She tried to summon "the saint-like eloquence of our minister" to evoke "*all the good, good to* the *poor,* the miserable, the idle, and the ignorant" that the school might achieve. "You have read Hannah More's life; you approve of her labours for the most degraded of England's paupers," Dix urged. "Why not when it can be done, without exposure or expense, let *me* rescue some of America's miserable children from vice and guilt, dependence on the Alms-house, and finally from what I fear will be their eternal misery."[54] In Dix's sweeping vision, teaching could satisfy her civic ideal of republican womanhood, her class-based hope for social authority, her religious sense of mission, and her desire to become for her pupils the sort of maternal mentor she had longed to find for herself.

As Dix's choice of role models indicated, her educational goals were more strictly ethical and religious than the aims of Rowson's fashionable finishing school or Willard's academic curriculum. While Rowson trained her pupils thoroughly in speaking and music and Willard emphasized the intellectual importance of mathematics, Dix cared relatively little about any of the secular subjects she taught. The courses of study varied in the small, informal classes she led for students of various ages, but her main goal was always to instill habits of discipline, perseverance, and seriousness of purpose. The teacher's moral example was decidedly the key text in Dix's school. "Give me to know that but one human being has been made better by my precepts, more virtuous by my example, and I shall possess a treasure that the world can never take from me," she rhapsodized.[55]

Dix taught her students with the same philosophy that she followed in improving her own haphazard education. Like any good Bostonian, she regularly attended public lectures, and she enjoyed learning about a variety of subjects on the broad, moralistic plane that informed the lyceum movement of the 1820s. She memorized acres of popular poetry, and she took a particular interest in the natural sciences as a demonstration of the divine order of the world, picking up enough astronomy and mineralogy to teach classes for older students.[56] Predictably, her special passion was botany, the standard Unitarian metaphor of self-cultivation, a vast classification of natural order, and the favorite hobby of the Boston social elite. Her love for flowers and ability to identify plants impressed friends throughout her life. She was considerably less adept at solving the arithmetic homework of her eleven-year-old brother Charles, a member of the lowest tier of students at the Boston Latin School. The important lesson, she insisted while struggling with one problem in addition, was that "it shall come right to me though if I try all night."[57]

While continuing to conduct her own classes, Dix assumed a new teaching post in April 1824 that aptly illustrated her ideas about education. Doubtless to the astonishment of her grandmother, she took charge of the afternoon program in plain and ornamental needlework at the Boston Female Monitorial School recently opened by William Bentley Fowle. She had initially declined Fowle's offer, and after she changed her mind she continued to anticipate her work "with an odd mixture of *pleasure* and *dread, like* and *dislike*."[58] But her qualms differed from the opposition that comparably ambitious women were beginning to express toward school instruction in feminine accomplishments like sewing. Dix considered the position daunting because she regarded embroidery as incidental to her administrative role in the exciting project of establishing a monitorial school.

Devised by English schoolteacher Joseph Lancaster, the monitorial method of instruction divided schools into small groups in which older children drilled younger children. The regimented system attempted to keep order through strategic classification of students and a schedule of constant activity rather than through the blunt physical discipline that Dix had meted out as a young teacher at Worcester. The use of student monitors also allowed one instructor to lead a large class; Dix taught needlework to about seventy girls at a time, mostly between the ages of seven and twelve. With effective management, she could vastly multiply the moral influence that she exercised in her school. As Fowle liked to emphasize, moreover, the training of the Boston Female Monitorial School potentially reached far beyond its own students, for the training that it provided to the monitors made it as close as any existing institution to a school that deliberately prepared women to become teachers.[59]

Dix's appointment to the Female Monitorial School, one of the most prominent educational undertakings in Boston, enhanced her already strong reputation as a teacher. The monitorial method stood near the peak of its prestige after rising in transatlantic influence since the beginning of the century, and Fowle ranked among its most highly regarded proponents. He had previously won acclaim in Boston for establishing a boys' monitorial school in which he firmly opposed corporal punishment and introduced such innovations as blackboards, maps, and written spelling lessons; at the girls' school, his morning classes featured impressively extensive scientific apparatus. The well-publicized design of the Female Monitorial School attracted the patronage of many distinguished Boston families. Dix devoted particular attention to Hollis Street minister John Pierpont's daughters Mary and Juliet, whom she may also have instructed privately.[60]

Shortly after Dix started teaching at the Female Monitorial School, her educational career bounded forward once again with the publication of her *Conversations on Common Things* in May 1824. Written during the previous winter, *Conversations* offered young readers a treasure trove of miscellaneous information in the popular format of a dialogue between a mother and her daughter. Dix's learned, upright, affectionate mother engaged her child's curiosity about topics like the weather, geography, and the making of everyday materials while interspersing lessons in initiative, diligence, and deportment. An effective working of a proven formula, *Conversations on Common Things* sold extremely well. It remained in print for at least forty years, with Dix's original references to Boston locales and institutions revised to reach readers throughout the country. Decades after its publication, she continued to list her right to a small royalty among her valuable assets.[61]

Conversations on Common Things repeatedly demonstrated Dix's immersion in her work. The book identified its author only as "A Teacher," and Dix highlighted her experience and commitment in both the preface, written for adults, and the dedication, addressed to her students. She featured a suitably impressive frontispiece quotation from John Locke, still the reigning authority on education in New England, although she acknowledged privately that she considered Biblical commentator Richard Stack "more interesting because less abstract" than Locke.[62] Aware of the competition in the market for children's books, she helpfully pointed out a similar British volume that *Conversations* should displace.

But despite Dix's strenuous self-identification as a teacher, *Conversations on Common Things* also revealed her failure to recognize emerging distinctions between the educational realms of the school and the home. She subtitled her book "For Use in Schools" and offered it as a classroom reader, but as one leading educational quarterly remarked in a laudatory review, "we know of few publications which are better adapted for the purpose of family instruction, or for enlivening a winter evening's fireside." The entertaining miscellany of information did not fit into even the informal curriculums of the day as a textbook but, at most, "as a reward for general diligence in the school."[63] Later editions of *Conversations* presented it "For the Use of Schools and Families." Dix never indicated that this modification of her original plan disturbed her. She had achieved a greater success than she could have dared to hope, if not precisely the success that she had intended.

— 6 —

Understandably, Dix passed her twenty-second summer and fall in an ebullient mood. "Prosperity certainly has been my attendant for a long season," she declared. Perhaps it was the brightening of her spirits that animated the vexatious rumor that she was engaged to her former French tutor. She denounced the "silly report" as groundless gossip, but her denial did not hint at any general repudiation of marriage. "It is not wise to think much of this matter," she concluded coyly.[64]

Dix's exuberance often clashed with the composure she sought to maintain. Delighted to be presented to Lafayette in August 1824 at a glittering party on Beacon Hill, the prize of the decade in Boston society, she could barely restrain her patriotic rapture and preserve a clenched dignity:

"What is the matter with you and why do you look so sober all evening?" an acquaintance asked after the guest of honor left.

"Because I *feel* and am only thinking of what has been," Dix answered, with evident effort.

"Do you think him handsome?"

"I did not criticise his features. I was thinking of his deeds," Dix retorted indignantly. The next morning she explained her suppressed turmoil to Anne Heath. "I long to see him; to be in the room with him and yet I hardly would trust myself," she told her beloved confidante. "My feelings . . . would be under *no* control; tears and tears only would make my greetings—and speak my heart's language."[65]

Dix's excitability and the tensions it created were not limited to pleasant moments. As she joined the Fragment Society's program of charitable visits to the homes of paupers, for example, an early excursion to "the abodes of want and disease" left her not only appalled by the misery she saw but "ashamed of myself" for losing her poise. "I never before got so much excited, so completely overcome," she reported to her mentor. Eager to channel her agitation into benevolent energy "if I can by any means render myself useful," she resolved to return the next day to resume both her assistance to the poor and her struggle for self-control.[66]

Dix addressed her passionate nature most directly late one night in September 1824 after reading a review of Letitia Elizabeth Landon's *The Improvisatrice* and promptly breaking into "a watery tribute to the genius of L. E. L." Although not ordinarily given to prolonged introspection, she recognized that her reaction to the maudlin poem typified her emotional sensibility. Invoking the feelings she had worked hardest to hide, she argued to Heath that her tendency toward sentimentality resulted from her painful childhood. "I was *early* taught by sorrow to shed tears," Dix explained cryptically, "and now when sudden joy lights up, or any unexpected sorrow strikes my heart I find it difficult to repress the full and swelling tide of feeling."[67]

Dix's tearful response to *The Improvisatrice,* however, revealed more than her susceptibility to pathos. The English review she was reading in her room at Orange Court—quite possibly written by Landon herself—also stirred her sense of ambition by emphasizing that L.E.L. illustrated the pure, vital spirit to be found in the maligned ranks of young women poets. "I worship *talents* almost," Dix scribbled excitedly. "I *sinfully dare mourn* that I possess them not." Her sin, she indicated, was not so much a neglect of her own more prosaic gifts but a craving for the sort of distinction that L.E.L. had earned, an aspiration that Dix found difficult to reconcile with her ideals of selfless womanhood. "I shrink sometimes from scrutinizing my own mind," she confessed to Heath. Although she disclaimed any desire for "the *world's* applause," she confided that she daydreamed about becoming "a fitting companion of the virtuous *great*" with "an intentness that threatens to annihilate the little stability that now sustains me."[68] Such a passionate outburst of ambition hardly maintained the level of discipline Dix enforced at the Boston Female Monitorial School, but she did not doubt that her own moral education was still continuing. With the aid of her sympathetic friend, she hoped that she might gradually resolve the clash between her temperament and her principles.

— 7 —

Dix's happiness began to crumble with the death of Anne Heath's younger sister Mary in December 1824. Although the twenty-year-old diabetic had long been regarded as an incurable invalid, her sudden death shocked the family. Anne, who was attending the dedication of a new Unitarian church in Salem when Mary began to decline abruptly, arrived home a few hours too late to see her sister before she died. For the next several months, she was overwhelmed with grief.[69]

Always the bereft and comforted half of her relationship with Anne, Dix struggled awkwardly to exchange parts. She immediately sensed that the calamity would draw the Heaths closer together and leave her desolate once again. She tried to contain her emotions in her initial letter of commiseration by copying inspirational verse, but at the funeral she collapsed into tears before the Heaths and Ezra Stiles Gannett. Apologizing for her failure to maintain "that degree of fortitude which is the test of Christian character," Dix explained that Mary's death and the tender strength of Anne's mother touched her own deep loneliness. She implored her friend to "think oh! think of the *treasure* you have still in possession. Anne, *I* have neither sister, nor *parent,* nor —. I am a being almost alone in this wide world."[70]

Dix and Heath started to grow apart during the winter of 1824–25. Dix's desperate pleas for pity and love only served to frustrate her hope to break through Heath's depression. She soon reflected that "we never feel our entire feebleness so effectually as when we find the voice of our affection lost upon the ear that has been wont to listen to its accents with joy." But she could not change her tone when her efforts failed. She continued to remind Heath that "I have *none* to *cling* to, none *that I dare love* in this world hardly" and begged her friend to resume that place. "Do not, pray do not withdraw yourself from me quite now Anne," she begged shortly after Mary's death. "The *living* have their claims and common charity would not allow you to forsake me."[71] Time and again she insisted that "*if ever* you are disposed to think your lot an unhappy one, or your heart desolate—think of her whose pathway is yet more thorny, and whose way is shared by *no* near and close connexions."[72]

The crack in Dix's closest relationship radiated throughout the relative contentment she had enjoyed since she met Heath. Although she urged her friend to count her blessings, for her own part Dix mourned that "I know not why I am so sad of late. I have daily and hourly cause of gratitude for numberless mercies, yet I feel there is a void that is most dreary."[73] The boardinghouse at Orange Court, always irritating, now seemed even bleaker. "I do live alone in reality," she sighed as new boarders came and went. "My room is becoming every day dearer to me, and I, every hour, more averse to visiting or company."[74] Her discontent compounded by winter illness, she closed her school and decided to limit her teaching to the Female Monitorial School.[75]

By the onset of spring Heath began to rebound from her grief, but her feelings toward Dix had changed permanently. Although she still admired her friend, she was weary of her relentless emotional demands. Heath retreated from her role as a maternal substitute in forming a strong attachment to her new Brookline acquaintance, Lydia Greene, a lively and relaxing conversationalist who was "not at all deficient in a taste for the ludicrous." The contrast between Dix and Greene manifested itself vividly when Dix invited herself to Heath Hill for a few days at the end of March 1825. Heath confided to her diary that she "came near denying her the privilege, but could not bring myself to act with such unwarrantable indecorum." Once again the friends read together and entertained Unitarian ministerial aspirants, this time David Hatch Barlow and Robert Wallcut, but the long weekend now seemed interminable to Heath. When Dix left on Monday, Heath recorded her ambivalence: "I love her—for I think her possessed of more good qualities than are often united in one person, but her presence here brings to my conscience (as Barlow says) an unsupportable burthen. The *farewell* was therefore uttered with a more cheerful accent, than any word which I spoke while she was here."[76]

Gradually, Dix saw that Heath was no longer withdrawing into grief but waning in affection. A variety of sudden complaints revealed Heath's deeper dissatisfaction. After receiving scores of letters, she began to criticize Dix's illegible handwriting and her occasional use of a pencil. She also admonished her to be more cheerful, and less candid, in her correspondence. As Dix prepared to publish a compilation of Unitarian hymns for children, Heath took her to task for changing the authors' words in several hymns. Most stunning to Dix, Heath began to address her as Miss Dix instead of Theodora in her increasingly rare notes.[77]

Dix also noticed that Heath was cultivating different friends. She expressed cordial praise for Lydia Greene, but she immediately assumed a skeptical attitude toward the next addition to the Heath Hill social circle, Elizabeth Palmer Peabody. The twenty-one-year-old Peabody and her younger sisters Mary and Sophia had fascinated Brookline society upon moving to the village in the spring. Catching a glimpse of them at church, Susan Heath noted that "nothing has been talked of for a month but these celebrated Ladies. They wear glasses & looked *interesting*."[78] The two sets of sisters soon met, and Anne became friendly with the inexhaustibly enthusiastic Elizabeth. They formed a lighthearted bond in June 1825 at a Brookline salute for the close of Lafayette's American tour when Elizabeth impetuously leaped onto the Marquis's carriage and kissed his hand. Peabody and Heath promptly vowed to meet on every anniversary of the occasion, a resolution they kept for many years. Dix regarded this youthful exuberance dimly. Looking back ten months to her own tongue-tied reverence for the Revolutionary hero, she explained that "I can imagine Miss Peabody's state of mind; but such feelings *I* would indulge but in the retirement and secrecy of my own closet. They are too sacred to be made an exhibition of: too exalted to be the theme of a giddy hour's conversation."[79] Heath's new vivacity excluded Dix no less than had her grief-stricken depression.

After pleading for sympathy and exhorting Heath to renew their intimacy, Dix at last confronted the collapse of her closest personal relationship. "I look back on the events of the past twelve months," she sighed,

> And mark how much one little year can do
> How much of Friendship that seemed made to last,
> Unwearied love, affection firm and true,
> Are now beheld no more except in fond review.[80]

She started to write to Heath less often, and she seldom visited Brookline. Midnight confidences about her dreams and anxieties faded from her reports on her activities. She confided to her journal that "*It would seem* as though of all *Idolatries,* the Infinite God smites with peculiar wrath the *Idolatry* of *the Affections.*"[81]

Dix nevertheless clung to the strained friendship as her most cherished tie. However intermittent and unsatisfying their relations became, she was content to leave the first place in her heart to Anne Heath while Heath gave the first place in her heart to Lydia Greene. Reopening Dix's childhood feelings of abandonment, the rupture strengthened her conviction that she was destined to a life of denial and solitude. She formed important new connections in the next few years, including relations with other female mentors, but she permanently submerged the hopeful dreams and the feelings of dependency that she had entrusted to Heath. Avoiding similar intimacy in the future, she found her chief social outlet in the esteem, concern, tempered affection, and guilt of her *"first love."*[82]

As her friendship with Heath withered, it became clear that Dix would never marry. Her ideal marital prospect dissolved into idle fantasy when she heard that Gannett was courting a young lady in Hingham. She jokingly relayed to Heath in the fall of 1825 that "this season had proved fatal to Bachelors, and that the few survivors were making hasty preparations for changing their *singleness of heart,*" but her gaiety fell flat. "This is nonsense," she concluded her report decisively.[83] As Dix later learned, the rumor of Gannett's romance was misleading. The pale young minister had indeed pursued Elizabeth Davis, but she had married Daniel Webster's law partner Alexander Bliss in June 1825; when Bliss died two years later, his widow again rejected Gannett before she eventually married the historian George Bancroft. But while Gannett thus remained eligible for years, Dix's infatuation was over. Although she still admired him tremendously, she began to watch the minister less intently. She respectfully demurred from the marital predictions of friends who observed that "if you were a Swedenborgian I should be sure you were spiritually united now, you are so much alike."[84]

Dix's changed attitude toward Gannett coincided with a more thorough renunciation of marriage despite the daunting economic and social consequences of spinsterhood in the early nineteenth century. Worried that her twenty-three-year-old granddaughter was passing through the prime wedding years without prospects and now without the resource of Heath Hill, Madam Dix pressed her to spend the winter of 1825–26 with relatives in Milton and Worcester. The presence of her cousin Edward Bangs no longer complicated this strategy, if it ever had, as he had married eighteen months earlier and moved to Boston as the Secretary of the Commonwealth. Dix acquiesced reluctantly in her grandmother's plan. *"Three whole months* spent in visiting!" she groaned. She worried that "this is very new business for me; I fear I shall acquit myself with poor grace. I should prefer being surrounded by my dear pupils, for I should be *more useful* to others."[85] Her gloom deepened as the date of her departure drew near. "Perhaps I may find more to edify and advance me on my rough path when I shall again come home," she thought in November 1825, shortly before she left Boston. "*Home* did I say! The world is my home, I am a wanderer in the land where my fathers dwelt; a pilgrim where their hearth fires blazed; an isolated being, 'who walk among the crowd, not of it.' "[86]

Once away from Orange Court, however, Dix undermined her grandmother's matchmaking scheme. Although she dutifully spent December with the family of her cousin Thaddeus William Harris in Milton, she insisted that "*Company* I refuse *altogether* (balls and parties I mean) . . . I feel no desire to add to my frailties that of wasting time."[87] Scheduled to spend the first week of January 1826 in Weston, she prolonged her stay for a full month to walk, ride, read, and sew with her friend Abby Gourgas. When she reached Worcester at last in February, she suddenly sank into illness. After a few days of influenza ended the strong health she had enjoyed since the fall, she spent the rest of her month-long stay in bed with "a severe attack of Inflammation on my lungs attended with symptoms of *Pleur*[*i*]*sy*." Dix had suffered intermittent sore throats and pulmonary complaints during the past two years, but she could not have better timed this indisposition to avoid the marital pressure of the Lynde clan. She reported herself fully recovered a few days after she left Worcester.[88]

Instead of a wedding, Dix's winter sojourn climaxed in her decision to leave home independently. Solicitude for her brother Charles no longer bound her to Orange Court; he had dropped out of the Boston Latin School and may have embarked already on the life at sea for which he had long pined. Dix nursed her eighty-year-old grandmother through a spring illness, but Mehetable Hathorne continued to attend to Madam Dix's routine needs and to run the boardinghouse. Dix saw no other reasons to endure the pinched desolation and inconvenience of Orange Court any longer. On May 1, 1826, four weeks after her twenty-fourth birthday, she moved into Monsieur and Madame Canda's boardinghouse at 44 Chestnut Street on the south slope of Beacon Hill, a well-known establishment that offered lessons as well as lodging for young ladies. Alone so often in her family homes, she would now live on her own.

$\leftrightharpoons 2 \rightleftharpoons$

Fixed as Fate

OPPORTUNITY welcomed Dix warmly to her new home. In early May 1826, a Boston publishing firm made "handsome offers" to her and Lydia Maria Francis to serve as coeditors of the first American magazine for children. During the same week, Dix met William Ellery Channing for the first time, and he invited her to lead a class in the Sunday school that his Federal Street church had recently organized. Dix declined both proposals. She answered that the Female Monitorial School absorbed her attention, that her health was precarious, that she needed time to study and improve herself.[1] Beyond these reasons for her refusals was a more general reluctance to consider new ideas and activities. Exhorting herself to follow the straight and narrow path, she was wary of diversions. Uncertainty and uncontrollable circumstances often changed her course—indeed, Channing and children's literature would soon become central to her life—but she remained steadfast in seeking to distinguish herself as a teacher of moral discipline.

— 1 —

The offer to work alongside Maria Francis provided a flattering measure of the reputation that Dix had earned through *Conversations on Common Things* and her children's hymnal. The twenty-four-year-old Francis was already a literary celebrity, the author of two important novels in addition to an educational dialogue similar to *Conversations*. Fellow lodgers at the Candas' boardinghouse during the spring of 1826, she and Dix continued to see each other during their Saturday drawing lessons at Chestnut Street after Francis returned to her native Watertown in the summer to edit the *Juvenile Miscellany* and teach. Dix enjoyed her company surprisingly well considering that the Heaths regarded Francis's gentle iconoclasm with "disgust." Francis, Dix thought, "has perhaps a *little too* much imagination but that will be lost as life advances. It is well to possess some in youth."[2] She recognized Francis as a peer worth watching, although she declined to become her editorial colleague and did not try to become her friend.

Pleased to be compared to Francis, Dix was thrilled to be noticed by Channing, the foremost religious and literary figure in the country. Only a few months earlier, Dix had noted that all of Boston was joining in "due praise" for the Federal Street pastor's essay on the Christian philosophy of John Milton.[3] The acclaim for Channing's delicately balanced compositions would sometimes puzzle later generations, but the fastidious minister exercised an extraordinary personal force over contemporaries. His onetime student Ralph Waldo Emerson, who acknowledged him as "our Bishop," wrote that "he could never be reported, for his eye and voice could not be printed, and his discourses lose their best in losing them."[4] Channing's most devoted disciple, Elizabeth Palmer Peabody, agreed that his sermons "without the *tones* in which they were uttered are like pictures faded."[5] Dix had of course included the premier preacher of Boston in her general reverence for the Unitarian clergy. Catching sight of him once at the Great and Thursday lecture—five feet tall and barely one hundred pounds, with a thin alabaster face—she quivered that "a saint-like spirit dwells in that frail tenement."[6]

For Dix, moreover, personal reverberations added a special intensity to Channing's appeal. She met him through her acquaintance with Jonathan Phillips, one of the wealthiest philanthropists in the city, a deacon of the Federal Street church, and Channing's closest friend since their days together at Harvard. Whether or not charitable patronage partly motivated them to recruit the daughter of their former classmate Joseph Dix, she surely saw the position on the select staff of the new Federal Street school as a chance to redeem some of her father's failures. When Channing and Phillips persisted in their solicitation, she quickly overcame the concerns for her health that she had cited in her initial refusal. With an ever increasing appreciation for "the great good *Teachers* might effect if they gave themselves earnestly to the labour," she agreed to form a Sunday school class comprised of "elder misses" at the Boston Female Monitorial School.[7]

Despite the attractions of the Sunday school post, however, Dix harbored significant reservations about Channing. Although she often deplored invidious comparisons of Unitarian clergymen, she indicated plainly that the ethereal, intellectual pastor did not represent her ideal of the ministry. As she started to attend services at Federal Street every week, his roseate ruminations about the infinitude of human potential impressed her much less than the strenuous piety of his assistant, Ezra Stiles Gannett. "Dr. Channing is I think from his little intercourse with society not always the best judge . . . ," she eventually concluded. "Wrapt in his own heavenly thoughts he is not sensible of the gradations in others."[8] She tried to avoid the teachers' private chance to hear Channing, their Friday meetings in his study, objecting that she disliked risking a walk in the evening air after the fatigue of her daily work.[9]

Like her hesitant attitude toward Maria Francis, Dix's absence from the teachers' audience with Channing demonstrated her coolness toward the intellectually stimulating companions available to her. She formed no close relations with fellow Sunday school teachers like the well-read, well-connected Eliza Lee Cabot or Harvard professor George Ticknor. She betrayed no interest in entering the serious-minded Beacon Hill society over which Ticknor gravely presided. She never overcame the tensions in her relations with Thaddeus Mason Harris or his son, Thaddeus William Harris, to benefit from them as Maria Francis's education had been assisted by her brother, Convers Francis. Although she groaned in June 1826 that "I must study *alone* as I am condemned to *do every* thing alone I believe, in this life," she demonstrated little inclination to remedy her complaint.[10]

Dix's awkward relationship with Elizabeth Palmer Peabody epitomized her intellectual isolation. Moving to Boston in the weeks before Dix left Orange Court, Peabody had begun to call frequently on her, and Dix guardedly observed that Anne Heath's former Brookline neighbor "improves much on acquaintance."[11] The two young women were in some ways well suited for friendship. Despite her affectedly careless manners, Peabody's ingrained respect for social convention made her a more congenial companion for Dix than the bolder Maria Francis. In addition to their passion for Unitarianism, Dix and Peabody shared similar family experiences as oldest sisters who remained unmarried, and they both aspired to distinguish themselves as teachers. Peabody's superior intellectual training and lively curiosity offered Dix an education that she could not obtain at the Candas' boardinghouse. Her relentless gregariousness also promised to draw out the reserved Dix. Recently chosen by Channing to teach his daughter and serve as his unpaid amanuensis, Peabody was fast becoming a central conduit in a remarkable social and intellectual network of Bostonians. Characteristically, she regularly attended the Friday evening meetings in Channing's study even though she did not teach in the Sunday school at Federal Street.

After moderating her initial disapproval, however, Dix did not become closer to Peabody. Although Peabody's earnest naïveté shined clearly through her impulsive enthusiasms, Dix continued to blanch at her "excentricities." She also objected that Peabody "has many peculiarities of *mind* as well as *manner.*" Perhaps intimidated, Dix refused to join her in exploring the connections between the intellectual currents of Unitarianism and European romanticism, a project that would position Peabody near the center of the gathering New England literary renaissance. Often thrown together with Peabody as they settled into the same neighborhood and parish, Dix was willing to repeat to Heath after a year that their mutual acquaintance had *"improved greatly"* since her arrival in Brookline.[12] But she never truly warmed to Peabody's persistent friendly overtures. Looking back later, she would insist that "Miss Peabody was *only* an *acquaintance:* never a friend or associate."[13] She did not imagine that Peabody—or Francis or Cabot or Ticknor— might have been a valuable teacher.

— 2 —

Despite her diffidence toward her chief intellectual contacts, Dix continued to build her reputation as one of the most industrious and accomplished young women in Boston. During the winter of 1826–27, she began to write *Evening Hours,* a chapbook serial that used the question-and-answer structure of *Conversations on Common Things* to guide children through the New Testament. Dix's design not only built on her previous success; it also took direct aim at Susanna Haswell Rowson's *Biblical Dia-*

logues between a Father and His Family, published two years before the best-selling author's death in 1824. The main rival of Unitarianism among the genteel classes of Boston, the Anglican faith of Rowson seemed to Dix deplorably lacking in religious intensity. After once attending a party with a half-dozen Episcopal ministers, she exclaimed that they were *"very different"* from the representatives of her "much reproached sect"; none of the group could even be identified as a clergyman except for one conspicuously "time-serving, insinuating" minister.[14]

Like the Alworth family of Rowson's *Biblical Dialogues,* the Alwyns of Dix's *Evening Hours* surveyed Biblical geography, history, and doctrines in conversations meant to be entertaining and instructive. Dix dramatized her pietistic strain of Unitarianism, however, by emphasizing the devotional discipline of scriptural reading. She chose for the motto of the series one of her favorite educational slogans: "Line upon line, precept upon precept." Whereas Rowson's Alworths discussed the major Bible stories without referring to specific texts, Dix's Alwyns worked their way chapter and verse through the gospels of Matthew and John, pausing when necessary over individual words. The framework not only provided religious information but also demonstrated Bible reading as a constitutive family activity. The young Alwyns opened each episode with a brief edifying adventure, then posed questions to their mother and reported on their own independent religious reading. Mrs. Alwyn, Dix's pious counterpart to Rowson's facile Justinian Alworth, adopted an orphaned niece during the series, metaphorically reaching out to children who were increasingly likely to sit alone with a chapbook like *Evening Hours* rather than read the Bible aloud with their families.[15]

Soon after she published the initial installments of *Evening Hours* in February 1827, Dix took the short step from educational dialogues to didactic children's stories. She agreed to write for the new chapbook series *Original Moral Tales for Children,* a collection that boasted Lydia Maria Francis among its other contributors. Dix's first story, "John Williams, or the Sailor Boy," traced the process of Unitarian conversion in a ten-year-old boy who ran away from the Boston almshouse after his mother died and his father fell into alcoholism. Taking charge of the homeless urchin, Dix's narrator sought to "eradicate the seeds of wickedness thus early sown in his heart, and in their place cultivate virtuous and religious principles." She emphasized that genuine reformation must be gradual, slowly beginning her year-long project with "the influence of steady kindness and discipline." As young John Williams repented his thievery, the guardian introduced Bible reading, religious instruction, and prayer. "First shame and then gratitude operated to subdue his sinful habits," she explained, "and this state of mind, I felt would be followed by better and higher motives." She stressed that "merely moral lives" could not withstand the temptations that had overwhelmed John's decent but irreligious father. When the boy achieved a Unitarian state of grace—reflected in part by his prolific reading of "good little books for children"—Dix's narrator granted his wish to become a sailor.[16]

Dix's literary efforts received gratifying approval from the lodestar of her own reading, the *Christian Examiner.* Henry Ware, Jr.'s organ of Unitarianism warmly recommended *Evening Hours* to parents and Sunday school teachers, and the editor encouraged Dix to extend the series after she completed the New Testament. The journal also singled out "John Williams" for special praise in welcoming the new *Original Moral Tales* series. Drawing on Ware's understanding of Dix's role in the raising of her brother Charles, the review added that the "excellent story" gained "peculiar interest from our knowing that it was in almost every incident true, or as children say, real."[17] Dix's other writings similarly imagined variations of her own experiences. She noted in *Evening Hours* that the young Alwyns repeated remarks she had heard from children while teaching at the Federal Street Sunday school. Mrs. Alwyn's oldest child, Charles, deciding between careers in medicine and the ministry as he entered Harvard, may well have described Dix's unfulfilled hopes for her own young charge of the same name, who like John Williams preferred to go to the sea.

Among the most important parallels between Dix and Mrs. Alwyn was their common susceptibility to illness. Dix's decision to write *Evening Hours* partly reflected her inability to teach regularly at the Female Monitorial School during the winter. She described herself in February 1827 as "an *embodied cough.*"[18] Alert to the danger of tuberculosis underlying her chronic pleurisy, the prominent Boston physician George Hayward had advised her a few years earlier that "Your lungs are not now actually diseased, but your future health depends on *present* care: the less you do . . . the better it will be for you."[19] When Dix suffered another attack of "rheumatism on my lungs" in the winter of 1826–27, Hayward prescribed cantharides and rest.[20]

Exasperated, Dix struggled to teach when she could. When William Bentley Fowle suggested that she "*give up* for a few weeks," Dix sighed, "that has been the reechoed song for *months.*"[21] At length she reluctantly resigned from the monitorial school. Her departure as head of the after-noon department did not altogether disappoint Fowle, who later reported that she "had failed to conduct it with success." According to the headmaster, the seventeen-year-old student monitor who eventually replaced Dix "soon spread over the school an air of order and industry which it had never exhibited before."[22]

Contrary to Dix's hopes that warm spring breezes would restore her to full strength, her health sank toward a crisis in April 1827. Only her ministers were permitted to see her, although Anne Heath gained admittance when she loyally called. Dix's condition improved somewhat toward the middle of the month, however, when she accepted William Ellery Channing's invitation to join his family for the summer at their retreat near Newport. There she could earn her keep during her convalescence by taking charge of the minister's nine-year-old daughter, Mary, and seven-year-old son, Willy. By the eve of her departure in June, Dix had recovered enough to pay a farewell visit to Heath Hill. Still feeble and visibly agitated by the memories associated with the house, she seemed to Susan Heath "so miserable that it is doubtful if she returns from Newport."[23]

— 3 —

Oakland, seven miles from Channing's native Newport, was the country seat of his extended family. The estate belonged to Sarah Gibbs, the sister of the minister's wife and first cousin, Ruth Channing, whose father had bequeathed the greatest fortune of Newport's commercial heyday. Miss Gibbs presided over Oakland with an easy, expansive hospitality, periodically adding extensions to the rambling colonial farmhouse as she welcomed strings of allied families. Almost invariably dressed in white cashmere or camel's hair and a pale shawl, she seemed to visitors "a sort of venerable fairy godmother."[24] She immediately took

Dix under her wing, and the young invalid began to regain strength walking through the orchards and fields on the property.

As she settled into Oakland, Dix grew at least as close to Sarah Gibbs and Ruth Channing as to William Ellery Channing. After leading the household religious service, the Federal Street pastor spent mornings in his study, descending occasionally to stroll along a garden path to the edge of the wood. He gave afternoons over to family outings, but he maintained the distant, self-absorbed concentration that even the most polished conversationalists found impenetrable. Dix remained intensely shy in his presence. She rarely dared to speak to Channing and blushed deeply when addressed. Although she tried to preserve a dignified manner, she nervously stooped to reduce the half-foot by which she stood above the minister.[25]

To the Channing children, Dix was as much a governess as a tutor. She led them on expeditions around Oakland, calling their attention to points of botany and natural history, but she apparently did not direct more formal studies. As usual, her chief lesson was her strict discipline. Frustrated by "that iron will from which it was hopeless to appeal," Mary Channing considered her "fixed as fate."[26] Mary's summer with Dix contrasted strikingly with her winter classes under Elizabeth Palmer Peabody, who worried that the severe Newport regimen would undercut her efforts to nurture the child's intuitive spirit. The pairing raised an appearance of competition, but Peabody and Dix were assuming quite different footing in their work for the Channings. While Peabody tried to apply current educational theories and could offer instruction in a dozen languages, Dix sought to provide the kind but firm hand of a family friend.

After returning from Newport in late October 1827, Dix decided to spend a season in Philadelphia rather than risk her improved health during another Boston winter. Sarah Gibbs's similar plans probably influenced her, as Dix knew nobody else in the city. She arranged for one letter of introduction, to Unitarian minister William Henry Furness, and on November 17 she left Boston for her first journey outside of New England.[27]

Dix's sojourn in Philadelphia traded her usual winter cough and sore throat for an acute case of homesickness. Although she prudently stayed indoors during the first raw, rainy months, she described herself as "not *really ill,* only a little indisposed." She achieved a mixed success in comforting herself with reminders of Boston. She saw a good deal of Sarah Gibbs, but the forty-five-year-old heiress was often indisposed herself. Anne Heath remained an unreliable correspondent, and William Ellery Channing frankly warned that he did not have time to answer Dix's letters. When he did write, he showed little sympathy for a debility attributed to Dix's rash overexertion. "You are of age, & have had experience, & have a conscience," the minister told her, "and if all these will not keep you right in such a plain matter as the care of your health, your friends will do you little good." He invited her to write to him only if she could make the effort "with a *good conscience.*"[28]

On a brighter side, Philadelphia pastor William Henry Furness delighted Dix almost as much as his Harvard classmate and close friend Ezra Stiles Gannett. Like most of his colleagues outside of his native Boston, Furness was facing a difficult task as a missionary of Unitarianism. Dix applauded his gradual progress. "I think I have never studied a character with more pleasure," she decided in December 1827. Facilitating the pastor's visits by moving to lodgings closer to his home, she pronounced him *"one of the best"* and judged Annis Furness "a *good minister's* wife."[29]

Dix established another valuable tie to Boston by opening a correspondence with her fellow Federal Street parishioner Mary Turner Torrey. The childless, lonely wife of a wealthy merchant and Federal Street deacon, Torrey was Ezra Stiles Gannett's chief patron in the church. She staunchly took the side of the junior minister in the unequal relations with Channing that had almost provoked Gannett to leave Boston for New York during the previous spring. Perhaps not coincidentally, she was also a confidante of Elizabeth Davis Bliss, whom Gannett now loved with renewed hope after the recent death of her husband. Recognizing their common religious interests, Dix set aside her customary reserve and began to write "with the unrestricted freedom of an old friend," although she had never called on Torrey in Boston.[30]

Dix's uncharacteristic initiative reflected not only her homesickness in Philadelphia but a deeper emotional void as well. Like the relationships that she did not cultivate with Boston women closer to her age, her assertion of familiarity with the thirty-five-year-old Torrey revealed a continued fear of personal rejection. Their epistolary friendship was sympathetic and steady but markedly detached. Dix occasionally tested this distance, surprising Torrey by enclosing flower petals in her letters and expressing her love, but she quickly fell back into embarrassment about her *"warm affections."* She informed her new acquaintance, somewhat inaccurately, that "one by one I have followed to the tomb those most endeared to me," and she explained that, as a result, "far from finding my affections buried with the dead joys of home, they flow forth and extend themselves more widely, like the fountain whose natural bounds are rent away and which then pours its waters far abroad."[31] Ordinarily vigilant about the privacy of her correspondence, Dix acknowledged the lack of intimacy in the relationship by permitting Torrey to show her letters to friends.

In part a substitute for attendance at church services during the winter, Dix's letters to Torrey presented one of the most sustained expositions of her religious thinking. She dwelt vigorously on a few broad ideas. Continuing to distrust theology, she concluded after a survey of her hesitant opinions about the divinity of Jesus that "I would be cautious in embracing or rejecting *doctrines.* Had they been essential to our salvation, they would have been more *explicitly declared* in the Gospels, where we are so well taught the practice of every good *word* and *work.*" Her vision of Unitarianism emphasized devout reverence and moral righteousness. She criticized Channing for slighting "heart-felt religion" in his glorification of personal virtue. "A man certainly cannot be religious without good morals," she maintained, "but one can have good morals without the essence of religion, *viz,* vital piety."[32]

Long one of Dix's favorite religious themes, Christian piety was particularly on her mind in Philadelphia as she worked on a new book, a manual of devotional exercises. Dedicated to the Boston friends who had cared for her during her illness, the passages she presented for daily meditation in *Private Hours* summarized some of the lessons she had drawn from her experiences. She proclaimed the solace of religion "though earthly friends forsake thee" and anticipated the eternal life in which "thou shalt not call thyself an orphan." Her repeated allusion to herself as an orphan notwithstanding, *Private Hours* reflected some of her parents' evangelicalism as well as the buoyancy more often associated with Unitarianism. Although in her letters she mentioned a Unitarian distaste for the notion that "the life of a Christian is ever one of hard warfare," in her prayers Dix asked: "Shall I refuse to engage in the christian's warfare?" She answered that "I must fight, if I would reign / . . . I'll bear the cross, endure the pain."[33] Subsequent editions of _Private Hours_ appended a hymn by Charles Wesley, the Methodist for whom her brother was named. The shifting moods of Dix's piety shared the same evangelical Protestant vernacular as her antipathy toward doctrines and creeds. Like many Unitarians, she preferred to regard her religion as a diffusive movement to improve individual spiritual discipline rather than a sharply defined denomination.[34]

Dix's attempt to articulate her beliefs provided her a way to participate from a distance in the clash between liberalism and orthodoxy that had resumed in Boston following the evangelical invasion led by Lyman Beecher in 1826. "The contests between those who call themselves Christians seem to rage with more bitterness than ever," Dix observed from Philadelphia. "Where has Religion fled, and where is the place of her rest?" In emphasizing pietistic, nonsectarian values, she typified the Unitarian response to the conflict and foreshadowed strategies that she would later adopt in her political career. Stung by the popularity of Beecher's church, Dix and other Unitarians sought to appropriate the main argument of their rivals while disdaining to acknowledge the ongoing competition. Dix called on liberalism to prove its "superior excellence" by rising above the "unkind, reproached and more uncourteous treatment" it received.[35] She enthusiastically applauded similar salvos, such as Henry Ware, Jr.'s reply to Lewis Tappan's explanation of his much-publicized conversion from Unitarianism to orthodoxy. Beneath her ecumenicism, however, Dix remained an ardent partisan. She criticized liberal ministers whose antisectarianism actually resembled impartiality, warning that "it is dangerous to be _neither hot nor cold._ Temporizing does not answer nowadays."[36]

Dix's correspondence with Torrey involved her indirectly in one active Unitarian response to the orthodox surge in Boston. In an effort to refute the charges that Unitarians suffered from "coldness & want of zeal, particularly in religious charities," Torrey helped to organize an "infant school" in the North End to rival an orthodox day-care center for children between eighteen months and six years of age. Dix provided useful assistance in the project. Going out more often as the weather brightened in the late winter, she toured several infant schools in Philadelphia and sent literature to Torrey on the popular movement of the late 1820s. The exercise and occupation only slightly alleviated her homesickness. She apologized for her meager travel sketches, confessing that "I enjoy *home* and those I love there so much more than any thing *here* that I am apt to speak of little else." After visiting the infant schools and the Pennsylvania Institution for the Deaf, she concluded that Philadelphia did not deserve its high reputation for civic charity.[37]

Although eager to return home, Dix eventually acquiesced in Gibbs's invitation to travel to Virginia for the spring. They left Philadelphia in the middle of April, perhaps accompanied by Harriet Clark Hare and her husband, Robert Hare, a distinguished chemistry professor at the University of Pennsylvania. The party stopped in Baltimore and Washington before going on to Richmond, Charlottesville, and the Natural Bridge. Circling back through the Shenandoah Valley, they reached Philadelphia again in May 1828. As Dix took leave of the city, she paused to meet Bronson Alcott, the former Connecticut schoolteacher appointed to head Mary Torrey's infant school. Alcott, preparing for his first job in Boston, thought Dix "much interested in the good cause of informative instruction," although it is doubtful he made clear his mystical goal of "emancipating the incipient intellect from the physical and moral slavery under which the ignorance and prejudice of ancestral pride have laid it."[38]

The arrangement of her own affairs in Boston still unresolved, Dix agreed to spend another summer at Oakland. She busied herself with an energy that obliterated any trace of her original reluctance to return. "We are not sent into this world merely to enjoy the loveliness therein, nor to sit us down in passing ease," she preached from the country estate in July 1828. "No, we were sent here for action—for constant action. The soul that seeks to do the will of God with a pure heart fervently, does not yield to the lethargy of ease."[39] Dix again took charge of the Channings' children, leading another round of marches to examine plants and insects. She and William Ellery Channing both taught classes in the Sunday school that Dix organized at the meetinghouse adjoining Oakland. Most of her time, however, she devoted to reading and writing. For unexpectedly, under the financial pressure of her respite from school-teaching, Dix had almost become a professional author.

41

— 4 —

"Was there ever such an age as this for authorship?" Dix asked in January 1828. "Every one's badge is a pen, and each one says, 'I too write.' *Readers* are overwhelmed, and may well give up in despair, as Volumes by hundreds and thousands are *showered* upon them."[40] Her own reading cautiously followed the revolution in the abundance and variety of printed materials that was transforming American culture. As *Evening Hours* indicated, close study of the Bible remained for her the marrow of literature, accompanied by the *Christian Examiner* and such traditional staples as sermons and devotional exercises. But she also indulged an omnivorous appetite for poetry, and she eagerly sought out biographies of exemplary women like Hannah More and Queen Elizabeth. She read and reread the life of the British translator Elizabeth Smith, sighing that "to be like her even in a humble degree would be sufficient."[41] Although more than many contemporary women she obeyed the strictures she echoed against popular novels, she inevitably kept up with Walter Scott, and she confirmed her distaste for Cooper and Irving by reading their early works. She excepted religious novels from her condemnation of fiction, applauding the efforts of Catharine Sedgwick, Harriet Cheney, and other authors to translate Unitarianism into imaginative literature. Henry Ware, Jr.'s *Recollections of Jotham Anderson* made the minister one of her favorite novelists as well as one of her favorite preachers.[42]

Dix's thorough assimilation of liberal literary conventions led to a promising start as an author. Even before the publication of *Private Hours,* her income from writing was sufficient to meet her meager living expenses.[43] Additional installments of *Evening Hours* continued to receive warm praise, and Dix also contributed more chapbooks to the well-regarded *Original Moral Tales* series. Sarah Josepha Hale, editor of the fashionable *Ladies' Magazine,* offered flattering encouragement in a brief notice of several stories by Dix. Herself a successful novelist before she assumed direction of the new Boston monthly, Hale recommended Dix as a children's author who "might, perhaps, would [she] attempt it, write a novel that would merit a labored review."[44]

While in Philadelphia, Dix involved herself more fully in the literary world by agreeing to edit a children's holiday annual to be called *The Pearl.* Giftbooks had lately become a central part of the American reading market, and Lydia Maria Francis had adapted the vogue for children during the previous winter. Dix's responsibility for a similar anthology soon led her to act and sound more like a professional author. She became friendly with the influential publisher Matthew Carey, with whom she shared additional interests in infant schools and other Philadelphia charities. She reconciled herself to Sarah Gibbs's southern excursion as an opportunity to collect "materials for my work." While in Philadelphia and at Oakland she wrote all of the stories and nonfiction sketches for the inaugural issue of *The Pearl,* which also included verses by Edward Everett and William Cullen Bryant. Upon its publication in November 1828, she sent copies to Henry Ware, Jr., and Catharine Sedgwick as well as literary friends like her former Hollis Street pastor John Pierpont.[45]

The Pearl amply demonstrated the talent for didactic fiction that had impressed Sarah Hale. Dix followed many of the standard formulas for moral tales. She rewarded the exemplary children and punished the wicked, often contrasting the fates of two siblings to dramatize her lesson. She warned that poverty or illness might strike anyone suddenly and pose an acid test of character. Betraying no subtlety or moral ambiguity, she hammered at familiar lessons of obedience, self-discipline, and industry. Like other American writers attempting to supplant Maria Edgeworth's moral tales, she promoted patriotism as a cardinal virtue. Several pieces in *The Pearl* also touched on current political issues in the United States. A sketch of Tecumseh criticized the dispossession of Indian tribes. A story drawn from Dix's travels in the Shenandoah Valley described the new Virginia Western Lunatic Asylum and praised the movement to replace jails and almshouses as accommodations for the insane.

In keeping with the literary values championed by Hale, Dix's writing continued to center on the redemptive power of women. Almost all of the stories in *The Pearl* highlighted the female influence that Dix had earlier depicted in her educational dialogues and chapbook tales. In the giftbook stories, one girl supported her family with her etchings after the bankruptcy of her wealthy father and, in a more exotic variation, a young Iberian girl rescued an imprisoned male cousin while her father, the military governor, hid in the castle. Perhaps the most striking example of this pattern was the tale that opened the anthology, a supposed legend in which the goddess Minerva appeared to the young George Washington and set him on the road to glory.

As in many Unitarian novels, Dix's celebration of female influence was inseparable from her religious convictions. In her writing no less than in her schoolteaching, she wholeheartedly embraced the idea that the superior piety and benevolence of women endowed them with a distinctive moral authority. Dix recorded a typical summary of this sentiment in her commonplace book in a verse entitled "Woman":

> Not she with trait'rous kiss the Saviour stung,—
> Not she denied him with unholy tongue;
> She when the Apostles shrunk, did danger brave,—
> *Last* at his *cross,* and *earliest* at his *Grave.*[46]

A female concept, the word "religion" took the pronoun "she" in *Private Hours.* Women dispensed redemption in Dix's moral tales while men at best occupied themselves with commerce or other mundane affairs. Her heroines handily appropriated traditional male attributes to unleash female prowess. The young Iberian protagonist asserted "her father's tone of proud command, now suddenly added to the feminine grace and loveliness which adorned her mother."[47] Only rarely did Dix hint at any impatience with this sacred division of sexual roles, confessing envy in one chapbook tale for the boys who frolicked in a snowstorm while the girls sewed and read at home.[48]

But if Dix continued to demonstrate her immersion in themes that animated major novels, she also revealed reasons to doubt Sarah Hale's opinion that she might write a more ambitious work. Hale's own review of *The Pearl* in December 1828 qualified her overall praise with a reproof of Dix's slipshod grammar and diction. A few months later, the editor complained that a new chapbook tale by Dix was ill designed to engage the interest of children. A survey of children's literature in the *Christian Examiner* ridiculed another of Dix's stories as illogical in its connection of the protagonist's error to his inevitable calamity.[49]

Together suggestive of her impatience with literature as a craft, these disparate criticisms also illustrated Dix's more fundamental awkwardness in putting her thoughts into words. She did not write or speak easily. Her personal letters tended toward a cryptic compression, much as her conversation often lapsed into heavy silence. After enough inward pressure accumulated, she would sometimes blurt out her views in a rush. Her extreme penchant for underscoring words vividly demonstrated her frustration in communicating her intensity. She conceived of genuine feeling as silent, like the flower petals that she enclosed in her letters to friends.

This ambivalence toward literature provided the premise of Dix's next project. Most comfortable when imitating a model, she imported from a popular British book the idea for a guide to the symbolic language of flowers. Each of her entries in *A Garland of Flora* provided basic botanical information, a description of the flower's traditional connotations, and "a storehouse of poetical sentiment and imagery."[50] On the subject of roses alone, she covered almost twenty pages with long excerpts from the works of approximately seventy writers. Curiously similar in its plan to Thaddeus Mason Harris's *Natural History of the Bible,* from which Dix drew much of her information, the attempt to edify readers through contemplation of flowers and poetry inadvertently illustrated the tendency of Unitarianism in the mid-nineteenth century to dissipate from a religion into a secular gentility.

A Garland of Flora brought Dix's writing to a new level of commercial sophistication, though it was apparently one of her less profitable works. Samuel G. Goodrich, a key figure in the growth of the American book market, published the anthology in early May 1829 as the flowers in Boston reached full bloom. Attractively bound in green leather and cloth, with gilt-edged pages and rare color plates, the book aimed to adorn any drawing room. A delighted Sarah Hale summarized the complimentary reviews. She acknowledged in her *Ladies' Magazine* that "a thorough Botanist would probably call the Garland a romance, and throw it disdainfully aside for Linneus," but she warmly recommended Dix's book to "those who love flowers and fine sentiments."[51] A few years after *A Garland of Flora* faded without a second printing, Hale candidly relied upon it to prepare her own floral dictionary, which sold out more than a dozen large editions and inspired several other imitators.[52]

Dix abruptly stopped writing after the publication of *A Garland of Flora.* She wrote no more chapbook tales, although a publisher later brought out a collection of her stories. She relinquished the editorship of *The Pearl,* and she broke off her *Evening Hours* serial despite its potential value as a book if she completed it. *A Garland of Flora* had evidently deepened her reservations about her drift toward literature by showing that professional writing led away from her primary goals of moral instruction. As much as she loved flowers and poetry, she confessed the anthology was *"not in all* respects, congenial to my feelings."[53] The decorative book typified "our own scribbling and 'degenerate days,' when there are more writers than readers, and more talkers than thinkers."[54] Like many comparable women authors, moreover, she worried that her literary efforts overstepped the accepted private bounds of female activity and improperly brought her into the public realm. *A Garland of Flora* adopted the standard solution for these anxieties, anonymity; the collection did not even hint at the identity of the compiler.[55] More conclusively, Dix resolved to return in the fall to the conventional work as a schoolteacher from which she had detoured into writing.

— 5 —

With literature behind her and teaching again ahead, Dix set out in June 1829 to "make the most of my last summer in the country." Accompanying the Channings on an excursion to Vermont before the minister's family joined Sarah Gibbs's larger group at Oakland, Dix found that the landscape of her childhood had "never before seemed half so lovely." She was certain that no scenery could be as exhilarating to her as the New England countryside. "Our 'native land' is always the true paradise in our eyes," she declared to Anne Heath. After a stormy passage across a Vermont lake, she sighed that "I never so wholly enjoyed a day; it was all 'spirituelle.' "[56]

The intimate traveling party also made William Ellery Channing seem more sublime. "Near him you may suppose that any one may, if they choose be happy," she told Heath. "He imparts the peace of his own spirit to those around him." Dix's estimate of the minister rose as she came to look on him as a personal mentor rather than a preacher. At Oakland she continued to relax gradually, much to the surprise of friends who had seen her shyness in his vestry meetings. Mary Torrey "rejoice[d] that you find such a friend in Mr. Channing" and enjoined Dix to "obey him in his parental character."[57]

While at Oakland for the third consecutive summer, Dix made significant plans for new living arrangements in Boston. She received a stream of reports from friends assessing the respectability of various boardinghouses and the prospects for a new school in each neighborhood. She also considered the short-lived proposal of Lydia Maria Francis— now Lydia Maria Child—to organize a "Protestant nunnery."[58] Ultimately, Dix decided to rent a house for herself and her brothers. Considerably more expensive than living in a boardinghouse, the arrangement demonstrated the financial success of her writings and suggested the income she could expect from teaching school. The decision also affirmed her renunciation of marriage. Although at twenty-seven she sometimes continued "to pay the penalty of being an attractive young lady," as Torrey sympathized, Dix's economic and emotional commitment to furnish her own home signaled that she would not undertake marital housekeeping.[59] Upon returning to Boston in late September 1829 she moved to Willow Street, around the corner from her old lodgings on Chestnut, with Charles and Joseph.

Dix enjoyed the family responsibilities that she assumed at Willow Street. She helped fourteen-year-old Joseph look for a job, and she tried to interest seventeen-year-old Charles in an occupation that would keep him from the sea voyages she always dreaded. Her school attracted young pupils despite intense competition in Boston. Notwithstanding William Bentley Fowle's doubts about her administrative ability, admiring mothers believed that "your neat needlework is much needed by my children, and your lovely gentle manners, and the influence you possess over their feelings and principles is just what I want for them."[60]

Dix's withdrawal from boardinghouse society also reflected her satisfaction with the friendships she had developed in the past few years. She still regretted that she and Anne Heath seemed to be "through coldness or neglect estranged," but she now contented herself with less emotional, more collegial relationships with women who had aided Mary Torrey in founding the infant school, including Martha and Elizabeth Higginson and Sarah Cary Tuckerman, the wife of Boston minister-at-large Joseph Tuckerman. Dix's most intimate friend was probably Helen Curtis Loring, a deeply benevolent but impishly teasing spinster from a prominent Boston family. An admirer of Dix since using her children's hymnal to teach Sunday school classes, Loring had met her by volunteering to nurse her during an illness. She steered two of her young nieces to Dix's school, but the strongest bond between the women was their cooperation in the religious education of Charles, who adopted Loring as his spiritual confidante. As Torrey once said to Dix, "he seems to regard her as your second self & she to look on him as a young brother."[61]

Dix's new duties at home did not extinguish the desire for public distinction that she had once confided to Heath. At Willow Street her ambition briefly turned in the direction of science. Refocusing the enthusiasm for botany that had informed her recent poetry collection, she took up the study of algae. In December 1829 she sent samples of the seaweeds she had collected at Newport to Yale professor Benjamin Silliman, the editor of the leading scientific journal in the country, and proposed to write an article on the subject. Silliman cordially welcomed a submission but warned that American botanists had achieved little success in analyzing "this family of cryptogamous plants." Dix worked intermittently on the project for several months, at the end of which she despaired "of saying much that is decidedly satisfactory." In June 1830 she told Silliman she saw better opportunities in the study of insects; she could "imagine nothing more interesting" than the metamorphosis of a caterpillar into a butterfly. Silliman duly published her observations on the process, along with her account of a spider that she and the Channing children had kept in a jar at Oakland during the previous summer.[62] The amateur contributions to the *American Journal of Science and Arts,* the peak of Dix's scientific researches, added little to the development of biology. The serious-minded publication furnished a penitent epitaph, however, for the literary career that had culminated in the frivolous *Garland of Flora.*

— 6 —

Making a brief visit to Oakland in August 1830, Dix accepted an invitation to join the Channings on a winter excursion to the Caribbean. She told Silliman that her primary motive in making the journey was "the study of Natural Science," but the chance to travel again with the minister's family doubtless entered more persuasively into her decision to give up her school and the expense of housekeeping on Willow Street. Of course for Dix, as for the Channings, the most obvious rationale for the voyage was therapeutic. Ruth Channing sought relief from her chronic rheumatism, and her husband's delicate constitution perpetually seemed to need rest. Dix had returned almost to full strength in the three years since the collapse that first sent her to Newport, but she had once again suffered "protracted indisposition" during the past winter in Boston. She now hoped to establish "confirmed health" in the tropics.[63]

After first considering Cuba, the travelers decided to spend the winter on the island of St. Croix in the Danish West Indies. On November 27, Dix, the four Channings, and a nurse boarded the schooner *Rice Plant* in Boston harbor and sailed south. The sixteen-day voyage was "safe, though boisterous." William Ellery Channing recorded that it induced more than the usual seasickness, but Dix concluded that "no vicissitudes . . . can wean the mind from admiration, if not positive love of the Ocean." She only wished the Atlantic vista was as expansive as her reading had led her to anticipate. "*Wideness* of view is all imaginary," she decided, even in calm waters. If the horizon seemed narrow to her, she fully enjoyed "the *solitude* of our passage." "One is probably never more conscious of the individuality of their own existence . . . ," she concluded, "than when consigned to a small vessel, far out of sight of land."[64]

The tropics proved to be as fascinating as the sea. William Ellery Channing wrote that his arrival in St. Croix "gave me the feeling of being transported into a region of fiction."[65] Because the minister preferred the country to the ocean, the party stayed in the port city of Frederiksted for only two days before moving to a sugar plantation in the interior of the island. The agricultural setting shocked Dix. "St. Croix has been the seat of man's violence; and rapacity has levelled its ancient forests," she sadly discovered. In place of the giant cocoa and royal palm trees described by visitors to "less *sacrificed*" Caribbean islands, she saw that "now upon every hill, and down every valley, and far over all the level country, are spread the unbroken surface of Cane plantations." Disappointed, she reminded herself that there was "*much* to admire, and much to study" in her tropical home despite the absence of lush vegetation and the limited opportunities to collect seashells.[66]

Her scrutiny inevitably turned to the dominant focus of attention on St. Croix, the black slaves who worked in the cane fields. The population of the island included more than 20,000 slaves, fewer than 2,000 whites, and several thousand free blacks in an intermediate legal and social status.[67] About 230 slaves lived on the plantation where Dix was staying, their village of huts spreading out only a few steps from the piazza. As William Ellery Channing later recalled, "Here was a volume on slavery opened always before my eyes, and how could I help learning some of its lessons?"[68]

Dix probably had not thought much about slavery before her visit to St. Croix. She presumably saw African Americans in bondage during her journey from Philadelphia to Richmond in 1828, but she did not report her impressions in her letters and did not indicate them in *The Pearl,* which drew heavily on her travels. Unlike some New England chapbook writers of the late 1820s, she did not criticize slavery in her moral tales for children. Her only allusion to the subject asserted that the African slave trade resulted largely from "the natural indolence of the negroes" on the Guinea coast, who lived by selling war prisoners to Europeans.[69] But if she did not devote her attention to slavery or anti-slavery movements, as a follower of English affairs she likely knew about the recent acceleration of efforts to abolish slavery in the British West Indies; if she did not, she surely heard about the campaign once she arrived in the Danish West Indies. Ripples of similar initiatives in Boston reached the Caribbean as Dix began to study the slaves around her. In December 1830, Mary Torrey approvingly told her of plans to establish an "African Infant School" in the North End, noting that the young abolitionist William Lloyd Garrison was to deliver a speech in support of the project.[70] On the first of January 1831, three weeks after Dix arrived in St. Croix, Garrison started to attract wider attention by publishing the first issue of *The Liberator.*

The growing criticism of slavery influenced Dix, but much less than her perception of the black ordeal on St. Croix as an exotic curiosity. "You have no idea how interesting the negros are here," she told Mary Torrey. "They have not what we are used to seeing in the descendants of Africans at the north—coarse features, a clumsy gait, and rough voices. They are in general handsome, much above the generality of whites; very fine figures, and graceful beyond any thing I have ever seen." She marveled at the "heartiness, simplicity, and ease" of their dancing and the musical tones of their voices, although she disliked the "shrill" harmonies chanted by the slave gangs as they cut the sugar cane. In fact, she showed little interest in any aspect of the labor that dominated the slaves' lives. She did not mention that during the crop season, when she was on St. Croix, rural slaves typically toiled from the summons of the conch at four o'clock in the morning until long after sunset. Her reports focused instead on their activities "during leisure hours." She painted an idyllic picture not only of the slaves' dancing and magic rituals, but also of the Sundays on which they worked to feed themselves by tending their small patches of vegetables and yams.[71]

Despite the "softly plaintive" slave accents that occasionally stirred Dix's sympathy, she concluded that "they are in reality cheerful and happy." She judged them "sufficiently well clothed, sheltered, and fed," although the brutal lives of slaves in the cane colony had contributed to a steady decline in their population during the three decades since Denmark banned further importations. Her verdict was not based on observation of an extraordinary plantation; she acknowledged that "managers, overseer, and too often their owners, are *very* corrupt." She naively believed, however, that the self-interest of slaveowners and the supervision of the government protected the slaves from abuse. Nor did she express outrage at the less palpable oppressions of slavery. She dissented from the recent official approval for the educational efforts of Moravian missionaries, a preliminary step toward the establishment of schools for slaves in the Danish West Indies. As slaves were *"not free agents,"* Dix maintained that "I would by no means teach them the distinctions of right and wrong. I would not enlighten them, to ensure *a tenfold* wretchedness *here,* and perhaps not make any progress in aiding them to be happier hereafter."[72]

Dix turned away from slavery on St. Croix as the concern of an alien society. Like the dearth of churches on the island, the indifferent observance of the Sabbath, the free consumption of alcohol, and the antipathy of white residents to strenuous exertion, slavery demonstrated the "beautiful atmosphere of moral depravity" in the Caribbean. Her mind did not move from the bondage she witnessed to a contemplation of slavery in the United States. For the traveler from Boston, the crucial lesson of her experience was instead to exercise self-control even over her passion for righteousness. "New Englanders you know are somewhat scrupulous and severe in judgment between right and wrong," she wrote to Mary Torrey in February 1831. Rather than acting in condemnation, she urged "a spirit of more fervent gratitude, and more earnest self-discipline when we feel our firmer principles rising in indignation at transgressions which perhaps only a more correct early education has taught us to view with proper disgust and horror."[73] Dix's balancing of this moral equation again demonstrated her principal axiom of conduct: the central challenge of life was to harness passionate impulses, not to emancipate oppressed spirits. She transmuted her disapproval of slavery into thanksgiving for her heritage and redoubled efforts to maintain her personal rectitude.

Dix's complacency paralleled her slow acclimation to the tropical heat. She noted that "I pant under the *weight* of muslins and Cambrics, and regard the happy little negro with a feeling of envy, as they stroll over the plantation with a single slight garment." Disinclined to go outdoors between nine o'clock in the morning and four in the afternoon, she spent much of her time resting on the couch or working on her large collection of marine plants. She confessed she was "the very picture of Sloth" although her health was now usually satisfactory. "How changed Miss Dix is," Mary Channing teased. "She used always to be busy and now she only says, 'Don't talk to me,' and throws herself on the bed twenty times a day." Dix's lethargy even drew some ribbing from the usually humorless William Ellery Channing. "My dear," he said to Ruth Channing, "Where can Miss Dix be? Oh, but I need not ask (with mock praise). She is doubtless very busy as usual. But pray what is that I see on yonder sopha? Some object shrouded in white. Oh! That is Miss Dix after all. Well, well, tell it not in Gath: how are the mighty fallen."[74]

As Dix's proud circulation of these jests indicated, her deepening intimacy with the Channings was the highlight of her journey to St. Croix. More than ever she saw the risible absent-mindedness and obsessive caution of the famous minister. Disturbed by a brisk draft while he attended a local Episcopal church, for example, he blithely put up his umbrella for the rest of the service. Accustomed to changing coats a half-dozen times a day in Boston "from motives of prudence," he amused Dix with the wide assortment of parasols and shawls he required to travel at St. Croix. The aloof, elusive Channing now seemed to her a personable guardian, his effeminate manners reminiscent of the older women mentors she cultivated. "When we ride in the small wagon nobody in the world would suspect we were not *three* ladies," she wrote, "for Dr. Channing wears a white straw hat lined with green, tied by a black ribbon to save it from being blown away. Round his shoulders is thrown a gown in the style of a shawl, and it being very light colour the effect is the more fantastic deception." She felt "more and more attached to him and his family," and she gratefully deferred to "the most careful and parental influence" that the minister and his wife exerted in supervising her convalescence.[75]

Interesting as Dix's sketches of Channing were to her Federal Street friends, Mary Torrey was stunned to see her slide so quickly past the problem of slavery. Although as politically conservative as Dix, she sent her friend a sharp reminder of "the *sin of slavery.*" "I would not set the world in an uproar by rash measures," Torrey wrote, "but I would have every heart & mind unite in judiciously preparing the way for removing this stain from the face of the earth, & giving to all the creatures of God their proper birth right. Do we not feel alike?"[76]

Prodded, Dix answered with the expected condemnation of slavery, but she also affirmed that she would not openly oppose the institution and expressed her distrust of social reformers who did. "Your views of Slavery coincide with my own," she reassured Torrey, quoting a famous passage from Laurence Sterne's *Sentimental Journey:* " 'Disguise thyself as thou wilt; still Slavery, still thou are a bitter draught'!" She vowed she would not aid the capture of runaways and predicted that "whatever be the form, or however remote the time, sure am I, that a retribution will fall on the Slave-merchant, the Slave-holder, and their children to the fourth generation."[77]

More telling than her hazy prophecy, however, she did not answer Torrey's modest plea for action. Although Dix had recently seen two captured runaways imprisoned in a sugar boiling house with spiked iron yokes fastened to their throats, she continued to believe that existing legal safeguards almost always ensured just and mild treatment for the slaves. In a comment about the ill-clad adults and naked children that summarized much of her thinking about slavery, she explained to Torrey that while "one's delicacy is at first shocked by such novel exhibitions," dominant local customs soon became *"habits of course"* and "feelings accommodate themselves to circumstances." She roundly criticized recent efforts by the new reformist Governor General, Peter Von Scholten, to ameliorate the plight of slaves and free blacks. Echoing local planters, she reported that Von Scholten was as willful "as a spoiled child; and has all the caprices of a weak mind, invested with uncontrolled powers." The fear of antislavery excesses continued to trouble her more

53

directly than the denial of freedom and equality. Aware that Torrey often showed letters from St. Croix to Dix's brothers and Helen Loring, Dix instructed her to keep private "this more than usually indulgent epistle." Similar silence would remain the hallmark of Dix's attitude toward slavery when she returned to the United States in time for the early stages of the controversy excited by radical abolitionism.[78]

Dix's response to slavery in the West Indies contrasted significantly with the experience of her fellow traveler William Ellery Channing, who felt he "passed through a regeneration" on the subject while in the tropics. His characteristically circumspect conversion to the antislavery movement proceeded far too slowly to satisfy abolitionists like Maria Weston Chapman, who fumed that Channing "had been selected by a set of money-making men as their representative for piety, as Edward Everett was their representative gentleman and scholar, Judge Story their representative jurist and companion in social life, and Daniel Webster their representative statesman."[79] But tentative as Channing was, Dix remained yet more disengaged. Although she shared much of his religious analysis of slavery, the moral duty to speak out against the institution became another of the vital issues on which she disagreed with the minister who had become so important in her personal life.

Dix's position on slavery reflected not only her social and political conservatism but the broader pattern of abstention she had traced since leaving Orange Court five years earlier. Like her indifference to valuable intellectual opportunities, her detached personal relationships, and her abruptly abandoned writing career, Dix's recoil from antislavery reform efforts showed the fixity of her original ambitions. At twenty-nine, she had passed over some of the most rewarding futures available to an ambitious single woman of her generation, as she had earlier ruled out marriage. If she reproached herself, however, it was because she could point to little progress in the occupation that still excited her most: teaching. Happy to sail back toward "the invigorating air of New England" in May 1831 with her strength restored, she resolved anew to throw all of her energy and hopes into establishing a school.[80]

Moral Power

RETURNING from St. Croix to Newport with the Channings in May 1831, Dix started once again to sift through reports of available Boston houses until a family crisis suddenly decided her plans. Mehetable Hathorne, Dorothy Dix's longtime caretaker, announced that she was leaving the Washington Street boardinghouse. The eighty-five-year-old Madam Dix's desire to remain in her home for her final years prompted sympathetic relatives and friends to suggest a variety of new arrangements. Claiming "the *full* privileges of *sisterhood,*" Helen Loring took the lead in encouraging her friend to move back to Orange Court. "The fact is, that Grandmother, Charles, & myself, are quite one family," she told Dix. "Do you not wish to be admitted to our circle?" Dix decided to return as the mistress of the house and to establish in it a boarding and day school for older girls. Her increased responsibilities and the renewal of her previously unhappy relations with her grandmother presented cause for anxiety; but, as Mary Torrey acknowledged, "I see not what else is to be done." Alluding to the most delicate aspect of the arrangement, the possible implications for Dix's inheritance and the future ownership of the mansion, Torrey added the consoling hope that "I trust there is reserved a bright reward for such devoted & faithful attention to those sacred ties of kindred, & claims of society."[1]

— 1 —

Dix was opening her most ambitious school at an exciting time in the history of women's education. In Boston, the recent closing of a short-lived public high school for girls had sharpened a vigorous debate over the instruction appropriate for young women beyond the skills taught in grammar schools. George B. Emerson, the headmaster of the leading private girls' high school in the city, summarized an increasingly popular viewpoint in a well-publicized speech to the American Institute of Instruction in August 1831: "Hitherto, it has been considered of more importance that men should be well educated, than that women should be. It is not so. With the exception of what belongs to the professions and to the business of government, it is more important to the community that women should be well educated." Educated women, he argued, "give a permanent impulse to the onward movement of the race" through their influence as mothers and schoolteachers. He outlined a model curriculum for advanced female students that included instruction in Latin, algebra and geometry, the physical sciences, and essay composition.[2]

In addition to Emerson's school and its Boston rivals, several nationally renowned institutions suggested useful blueprints for Dix's efforts. Emma Willard's Troy Female Seminary and Catharine Beecher's Hartford Female Seminary not only served as secondary schools for women but aimed to match the instructional level of men's colleges. Like Emerson, these teachers maintained that the social role of American women demanded training at least as rigorous as that received by young men. "_Away_ with French & Music & Painting from _our_ school," declared the prominent educator Zilpah Grant, who resigned in protest when the trustees of her academy added dancing to the curriculum.[3] While Dix was opening her school at Orange Court, Grant's assistant Mary Lyon was drawing up plans for a "New England Female Seminary for Teachers," a project that resulted several years later in the founding of Mount Holyoke College.

Dix's school was no less serious an enterprise than the well-known female seminaries. She charged a phenomenal fee of $80 for a twelve-week quarter, a figure that students might double by additional charges for lodging, clothes, laundry, stationary, church seats, transportation, and specialized tutors. Even without any of these extra fees, Dix's school was four times as expensive as the Female Monitorial School.[4] Not surprisingly, Dix drew most of her students from affluent Boston families. Relying on personal connections rather than broadsides or newspaper advertisements, she enrolled former pupils from William Bentley Fowle's school, daughters of fellow Federal Street parishioners, and girls directed to her by friends.

As when she taught younger girls at the Female Monitorial School, Dix offered a more traditional preparation for womanhood than the training advocated by her celebrated contemporaries. The program of study at her school on Washington Street did not include algebra or Latin; it resembled Emerson's model mainly in Dix's attention to botany and other branches of natural history. She drilled her students in Lindley Murray's mannered grammar text, a classroom standard that Grant and Lyon used but required their students to criticize. She taught composition mainly by assigning students to write letters to her, preparing them for the correspondence duties of a lady, and she emphasized neat penmanship even though her own hasty, slashing scribble often defied readers. She furnished a tutor in French and, for additional fees, tutors in music and drawing. For another surcharge, her students took dancing lessons in Lorenzo Papanti's classes, which were rapidly becoming an essential phase in the youth of proper Bostonians.[5]

Dix's institutional conception of her school was as conservative as her curriculum. Contrary to Catharine Beecher's recommendations for girls' academies, she did not give her school a name, incorporate it, or solicit an endowment. She hired no employees apart from her arrangements with the specialized tutors, relying on older students to act as her assistants. Although pupils became uncomfortably crowded while writing their lessons around the long dining-room table in the Dix mansion, she did not seek to expand to a facility outside of her home.

Boundaries of school and family frequently blurred at Orange Court. Stately Madam Dix and the household dog Benjie were familiar figures to the students, and Charles, a few years older than the young women, amiably enlivened their afternoon tea. Dix eagerly assumed the role of mature confidante and mentor. One sixteen-year-old pupil later recalled that the teacher "fascinated me from the first, as she had done many of my class before me. Next to my mother, I thought her the most beautiful woman I had ever seen."[6] Dix actively encouraged similar comparisons, calling her students by pet names and referring to them as her children. Concerned about her friend's attachment to one student, Mary Torrey warned, "I fear indeed you are making her your *'idol.'* You must not love her so much . . . Her parents cannot spare her to you always, & if you make her so necessary to your happiness, both you & she will suffer."[7] Dix carried the familial metaphor to an extreme in seeking to adopt her twelve-year-old cousin Marianna Davenport Cutter, the youngest student in the school. When the girl's mother refused, Dix simply addressed her cousin as Marianna Davenport Dix Cutter for the rest of her life.[8]

The emotional intensity of Dix's relations with students fueled the central mission of the school, her efforts to ignite a Unitarian awakening. She conducted morning and evening religious services, along with a session that one student described as "the never to be forgotten 'GRACE CLASS.' "[9] Private conferences on Saturday evenings prepared boarders individually for the Sunday services they attended together at the Federal Street church. The spiritual crucible of the school, however, was a large seashell from St. Croix. The girls left notes in the conch detailing their examinations of their consciences, and Dix answered with exhortations to pursue self-improvement. "I *will do* and *be* all you expect from your child," wrote one student, quoting a sermon in which Ezra Stiles Gannett declared that "an iron *will* can accomplish *everything.*" Feverish letters implored: "Please write me a note, dear teacher . . . The *casket* is ready, please fill it with *jewels.*"[10] Eventually, the membership list of the Federal Street church began to add the names of young women in Dix's school. One father noted that he had been uneasy about his daughter's precocious religious commitment, but that "with you for her friend, guide and counsellor I have nothing to fear."[11]

Dix best expressed the career goals animating her school in a letter to Andrews Norton, until recently a professor at the Harvard Divinity School. "It is your happiness to be the Teacher of *Teachers,* the Apostle to Apostles," she complimented him. She assured Norton that "your labors, though they may seem at first glance to be somewhat confined, are in fact *not to be measured*" because a generation of Unitarian ministers was spreading "the moral power *you* have *strengthened* and *created,* to hundreds and thousands."[12] Her description of Norton's achievement closely resembled George B. Emerson's vision of women's education rippling through the community. Now her own academy would seek to fill for women, the backbone of the church, a role like that of the Harvard Divinity School. Dix's pupils would spread her influence in their future roles as mothers, schoolteachers, and benevolent volunteers. Like Norton, she would be a teacher of teachers, and her school at Orange Court would be a beacon of "moral power."

— 2 —

Dix's school fit well into the Boston educational market. Her excellent reputation and conventional curriculum helped meet the tremendous demand for girls' academies that the public high school controversy had demonstrated and intensified. Prospering, Dix wrote in April 1833 to the prominent banker Thomas Wren Ward, the father of a former pupil at the Female Monitorial School, to ask how to invest her savings. Ward evidently advised her to buy annuities issued by the Massachusetts Hospital Life Insurance Company, and Dix wisely followed his recommendation. Like some other proprietors of similar schools, she was compounding an income that considerably exceeded the annual salary of $200 to $250 paid to women who taught in the public grammar schools.[13]

But while Dix's school seemed sound to the parents who paid the bills, many of her students loathed their experience on Washington Street. Mary Channing later reported that students "disliked extremely" Dix's "strict and inflexible" discipline. Others complained she was "irascible." The letters in the St. Croix seashell vividly expressed the nervous anxiety incited by the demanding teacher. "I feel the need of some one to whom I can pour forth my feelings, they have been pent up so long," one girl cried. "You may, perhaps, laugh when I tell you I have a *disease,* not of body but of mind. This is *unhappiness* . . . I am in constant fear of my lessons, I am so afraid I shall miss them. And I think that if I do, I shall lose my place in the school, and you will be displeased with me." Intimidated by Dix's relentless criticisms, students took little comfort in seeing that she was equally harsh in her judgment of her own improvement. "If you are not satisfied in some measure with yourself . . . I don't know what I shall do," one girl pointed out.[14]

Dix interpreted the complaints as affirmation of her uncompromising

59

standards. Rather than softening her manner, she stiffened her resolve and waited for the young students to recognize the wisdom of her ways. "I *never* doubted but the time would arrive when you would *own* the usefulness of my unwelcome discipline," she told one repentant critic. "I have but one object in teaching; it is to aid the *spirit upward. Whatever* tends to the accomplishment of this end, I adopt, however *unpopular* it may be for the *time being*."[15] Refusing to modify her approach for particularly promising young women, she expelled one of her brightest students, the budding Transcendentalist poet and socialite Caroline Sturgis.[16]

By the spring of 1834, these tensions were destroying the school. "It is amazing that Miss Dix has any success. The students dislike her very much," Elizabeth Palmer Peabody commented in May.[17] Although she might have been expected to feel a competitive sense of vindication, Peabody recognized that the rigid schoolmistress's unpopularity was a matter for compassion rather than scorn or ridicule. Still a regular visitor to Orange Court, she saw that Dix's righteous ideals had virtually consumed her personality. "I particularly detest such a character as Miss Dix," Peabody noted in her diary in a perceptive analysis. "I don't detest Miss Dix herself however. I think she is rather better than her character—if such a discrimination can be made—and this discrimination can be made."[18]

The loyal admiration of some pupils brought out the more appealing side of Dix that Peabody recognized. While discontented students began to leave the school, others competed to offer the teacher her favorite crust of bread at breakfast and gratefully received her blessing and kiss at the evening service. Speaking for these students, one girl assured Dix that she was "in a manner your child, made so by mutual love, and on one side, unvaried kindness."[19] The embattled Dix saw "much that was bright, consoling, and satisfactory" as the school declined. "The high moral and religious principle exercised by so youthful a circle" provided bittersweet comfort when she thought of herself, barely past thirty, "as one of that band, as its leader, guide, and guard."[20]

The burden of caring for her charges on a daily basis added to the emotional strain of teaching. A young boarder later recalled that the schoolmistress "not only relieved all my real needs but often imagined others."[21] Dix once spoke of cooking for a household of thirty at Orange Court, although at the beginning of January 1835 she counted only nine girls with her.²² Periodic crises piled onto her routine responsibilities for her lodgers; Dix nursed some of her most beloved students during grave illnesses. For assistance she took in a young apprentice from the Boston poorhouse, engaging to teach her "the art and mystery of knitting and sewing" and "all branches of good housewifery."²³

Family duties were perhaps the most oppressive of Dix's domestic burdens, especially when Charles took a place on a merchant vessel to Europe and Joseph sailed to Asia during 1834 and 1835. Often ill as she neared the age of ninety, Madam Dix "now felt the need of indulgences of which she would not *before this* have accepted." But she had not lost her knack for probing her granddaughter's most sensitive feelings. Upon Dix's return to Orange Court, Madam Dix had openly predicted a quarrel with Helen Loring reminiscent of the rupture with Anne Heath. She continued to complain that her namesake "would not let those who love you, be happy, because you were constantly making yourself sick by imprudent exertion."²⁴ Left without a refuge from her home or her work, Dix felt overtaxed and unappreciated.

Dix's unpleasant relations with her grandmother sharpened the sorrow she felt when Mary Biglow Dix died in New Hampshire in September 1834.²⁵ Although Dix had distanced herself as much as she could from her mother, she tempered her final judgment with forgiveness and sentimental memories. A year later, she envisioned her mother as a reformed, loving guardian:

> Blest, she discerns the unsearch'd ways of heaven,
> And learns its chastisements "for good" are given
> And angel now, she watches o'er thy ways,
> Whispering in dreams the joys of other days.

Her sadness marked a peaceful dismissal of her mother rather than a coming to terms with her role in Dix's life. Almost never mentioning her mother again, she did not try to connect the "chastisements" suffered by Mary Biglow Dix to her own quest for the "ways of heaven," and her references to her childhood usually acknowledged little of "the joys of other days."²⁶

More commonly than nostalgia, redoubled piety and benevolent exertions provided an outlet for Dix's frustrations. Finding that writing hymns "beguiled me of pain," she filled her notebooks with effusive paraphrases of the Psalms and other scriptural texts. She published many of her verses in the *Christian Register,* the weekly newspaper of Unitarianism, but she showed no regret for her forsaken literary career. "I am too busy, even if I had the knowledge or the talent, to permit myself to be called an author," she declared.[27] One of the projects that kept her busiest was the charity school she established in the coach house at Orange Court in 1835, a fulfillment of the ambition to emulate Hannah More that Dix had expressed more than a decade ago. "The Hope-well Mansion School," as she christened the makeshift classroom, imparted moral instruction to poor children and provided useful teaching experience for the young women at Orange Court. She and her students also helped to organize a similar evening school for young workingmen and -women. Located in the basement of Thaddeus Mason Harris's church, the school was superintended by his junior colleague, Nathaniel Hall, later the husband of Dix's prize pupil, Sarah Coffin.[28]

But while Dix intensified her outside activities, the problem of her unpopularity at Orange Court continued to mount. Elizabeth Parsons Channing, an intelligent student and the niece of the Federal Street pastor, left the school after one year despite an offer to remain without charge. Dix repeated the proposal to Channing's sister, but she also declined. By March 1835, Dix was forced to solicit an endorsement from Helen Loring's brother Charles G. Loring, one of the most prominent lawyers in Boston. He kindly wished the testimonial letters had "a talismanic power, to speak . . . of the satisfaction we feel in the advancing improvement & happiness of our children, and our confidence and esteem for their instructress." Despite the compliment, however, Dix doubtless saw the resort to advertising as a desperate confession of looming failure.[29]

Dix's outlook darkened and her pace quickened further during the next several months, accompanied now by a downturn in her health. She eagerly seized Anne Heath's rare greetings at the time of her thirty-third birthday in April as the opening of a reconciliation after "we have lived whole years *seemingly* estranged." Wistfully, Dix looked forward to an afterlife "where our employments will be wholly congenial."[30] Paying a spring visit to Brookline, she struck Susan Heath as enervated and unwell. During the summer, Dix complained of painful headaches, possibly nervous in origin. By September she had rebounded markedly, but her condition and bustling pace still alarmed George B. Emerson when she told him about the Hope-well School in November 1835. "You are doing too much for others and not enough to take care of yourself . . . ," the schoolmaster soberly warned. "I am afraid that unless you will listen to the admonition you have already received, that you are doing too much, that you will have the claim pressed upon you in language from which you will not be able to turn away."[31]

Dix's hymns suggested a different explanation for her conduct than the runaway altruism that Emerson described. When she peered into "the mirror [that] . . . brings my secret sins to view," she did not tie her impending physical collapse to philanthropic instincts but to feelings of despair. "In want and pain the spirit winds," she wrote in January 1836, "and griefs descend as summer rain."[32] The Hope-well School and similar exertions had become not merely a distraction from Dix's unhappiness at Orange Court but a means to escape into exhaustion. Guided more by religious reflex than deliberate strategy, she sought a martyred relief through her intensified conscientiousness.

In late March came the breakdown that acquaintances had anticipated. Dix announced she was critically, very likely terminally, ill and would sail as soon as possible for Europe. She left unclear the exact nature of her illness. While acknowledging that to all outward appearances "long years were probably before me," she asserted that "I have no reason to believe it." She reported only that "I have had medical advice," drawing a curtain across the diagnosis. "I have the promise of the few who know how really ill I am, to meet my wish and be silent." If she discussed her malady, she added, friends offering "advice, . . . remedies, and alleviations" would destroy her tranquil acceptance of her lot.[33]

She was more forthcoming about the severity of her condition. Dix repeatedly confided that "the conviction is, and has long been strong that the veil which divides me from 'my home' would soon fall." She was pleased to find herself "calm, happy in this view." Observers were less certain that she was dying. As sympathetic a friend as Mary Torrey suggested that Dix was suffering from the winter weather and expressed no doubt that she would be "refreshed and invigorated by the relaxation and the change" of a vacation in Europe.[34]

For two weeks, Dix scrambled to be ready to sail across the Atlantic with the family of her pupil Joaquina Fesser. She once again pressed the

Heaths into service, this time to sew her nightcaps. She asked George B. Emerson to watch over "the Hope," leaving the schoolmaster a warm letter of gratitude for "the composing influence of your friendship," to be opened if she became "more seriously and permanently indisposed."[35] From William Ellery Channing she solicited several introductions, including letters to two of her favorite British authors, Lucy Aikin and Joanna Baillie. The minister's note to Baillie mentioned Dix's long association with his family, her fine reputation as a teacher, and the poor health she had incurred "by her singular devotion to her work." "Her history is one of the most remarkable examples of what may be accomplished by energy & a high sense of duty," Channing remarked, tacitly apologetic that he could not recommend the visitor for more brilliant virtues.[36]

Dix's tearless departure underscored the failure of her most important efforts to forge personal relationships in Boston. Exchanging farewells, Anne Heath asked her old friend to "forgive me for ever having pained you" and called on her to remember the happier past that provided them a continuing fund of affection. Dix in return enjoined Heath to "think of me as an invalid but not troubled."[37] After she left Boston on April 16, George B. Emerson acted as her educational executor, counseling several Orange Court pupils who scattered to schools around Boston, including his own academy. As he evaluated the students and heard their reminiscences, the schoolmaster formed a perceptive final judgment of Dix's last four-and-a-half years. "Miss Dix was a thorough, successful Teacher, and got rich," Emerson concluded, "but she did not succeed in making her scholars *love her*."[38]

— 3 —

Dix's voyage across the Atlantic in *The Virginian* raised an excellent prospect of relief from her frustrations at home. She "formed at once a pleasant social circle" with the Fessers, some Baltimore friends of the Channings that she knew from Oakland, and several other travelers from Boston, including the textile magnate William Lawrence.[39] Her health held up fairly well, although Edward Fesser felt obliged to take away her pens and paper to conserve her strength. She even found an opportunity to make herself useful on the ship, nursing a young woman who died soon after the crossing. One of her new acquaintances marveled that "the Poet makes a merit of forgetting his griefs to be happy with his friends, but you forget your own ills to watch over the sick bed of a stranger!"[40] When *The Virginian* arrived at Liverpool, however, Dix collapsed. The Fessers tended to her at a hotel until Edward Fesser's business obligations obliged the family to proceed to London. Reluctantly, they left Dix in the care of the prominent Rathbone family.

The Rathbones were accustomed to welcoming American visitors generously. Greenbank, their Strawberry Hill Gothic manor three miles from Liverpool, offered travelers a comfortable and convenient resting place near the major transatlantic port of entry. The Rathbones' well-known hospitality was partly a sensible business practice. Their mercantile firm had long been actively engaged in American trade, acting as the consignment agent for the first shipment of cotton exported from the United States. But to forty-nine-year-old William Rathbone, the fifth head of the family to bear that name, the cultural exchange between the two countries was more interesting than the development of commercial connections. A decade earlier, he had contributed significantly to the launching of the career of John James Audubon. A convert from his family's Quaker heritage to the Unitarianism of his wife Elizabeth, Rathbone especially admired William Ellery Channing. He proudly hosted the minister at Greenbank, and they regularly swapped introductions of travelers. When Rathbone learned that Dix was ill at a Liverpool hotel with letters of introduction from Channing, he hastened to extend his assistance.[41]

After a few days at Greenbank and Woodcroft, the nearby family cottage, Dix decided she would go no further. "My restoration will undoubtedly be very gradual," she predicted in early June 1836.[42] Explaining that she could not ride more than twenty miles a day, she canceled plans to accompany her shipmates in a traveling party to the continent. After the Fessers returned her belongings, Dix declined invitations to join another pupil's family in London and to travel in Scotland with Sarah Gibbs. She left Liverpool only once during the summer, for a two-week excursion to see the Lake District with the family of her physician, William Reynolds, a relative and neighbor of the Rathbones. In September her slow improvement in strength reversed, and on the advice of Reynolds and another doctor, she confined herself to a bed at Greenbank.

Dix's prolonged debility baffled the friends who had seen her leave Boston. "What can have caused it?" Helen Loring asked incredulously. Ceaseless in her own charitable activities although poor health had rendered her "a mere shadow," Loring expressed touching disappointment that the trip was not providing her friend "renewed strength for many more years of moral energy."[43] Anne Heath, who had expected Dix to journey to the Holy Land, assumed the Atlantic crossing must have necessitated the lengthy convalescence; Madam Dix blamed the harsh weather of Liverpool. William Ellery Channing was readier to attribute Dix's feebleness to overexertion, but only because he suggested that her trouble was primarily psychological. "Did you never hear the comparison of certain invalids to a spinning top, which is kept up by perpetual whirling?" he reproached her, echoing his comments on the collapse that had forced her to quit the Boston Female Monitorial School nine years ago. "It was very natural that you should fall, when exciting motion ceased. When you begin to spin again, I trust, it will be with a gentler movement."[44]

Annoyed by these unsympathetic doubts, Dix wished that her friends "felt less of surprise and disappointment at my being so ill, and *not* being restored by a voyage and travelling." She assured correspondents that "I was very sick when I left America—only I did not yield to it." "I hope you will not think me wrong in refraining from telling you how much I suffered, and how really very ill I was," she told her grandmother, adding that "it could not have amended my strength to impart to others the knowledge of my great pain and suffering."[45]

Dix provided few additional details, however, about the nature of her affliction. "Not a great sufferer by any means" in early October, she explained that "confinement to my apartment, and much to my bed, is for the most part remedial; cautionary rather than through excessive illness." Unable to sit up for more than a few hours at a time, she wrote letters while braced by pillows "in a very Oriental luxury of position." Six more weeks brought no change in her condition. Free from pain, she observed that "weakness is its own burthen." She concluded that "*rest* seems to be my necessity—long *positive inactivity,*" emphasizing that she was faithfully following the counsel of her physicians.[46]

Although she maintained that similar rest would not have benefited her "*in our climate,*" Dix had to admit Liverpool was an unlikely resort

for an invalid, especially as winter descended. In November she acknowledged she had "vainly sought, thus far, to discern the *difference* of climate
from that of New-England." The spring chill, summer heat, and autumn
storms, together with the snow and ice that had already set in, presented
variable extremes "not exceeded in our much abused country." But she
argued that travel would be even less salutary, especially on the newly
introduced railroads and steamboats, "the two worst modes of convey-
ance that ever were devised where more than *mere* expedition are
required." While pleased to note that "the imperial city will this year
be well nigh colonized from the land of liberty and puritanism," she
declined to join her many Boston acquaintances spending the winter in
Rome.[47]

Aside from Dix's medical rationale for staying in Liverpool, she was
enjoying herself too much to leave Greenbank. She found consolation
for her illness, she said, in "a uniform state of cheerfulness." A visitor
from Boston teased that the invalid was not Dix at all because she had
lost the gravity that characterized her at home.[48] Confined to her room,
rarely reading anything that she had not read before, Dix delighted in
the visits she received throughout the day from the members of the
Rathbone family. She affirmed that Anne Heath saw the situation correctly. "Surrounded by numbers, you have hitherto lived without companionship . . .," Heath noted. "The pleasure of agreeable, social con-
verse, and interchange of sympathy, I doubt not, you have enjoyed more
entirely in England than ever before."[49] Although urged to write sparingly to conserve her strength, Dix penned numerous poetic tributes to
William and Elizabeth Rathbone, their four young adult children, and
the local relatives of the family.

Hungry for love, Dix seized the Rathbone's hospitality as the family
bond that she had often craved. "Of the excellent family who so affectionately number me as one of their *'own,'* I should never tire of speaking,"
she declared. "They are all, and every thing in themselves, which can render the social and domestic state happy and improving."[50] She recorded
in her journal that she felt "Folded as infant dear in parent-arms, / Hushed
are life's griefs, and stilled, its dread alarms." Fond of the entire family,
she especially admired forty-six-year-old Elizabeth Rathbone. "I never saw
her excelled," Dix tactlessly told her grandmother. "I hardly know if I
have seen her equal, embracing all qualities of the mind, and heart." A

67

conscientious, strong-willed contributor to Liverpool charities and educational enterprises, she, rather than her gruff and slow-witted husband, was the family successor to the fourth William Rathbone, a distinguished philanthropist. Dix rhapsodized that "in strength of mind she always secures and arrests attention, her cheerfulness is invariable, and her self-sacrificing benevolence untiring. She is the light and joy of her husband and children; indeed of all who know her."[51]

Occasionally, Dix explicitly voiced the dissatisfactions with her own family that her praise for the Rathbones suggested. Although she inscribed herself "your affectionate child" in her letters to Madam Dix, she complained that her grandmother had shown little sympathy for her travails at Orange Court. "There have been times within my memory, at no long past date, when it [sympathy] might have been kindly bestowed, and where it might naturally have been looked for, but *was not,*" she recalled. She warned that Madam Dix should not expect to see her again, and when she wrote that she liked to envision her grandmother sleeping, it was not unreasonable to infer that she wished the old woman would die.[52] Friends reported that Madam Dix remained remarkably well, however, and Dix ambivalently urged them to call often. She beseeched Anne Heath: "Visit my Grandmother if you can summon moral and physical courage to face the Medusa! The flinty mask may *yet* be *softened.*"[53] No better appreciated at home despite her absence and illness, she sighed that the infrequency of mail left her "heart-weary of asking for letters."[54] For her own part, she wrote as rarely as she deemed polite to her uncongenial relatives in the family of Thaddeus Mason Harris.

Beyond her intimacy with the Rathbones, Dix participated selectively in the social whirl of Greenbank, which she called "but another name for the *Travellers'* and *Strangers' Home.*"[55] Her confinement to her room caused her to meet few of the guests whom the Rathbones entertained almost every day. But before her isolation she earnestly importuned William Rathbone's aged mother for an introduction to her fellow Quaker, the legendary prison reformer Elizabeth Fry.[56] Later, Dix made a point of meeting Greenbank favorite Joseph Blanco White, a former Catholic priest whose adoption of Unitarianism was considered a triumph for the religion. She developed a closer relationship with the young Liverpool minister John Hamilton Thom, soon to marry into the Rathbone family. An admirer of Channing and deeply influenced by Boston minister-at-large Joseph Tuckerman's description of his charitable mission while on a recent visit to Greenbank, Thom eagerly discussed the celebrated Boston clergy with Dix and shared the recent issues of the *Christian Examiner.* He also welcomed the chance to develop his pastoral skills, flattering himself that he had been "admitted to the confidence of your mind in circumstances in many respects peculiar and trying."[57]

For the most part, however, Dix's new contacts outside of the Rathbone family were not her hosts' English friends but other visitors from Boston. Shortly before Dix established herself indefinitely at Greenbank in September 1836, Joseph Tuckerman's twenty-three-year-old daughter, Sarah, joined the household, an addition that multiplied the Rathbones' ties to Unitarian travelers. Friendly with the minister's wife, Dix saw Sarah daily, and she showed her and other Boston guests a sociability she had suppressed at home. Introducing a returning physician to Madam Dix, she noted that "*distance* from one's country make those who were unknown almost at once on easy or familiar terms."[58] Even when otherwise unable to receive company, she welcomed "without hesitation" long visits from Boston writer Eliza Farrar, the author of a Sunday school profile of prison reformer John Howard and an influential etiquette book for young ladies. In addition to the steady flow of guests, Dix explained that she liked to stay in Liverpool because the mail packets offered "the means of hearing frequently from Boston." She also kept in correspondence with many Bostonians on the Continent, including Sarah Gibbs, the Ticknors, and the families of several of her former pupils.[59]

Lingering in Liverpool, Dix presented a striking variation on the familiar nineteenth-century figure of the ailing American seeking renewal in Europe. Like many voyagers, she counted her journey as the happiest phase of her life, although she traveled only a few miles from the dock. To an extreme degree, her pleasure was not in what she found overseas but in the mixture of what she left behind and what she brought with her. Freed from her compulsive sense of duty, her frustrations in teaching, and her discontent with her family, she unlocked her social disposition and relished her identity as a Bostonian. Only by going abroad had she learned to enjoy home.

— 4 —

Dix's condition worsened before she started to recover. Her health deteriorated sharply in mid-November 1836, perhaps from a case of pneumonia. For the next two months her deepening fatigue was accompanied by pain in her side and a persistent cough, her phlegm sometimes streaked with blood. Fluid rushed to her chest when she tried to move, compelling her to remain bedridden. She showed signs of improvement in January 1837 and started to walk around her room for the first time since September. She also began to think gradually about leaving Greenbank. "There is danger perhaps of my getting a little *spoiled* with so much caressing and petting," she conceded to her grandmother, acknowledging that "so completely am I adopted into this circle of loving spirits that I sometimes forget I really am . . . to consider the bonds transient."[60]

She continued to forbear reassessment of the overall direction of her life. "My state is so very precarious that I form no plans, and indulge in no day-dreams for the future," she repeatedly explained.[61] Without considering specifics, she hoped to resume her teaching career eventually, for her ambition to exert influence through schools had not abated. Breaking off a letter outlining educational policy as "too absorbing," she remained firm that "*moral culture* should hold a more absolute place, and more care should be taken that the domestic influence which the lower class are expose[d] to be *early* counteracted." She also retained a deep affection for her students—"my most engrossing objects of heart-interest"— several of whom wrote regularly to her. She admitted that in looking back on her work at Orange Court she saw "much to lament in deficient performance," but she resolved "to keep *unprofitable* regrets out of sight." She told friends she was praying for "renovated health and vigour to resume my labours as a Teacher," although she warned them, and herself, that she might have to relinquish her goal.[62]

As she slowly regained strength, Dix seemed likely to remain for some time engaged in the main alternative she saw to teaching, the life of an invalid. In February she announced that she would probably remain abroad for another year. The arrival of spring and Dix's emergence from her bedchamber soon brought renewed invitations to travel. But unwilling to leave the Rathbones, she started instead to look for a cottage in the vicinity of Greenbank, where she could "fix myself independently, near the dear friends who have been parents, and kindred, and Christian friends to me."[63]

Aware that her friends in Boston considered her accounts of herself "liable to deception," Dix commissioned John Hamilton Thom to report to William Ellery Channing on her health and prospects in April 1837. Three days after the anniversary of Dix's departure from Boston, Thom relayed that her physician William Reynolds "speaks positively as to no symptoms of pulmonary disease having yet manifested itself." The doctor saw "no reason to doubt a partial recovery" and thought "an entire recovery of strength" was possible. But on the whole, Thom wrote, Reynolds believed that "the active part of her life must be considered over." Dix could not again expect to be "robust & energetic . . . if she has ever been so." At most, her health would enable her to "enjoy life &, through the mind, be engaged again in that quiet usefulness without which to enjoy life is not possible."[64]

Turning from Reynolds's diagnosis to his own, Thom offered an evaluation of Dix's spiritual condition. "It is impossible to see any thing of so devotional a spirit, & so pure a conscientiousness without a strengthened confidence in the power & beauty of those principles of mind," he noted. "She has made many friends here . . . & she has left the impression of her own character on many minds that I am sure will cherish the remembrance of it as an influence." At the same time, he hinted carefully, "There is in her conscientiousness something of morbidness." He confided to her pastor that "I should fear that even in her most active benevolence there had been a want of that self forgetfulness which is the healthiest condition of the mind. I do not mean this in a *selfish* sense, far from it—but that her plans & hopes for others were too much regarded as proceeding from herself—& never sufficiently separated from the thought of her own individuality." He hoped illness had presented "a most useful & perhaps required discipline."[65]

A few days after Thom sent Channing his insightful, if overly optimistic, analysis, a sudden relapse brought the most severe trial of Dix's sojourn. Again confined to her room, she found that "now it is less easy to maintain a perfectly regulated and tranquil mind than through the winter." She was tired of indisposition. When she received a letter from Mary Torrey reporting on Channing's uncharacteristic pastoral energy after a stroke crippled the indefatigable Ezra Stiles Gannett, Dix observed with satisfaction that "there is a time when all Invalids require rousing from what originally was needed rest." She now expected that she too would benefit from exertion, and she started riding again within a few weeks of the unexpected downturn.[66]

Even more than Torrey's description of the contrasting Federal Street ministers, news of Helen Loring's continued decline came to Dix as a tacit reproach. Throughout her stay at Greenbank, her brother Charles and others had sent eulogies to her cheerful, self-sacrificing friend. Sensitive to the implicit comparison, Dix at first maintained she was feebler than Loring. "I little deemed she would outlast me," she had told Torrey. "It will be her privilege to die in the *exercise* of ministration to others: strange that is is mine, only to be ministered to."[67] But as she recovered and Loring continued to waste away, Dix pointed to a deeper lesson in their parallel situations. She observed that "it seems to me [Loring] mistakes duty sometimes; but it is not easy to judge for others, except we can take in, and carefully weigh, all circumstances, and indeed know what few can, the secret springs of action." Reflecting her belief that friends in Boston had failed to appreciate her own condition, Dix commented: "It *is* marvellous that when we feel the impossibility of being understood in society at large . . . we are so ready to censure mentally or audibly, the conduct of others. A knowledge of *motives* would full often strangely revolutionize our opinions."[68]

If Dix felt increasingly inclined to get on with her life, the dreary prospect awaiting her at home remained a powerful incentive to remain in Europe. In March she had sent her grandmother a pointed acknowledgment of "the first and only expression of affectionate remembrance from you since parting." Shortly afterward, Madam Dix dictated a letter urging her to return home. She had expressed through visitors her desire to see her namesake again, and to Dix she added that the long stay at Greenbank had resulted in little benefit while imposing a heavy burden on the Rathbones. Her granddaughter testily replied on May 16 that "it was not less surprizing than painful to know you indulged so much solicitude on that point." She stood by her decision to leave Boston. "That results have not answered expectation is not to prove that there was error in adopting the [medical] advice," she argued. Confident the Harris family was meeting Madam Dix's "every want and comfort" and emphatic that a voyage back across the Atlantic was "absolutely out of the question as impracticable," she rejected the plea to return. To the contrary, she announced that she would probably travel abroad for a while.[69]

Dix soon learned that her grandmother had died two weeks earlier. As Helen Loring noted, the news "could hardly have been sudden intelligence" despite recent reports of the nonagenarian's recovery from a long winter of influenza. Dix reacted calmly. She characterized her meditations as "not deeply sad," although "more than usually wandering." She felt her grandmother's death had "divided the only link, save the yet closer one of fraternal bonds, which allied me to kindred," but she unhesitatingly pledged that "in the lot appointed for me on earth I hope to abide in submissive trust." Reversing her recent plans, she now struggled to restrain the "first wish of my mind to return to America at once" and quickly found that Sarah Tuckerman, Sarah Gibbs, and Harriet Hare were all planning summer return voyages that she might join.[70]

Fond of making dramatic appearances, Dix embarked on the ocean crossing on August 24 without notifying her friends in Boston. The Rathbones bid her a gracious farewell, promising to obey her injunction to write regularly. "Do not hope to do great good alone," John Hamilton Thom exhorted in a futile final blessing. "Do not seek *in this way* to be morally independent. Make others happy by permitting them to feel that they are necessary *to your* happiness."[71] Dix may have sailed with Sarah Gibbs, as she proceeded directly to Oakland upon her arrival in the United States. In any event, the chance to talk about the Rathbones doubtless made the initial visit to the Channings especially appealing. She rested near Newport for the remaining weeks of the season before heading to Boston, her health much the same as when she had departed.[72]

4

I Tell What I Have Seen!

IN OCTOBER 1837, eighteen months after she sailed for Europe, Dix returned to her family home. As one of her younger cousins observed, her appearance at Washington Street personified an ideal of American womanhood. The rare adventure of foreign travel seemed a characteristic experience for the "tall slender young woman of erect graceful figure and deliberate gentle movements, with an appearance of delicate health." Her fine merino dress was ornamented only by a white ruffle, "which well became the slender neck and delicate face above it." She had started to arrange her chestnut hair in the fashion she would favor for the rest of her life, gathered to a coil in long loops. The conservative style neatly framed her blue-grey eyes and "a sweet grave face, lighted up by not too frequent smiles." Dix's cousin later told her that "there was a little more of a *stir* in the domestic circle when your arrival was spoken of, than was common in our house at the reception of a guest."[1]

— 1 —

The unusual stir evident to a child at Washington Street was the muffled sound of family upheaval. Dix returned to find that she no longer had a home where she had lived and worked for the five years before her journey to England. Madam Dix, whose will had long provided for the equal partition of her real estate between her Harris grandchildren and the children of Joseph Dix, had written additional testamentary instructions in August 1836 offering free use of the Washington Street house to Mary and Thaddeus Mason Harris for the rest of their lives. Upon Madam Dix's death, her executor simply sold the house on favorable terms to the minister, who had retired from his pulpit and now moved from his Dorchester estate into Boston. Dix hoped for an "opportunity of creating a *kind* and *kindred* sentiment of *rational, permanent good feeling*" with the unctuous Harris and his imperious wife, but they offered no lasting welcome to their niece. Nor could Dix establish a common household with her brother Charles, who was almost constantly on voyages at sea, or with Joseph, who remained with the Harrises. She stored her share of the heirloom furniture, sent many of her grandmother's books to Elizabeth Rathbone, and left Washington Street forever.[2]

Financially, Dix was fairly well prepared for independence. To her considerable savings from teaching and writing she now added her inheritance of a one-sixth interest in the Orange Court garden and in the proceeds from the sale of the mansion to Harris. Her portion of her grandmother's estate was valued at approximately $4,000, and she could reasonably look forward to benefiting at least in part from the equal shares of her brothers. She was not wealthy, but her austere tastes and prudent management would enable her to live comfortably on the income from her capital.[3]

Sympathetic friends tried to help Dix find a new place to live in Boston. Nineteen-year-old Mary Channing urged her to move into her father's house, but Dix declined to go there while the minister and his wife were traveling. The Heaths lamented that they did not want her to stay in a boardinghouse but were too crowded to accommodate her indefinitely. "She would be a real acquisition," Susan Heath noted in her diary when Dix stayed in Brookline for several weeks in the fall. "She is a remarkable character! A perfect mystery." Anne Heath suggested that Dix take rooms with a neighboring family, but she recognized that such an arrangement was not "the inducement which would keep you: a *home* where your affections may securely repose, & find an answering voice."[4]

As winter approached, Dix decided to seek the warmer air of the South. In January 1838, she left Boston again, expecting to be away for two or three years. She planned tentatively to go to Charleston, South Carolina, but her destination was less important than her point of departure. Her lonely, frustrating return to Boston, dramatized by the contrast with her happiness in Liverpool, was such a painful experience that she sought to "banish it, by resolutely applying the thoughts to other subjects" and to cultivate toward her Harris relatives "a spirit of forgiveness and forbearance,—and as far as possible of forgetfulness." Three months before her thirty-sixth birthday, she was completely alone. In an emotional farewell letter, Heath wrote that "if you send me only a little poetry & the rest blank paper, I shall conclude you returned to your native planet. I never thought this world your home, & I still think of you as something bright, high & distant, but unapproachable."[5]

After a brief pause in New York, Dix proceeded to Washington. There she was welcomed into the home of William Jones, a friend of the Channings, and her intended stopover lengthened into a sojourn of two months. Finding it easy to avoid social calls in a city where she knew almost nobody, Dix gratefully occupied herself with reading, sewing, and walking. She took rooms in Georgetown for a week and toured the college, the orphanage asylum, the Catholic convent, and the Protestant female seminary. She visited the Capitol twice, but she preferred to follow politics less closely, through the newspapers. She most enjoyed the Library of Congress, which she concluded "would make a very attractive apartment were it less often resorted to by the Members and others who make it too public for ladies to desire to spend much time there." In March 1838 she learned that her old friend Elizabeth Higginson, who had married minister Reuel Keith, was now living nearby in Virginia, and for the next several months she moved to the seminary at which Keith taught. Despite the heat of spring and summer, she reported in July that "I have no recollection of any season at the north less oppressive than has been the present here."[6]

As much as she enjoyed her southern excursion, Dix recognized that her travels lacked a purpose. Her quiet habits in Washington and Alexandria were difficult to reconcile with her declarations that "life is not to be expended in vain regrets—self is not to be the object of contemplation—individual trials are not to be admitted to fill the mind to the exclusion of the sufferings of the *many*." She maintained that life "cannot be granted to any, but for some wise and good end. What that end be, it is ours diligently to inquire." Although she hoped that she was strengthening her health for future usefulness, by midsummer she was again suffering from pain and swelling. Moreover, the lodgings available in Boston began to look more acceptable as she learned her alternatives in strange cities. She quickly developed "a disgust of what are called private Boarding Houses (strange misnomer)," but she knew no family with whom she could remain happily for more than an extended visit. After a tour with the Keiths through western Pennsylvania and Niagara Falls, she returned to Boston in the fall as a boarder with the family of schoolteacher Joseph Hale Abbot.[7]

For the next year, Dix remained helplessly adrift. She was, she confessed in November 1838, "a floating wad upon the ocean of each day's events." Overwhelmed when she entered a church in Boston for the first time in three years, she was barely able to remain and wonder, "Where, where are the severed links?"[8] Her social connections in the city had dwindled sadly. Helen Loring ended her long decline shortly after watching Charles Dix embark on a voyage to Africa in June 1838. Sarah Tuckerman's mother died in September. Martha Higginson, like her sister, had married a minister and left Boston. Dix left her nominal residence with the Abbots whenever possible to visit friends in Maine, Rhode Island, New Hampshire, and western Massachusetts. When Martha Higginson and her husband, Ichabod Nicols, invited her to prolong a visit to Portland in October 1839, Dix gladly stayed, explaining that in Boston "my presence does little good, and to myself, much harm."[9]

Dix did not fail to notice that the spectacular cultural flowering underway in Boston offered many examples of women inventing new forms of active, independent lives. For the most part, however, she sternly disapproved of their causes and methods. She and Mary Torrey raised a mutual eyebrow at Channing's enthusiasm for Angelina Grimké's unprecedented public lectures, together wishing that women "would understand what their *real* rights are!" They shared outrage at the abolitionist agitation led by Federal Street Church parishioner Maria Weston Chapman, whose life-threatening "brain fever" seemed "the natural result of such unfeminine & mischievious conduct." Appalled by "the German & Emerson Mania" that was attacking *"sound doctrine,"* neither woman would join the Transcendentalist *"conversation class"* that Margaret Fuller conducted in the winter of 1839. Indeed, when Ralph Waldo Emerson later suggested that the *Dial* review a new edition of *Private Hours,* Fuller correctly predicted that Dix probably would not give her a copy of the prayerbook.[10]

In December 1839, Dix drifted back into a life centered around the

Channing family, accepting Sarah Gibbs's renewed invitation to join her household. Perched near the summit of Beacon Hill, Gibbs's mansion at 85 Mount Vernon Street was one of the most magnificent homes in Boston, a masterpiece of Federal architecture that Charles Bulfinch had designed for Harrison Gray Otis, the soul of the codfish aristocracy. In her dining room, Gibbs displayed Washington Allston's monumental canvas of the prophet Jeremiah dictating to a scribe, a somewhat incongruous decoration but a perfect image of the aspirations that William Ellery Channing brought to the conversational table. The pastor, who also lived on Mount Vernon Street and was soon to move into a townhouse on Gibbs's land, used his sister-in-law's house as his domestic retreat, an Oakland in the city.[11]

Within a month of her return to the Channing circle, Dix felt *"at home,* and *at ease"* for the first time since leaving Liverpool. She confided that she would likely remain indefinitely at Mount Vernon Street. She still took no interest in the brilliant society around Channing. "I visit very little," she told the dazzled Heath, "finding no more pleasure in [an] evening so spent than in days gone by, when parties were contemplated from a *distance."* Instead, she enjoyed a quiet, comfortable relationship with the minister. Reading to him became one of her central pleasures, as did the remembrance of shared friends at Greenbank. Channing's preaching, too, appealed freshly to Dix. When he delivered an address on the education of the laboring classes that sparked controversy by calling on workers to renounce collective action and rely on self-improvement to penetrate through hardening class barriers, she attended her first public lecture in years and reported that "I never listened to Dr. C. with more pleasure."[12]

Once settled into Mount Vernon Street, Dix started to look again for opportunities for social usefulness. Her health now usually excellent, she joined several benevolent enterprises. Most notably, she began to teach a Sunday school for teenage boys at the Charlestown Navy Yard, her first class since she disbanded her school at Orange Court. "It is a great satisfaction again to teach," she observed. "It is a great satisfaction again to be not quite idle, to feel that I am not wholly a burthen in the social circle."[13] The trial of aimlessness was apparently ending. Teaching would yet enable Dix to complement the sense of fulfillment that she was at last finding in her domestic life.

— 2 —

In March 1841, Dix's renewed teaching ambitions prompted her to visit two interesting local institutions. On March 11, she toured the Massachusetts State Normal School in Lexington. Established two years earlier as the first state program in American history for the training of teachers, Lexington was a centerpiece of the reforms initiated by Massachusetts' dynamic Secretary of Education, Horace Mann. The attempt of the State Normal School to professionalize and improve public education was widely recognized as one of the most important social experiments of the age. Prominent reformers Lucretia Mott, Samuel Gridley Howe, and Robert Rantoul, Jr., helped select the first classes of students. Mann persuaded Cyrus Peirce, one of the leading teachers in the state, to become the principal of the school or, more precisely, to serve as the administrator, instructor, and janitor responsible for realizing the anticipated success of the woefully underfunded institution.[14]

Often dubious about his progress with the students, Peirce warmly welcomed Dix as a visitor who was "intimate in Dr. Channing's family and celebrated in the School line." He suspected that her praise for the school concealed criticisms similar to his own reservations, commenting to Mann that "I have (enter nos) some curiousity to know whether she thought as well of us after she got to the city as she professed to do here." Peirce had for some time thought that the school, which was restricted to women students, would benefit from the addition of a matron "as the older friend and adviser of the young ladies." He now saw that Dix might be perfect for that position.[15]

On March 28, Dix made another educational inspection, this time at the Middlesex County House of Correction in East Cambridge, when Harvard Divinity School student John Taylor Gilman Nichols asked her to take over his Sunday school class at the prison. Nichols later recalled that he invited Dix, on the recommendation of his stepmother Martha Higginson Nichols, because he felt incompetent to teach the young women assigned to him.[16] As the Divinity School's Philanthropic Society, which organized the prison Sunday school, had become primarily a debating club, he may also have been influenced by the distraction of preparing a major essay on temperance for debate before the Society on the following Wednesday.[17] Whatever his motives, he found a willing substitute in Dix, who had occasionally taught Sunday school in the Charlestown state prison when she was living at Washington Street.

After leading class for an hour, Dix crossed the yard from the House of Correction for sentenced prisoners to the smaller jail. Designed by Charles Bulfinch a few years after he built Sarah Gibbs's home, the jail resembled a simplified version of her Federal mansion on Beacon Hill. It provided a detention facility for inebriates, defendants awaiting trial, witnesses, and debtors making shoes to repay their creditors. Among its many functions, the jail helped Middlesex County comply with a state law requiring each county to provide within the precincts of its house of correction "a suitable and convenient apartment or receptacle for idiots and lunatic or insane persons, not furiously mad" to accommodate overflow from the crowded state mental hospital in Worcester. About a dozen such inmates lived at East Cambridge when Dix visited in late March. She noticed some of them in the jail and asked the warden to provide them with a fire. When he replied that a flame was unnecessary and unsafe, Dix complained at the adjacent county courthouse and arranged for heat in the cells.[18]

The visit to the Middlesex County jail spurred Dix's interest in the moral education of prisoners and her sympathy for the insane. She began to teach regularly in the East Cambridge Sunday school, furnish religious tracts to the inmates, arrange for ministers to preach at the prison, and examine similar institutions in the area. Passing through Boston on a tour of the United States, William Rathbone, Jr., reported to Greenbank in June 1841 that "Miss Dix is pretty well and I think might be perfectly so if she would only be moderately prudent" but that she was routinely making weekday visits to prisons and other institutions. Showing the young tourist the local sites of interest to her, Dix brought Rathbone to a botanical garden and to the complex of facilities in South Boston, including the Suffolk County House of Correction, the Perkins Institute for the Blind, and the new Boston Lunatic Hospital for city paupers who were unable to obtain a place in the Worcester State Lunatic Hospital.[19]

Although friends worried that she was overtaxing her strength, Dix further expanded her prison work in July, asking fellow Federal Street parishioner Nathan Appleton for aid in establishing a permanent library of uplifting literature at East Cambridge. The appeal diverted her attention almost entirely from the prison. In commending the charity to the textile magnate, she pointedly observed that many of the male prisoners and almost all of the women had worked in the Lowell mills. Appleton strenuously denied her aspersions on the oft-repeated claims that his business provided a wholesome influence in the maturation of young women. He presented a certificate from the Lowell police court to rebut Dix's charges and supplemented his polite reply to her letter with the blunt response of an assistant who sought to give Dix "a lesson to be more cautious in making sweeping charges against whole classes of persons." The outraged Dix in turn sent back Appleton's donated books as morally inappropriate and started intermittent research to prove the degrading tendency of industrial labor.[20]

While Dix's project at East Cambridge advanced unevenly, a much larger opportunity presented itself in Lexington. In August 1841, Peirce broached to Mann the appointment of a matron, and they soon identified Dix as the leading candidate.[21] The matron would take charge of the school's boardinghouse and direct the students' personal development, which Mann and Peirce believed to be no less fundamental than the acquisition of pedagogical skills. The role potentially commended a vast influence. The guidance of the matron would radiate throughout the Normal School and define the professional character of schoolteachers throughout Massachusetts, the state that shaped education throughout the country. Here was the main chance of Dix's teaching career. The Normal School, at a critical stage of development in one of the most important educational innovations in the United States, offered a position in which she could make a contribution to her field comparable to the achievements of such contemporaries as Catharine Beecher and Mary Lyon. She could become, as she had hoped to be at her Orange Court school, a teacher of teachers.

Dix jumped at the opportunity. She could not bring herself to surrender abruptly her home at Mount Vernon Street, but she proposed to establish herself almost equally in Lexington. She promised to come to the Normal School at least two or three times each week. She planned to hire a steward to manage the boardinghouse on a daily basis and a young woman to supervise the students and act as a counselor. The house would be "made a *good Boarding Establishment decidedly* in every respect," for which students would pay $2 per week. Dix would personally meet any additional expenses, an important consideration for the financially struggling school.[22]

Peirce was overwhelmed by Dix's plans, which he recognized as the basis for a powerful independent authority in the Normal School. "It is rather too much a wheel within a wheel," he objected. He maintained that "as . . . the earth can have but one sun, so there can be but one head in the administration of the Normalty." The tenor as well as the scope of Dix's potential influence disturbed Peirce. Dix hoped to create in her boardinghouse the discipline of a convent. Not only would she ban riding and walking with gentlemen; she would also prohibit all calls from any males except relatives. She did not want her girls to appear in public even to pick up letters from the post office. But if Dix envisioned the Normal School as a vocational community instilling feminine solidarity and commitment, Peirce worried that her plans contemplated a pernicious and impossible isolation from society. "The good lady must not expect to make these normalers *young ladies* in the sense in which her own scholars were," he argued to Mann. "They are designed for a somewhat different sphere & must see & encounter more of the roughness of Life." Peirce recalled Dix's unpopularity among her students at the Orange Court school and predicted that "her nice notions and straitlaced prudery may render her somewhat disagreeable to the young folks, who must sometimes *laugh loud,* and run and jump, as well as study and sit up *prim.*"[23] He and Mann quickly decided to back away from their offer.

Samuel Gridley Howe, one of Mann's best friends and a slight acquaintance of Dix, assumed the delicate task of deflecting her interest in the Normal School. The assignment was ironic, for although Howe was perhaps the most celebrated humanitarian in the United States, he privately shared Dix's anxious search for satisfying work. The American hero of the Greek Revolution as a physician, a guerilla warrior, and an administrator of charitable donations, Howe had returned to Boston with Byron's helmet and a flamboyant passion for grand chivalry in the service of philanthropy. His subsequent triumph as director of the Perkins Institute for the Blind, particularly in training the blind, deaf, and mute Laura Bridgman, had captured the imagination of the Western world as a symbol of the irrepressible human spirit. But as he approached forty, Howe was losing interest in the education of the blind and was eager to find a new challenge. In the spring of 1841 he had applied for a diplomatic post in Madrid, a step that his close friend Charles Sumner easily recognized as a sign of his restlessness. Sumner encouraged Howe to direct his energies instead to his tempestuous courtship of twenty-two-year-old Julia Ward, whom Howe had met a few months before he took up Dix's plan to join the Normal School.[24]

Howe rebuffed Dix's proposal in September 1841 with his usual air of gallantry. Her plan was "too generous & self-sacrificing on your part to be accepted." He, Mann, and Peirce "thought we knew so much better than you could what a great weight of care and anxiety it would devolve upon you—& therefore decided for you." Howe assured Dix that she was welcome to the position if she truly wanted the burden, but he added for the first time that if she accepted it she would have to pay to furnish the boardinghouse. As an alternative to the Normal School he hinted, oblivious to Dix's traumatic experience at Orange Court, that the true priority in educational reform was the establishment of model schools "to prove by *demonstration* what a school for children well managed can do."[25]

Howe was also quick to encourage Dix's work in East Cambridge, where she had asked the humanitarian physician to intervene on behalf of a mildly disturbed young woman who was confined with a furiously mad cellmate. Howe readily agreed, noting that "the dreadful condition of the Insane in Cambridge & the neighborhood is such as demands a public exposition." He soon visited the jail with Sumner and arranged for the young woman to be moved to another cell. Howe's restlessness and his compassion for the downtrodden converged perfectly with his task for the State Normal School. After returning from East Cambridge, he suggested to Dix that they discuss further the problem of the unhospitalized insane. Meanwhile, Mann and Peirce hired a different matron at Lexington.[26]

— 3 —

Her hopes for the Normal School dashed, Dix threw herself wholly into the life of the prison. She supported the construction of a chapel in the house of correction and heightened the intensity of her Sunday school.

This religious instruction was directed both toward the inmates and toward the Harvard Divinity School students who continued to visit the prison. She urged the future ministers to preach extemporaneously in order to express immediate piety, and she criticized any deficiencies of fervor in their sermons. One student who felt renewed by Dix's example told his father that "speaking so kindly as she does both to us and of us is a sort of constant rebuke, when we think of what she is doing." He described Dix as a "warmly interested" speaker who "went on talking until she was quite exhausted" in her appeals to the prisoners awaiting trial.[27] By December 1841, her friends were united in calling for her to rest. Heath pressed Dix to defer to Channing and stay home until spring, urging that "he is rational, and you, a little given to extravagance." Dix retired to Mount Vernon Street to regain strength, but continued to follow the spiritual progress of the prison through the reports of the divinity students.[28]

During the winter Dix saw little of Howe, who traveled to Kentucky to lobby for the construction of a state school similar to the Perkins Institute. Their mutual project for the insane continued to develop, however, through Howe's contact with Edward Jarvis, a young physician from Boston who had settled in Louisville. Jarvis was urging the state legislature to convert the state insane asylum from a purely custodial institution to a modern mental hospital. His pamphlet *Insanity and Insane Asylums* capably summarized contemporary medical thought about mental disorders. He described in detail the clinical regimen known as "moral treatment," which had superseded the "heroic treatment" of insanity by bloodletting and other aggressive measures that were intended to exhaust or overpower mental patients. Developed simultaneously in France and England in the early nineteenth century, the moral treatment attempted to inculcate self-control in patients rather than impose violent coercion. The critical instrument in this therapy was the insane asylum. Proponents of the moral treatment envisioned the asylum as a curative milieu that would instill discipline through the gentle influence of a carefully regulated, meticulously sane environment. They expected the insane to benefit from the order of a daily routine, the satisfaction of meaningful employment, the intellectual stimulation of diversions, an identity in the asylum community, and above all, the personal guidance of the asylum superintendent.[29]

Howe

Dix undoubtedly read *Insanity and Insane Asylums,* which reinforced and refined her existing ideas.[30] She had long shared in the broad public understanding of the moral treatment, endorsing the asylum movement a dozen years earlier in *The Pearl,* and she had recently seen the holistic therapy demonstrated at the Worcester State Lunatic Hospital, the Boston Lunatic Hospital, and the McLean Asylum of the Massachusetts General Hospital. Most important in her thinking, however, the moral treatment closely resembled the principles she had ardently promoted as a schoolteacher. As one historian has recently pointed out, academies like Dix's boarding school at Orange Court were "quasi-custodial institutions" that shared much of the ideology underlying asylums.[31] Her plans for the boardinghouse at the Massachusetts State Normal School similarly envisioned an ideal environment for the cultivation of self-discipline. Dix's combination of interests in moral education and the moral treatment was not unusual. Horace Mann, for example, had won his first fame as a young state legislator by sponsoring the establishment of the Worcester State Lunatic Hospital in 1830.

Howe and Dix launched their campaign in earnest in June 1842. Howe arranged for John Gorham Palfrey, editor of the prestigious *North American Review,* to commission him to review Jarvis's pamphlet in a lengthy article about the condition of the unhospitalized insane.[32] Dix began to visit jails and almshouses in eastern and central Massachusetts to gather information. This summer tour was much more extensive and more deliberately planned than her previous informal inquiries into a few major institutions outside of East Cambridge. Her concerns, however, remained the same as they had been since her first visit to the Middlesex County jail. She counted the insane, noted their general condition, and tried to alleviate individual suffering when possible. She took special interest in the provisions for religious instruction, the frequency of pastoral visits, and the availability of uplifting literature.[33] She passed her observations along to Howe, and he followed her leads to the worst facilities. When she suggested that he return to East Cambridge, where the number of insane inmates had doubled in a year, he brought along Jarvis, who had recently moved back to Boston, and Jarvis promptly sent an anonymous paragraph to the Boston *Courier* deploring the situation. Dix apparently did not plan to write an independent report on the condition of the insane; to the contrary, she told Howe in late August

1842 that she was at last turning her attention more fully to the mill girls at Lowell.[34]

The next few weeks changed Dix's plans forever. On September 8, Howe published a sensational article in the Boston *Daily Advertiser* exposing the treatment of the insane at East Cambridge as "disgraceful in the highest degree to a Christian community." The renowned humanitarian's charges immediately ignited a controversy. Two days after Howe's article appeared, the state legislature appointed a special investigatory committee, which quickly reported that the accommodations for the insane at East Cambridge were inadequate. Prison physician Anson Hooker responded with a public letter sharply denying that the conditions were as bad as Howe had alleged. Always eager to rise to a challenge, Howe replied in extensive detail, and a fierce newspaper debate continued for a month. To support his charges, Howe sought corroboration from Sumner, Jarvis, and Dix.[35]

Agreeing to confirm Howe's account, Dix offered to write an article for the *Daily Advertiser* that would broaden the public debate from the mistreatment of the insane in East Cambridge to the problem throughout Massachusetts. But editor Nathan Hale rejected the report, and Howe told Dix that he "did not choose to urge what I think [Hale] should have been ready to solicit." Howe assured her that his article for the *North American Review* would make full use of her research. "I shall follow in your footsteps," he promised, "and gather all the information I can respecting the condition of these poor creatures, and put it with yours, in such a shape as will, I trust, effectually cure the evil." He warned Palfrey to expect controversy about the essay, now postponed from the October 1842 to the January 1843 issue of the quarterly.[36]

As Dix decided whether to continue to work solely through Howe or to pursue the independent course charted by her proposed article, the underlying tranquillity of her private life suddenly shattered. During the week that Howe published his exposé in the *Daily Advertiser,* William Ellery Channing suffered an attack of typhoid fever while on vacation near Dix's childhood home in Bennington. He quickly began to sink, and Mount Vernon Street took up a death watch through September for the stricken minister in Vermont. The end that his admirers expected came when he died on October 2.

Dix felt Channing's death deeply.[37] Unitarianism had lost its brightest light, and her longtime pastor was silent at a pivotal juncture of her life. Her beloved home at Mount Vernon Street was also likely to break up, as Sarah Gibbs would obviously form a common household with her widowed sister. But, true to her faith, Dix's mourning competed with rejoicing for the immortal life achieved by Channing. And mingled with her pain was a sense of liberation from the obsessively prudent guardian who had thought of Dix as a perilously spinning top. Shortly after Channing's death, Susan Heath was surprised to notice that Dix was "uncommonly agreeable and communicative" despite her grief.[38]

Amid the swirl of emotions, Dix determined to expand her proposed newspaper article about the insane. On the day of Channing's death she wrote a terse corroboration of Howe's charges that was published the next day. Her letter declared that the appalling conditions at East Cambridge were better than the treatment of insane paupers elsewhere in Massachusetts, and she promised that the deplorable situation throughout the state would soon be placed before the public.[39]

Dix now began a dramatic escalation of her visits to jails and almshouses. She crisscrossed Massachusetts during the last three months of 1842, inspecting town and county institutions from the western Berkshire mountains to the tip of Cape Cod. In one week alone she visited thirty-five towns. Traveling constantly, she returned to Boston only on Sundays. "If I fail in this work," she vowed, "it shall be through no negligence of mine."[40] Her exhaustive survey carried to an unprecedented degree the reckless zeal that Channing had always disapproved of. Even Howe, who admired Dix's robust display of energy, felt obliged to dissuade her from sailing to Nantucket and Martha's Vineyard to complete her circuit.

Going far beyond her work during the summer, Dix's autumn tour squarely anticipated her independent participation in the public discussion that Howe hoped to provoke through his article in the *North American Review.* Meanwhile Howe, reasoning that "we shall need some humane & energetic person to put himself at the head of the movement" in the Massachusetts legislature, won election as a Whig member of the state House of Representatives.[41] He promptly encouraged Dix to summarize "the result of your painful & toilsome tour" in a memorial to the legislature.[42] She wrote the report at Mount Vernon Street in the first few weeks of January 1843, showing drafts to Howe as she worked. He repeatedly urged her to eliminate all hearsay evidence and eased her apprehensions about the propriety of some of her statements. "I have not seen an intimation that the most squeamish would stickle at," he assured her.[43] Dix completed the memorial in time for the opening of the session, and Howe presented it to the legislature at the first meeting on January 19.

— 4 —

Dix's _Memorial to the Legislature of Massachusetts_ was one of the most remarkable documents of the era. Part legislative petition, part Unitarian sermon, part personal justification, the thirty-page petition transformed her study of prison and almshouse conditions into a fascinating exploration of American society. Her gripping narrative contrasted sharply with Howe's forceful but prosaic essay in the _North American Review_ and fulfilled the literary potential that she had long ago suggested in her children's tales. The polemical, religious, and autobiographical strands of the memorial united dramatically in Dix's conclusion that the plight of the insane compelled her to transform traditional ideals of womanhood and enter actively into public life.

Discarding her September draft for the _Daily Advertiser_, Dix adopted a new approach to present the results of her investigation. In her newspaper submission she planned to analyze the state law requiring confinement of unhospitalized insane paupers in county jails and to tabulate the number of local institutions in which she had found insane inmates suffering; anecdotal evidence merely illustrated her point that "these places _cannot be made_, crowded as they are, _either decent or comfortable._"[44] In contrast, the legislative memorial argued through significant details culled from Dix's survey rather than through a statistical summary of her findings. Howe, whose article estimated at length the insane population of Massachusetts, urged Dix to provide an updated count from her tour, but the memorial stated only that she had seen "hundreds of insane persons in every variety of circumstance and condition" in her three months traversing the state and almost two years of interest in the subject. The situation of most of the insane, she conceded, "could not and need not be improved." Her memorial sought solely to demonstrate the condition of the substantial minority "whose lives are the saddest picture of human suffering and degradation."[45]

Instead of an overview, Dix presented a series of representative cases. After establishing the scope of her investigation through short notes on the treatment of the insane in thirty widely scattered communities, she devoted the bulk of the memorial to close accounts of almshouses and prisons in twelve towns. Dix named the places she discussed and often gave the dates of her visits, unlike Howe, whose article briefly described several of the same scenes. She emphasized repeatedly that she had accepted no secondhand accounts. *"I tell what I have seen!"* she promised, warning that she "would "speak with great plainness" about "many things revolting to the taste."[46]

The memorial was an unforgettable kaleidoscope of horror, describing in painful detail "the *present* state of Insane Persons confined within this Commonwealth, in *cages, closets, cellars, stalls, pens! Chained, naked, beaten with rods,* and *lashed* into obedience!" Dix opened with a graphic account of a Danvers woman in "the horrid process of tearing off her skin by inches; her face, neck, and person, were thus disfigured to hideousness." She went next to the Newburyport almshouse, where a man was kept in an out-building alongside " 'the dead room,' affording in lieu of companionship with the living, a contemplation of corpses!" The memorial continued in a relentless succession of insane men and women paralyzed by cold, wallowing in filth, and confined in plank sheds without light. Dix professed to believe that most wardens and almshouse keepers were innocent of deliberate cruelty, but her descriptions accused them of brutal indifference to the welfare of their charges. The sole principles for care of the insane were stringent economy and the prevention of escape. Few insane inmates had heat or clothes or more furniture than a handful of straw or a lock of hay. Dix reported that she had seen inmates beaten "both passionately and repeatedly." She depicted a young woman chained to a wall in Westford and a man throttled by an iron collar in Groton. In Newton she found "something I was told was a man, I could not tell, as likely it might have been a wild animal." Through the neglect of an almshouse keeper, the inmate's feet had frozen and been amputated, "yet from these stumps, these maimed members were swinging chains, fastened to the side of the building."[47]

Dix disdained to subordinate these images to "earnest persuasion, or stubborn argument." Most conspicuously, she did not join Howe in arguing that the state was obliged to care for the insane because mental

disorders reflected the "imperfect or vicious social institutions and obser-
vances" of modern civilization.[48] She maintained that the causes of insanity were irrelevant and declared without apology that she had not investigated them. The duty of society, she asserted, was identical whether
insanity came from a life of sin or from pure misfortune. Nor did Dix
dwell on the prospects for curing the insane in a state hospital rather
than in local jails and almshouses. Emphasizing potential recoveries,
Howe merely acknowledged a public interest in the incurable insane;
Dix concentrated almost exclusively on hopeless medical cases. She
promised that the insane would be safe, comfortable, and peaceful if
removed from jails and almshouses, but she did not claim that all of
these inmates would regain rationality. Her most specific recommendation for legislative action was that "we need an Asylum for this class,
the incurable, where conflicting duties shall not admit of such examples
of privations and misery."[49] She did not mention the long-term savings
offered by state institutions that would heal the insane, a point that
Howe raised with studied diffidence for the mingling of economy and
philanthropy.

But although Dix presented her appalling descriptions as a random
sample of her survey, without generalizing overviews or supporting arguments, the memorial was as carefully designed as Howe's closely reasoned
essay. In place of Howe's policy analysis, Dix unified her petition as an
allegorical sermon to the legislators. The conditions in the jails and
almshouses served as her text for a pietistic Unitarian interpretation of
the insane that affirmed the primacy of the emotional affections as the
basis of moral nature and illustrated the hope of redemption for a humanity that all too easily lost control of emotions and fell into a maelstrom
of passion.[50]

Dix clearly echoed Channing's last address in her insistence that the
insane shared a capacity for emotional response, and that emotions were
more fundamental and more enduring than human powers of reason.
Two months before his death, while Dix was touring jails and almshouses, Channing had pointed to the soothing effects of kindness on the
insane as proof that love was the divine plan for all earthly relations.
Dix similarly emphasized that merely "the mortal part" was lost "when
the temple of reason falls in ruins."[51] Although the incurable insane were
treated as animals or as wholly impervious to their surroundings, they

retained the essence of true immortal life and responded to kindness as to the warmth of a fire. Improving the condition of these inmates was not for Dix, as it was for Howe, "only, as it were, twining fresh flowers on the graves of the dead."[52] For Dix, the emotional attributes that entitled the insane to respect were the higher rather than the lower faculties of humanity.

But Dix's subjects also illustrated the opposite of the blessed affections. The deserted, helpless insane in the jails and almshouses were denizens of a spiritual underworld estranged from God. Dix dramatically introduced this theme after her accounts of the self-mortifying woman in Danvers and the "dead room" in Newburyport. She narrated in detail her descent into the cellar of the Newburyport almshouse, where she found a woman partially wrapped in blankets who presented "the image of distress" in the most familiar form. Dix wrote that "mournfully she extended her arms and appealed to me, 'why am I consigned to hell? . . . my God! my God! why hast *thou* forsaken me!'" Following this re-envisioned crucifixion, the scenes of Dix's memorial unfolded in a place where "it seemed as if the ancient doctrine of the possession of demons was here illustrated." The blasphemies and uncontrolled rage of the inmates gave "reality to that blackness of darkness, which it is said might convert a heaven into a hell." Dix imagined the insane crying in the words of the abandoned Job: "'Have pity upon me! have pity upon me! for the hand of the Lord hath smitten me.' 'My kinsfolk have failed, and my own familiar friend hath forgotten me.'"[53]

The governing law of the insane in Dix's memorial was unchecked passion. "It may be supposed that paroxysms of frenzy are often exhibited," she confirmed, "and that the tranquil state is rare in comparison with that which incites to violence." She detailed a crushing variety of uncontrollable outbursts. The shouts of the insane often convulsed entire neighborhoods and guided her to them from a distance. Her subjects mutilated themselves, destroyed their meager provisons, and occasionally threatened other people. In turn, brutal caretakers perpetuated "the passions which an iron rule might be expected to stimulate and sustain."[54]

Teetering between sinful passions and redeeming affections, the insane brilliantly demonstrated the central tenet of Dix's strain of Unitarianism, the promise that religious piety could channel ardor into the achievement of self-control.[55] The spiritual restoration of this lost self-control, rather than the medical cure of insanity, was Dix's goal for her subjects. The memorial pointed to several examples of inmates who had achieved peace and stability, although by no means recovering their reason, and had thereby reconnected the severed link with God that insanity represented.[56] Shortly after publication of the memorial, Dix added that she had never seen an inmate, however fierce or disturbed, whom she could not calm with Scripture or prayer uttered in low, gentle tones.[57]

Dix placed herself at the center of this extraordinary narrative of Unitarian conversion. Despite a prefatory promise that "the memorialist will be speedily forgotten in the memorial," she portrayed herself as deliberately and as significantly as she described the insane. Her September draft and Howe's essay made only oblique self-references to prove firsthand knowledge of the conditions reported. In contrast, the memorial maintained a constant focus on Dix to guide her readers' response to those conditions. She showed herself circulating through the institutions dressed in mourning for Channing, distributing books and religious tracts, reading aloud from the Bible, conversing with the inmates and caretakers, and reacting to what she saw. In an encounter with an insane former state legislator in the Ipswich almshouse, for example, she compared her own isolation with his doleful solitude:

> "And have you too lost all your dear friends?" Perhaps my mourning apparel excited his inquiry.
> "Not all."
> "Have you any dear father and mother to love you?" and then he sighed and laughed and traversed the limited stall.[58]

Dix introduced her own character into the memorial as the representative of the gendered values needed to address the problem of the insane. To judge whether conditions were humane in the jails and almshouses, she offered the "peculiar sensitiveness" of "my woman's nature." To vindicate the religious imperative of self-control, she applied her "calm and deep convictions of duty" rather than the "spirit of selfishness and self-seeking" that ordinarily characterized the men of the legislature. She maintained that she could be trusted not to "quicken your sensibilities into short-lived action, to pour forth passionate exclamation, nor yet to move your indignation" against the culpable local officials. But even temperate political intervention required Dix to surrender "my habitual views of what is womanly and becoming." Accordingly, the pivotal drama of the memorial was the course by which Dix justified her entry into public life.[59]

Arranged without regard to the actual chronology of Dix's visits to the jails and almshouses, the scenes of the memorial traced her political awakening. The responses to the insane reported at the outset of her account were sympathetic but tentative. She refrained from protesting to caretakers about their deplorable institutions, resisting the emotional temptation presented by sights that "might have roused to indignation one not dispossessed of reason, and owning self-control." She began to speak out when she met the almshouse keeper who had devised an iron collar that previously horrified her, and thereafter she tried to obtain direct relief for the inmates in every institution she described. The usual result, she ruefully admitted, was that "I made no impression." The futility of her efforts was made clear when a sane inmate in the Newton almshouse refused her request to afford privacy to a raging, almost nude woman kept next to his apartment. Dix, who had been unable to hold her eyes on some of the insane, found that she was now "almost incapable of retreating."[60]

The culmination of Dix's progress toward action in the memorial took place in the inner circle of lost self-control that she saved for her ultimate example of the degraded condition of the insane. As she had foreshadowed in her first vignette, she discovered a "lunatic pauper of decent life and respectable family" in the Worcester almshouse "negligently bearing in her arms a young infant, of which I was told she was the unconscious parent!"[61] This picture was precisely the opposite of the equally charged sexual image that Howe had chosen to close his essay. He asked his readers to remember above all a "poor, trembling, comely girl" who was not insane "but only *silly,*" confined next to a "half naked, yelling maniac" whom Howe imagined "smiting with heavy fists upon the boards which make their only separation."[62] Howe's description—a startlingly different account of the pathetic former legislator at Ipswich who had asked Dix about her family—envisioned insanity as a restless, powerful aggression that threatened rational society. Dix, in contrast, presented insanity as a heightened weakness that necessitated the removal of the afflicted to protect them from the predatory forces of society.

Following the Worcester example, Dix's memorial shifted from a report of abuses to an appeal for reform based on the moral authority of her femininity: "Men of Massachusetts, I beg, I implore, I demand, pity and protection for these of my suffering and outraged sex!" Abandoning her antipathy to public life, she urged the "Fathers, Husbands, Brothers" of the legislature to embrace the values of sensitivity and self-control that she personified.[63] In the brief final section of the memorial, she acted on this lesson of her personal journey by starting to move from the stance of a moral critic to that of a participant in the politics of reform. She presented a series of complaints that she had solicited from municipal officials pressing the state government to assume care of the insane. She analyzed and rejected the suggestion that expanded county institutions might solve the problem she had identified. She discussed the state's interest in removing the insane from prisons to promote the rehabilitation of criminals and suggested that prisoners might sue to challenge their incarceration alongside the insane. With each of these concluding arguments, injecting into the memorial a policy perspective similar to Howe's essay, Dix indicated that she would be not only a humanitarian missionary on behalf of the insane but also their public representative.

— 5 —

Dix's memorial, immediately reprinted as a pamphlet and excerpted in newspapers around the state, was far more controversial than the legislation it supported. Not that the campaign to expand state accommodations for the insane lacked powerful opposition: fiscal retrenchment was the keynote of Governor Marcus Morton's opening address to the legislature and the strongest bond of the Democratic majority. Howe's essay had estimated that construction of a new asylum equal in size to the Worcester hospital would require a new appropriation of $100,000, or approximately one-fourth of the state's ordinary annual expenditures. Alternatively, he had suggested that an available private bequest would enable Massachusetts almost to double the capacity of the Worcester hospital for an appropriation of $25,000. But even this sum represented a significant outlay for a legislature determined to cut expenses. Charles Francis Adams, a leading Whig member of the House of Representatives, predicted that proposed measures for the insane would be defeated by strategic procrastination hidden beneath protestations of sympathy for the humanitarian cause.[64]

For the general public, however, the furor over Dix's memorial overshadowed these budgetary debates. Several communities angrily disputed Dix's descriptions of their care for the insane. Officials in Danvers, claiming that Dix had been in their almshouse for only five minutes, prepared a countermemorial arguing that she had described *"the high wrought fancies of [her] imagination, instead of the practical realities of life."* Shelburne selectmen and overseers of the poor echoed that Dix was "looking forward for something more marvelous than is to be discovered in real life; and because the things themselves will not come up to this pitch of the imagination, the imagination is brought down to them, and has a world of its own creating." Her memorial, they maintained, was a tissue of "bare-faced falsehoods, false impressions, and false statements."[65]

Some supporters of Dix's cause voiced reservations about the memorial that were more difficult to dismiss as self-serving. The Boston *Courier,* which had warmly endorsed reform and reprinted lengthy excerpts from Howe's essay, judged that "the public will be quite liberal, if they receive her facts at a discount of about fifty per cent."[66] Sympathetic William Bentley Fowle, now in the state legislature, expressed confidence in Dix in a newspaper editorial but privately asked his former assistant at the Boston Female Monitorial School how much information about humane treatment she had suppressed and how accurately her sensational examples reflected the overall condition of the unhospitalized insane.[67]

Dix's firmer admirers avoided disputes about specific almshouse conditions and emphasized the image of female benevolence that her memorial so magnificently expressed. Noting that "the degree of feeling, hostile to that lady," was "not extraordinary, considering the character of the pamphlet," the Boston *Mercantile Journal* conceded that Dix may have occasionally missed "mitigating circumstances" in the scenes she described. But the newspaper also saw "much reason to fear" she was equally unaware of "some cases more shocking to humanity." The central point was Dix's sterling character as a witness "distinguished for cherishing a principle of *active benevolence,* and . . . a well-cultivated mind of a superior order." Moreover, as a woman ineligible for political advantage Dix was disinterested as well as dispassionate. "There appears to be no possible _motive_ for this lady to misrepresent," the newspaper maintained.[68]

Gratifying private congratulations echoed this analysis. The distinguished Baptist minister Daniel Sharp saluted Dix for demonstrating the role respectable women should play in politics. "I have been rather sensative [_sic_] in regard to the claims which some have asserted for females," he told her, reporting that he had urged his state representatives to support asylum legislation, "but if they will go on such a ministry of mercy as you have been, I shall not quarrel with them." Mary Torrey's uncle L. M. Sargent, a nationally prominent temperance advocate, urged Dix not to "suffer a moment's disquietude, from a consideration, that there is a morbid sensibility abroad, which may question the propriety of such an investigation, by one of your sex." Drawing on the conventional religious vision of female benevolence that inspired Dix, he assured her: "Woman was last at the cross & first at the tomb, & she is never more in her appropriate station, than when placed precisely as you are at this moment."[69]

The most balanced and thoughtful response to Dix's memorial came from Thomas Bayley Fox, editor of the Newburyport _Herald._ In an editorial calling for immediate expansion of state facilities for the insane, he declared that Dix's "noble work" showed "that the heart of one woman is worth more than all the heads and hearts in the capitol." But when Dix took issue with the editor's identification of minor inaccuracies, Fox sent her a long private letter reviewing her description of the mad woman crying out in the Newburyport almshouse cellar. He concluded that Dix's details may have been literally accurate, but that "the picture your account would give to any reader, does not correspond to reality." To Fox, Dix's spiritual underworld was a spacious kitchen-cellar, "such as can be found in many good houses," with ordinary light and ventilation; the inmate's haunting echo of Jesus on the cross did not express her condition but merely confirmed that her "mania is of a religious style."[70] The conflicting perceptions of Dix and Fox illustrated the unique vision that informed the memorial, an interpretive imagination that sustained Dix but struck even some of her earnest allies as exaggerated and distorted.

Dix fiercely resisted all criticisms of the memorial as personal insults animated by the "passionate excitement" of the officials whose conduct she had exposed.[71] Her response to the mild complaint of Anson Hooker aptly measured her tenacity. Hooker pointed out that the memorial misquoted a letter in which he had said that insane inmates in the East Cambridge jail occupied rooms adjacent to the cells for convicts; according to Dix's memorial, Hooker had admitted that the insane shared individual cells with prisoners, which he had steadfastly denied in his newspaper debate with Howe. Dix scribbled on Hooker's complaint that her version "would be borne out by *facts,*" and she answered the prison physician that a typographical error in her memorial had improved the accuracy of his statement. She declined Hooker's request to correct the misquotation in the reprinting of the memorial. To his surprise, she suggested that he had lost the emotional balance to consider the issue in a civil manner.[72]

Dix's principal ally, Howe, defended the memorial with uncharacteristic timidity. Upon presenting it to the legislature, he had urged her to "select some newspaper as your cannon, from which you will discharge often red-hot shots into the very hearts of the people."[73] But as the controversy grew, his melodramatic fervor soon faded into caution. When Danvers officials opened the attack on the memorial, Howe and minister Robert Cassie Waterston published a letter with their own appalled impressions of the town almshouse. On the specific allegations controverted, however, Howe lost the zeal for point-by-point vindication that had characterized his protracted exchange with Hooker. "From the very nature of things," he equivocated, "the suffering of the insane must be more or less aggravated at different times; the visitor will find them on one day comparatively clean and quiet; on another filthy and furious."[74] Howe never revealed that he had inspected many of the institutions highlighted in Dix's memorial immediately after her visits, and he never offered the unqualified corroboration with which Sumner responded to the criticism of Dix by officials in Shelburne.[75]

As sponsor of the proposal to build new state facilities for the insane, Howe tried to keep the legislature from veering into the public debate over Dix's accuracy. In recognition of his work at the Perkins Institute he was named chairman of the Committee on Public Charitable Institutions, to which Dix's memorial was referred. The committee declined her offer to present additional evidence and her request for a further investigation of the protesting towns in justice to herself as well as the insane. Howe's report for the committee did not mention Dix; its description of the unhospitalized insane relied instead on the statement of Samuel Woodward, the superintendent at Worcester, and on the personal knowledge of the committee. Embarrassed by his failure to vindicate her, Howe called on Dix to ignore "the modicum of censure which is cast upon you." When the legislature brought up her memorial, he rationalized its possible errors, questioned the motives of her critics, emphasized the independence of the committee's findings, and maintained only that Dix's account was "in all its main features true."[76]

The value of Dix's memorial as a polemic was debatable, but its failure as a policy proposal was indisputable. Her recommendation that Massachusetts build an asylum for the incurable insane rather than additional hospital facilities received no serious attention. As Howe had anticipated in his essay, reform advocates instead debated whether to press for a second state mental hospital or to support expansion of the asylum at Worcester. They reluctantly adopted the latter strategy, although they recognized that it would make the state mental hospital too large for inmates to receive the personal attention of the superintendent that was at the heart of the moral treatment.

Refusing to be relegated to the periphery of the legislative contest despite the doubts about her evidence and the rejection of her recommendation, Dix tried to fulfill the promise of her memorial and participate actively in the political fate of the insane poor. In the early days of the session, she solicited letters from superintendents of mental hospitals around New England to support the construction of a new asylum.[77] She attended the legislative debates, providing Howe with additional information, and she discussed the proceedings several times with Palfrey, another of the Boston representatives in the state legislature.[78] On the eve of a crucial vote, she wrote a letter to the leading opponent of the measure, Samuel Allen, supplementing the exhortations of the memorial with an analogy to the central issue of the session, movements to bar participation by state employees or use of state property in the rendition of fugitive slaves to the South and to call for amendments to the federal Constitution that would separate Massachusetts from all connection with slavery. "We appeal *feebly* to our Southern Countrymen to break the bonds of the slave and bid him go free, while *here* we hold men in dungeons," Dix argued, with evident lack of sympathy for the issue that competed against her cause for the attention of legislators.[79]

Dix's emergence astonished observers who had known her earlier. Anne Heath wrote that she could "almost envy your ability to furnish yourself with engrossing, useful employment." A surprised Lydia Maria Child, now one of the leading journalists and reformers in the nation, praised her former housemate for overcoming "her fastidious propriety, and almost excessive reserve of character." Dix thought she was best understood by Horace Mann, although she had met him only recently in the embarrassment over the State Normal School. She beamed when Mann found in her efforts a renewal of the inspiration he had felt in founding the State Lunatic Hospital, a conviction that "all personal enjoyments were criminal until [the insane] were relieved."[80]

On the last day of the session, the legislature narrowly enacted a compromise bill to enlarge the Worcester asylum. The measure added room for 150 more residents, raising the capacity of the hospital to approximately 400 patients. Although the facility would then be much larger than most asylum superintendents thought appropriate for an effective program of moral treatment, reformers saw the growing acknowledgment of state responsibility for the insane poor as an important victory. "Glory—glory & good tidings for all sane & insane," Howe exulted to Sumner. For Dix, the legislation vindicated her difficult entry into public life. Despite the controversy over her memorial and the failure of her policy recommendations, she would later point to the expansion of the Worcester State Lunatic Hospital as her first achievement on behalf of the insane.[81]

On May 1, 1843, one month after the reformers' triumph in the Massachusetts legislature, Mann left for Europe on a honeymoon with his new wife, Elizabeth Palmer Peabody's sister Mary. They were joined by Samuel Gridley Howe and his new wife, who after many serious disagreements had become engaged in the week that the Worcester proposal passed its first significant test in the state House of Representatives. "I am glad to find that Howe managed the case of the Insane so well," Julia Ward joked in accepting Sumner's congratulations. "It gives me less anxiety about his ability to manage such a rattle-head as me."[82]

Dix, too, was embarking on a journey. The death of Channing had left her homeless once again, but this time she had a lasting solution. After years of disappointment in teaching school, she had at last found her vocation. "My painful task is but begun," she told Mann shortly after she completed her memorial. "I put aside myself, and go forth again alone upon that most sad investigation" into the plight of the abandoned insane.[83] She would not end that investigation, or settle permanently into another home, for almost forty years.

5

This Mighty Vortex of Labor

DIX HAD COME to her mission late, not only in transforming her life at the age of forty but also in dedicating herself to a reform movement that had already matured. By 1843, twelve public asylums in the United States provided the moral treatment for the insane poor; another five private institutions had been specializing in the therapy for a quarter-century.[1] As Dix's work on the expansion of the Worcester State Lunatic Hospital indicated, she and others interested in insanity now faced a second generation of issues and challenges: the contest for leadership of the asylum movement, the mobilization of public support to make the moral treatment more widely available without compromising the standards considered essential to its success, and the fate of those individuals that the therapy could not cure. Calling on her audiences to live up to a broadly acknowledged duty of care for the insane, popularizing and enforcing conventional norms as she had in her work as a schoolteacher and a writer, Dix shifted her original aspirations to the new realm of politics.

— 1 —

Dix's activities immediately after the passage of the Worcester hospital bill interwove her past schoolteaching career and the future she was pursuing as a reformer. Spending six months examining public institutions in Vermont, New Hampshire, Rhode Island, and Canada, she inspected schools as well as almshouses, jails, and hospitals. She distributed copies of George B. Emerson's lecture on women's education along with copies of her own memorial to the Massachusetts legislature. As she had no close relations with any experts on welfare institutions, prison reform, or insanity, the Boston schoolmaster served as her chief counselor. Dix asked him to write a preface for a new edition of her memorial and consulted him for advice on "which way to go next."[2]

She was most active in Rhode Island, where she achieved an exhilarating success. Interest in the establishment of an asylum near Providence for insane paupers had recently been stimulated by a bequest of $30,000 for that purpose from Nicholas Brown, whose gifts to the former Rhode Island College had prompted the renaming of the school in his honor. Using Oakland as a base, Dix traveled to all of the towns in the small state to survey "the actual condition of the Insane."[3] Through Providence minister Edward Brooks Hall, the brother of her former coadjutor in the Hope-well Mansion School, she met civic leaders eager to raise the necessary additional financing for the asylum, including Governor James Fenner and Brown College president Francis Wayland. When she reported her findings to the group, one ally marveled that "she has ferreted out some cases of human suffering almost beyond conception or belief."[4]

Dix learned that Cyrus Butler, an aging, childless millionaire, was a promising candidate to solicit for funds except that he had a reputation for brusque indifference to charity. Undaunted, she asked Hall to escort her to Butler's home for a private interview. Neither of the two participants recorded the conversation, but Dix's persuasive powers evidently proved decisive. Already during her Rhode Island tour, the force of her "beautiful, strong nature, shining through a genuine womanhood," had overwhelmed the preconceived antipathy of Hall's wife toward the "self-appointed critic."[5] Butler soon donated $40,000 toward the establishment of a facility for the indigent insane, contingent on public subscription of a matching endowment. The matching funds were soon collected, and for the rest of Dix's life, one of her favorite reminiscences was the story of her conversion of a miser into a founder of the Butler Hospital for the Insane.[6]

In the fall of 1843, Dix decided to undertake a much larger project in New York, where the care of the insane poor had also attracted recent public attention. The opening of the New York State Lunatic Asylum at Utica in January 1843, seven years after the state legislature approved its construction, revitalized the controversy that the institution was intended to resolve. Originally appropriated $50,000 for construction, the building commissioners adopted plans to spend $431,636 for four separate wings that could accommodate more than 1,000 patients. The vast project became a perennial subject of conflict in the state legislature. Noting that the census of 1840 counted approximately 2,300 insane New York residents and more than 700 insane paupers supported by taxpayers in county almshouses across the state, eastern financial interests argued that the commissioners' centralized plan would minimize public expenditures for the care of the insane. Western delegates responded that they wanted a comparable government institution in their region. Physicians, who had been instrumental in pushing the legislature to establish the Utica asylum, called for smaller mental hospitals that would enable superintendents to monitor each patient and would create additional top-level positions for doctors. The opening of the first wing at Utica, providing a program of moral therapy for 225 patients after a state expenditure of more than $200,000, ensured another round of controversy at the next meeting of the Albany legislature.[7]

For Dix, the contest offered a chance to renew the proposal that she had advanced without success in Massachusetts. Like the Worcester State Lunatic Asylum, the Utica hospital concentrated on so-called "curable" cases. Because specialists unanimously agreed that the moral treatment worked best immediately after the onset of insanity, admission to the new hospital was limited to patients afflicted within the past two years. Chronically insane paupers were to remain in county almshouses or outside of institutions. Dix resolved to prepare an exposé on the condition of the insane in the poorhouses and to seek state funding for the incurable cases.

In late September 1843, Dix launched a comprehensive inspection tour through New York. Her ten-week journey across almost sixty counties was a rigorous expedition. Many remote corners of the large state could be reached only in uncomfortable vehicles that followed tortuous routes. From a boat on Lake Erie in mid-November, she reported that "the travelling has been indescribably bad, chiefly plunging through mud-sloughs in mud-wagons or lumber-wagons—or breaking roads through snow-drifts in *sleds:* all sorts of weather except sunny skies. I journey day and night in order to count a little advance." Invigorated by her work, however, she added that "I encounter nothing which a determined will, created by the necessities of the cause I advocate, does not enable me to vanquish."[8]

As she had expected, Dix found "a terrible field of investigation in New York."[9] In some county poorhouses, she saw insane paupers confined to dank cellars, exposed to the winter frost, chained to their beds, or scarred by beatings. But other almshouses demonstrated that humanitarian attitudes toward the insane were penetrating local as well as state institutions. Although Dix never doubted that the establishment of specialized asylums would improve the situation of the insane, she conceded that in several county poorhouses a visitor could "almost forget here the defects of the general system, so excellent are the domestic arrangements." Even in unsatisfactory almshouses, the problem tended to be a pervasive neglect of all residents more than a particular abuse of the insane.[10]

In addition to gathering information, Dix made a few other political preparations for the upcoming legislative contest as she circled through New York. She planned her itinerary with the aid of Theodric Romeyn Beck, one of the two doctors on the Utica board of trustees, and arranged for him to present her findings to the board and the legislature. On her route east through Cayuga County, she paused in Auburn to seek the counsel of former governor William H. Seward, a strong proponent of the state asylum during his recent administration. In Manhattan several days later, she sat for an interview with Lydia Maria Child, who published the first magazine profile of her former housemate in mid-December. Child drew a dramatic portrait of Dix as a "missionary of mercy" who calmed raving, dangerous maniacs by reading "with serene countenance and gentle voice, certain passages of Scripture filled with the spirit of tenderness." "Hush!—there are angels with you!" Child quoted one insane young man. "They have given you their voice!"[11]

Dix submitted the results of her investigation to the New York legislature in January 1844 as an appendix to the first annual report of the

Utica asylum. In style, the sixty-page memorial differed markedly from her controversial appeal to the Massachusetts legislature one year earlier. She abandoned her imaginative religious account of the insane and presented a more conventional public report. Declaring that she would not "consume time by narrating individual histories," the strategy that comprised the bulk of the Massachusetts memorial, she provided capsule evaluations of each county almshouse rather than a swirl of representative episodes. Although she described some of the same conditions that she had seen in Massachusetts, she rarely developed the details as metaphors. Revealing little of her emotional experience except for outbursts of shock and indignation at the worst conditions, she did not attempt to unify the separate summaries of each almshouse through the evolution of her consciousness. A straightforward argument rather than a spiritual narrative, the New York memorial responded to the sharp criticism that had raised doubts about the credibility of her first legislative petition.[12]

Although different in design, Dix's appeal to the New York legislature elaborated the same policy analysis that she had sketched in Massachusetts. She enthusiastically praised the Utica hospital and the older Bloomingdale Asylum, a government-subsidized unit of the New York Hospital, but she noted that the curable insane population of the state far exceeded the combined capacity of both institutions. Furthermore, she emphasized, the recent cases eligible for treatment in these asylums were less numerous than the chronically insane paupers, who could achieve emotional stability through moral management even if they would never regain their reason. "My earnest, my importunate intercession, then," she told the legislature, "is in behalf of the *incurable insane*, who, lost for life to the exercise of a sound understanding, exposed to suffering and degradation, to neglect and abuse, and often abandoned of friends, are at once the most dependent and most unfortunate of human beings."[13]

Dix argued that the existing system for accommodation of chronically insane paupers—the county almshouses—did not and could not provide adequate care. The memorial offered scathing descriptions of several county institutions. She maintained that "the prisons of the Court of Inquisition before their destruction, afforded no more heart-rending spectacles than the dungeons . . . of the Albany alms-house." But her main target was the idea of the almshouse rather than deplorable conditions at particular institutions. Acknowledging that the facilities for the insane in the Westchester almshouse rivaled the Utica and Bloomingdale asylums, she declared that "if any thing could ever reconcile me to subordinate institutions, this certainly would do so; but nothing can."[14]

Even the best county institutions failed, Dix asserted, because almshouses were "*compound* and *complex* in their plans and objects," mixing the functions of insane asylums, orphanages, houses of correction, and retreats for the aged, invalid, and helpless poor.[15] Because few officials possessed the range of skills necessary to direct such diverse institutions, she argued, the management of poorhouses was inevitably inadequate. Moreover, administrative and structural improvement of the almshouses to provide appropriate care for the insane would be prohibitively expensive in light of the taxes already assessed for public charities like the Utica hospital.

As in her Massachusetts memorial, Dix concluded that New York should create new state facilities for the incurable insane. She urged the legislature to establish several asylums in different parts of the state "upon a *cheaper plan,* which, while it *assures every needed comfort* and most *careful attendance,* will not need the many extra provisions absolutely essential to a curative institution." Although broadly supervised by physicians, these asylums would not be hospitals like the expensive Utica asylum. Dix envisioned a moral environment for the incurable insane that fostered tranquillity without active medical intervention. The new system would be "somewhat on the plan of the celebrated and successful establishment of *Ghiel.*"[16]

Dix's proposed model underscored her fundamentally nonmedical approach to insanity. The Belgian town of Geel had become famous during the Middle Ages as a shrine for lunatics seeking divine relief. Many pilgrims remained permanently, forming a large working colony administered by the town. Although, as Dix noted, the colony was loosely affiliated with the nearby Antwerp hospital, the simple cottages at Geel symbolized the antithesis of medical therapy in nineteenth-century discussions of social policy toward the insane.[17]

Dix's proposal clashed directly with the position of almost all physicians interested in insanity. Asylum doctors were acutely aware that the program of moral treatment, which had originated largely as a lay revolt against the ineffective, dangerous medical practices of heroic treatment, threatened to undermine their jurisdiction over the care of mental disorders. In the half-century since Quaker merchant William Tuke opened his York Retreat in England, no clear rationale had emerged for a medical monopoly over administration of the moral treatment. The therapy shared common holistic principles with other popular alternatives to medicine, including water cures and homeopathy, and its theoretical rationalization frequently intersected with pseudoscientific fads like phrenology, animal magnetism, and spiritualism. The weakness of the links between treatment of the insane and the primacy of doctors had spurred the professional self-consciousness of physicians interested in insanity. Asylum doctors worked diligently to substitute medical management for the lay structure of the York Retreat, the model for most early American institutions for the insane. Their efforts had placed doctors in charge of most asylums before Dix became interested in insanity. But the triumph of medical sovereignty remained incomplete in the early 1840s, and asylum doctors remained highly sensitive to threats against their role in the governance of deviant social behavior. The most important manifestation of this anxiety was the founding of the Association of Medical Superintendents of American Institutions for the Insane in October 1844. The association, the first national organization of physicians in the United States, epitomized the determination that physicians should control institutions for the insane, a position that asylum doctors justified by arguing that their prompt treatment could cure almost all cases of insanity. By calling for nonmedical public asylums on the basis of the contrary observation that insanity often remained a permanent, incurable condition, Dix's recommendation to the New York legislature in January 1844 challenged the growing professional consensus.[18]

Dix had not intended to attack medical authority. To the contrary, she had tried to establish strong relations with the key New York physicians interested in insanity. She sought to cast Theodric Romeyn Beck as the sponsor of her survey, and she actively cultivated the support of Utica medical superintendent Amariah Brigham. Previously the director of the influential Hartford Retreat, Brigham was one of the foremost specialists in the treatment of insanity. Dix saluted "the vigilant and successful superintendent" in her memorial and quoted from his writings on moral treatment.[19] She saw no contradiction between her plan and a broad acknowledgment of medical expertise. In responding to her circular letter to asylum superintendents during the Massachusetts campaign, the distinguished specialist Isaac Ray of the Maine Insane Asylum had endorsed the idea of separate institutions for incurable cases, which he considered "only an incidental point." Dix did not appreciate that Ray, often considered a maverick by his colleagues, was an exception to a coalescent orthodoxy that saw incurable cases as a dangerous embarrassment to the premise of curability underlying the asylum ideology.[20] Her recommendation had inadvertently struck an exposed nerve in a profession unsure of its control over the insane.

Two days after Dix submitted her memorial to the New York legislature, Amariah Brigham sent her a declaration of his opposition. His letter ably summarized the dominant attitude of doctors toward lay institutions for the insane. Indeed, a few months later, he published the statement as a manifesto in the first issue of his _American Journal of Insanity,_ soon to become the organ of the Association of Medical Superintendents. Brigham argued that institutions for the incurable were self-defeating because nobody could identify incurable cases with perfect accuracy, and he confidently asserted that no patient would recover without medical attention. He maintained that "this fact, that the chances of recovery would be diminished, to even but a few, is enough to make us hesitate before establishing such asylums." Although he agreed with Dix's assessment that the almshouse system was inadequate, he saw no reason to expect that her proposed state asylums would be better. Whereas she had envisioned facilities for chronically insane paupers as idyllic communities like the pilgrim colony at Geel, he described such institutions as "infernal regions, where no patient is expected to leave until dead, where hope never comes." He argued that the state should build hospitals in which doctors would restore reason to the curable patients and provide at least an illusion of hope for the permanent residents. "Provide good asylums for all," he urged, "and let all have the same kind care, and indulge the same hopes (even if delusive to many) of ultimate recovery, but do not drive them to despair by pronouncing them incurable."[21]

Brigham's opposition immediately doomed Dix's proposal. An enthusiastic and experienced political advocate, he skillfully circulated his letter to Governor William Bouck and selected legislators. His position was expressed in the state assembly by a delegate who argued that a nonmedical asylum would be "a mad-house—a mad poorhouse—a den of filth and misery, and an object of abhorrence and disgust."[22] Notwithstanding Brigham's own dissatisfaction with the county almshouses, he attacked the reliability of Dix's criticisms as well as her policy recommendation. "By coloring and not accurately observing," he maintained, "she was often mistaken and this has thrown a doubt over all her statements with many."[23]

Dix played no significant part in the legislative contest over additional state facilities for the insane. As Brigham pressed for the expansion of his own institution, Dix joined the faction calling for smaller, regional hospitals under medical supervision. She underscored "the great disadvantage of enlarging the Hospital at Utica" and the necessity of establishing scattered institutions that could "readily be reached by all who need the care they supply." She offered to lobby for this second-choice policy if it would "avail any thing for the *best* good of the cause I have so much at heart," but she had little influence to exert.[24] In March the legislature adopted the expansion plan she least favored, the construction of additional wings, doubling the capacity of the Utica asylum.

As in Massachusetts, addition of new state facilities for the moral treatment of the insane offered some consolation for the failure of Dix's own proposal, but her experience in New York afforded a much more hollow satisfaction. Her personal defeat was underscored when the Albany legislature, upon the objection of a representative criticizing the accuracy of her memorial, blocked a resolution to thank her for her efforts.[25] Her grueling journey through the mud and snow to every county poorhouse in the state had led only to another disappointment.

— 3 —

With impressive resilience, Dix picked herself up and tried again. She started by returning to her most noteworthy success, venting her frustration as she aided the campaign for a public endowment to match Cyrus Butler's asylum donation in Rhode Island. In April 1844 she published an article in the Providence *Journal* on the "Astonishing Tenacity of Life" demonstrated by Abram Simmons, an insane man "confined for several years in a dungeon in the town of Little Compton."

Flashing her capacity for biting sarcasm, Dix wrote that the citizens of Little Compton "profess the Christian religion, and it is even said that they have adopted some forms and ceremonies which they call worship" but that "their worship, mingling with the prayers of agony which [Simmons] shrieks forth from his dreary abode, would make strange discord in the ear of that Almighty Being, in whose keeping sleeps the vengeance due to all his wrongs."[26] She met with state legislators to urge that Simmons be removed from the care of the town, but her apparent progress was ended by the sudden announcement of his death. Approached by the delegates from Little Compton, she startled them by "imputing to the town's people—the crime of *murder* in the second degree."[27] She returned only briefly to Boston before setting off in June for her next major project, in Pennsylvania.

Once again Dix hoped to build on recent efforts to promote the moral treatment. Four years earlier, the Pennsylvania legislature had approved the construction of a state asylum for the insane paupers presently kept in almshouses and (unlike New York, where state law prohibited counties from incarcerating the insane) local jails. The governor vetoed the bill on financial grounds, as the national economic downturn had transformed Pennsylvania's canal construction program into a river of state debt. Dix now sought to work with the asylum advocates, who wanted a public institution to supplement the private facilities at the Friends Asylum in Frankford and the Pennsylvania Hospital for the Insane in Philadelphia.

Painfully aware that Brigham's opposition had ruined her plans in New York, Dix sought from the outset to ally herself with the medical core of the asylum movement. She asked superintendent Luther Bell of the McLean Asylum in Boston to provide her with an introduction to Thomas Kirkbride of the prestigious Pennsylvania Hospital for the Insane, soon to become the influential secretary of the Association of Medical Superintendents. Meeting Kirkbride shortly after her arrival in Philadelphia, she made an ingratiating appeal to his expertise. "I do not consider that the best results are reached through taking counsel with *many,*" she noted, more eager for his sanction than his advice. As she planned her survey of the state, she was careful to seek out community physicians and ask their view of the local condition of the insane.[28]

Dix's travels quickly showed that her reputation for benevolence had already introduced her to many civic leaders who might aid her work. Awaiting an early morning change of trains in New York City on her way to Pennsylvania, she ventured into New Jersey, "believing I ought not to lose the opportunity of making myself acquainted with its wants," and examined the Jersey City almshouse. For more information, she rang at 7:15 in the morning at the door of a "stately mansion" where "the exterior of the dwelling announced that the occupants could not be unacquainted with the civil and social state of the country." When without introducing herself she asked about the local condition of almshouses, jails, and the insane, the homeowner exclaimed, "Ah, you are then Miss Dix," and welcomed her to his house and to the state. After a lengthy conversation about the need for a public asylum in New Jersey, which almost caused Dix to miss her train, she discovered that her congenial new acquaintance was the mayor of Jersey City. Similar scenes were repeated in Pennsylvania. After she had traversed sixteen counties, she reported back to George B. Emerson that "I see all the *best minds; physicians*, lawyers, judges, &c."[29]

Pleased by her reception, Dix turned her tour of Pennsylvania into a series of municipal reform efforts as well as a survey for presentation to the state legislature in January. When she called for improvements in the Lancaster County poorhouse, prominent citizens asked her to address the subject in the local newspaper, urging that "you will be listened to, and exert an influence which no one else will." She consented, and regularly began to write articles for county newspapers about the institutions she visited. She took a more forceful course in Washington County, petitioning a grand jury to order immediate repairs, administrative changes, and "a more frequent application of *White-wash*" in the jail and almshouse. Asked to settle disputes at two other institutions, she saw that she now exercised an independent power in the administration of local charities: "I am asked to interpose between physicians and Trustees—between Wardens Chaplains and Managers—between the public and the establishments."[30]

Dix's attention to county institutions provided her some assurance that her efforts would not again be wasted as they were in New York. Fearing another setback ahead in the Pennsylvania legislature, she consoled herself that "if I do not succeed in getting a State Hospital I shall feel amply rewarded by what I am able to effect in prisons and almshouses." At the same time, she recognized that her local projects, and her work on the numerous individual cases brought before her, threatened to distract her from the asylum campaign. "I do not see how I shall get through this state by January with all the talking and writing I have to do," she worried at the beginning of September.[31]

Scrambling to canvass all fifty-eight Pennsylvania counties while she urged reforms at jails and almshouses and made periodic detours into Ohio, Virginia, and Maryland, Dix immersed herself fully in her work. She traveled by overnight stagecoaches to save the daylight hours for more inspections and meetings. She rarely spent time on anything else. When she forgot a promise to send friends an account of her travels, she explained that "all other purposes were lost in this *mighty vortex* of labor."[32] She apologized for "egotism" in the letters she did write, but she declared that "I can say nothing which does not savor of *my calling*." "Prisons and Hospitals, Jails and Poor-houses fill the reach of my mental vision," she told Emerson, acknowledging a "wide ignorance" about the other events of the day. Compression heightened the intensity of her already strenuous character. Although concerned that her progress was too slow, she completed in six weeks a list of assignments she had expected to take twice as long.[33]

In late October, Dix doubled the work before her by deciding to follow her travels through Pennsylvania with a rapid tour of New Jersey. The sudden change of plans, though it had perhaps been percolating in her mind since her initial visit to Jersey City, was prompted by a letter she received from a Quaker in Salem decrying the condition of the insane in her county and the recent refusals of the state legislature to establish a public mental hospital. Dix's informant reported expectations that the legislature would again consider the issue, as it had in every session for the past five years at the instigation of the state medical society.[34] Able to complete her survey of Pennsylvania in early November "by being very active," Dix concluded within a few days of her arrival in New Jersey that "*here* I feel almost sure of gaining what I solicit," whereas she could "hardly indulge a faint hope of success this year" in Pennsylvania.[35]

After Dix hurriedly examined twenty-nine New Jersey jails and poorhouses in November 1844, the return of her winter cough and the imminent assembly of the Pennsylvania and New Jersey legislatures brought her journeys to a halt in December. She retreated temporarily to the Philadelphia home of Harriet Hare, a childhood friend of the Channings and the Gibbses with whom she had often stayed during the past six months. "I am going now to be shut up and very busy going over notes," Dix announced. For the next several weeks, she prepared her dual legislative campaigns for the establishment of state insane asylums.[36]

— 4 —

Dix's lobbying technique again began with legislative memorials. In many respects, the parallel petitions she drafted in the first weeks of 1845 were similar to the memorial she had prepared in New York one year earlier. The lengthy documents provided summary reports on each of the jails and poorhouses she had visited. Prefatory and concluding exhortations aimed to touch every sympathetic chord. She told the Pennsylvania legislature, "I appeal to your hearts and your understanding; to your moral and to your intellectual perceptions; I appeal to you as legislators and as citizens; I appeal to you as men, and as fathers, sons, and brothers." Reviewing the unsuccessful previous efforts to establish public asylums, she emphasized that both states had fallen "*behind* the age" in their welfare policies.[37]

Dix's memorials in Pennsylvania and New Jersey differed sharply from her previous petitions, however, in her pervasive efforts to show that she expressed the views of leading doctors. Her New Jersey petition opened with an "appeal to medical men . . . to unite their testimony with mine." For the first time, she devoted much of her memorials to expounding standard medical conceptions of insanity. She described insanity as a "physical disease affecting and disturbing the natural and healthful functions of the brain," and she attributed mental disorders to "lesion of the brain, or organic malconstruction" rather than flaws in a disembodied mind or soul. She traced the rise of the moral treatment to French physician Philippe Pinel, "the great and good Pinel," passing quickly over the simultaneous lay development of the moral treatment at the York Retreat. Morality merged with medicine in her tribute to Pinel's "great triumph of humanity and skill, over ferocity and ignorance," culminating in her dramatic account of the physician's legendary decision to unchain the insane inmates at the Bicêtre asylum during the French Revolution.[38]

Dix's new approach depended heavily on the claims of asylum physicians that "a new era has dawned on this department of medical science." Shifting from her earlier focus on neglected chronic patients, she built her memorials on the premise that prompt therapy cured most cases of insanity. For evidence, she cited numerous annual reports in which Amariah Brigham, Thomas Kirkbride, and other prominent asylum superintendents buoyantly described their institutions to taxpayers, potential patrons, and the general public. She reproduced charts from two asylum reports to show that mental hospitals, although initially more costly than almshouses or other nontherapeutic institutions, would quickly repay the taxpayers' investment as patients were restored to reason and removed from the public assistance rolls. "On the ground of a discreet economy alone," Dix maintained, "it is wise to establish a State Hospital." Recasting the fiscal argument as a moral calculus, she concluded: "there is then but one alternative—condemn your needy citizens to become the life-long victims of a terrible disease, or provide remedial care in a State Hospital."[39]

Scientific expertise now moved to the center of Dix's vision of the asylum. She no longer reported instances of irrational men and women who had recovered their emotional tranquillity through kind, firm discipline outside of a hospital. Most important, she abandoned her proposal for a specialized but nontherapeutic institution similar to the colony of insane at Geel. Instead, she urged both Pennsylvania and New Jersey to establish state mental hospitals under the direction of medical superintendents.

Although Dix thus gave up her original policy goal, her compromise did not change her basic ideas or bring her into full agreement with medical specialists. She merely acquiesced in the authority of doctors to administer the moral treatment, which she still understood as a holistic process of spiritual, rather than somatic, healing. She later noted that "pure religion, more than any other power, tends to arrest, and assists to cure insanity." While careful not to challenge this common view of asylum therapy, most physicians took a broader view of their expertise and often combined the moral regimen with various forms of medical intervention, especially the prescription of narcotic and purgative drugs.

Dix dismissed such measures as merely incidental in sound practice. In addition to piety, she looked to "the sentiment of satisfaction in being useful" as the key to self-respect and ultimately to self-control. "A farm is as necessary as a physician," she once observed, "and more valuable than all the drugs of the apothecary."[40]

Dix's doubts about drug therapy might have suggested important tensions between religious and medical justifications for the asylum, but the areas of agreement overshadowed the potential conflict. Leading doctors believed earnestly in the efficacy of the moral treatment. Dix approvingly quoted one asylum superintendent's observation that "the great feature which characterizes the management of modern hospitals for the insane, is the extensive use of labor as a means of moral treatment." She also included a detailed description of the crops produced at the Bloomingdale Asylum, where superintendent Pliny Earle demanded authority to compel patients to work as the therapeutic equivalent of requiring them to eat.[41] And aside from the clinical views they shared with Dix, interested physicians could find much to applaud in her promotion of the insane asylum as a major civic institution under medical control, the largest and most complex variation of the emerging American idea of the hospital.

Presented to the New Jersey legislature on January 23 and to the Pennsylvania legislature on February 3, Dix's memorials in some ways added little to the previous campaigns for state mental hospitals. The information she offered on the condition of the insane in county institutions scarcely repaid her enormous exertions to gather it. Her expanded discussion of the medical aspects of insanity left less space for descriptions of the jails and poorhouses she visited. Besides, government-commissioned asylum advocates had recently surveyed the same ground in both states. Dix's evidence mainly added details and amplified the earlier reports to the legislatures on the well-known workings of the existing welfare systems. She originally planned to furnish a current count of the insane, but she ultimately did not collect population statistics to support her arguments.[42]

Also diminishing the evidentiary value of the memorials, controversy continued to mar Dix's efforts to highlight deplorable conditions in local institutions. When she reported that the "intolerable grossness and barbarity" of the almshouse in Washington County, Pennsylvania, was a "monstrous outrage on decency and morals," the local overseers of the poor retorted that she had seen the institution for no more than fifteen minutes. "She either knows nothing about what she is writing or . . . [is] purposely unjust," they charged in a lengthy rebuttal seconded by the local physician responsible for the care of insane paupers. The county senator delivered a speech suggesting that Dix's reform enthusiasm was "so great as to 'unbalance' her 'mind.' "[43] Such controversies were diminishing, but mainly because Dix presented markedly less sensational findings in her memorials than she had in Massachusetts and New York.

Nor did Dix appeal to the New Jersey and Pennsylvania legislatures with original or powerful logic. Her new emphasis on the curability of insanity typified her espousal of commonplace arguments for the establishment of mental hospitals. She had already moved in this direction in her New York memorial, which reprinted a lengthy passage from Samuel Gridley Howe's essay in the *North American Review*.[44] Now, facile reasoning increasingly obscured Dix's genuine opinions. She explained privately that "it is a difficult and delicate task to work out reforms *indirectly;* to announce abuses in such a way as to preserve the self-esteem of those in fault and error, from being changed into wrath and bitterness. So I ponder and devise."[45] Her memorials mixed a vast assortment of stock rationales with little regard to the force or consistency of her different claims. Repeating the cliché that insanity reflected the artificial pressures of society rather than the innate weakness of humanity, she asked the Pennsylvania legislature: "Is it not to the habits, the customs, the temptations of civilized life and society, that we owe most of these calamities? Should not society, then, make the compensation which alone can be made for these disastrous fruits of social organization?" At the same time, however, she held fast to her sterner judgment that "many of [the insane] are unworthy; in all probability the majority may have abused their privileges, wasted property, and impaired their health by indulgences and excesses, which must be condemned."[46]

Dix's memorials were most effective in arousing public support for state asylums. Printed in large editions by both legislatures and excerpted in newspapers, the accounts of the "inappropriate, unjust, and *sometimes* barbarous treatment of the insane poor" reached a wide readership. Wealthy Philadelphia merchant Thomas P. Cope, a key civic supporter of the Pennsylvania asylum bill vetoed five years earlier, noted admiringly that Dix's appeal was "written with spirit & feeling & dis-clos[es] sad scenes of wretchedness." In New Jersey, a reader wrote to the Trenton *State Gazette* that "if the representatives of the people, after reading this memorial through, and contemplating the thrilling scenes therein depicted, do not feel a responsibility resting upon them, para-mount to all pecuniary considerations, they must have hearts which cannot be touched by the *wailings of misery* or the *cry of distress.*" News-paper editorials seconded this view, and the New Jersey legislature received a tide of petitions in support of a state asylum.[47]

As Dix had told Thomas Kirkbride, however, she hardly envisioned herself as a grassroots lobbyist. She expected her memorials, newspaper articles, and travels "will gradually leaven the whole mass," but she did not seek to rely on public support for the new mental hospitals. While her opponents loudly doubted that voters approved the proposed state expenditures, she was content to assure the Trenton legislature that "through the length and breadth of New Jersey, I have heard but one and the same opinion . . . 'We need a hospital.' "[48] She offered no specu-lation about public opinion in Pennsylvania. She did not collect mass petitions or solicit newspaper endorsements, devoting her own county newspaper articles primarily to the improvement of local institutions rather than the statewide hospital campaigns. She never again pursued her Massachusetts strategy of orchestrating pleas from almshouse and jail officials for relief from the care of the insane.

When Dix did try to coordinate support for the new hospitals, she achieved little success. She hoped to join forces with Kirkbride, but forewarned by Amariah Brigham that Dix's unreliable testimony might rebound against asylum advocates, the Pennsylvania Hospital superin-tendent maintained a wary distance despite his own hopes for the estab-lishment of a public mental institution.[49] She also approached Thomas P. Cope, who was sympathetic but pessimistic about Dix's prospects amid the ongoing fiscal woes of Pennsylvania, and asked him to donate $10,000 to induce passage of a hospital appropriation. Astonished by "her 'modest' tax on my means," the patrician Quaker declined.[50] In New Jersey, Dix solicited the endorsement of U.S. senator Theodore Frelinghuysen, who agreed only to speak with any wavering friends, a vague promise further rendered unsatisfactory because it was addressed to "Mr. D. L. Dix." She noted with surprise that Frelinghuysen "rather singularly supposes his correspondent a *Gentleman*" despite the extensive publicity surrounding her campaign.[51]

But if Dix's evidence was unimpressive, her arguments hackneyed, and her allies disorganized, her personality added an overwhelming force to the asylum movement. Although less visible than her memorials, Dix's direct appeals to state legislators were the most important factor distinguishing her hospital campaigns in New Jersey and Pennsylvania from previous unsuccessful efforts. She shuttled briskly between Trenton and Harrisburg during the first months of 1845. "You cannot imagine the labor of conversing and convincing," she told Harriet Hare. "Some evenings I had at once, twenty gentlemen for three hours, *steady* conversation." She did not offer new information or reasoning in these meetings in her hotel parlor; often she read from her memorial and described in detail the principles of moral treatment. But few legislators could resist her direct intercession. "Though they appeared perfectly unimpressible at first, the ice melted from their hearts," she reported.[52]

Dix's power in these confrontations derived from her embodiment of the values of benevolent womanhood, her growing fame, and her dominating will. One legislator who thought her campaign was "all humbug" listened spellbound in her parlor for an hour and a half before announcing, "*I am convinced;* you've conquered me out and out; *I shall vote for the Hospital.* If you'll come to the House and talk there as you've done here, no man that is'nt a brute can withstand you." Another delegate vividly summarized the response of many politicians when he explained that he surrendered his opposition because he had been "Miss Dix-ed a little." Upon learning that the Pennsylvania House of Representatives had passed Dix's hospital bill, Thomas P. Cope wryly noted in his diary: "she is a persevering woman."[53]

Asylum supporters and opponents agreed that Dix's efforts had been decisive when the New Jersey legislature voted almost unanimously in March 1845 to establish a state mental hospital and the Pennsylvania legislature followed suit one month later. A Pennsylvania admirer exclaimed that "no man nor woman, other than yourself, from Maine to Louisiana could have passed the bill under the discouraging circumstances with which you had to contend."[54] A supporter of the New Jersey asylum admitted that "if she had never entered the state, this institution would not have been established." Opponents of "these random follies, these frantic projects" echoed the analysis with equal certainty. One chagrined legislator grumbled that "if that Miss Dix had been paid $500 or $600 and escorted over the Delaware, or to Philadelphia, or even a thousand dollars and taken to Washington city, and if you choose, enshrined in the White House, it would have been money well laid out."[55]

— 5 —

After a fitful series of stops and starts, Dix's new career as a reformer was now gaining remarkable momentum. In addition to the New Jersey and Pennsylvania mental hospitals, she calculated that she had arranged for the construction of four new county poorhouses and the reorganization of twenty-one jails. Extending his congratulations, Samuel Gridley Howe could hardly believe that the schoolmistress he deflected from the Massachusetts State Normal School had accomplished so much. "I recollect what you were then," he told Dix, "I think of your noble career since, & I say, God grant me to look back upon some three years of my life with a part of the self approval you must feel!" William M. Awl, the superintendent of the Ohio Lunatic Asylum and one of the founders of the Association of Medical Superintendents, invited her in April 1845 to turn next to "the destitution and suffering of the insane in the great West." He confidently predicted that Dix's lobbying could complete his own efforts to promote a state asylum in Indiana. "They only want *a Memorial* to set them a going," he assured her.[56]

Dix eagerly looked forward to following Awl's suggestion, but officials in both New Jersey and Pennsylvania first asked her to work with the government commissions overseeing the construction of the new state mental hospitals. As the example of New York starkly demonstrated, passage of legislation establishing an asylum was only the first step in a difficult and potentially long road to the opening of an institution. The locations of the hospitals, the design of the facilities, and the selection of administrators were only the most obvious of the many crucial issues still left to be resolved. Asylum advocates well knew, if some legislators later denied understanding, that much more state funding would have to be approved before the hospitals could receive patients and, in theory, rely on county-supported paupers to provide operating revenues. For all of these difficult tasks, the state commissioners gratefully welcomed

Dix's "superior judgment & experience" and her lobbying and negotiating assistance.[57]

Dix promptly threw herself into the building process. Usually rising at 5:00 in the morning, she participated actively in the commission meetings in Trenton and Harrisburg. She inspected potential sites with the commissioners and furnished them with letters of introduction when they traveled to Massachusetts to examine model institutions. She aided in the purchase of the farm near Trenton chosen for the site of the New Jersey asylum when a collaborator urged that she could obtain it "several thousand dollars lower than any of the Commission." Worried that the Pennsylvania legislature would not provide enough money for a first-rate institution, she launched a campaign to obtain supplemental private funding. The resulting endowment, which she directly controlled, added significantly to her influence. Philanthropist Thomas P. Cope headed the subscription list with the same mixed feelings he had developed toward Dix during the legislative contest. Admiring her zeal but wishing that she had undertaken her project at another time, he sighed that "she is not, however, very easily deterred or diverted from her purpose. Discretion is said to be the better part of valour. Constant excitement in the pursuit of even a praiseworthy object may warp the judgement & impair the intellect."[58]

Dix's emergence as the most celebrated advocate of moral treatment brought her a new respect from the physicians who had previously led the asylum movement. Her reform crusade more clearly advanced the goals of medical specialists now that she had set aside her plan for nontherapeutic custodial institutions, and doctors could not fail to see that she would play a key role in asylum politics when insiders were assuring her that "your wishes . . . will be *laws*" to state officials. That prediction was an exaggeration—for example, Kirkbride's protégé John Curwen won the post of superintendent at Harrisburg over Dix's candidate—but she was certainly influential enough to merit careful deference.

Dix's rapprochement with Kirkbride, probably the most influential asylum superintendent in the country, epitomized her recognition by medical specialists. They exchanged letters dismissing the previous coolness between them as the result of a misunderstanding, and Dix helped arrange for Kirkbride to serve as a design consultant for the New Jersey asylum, a key commission in his rise to dominance of American mental hospital architecture.[59] They soon formed a lasting personal friendship and a powerful partnership between the humanitarian and medical constituencies for the spread of asylums.

Gratifying as Dix's important work with the Trenton and Harrisburg commissions was, she found it no less exasperating. Cooperation with the commissioners sorely tried her patience. "You cannot exactly comprehend the inevitable anxieties that beset me in being *obliged* to act *with* others," she told Emerson in July 1845. "The habit of delay, of declining responsibility, of prolonged discussion conducing to no conclusions" seemed to her inherent in all committees and associations. "I wish the State Commissioners for the new Hospitals could be resolved into one energetic *heart*-working person," she grumbled. When the *"leisurely"* commissioners planned to meet at 10:00 in the morning, she proposed 8:00. Kept waiting by the governor of New Jersey before one meeting, she felt "too much provoked and murmured something about the value of time and Washington's punctuality." Only a few months after the boards had been constituted, she seethed that "two or three times, I have almost been on the point of asking to build the Hospitals myself."[60]

Dix's disgust with the asylum commissions left her in a dilemma. Solicitous about every detail relating to the institutions, she could easily foresee "a year's advantageous employment" in Trenton and Harrisburg, enhanced by excursions into Maryland and Delaware. Both sets of state commissioners implored her to help negotiate for building materials, transportation costs, and "twenty other things beside." She especially worried about leaving difficult tasks to the Pennsylvania board, which she rightfully judged incompetent. At the same time, she felt "a good deal impatient concerning the work at the *west*" that she had originally planned to undertake during the summer.[61]

Dix decided to go. She admitted to "some misgivings," and even her friend Harriet Hare criticized her for abandoning the Pennsylvania asylum. As it turned out, the state mental hospital near Harrisburg would not open for another six years and would be widely condemned by asylum advocates as a botched work of construction. Long before then, Dix denied that she could have saved the hapless commission from failure.

"I *knew* it would be lost time and money to linger longer," she told Hare. But more important, she had other priorities than the fruition of her political labors. She was determined to extend her mission, and she felt restless at the "binding of me to two places." She could not stop now to dwell on the Pennsylvania asylum, or even to watch over the New Jersey institution that she was coming to regard as "my first-born child."[62]

⟣ 6 ⟢

A Happiness Which Goes with You

IN AUGUST 1845, Dix estimated that she had traveled more than 10,000 miles during the previous three years. She had visited over 500 almshouses, approximately 300 county jails, 18 state penitentiaries, and an indeterminate number of hospitals. The relentless journey—mostly by stagecoach, when possible by the railroads and steamboats beginning to cross the countryside—was staggeringly arduous. "Sometimes I fancy my strength is wearing out," she observed, "but then I revive from fatigue both of mind and body, in a way I do not comprehend."[1] This unconscious renewal of power flowed partly from aims other than the insane paupers, welfare institutions, and state legislatures toward which she directed her travels. Declaration of her independence and test of her sacred calling, Dix's solitary pilgrimage across America was in itself one of her most important ends.

— 1 —

Dix's journey was mapped by places and feelings she wanted to escape as well as the destinations she approached. To be sure, the insane paupers she saw in jails and poorhouses presented revitalizing reminders of her singular mission.[2] But defiant self-reliance also remained a crucial animating force in her character. She attributed her success to "a certain sort of obstinancy that some people make the blunder of calling zeal; and the yet greater blunder of naming the first inciting cause philanthropy." When tired, *"opposition"* was the *"tonic"* she sought to restore her strength. Sensing Dix's inner restlessness, Lydia Maria Child slyly compared her to a comedian who could make anyone forget sorrow and anxiety but was himself deeply depressed. Similarly, Dix created homes for the insane only after she had forsaken any home for herself.[3]

Dix's estrangement from Boston expressed her renunciation most clearly. She maintained few close ties to her home city and her family. In February 1844 she learned that her beloved brother Charles had died five months earlier in Africa on one of his long ocean voyages.[4] She had never felt the same fusion of sisterly and maternal tenderness toward her younger brother, Joseph. Their correspondence quickened after he married "a plain sensible girl" in the summer of 1845, but Dix readily confessed that she did not know him well.[5] She showed little interest in most of her extended family. "I certainly have never from early childhood to this time experienced such acts and dispositions from relations as to create the wish to see them multiplied," she told her brother. She cordially despised her most prominent Boston cousin, Thaddeus Mason Harris's son Thaddeus William Harris, a distinguished scientist and passionate genealogist who inherited the minister's prominent position in the antiquarian community.[6]

Dix's long-standing friendships in Boston similarly seemed empty to her. Although Ruth Channing and Sarah Gibbs still regarded her fondly, she drifted apart from the sisters soon after the death of William Ellery Channing; for the most part, she kept up with them through Harriet Hare. She counted Mary Torrey as her most valuable correspondent in New England, but their common interests in the Federal Street church had never created an intimate personal attachment. "*You* are not in a poor-house or a Jail, and do not *need* me," Dix pointedly wrote from New Jersey, explaining her absorption in her work. She once complained that Torrey "is always cordial in her friendliness" but that "within her house is no place for a friend, beyond a *transient* call."[7]

Most poignantly, Anne Heath passed in and out of Dix's affections like a ghost. Mortified that she had to learn about her old friend through others, Heath bitterly repented her rupture of their intimacy. "The *mistake* I must of course deplore while this life remains and through the future also," she wrote in a wistful plea to renew their relationship. "When having eyes, we see not, the penalty of suffering must be paid."[8] Their friendship gradually became less erratic than it had been in the previous twenty years, but it always lived through the momentum of its earliest days. Although flashes of affection returned to their letters, Dix often thought her old confidante unloving and "the most negligent correspondent I have ever ranked as a friend." Despite Heath's often perceptive insights, Dix maintained that "*you* dear Anne do not know or understand me: and this is not strange; for an intercourse so broken reveals but little of the growth and changes of character."[9]

Dissatisfied with her old friendships, Dix did not try to establish new attachments in her home city. Her simultaneous immersion in social reform and departure from Boston was a striking anomaly in the hub of nineteenth-century reform movements. Her collaboration with Samuel Gridley Howe had introduced her to a remarkable set of acquaintances whose interests closely matched her own, including the Howes, the Manns, John G. Palfrey, and Charles Sumner. Significantly, she did not seek a place in this brilliant circle. She was far more staid than the ebullient Chevalier, as Howe styled himself, but other members of the clique suited her temperament splendidly. Her discontent with Boston society particularly puzzled Sumner's law partner George Hillard, who assured her at one point that "you have warm and true friends here, though . . . one might infer that you thought you had none."[10]

Although Dix did not lack sympathetic acquaintances or appealing reform opportunities in Boston, she saw her departure as a necessary escape from home. She believed that "I *never* was *understood* or known *in Boston* at any time." "I found neither moral or intellectual companionship," she claimed. "Many were wiser and better than myself but they were not especially suited to me nor I to them."[11] Genuine as her loneliness and frustration had often been, this sustaining conviction was also a self-delusion. Dix was never understood anywhere better than in Boston. She personified the highest ideals of Beacon Hill society, from her Unitarian conscience to her Yankee reserve to her feminine conventions to her prudent investments in the Massachusetts Hospital Life Insurance Company. For the rest of her life, many of her closest friends would be transplanted New Englanders. In no respect was she more emblematic of the city upon a hill than in the inner disquiet that inspired her to follow her Puritan ancestors into exile. Friends repeatedly urged that the insane of Massachusetts needed another asylum campaign, but she invariably found that "the *call* is louder elsewhere."[12]

"A little disposed to pour forth in one strong expression what most diffuse over their daily lives," Dix revealed her submerged longings for home in emotional letters to George B. Emerson. She told the sober schoolmaster he had "taken the place of Dr. Channing in my respect and affections" and become the brightest of "the guiding stars of my journeyings through the highway of existence." Imagining herself "as a weary child," she would write to "covet a caressing hand and affectionate parental voices." "Not often do I allow the thought of aloneness and orphanage to dwell upon my memory," she sighed during her journey through Pennsylvania, "but sometimes (it may be a woman's weakness) my strength of will threatens, as at this hour, to be insufficient for my stern purposes of self-extinction." When she visited Emerson during a rare visit to Boston, her envy of his daughters irritated her "beyond the power of that control I always endeavor to preserve. I did not wish their happiness less, but craved a filial relationship which I can never possess."[13]

Although startled by the intensity of Dix's letters, Emerson understood the encouragement she wanted to hear as she rode from one town to the next. Willing to extend "an affectionate voice if it may not be a parental one," he assured her that "your going about to do good preaches to me more loudly than any sermons I ever heard or read." He compared her asylum campaign to the educational reforms of Catharine Beecher, to which Dix blushingly demurred that the great evangelist of benevolent womanhood was "doing more and better than I." Appreciatively, she told him on looking back over her successful efforts in Pennsylvania and New Jersey that "you have been necessary to me, have largely added to my comfort and happiness. I am necessary to none—except the world at large."[14]

Dix's correspondence with Emerson elaborated not only her rejection of Boston but her broader alienation from all society. Contrary to the popular caricature of roseate religious liberalism, she considered most men and women shockingly depraved. Although she believed firmly in the spiritual potential of the redeemed soul, she maintained that "man perpetually in all tribes and natures, seems seeking an escape from the higher ends, and aims, and capacities of physical and intellectual being." Emerson repeatedly expressed amazement that a renowned humanitarian and fellow Unitarian could be so misanthropic. "I am no *humanity*-hater," Dix answered, "but I never feel drawn nigher to God and high spiritual attainment with society. It gives me no impulse—it crushes and depresses me—and only when acting, and cut off from these influences chiefly, do I feel myself *rising*."[15]

The progress of Dix's pilgrimage across the United States traced these evangelical convictions on a fantastic scale. The exaltation she found in her quest more than compensated for the hours of desolation. Although she had called schoolteaching an avocation even when most absorbed in her work, she soon began to refer to her new reform career as a vocation in the fullest sense. She developed an empathy with Catholic nuns, whose "*quiet* but active lives conquer hard hearts and take captive the many." The rigor as well as the solitude of her journey reinforced her faith in "the work which I believe is appointed for me to do," and she pointed to her deliverance from the dangers of travel as confirmation of her mission.[16]

Dix implemented this vision in the overall design and daily details of her work. Determined to keep moving and to reach the entire country, she could not linger to oversee the construction of her asylums in New Jersey and Pennsylvania, or remain in New York, much less Massachusetts, to improve upon unsatisfactory legislative compromises. She spurned companionship and declined letters of introduction during her statewide surveys because, as she confided to Emerson, "I confess I have great satisfaction in making my own way."[17] She often strode into public institutions or started to interrogate officials without identifying herself, preferring to appear as an anonymous incarnation of moral authority. In conducting an active publicity campaign but eschewing grassroots organizing, she sought to exert influence through moral diffusion rather than political pressure. And in her personal lobbying, she drew on a willpower backed by her confidence that she had surmounted the innate weakness of humanity and was fulfilling a divine mandate.

A profound source of inner strength, Dix's view of her reform crusade also promoted several disturbing tendencies. Her career widened but did not deepen. The conditions of insane paupers in almshouses and jails, the empirical basis for her asylum campaigns, received noticeably less attention in her letters after the first year of her work, certainly much less than the adventures of travel. When she did discuss her work, she now preferred to dwell on the "beautiful, almost holy" sight of the patients in the mental hospitals she visited.[18] This shift of focus paralleled the rapid decline in her efforts to learn about insanity after a brief initial flurry of reading in standard works of medical authorities. She did not question the prevailing definitions of insanity, probe the full workings of asylum medicine, scrutinize superintendents' dubious claims of success in curing patients, consider the value of alternative institutions, or interest herself in the legal rights of mental incompetents. Relying on the broad ideal of moral treatment with which she had begun her new career, she left most specialized issues to her friends in the Association of Medical Superintendents.

Moreover, Dix's self-conception lent itself to feelings of independence and power belied by her early failures. Because she saw herself as a disaffected critic of society rather than a representative of conventional morality, she treated her success as even more personal than it was. At times her sense of mission swelled to astonishing proportions. "In the Providence of God," she proclaimed, "I am the voice of the maniac whose piercing cries from the dungeons of your jail penetrate not your Halls of Legislation. I am the Hope of the poor crazed beings who pine in the cells, and stalls, and cages, and waste-rooms of your poor-houses. I am the Revelation of hundreds of wailing, suffering creatures."[19] Arguing in her New Jersey memorial that insanity did not destroy all perceptive faculties, she pointed as proof to three "poor maniacs" who recognized her as a divinely appointed emissary. She reported that one almshouse inmate prophesied, "God's spirit bids this message to you, saying, it is his work you are doing; lo, it shall prosper in your hands!"[20] That prediction now realized by her successes in New Jersey and Pennsylvania, Dix confidently prepared to move further onward and inward.

— 2 —

Eager as she was to head west and preoccupied as she was with the Pennsylvania and New Jersey asylum commissions, Dix made time in the summer of 1845 for another major project, a book about prison reform. Her basic interest in the subject demonstrated the similarity of hospitals and prisons in her ideas about moral reform. Like many contemporaries, she saw the two emerging social institutions as parallel environments for the redirection of deviant behavior. Her decision to enter the debate over prison discipline at this particular juncture, however, also revealed her deep personal isolation and her hostility toward Boston society.

Dix's work in Pennsylvania had reawakened the interest in the spiritual welfare of prisoners that predated her devotion to the insane. During her first month in the state, fresh from her frustration in New York, she started a study of prison administration that briefly competed for priority with her asylum crusade. She visited the Eastern Penitentiary near Philadelphia every day for two weeks, "coming in the early morning, and going away only in the afternoon when I could no longer use my voice."[21] In addition to collecting information from the convicts and officials, she began to conduct Sunday school, as she had before at the East Cambridge jail and the Massachusetts State Prison at Charlestown. Upon her departure for her statewide survey of the insane she published an address to the inmates summarizing her teachings, and throughout her stay in Pennsylvania and New Jersey she regularly preached on Sundays at the Eastern Penitentiary or a county prison.[22]

Dix offered prisoners the same message of self-discipline and redemptive labor she had delivered since her days as a schoolteacher. Echoing the motto of *Conversations on Common Things,* she often remarked that convicts primarily needed to be instructed "line upon line, and precept upon precept."[23] She argued to the prisoners that crime was weak self-indulgence and exhorted them to dominate themselves through tests of will, such as temperance, efficiency in manual labor, or memorization of poetry. She reasoned that convicts would thereby become reformed citizens, rather than well-disciplined malefactors, because "self-respect implanted, conducts to the desire of possessing the respect and confidence of others, and through these paths grow up moral sentiments, gradually increasing and gaining strength."[24]

But if Dix's sermons mostly reflected her unchanging moral code, her study of Pennsylvania's prison administration marked a new step from religious precepts to government policy. The Eastern Penitentiary was the central institution in a fierce debate between advocates of the "separate" system of imprisonment and proponents of the "congregate" system. Both models of prison discipline aimed to rehabilitate convicts through a grueling ordeal of isolation, regimentation, moral indoctrination, and labor. Under the separate system developed at the Eastern Penitentiary, inmates remained in solitary confinement at all times; during the day they performed piecework labor or gardened in small yards attached to their cells. The congregate system also isolated prisoners at night, but during the day had them work together in a factory, march in lockstep, and eat in a common mess. While these activities went on, prison guards sought to enforce absolute silence, often with a whip. The rivalry between the penitentiary systems, among the first American social innovations to attract extensive European study and emulation, had recently reached a vast popular audience through Charles Dickens's searing description of the Eastern Penitentiary in his *American Notes*. [25]

From the outset, Dix planned her prison research as groundwork for an essay "in favor of the *Separate system* of Imprisonment," known on both sides of the Atlantic as the Pennsylvania or Philadelphia system. No less important, she aimed to attack the congregate system, headquartered in Boston, though called the Auburn system because it had originated at the New York state penitentiary. Led by Louis Dwight, the most influential prison reformer in the United States, the Boston Prison Discipline Society sharply criticized the Pennsylvania system in a series of widely circulated reports on public institutions. Dix expressed "astonishment" that Dwight had "ventured to publish such representations." She told Emerson that "I feel it is a duty I owe to society to write a plain statement of the general ordering and discipline" of the Eastern Penitentiary. [26]

Dix kept a severe eye on her Boston target as she visited the Eastern Penitentiary and other Pennsylvania prisons, collected prison reports, corresponded with prison officials around the country, and detoured from her survey of the insane to examine every state penitentiary as far west as Ohio and as far south as Virginia. Emerson, sympathetic to her advocacy of the separate system, inadvertently reinforced her view of the prison debate as part of a deeper break with Boston. His accounts of Dwight's "indolent life" underscored Dix's relentless exertions to see institutions; Emerson reported that "of three or four such examinations he speaks as emphatically as you do of sixteen counties." [27] Planning a direct assault on the citadel of Boston opinion, Dix asked Emerson to arrange for publication of her essay in the *North American Review*. "Do I write well enough for the *North American?*" she asked uneasily. The schoolmaster assured her that "you write well enough, when you are in earnest and not thinking of the writing, for kings & queens or, what is infinitely more, for men and Christians," but when he did not receive an immediate answer from the prestigious journal, Dix obtained an invitation to publish her findings in the *Christian Examiner,* now edited by Ezra Stiles Gannett.[28]

Dix gradually turned away from the debate between the separate and congregate systems after these active preparations. Increasingly absorbed in her Pennsylvania asylum campaign and her efforts to reform local jails and almshouses, she postponed the planned essay indefinitely upon launching her New Jersey asylum campaign. "You must not think I have forgotten the Article relating to Prisons," she told Emerson. "I only am waiting for time to accomplish that and other subjects for the pen."[29] She visited several more state penitentiaries after she completed her surveys of the insane, and her Pennsylvania and New Jersey asylum memorials included vigorous endorsements of the Philadelphia penitentiary system. But her spectacular twin legislative victories seemed to leave less time and perhaps less need for her to seek a prominent role in prison reform.[30]

In May 1845, however, Dix suddenly resumed her focus on penal reform in the aftermath of an explosion in the Boston Prison Discipline Society. At the annual meeting of the society on May 18, Charles Sumner launched his own long-planned assault on Louis Dwight by denouncing the society's opposition to the Pennsylvania system and demanding a special inquiry into the relative merits of the two regimes. He emphasized that Dix, whom he called "a witness more worthy of consideration than anyone else living," favored the separate system.[31]

Dix immediately wrote Sumner to ask that he publish her study of prison discipline.[32] She did not know her former ally in the Worcester hospital campaign well, but she recognized that they opposed Dwight for similar reasons. Also deeply influenced by Channing, Sumner claimed to be opposing the orthodox Calvinism of Dwight, a former agent of the American Bible Society. Other allies stressed the same point to Dix, although some prominent Unitarians supported the Auburn system. Following the tense sectarian pattern of New England debates about criminal punishment, liberals argued that the Auburn system reflected Calvinist notions of ineradicable human depravity because congregate prisons used the lash to break the will of inmates. George Hillard, a deacon at the Federal Street Church, assured Dix that Dwight was an "evangelical peacock." Emerson urged her to emphasize the brutality of congregate prisons in her essay because "the contrast between this extreme severity and the merciful character of the Gospel must be pointed out."[33]

Beneath this religious reasoning Dix could also find personal motives that she shared with Sumner. The Prison Discipline Society stood near the center of Boston civic life. Secretary Dwight and treasurer Samuel A. Eliot, the former mayor whom Daniel Webster once called "the impersonation of Boston," were but two of the key members from the highest echelons of Beacon Hill; names like Appleton, Jackson, Lawrence, and Lowell dominated the list of directors. Like Dix, Sumner had recently become deeply disillusioned with Boston, and their attack against the Prison Discipline Society expressed their rebellion. Hillard astutely identified his law partner's target when he told Dix that Sumner's strongest adversary was "the social position and force of will of Mr. Sam Eliot, who is more than any one answerable for the one sided position of the Society." Howe welcomed her to "quite a war" in June 1845 with a warning that "we are in danger of being pulverised" by Eliot.[34]

Still spending her Sundays teaching at the Eastern Penitentiary, Dix resumed her essay about prison discipline during the summer hours she could spare from the Trenton and Harrisburg asylum commissions. In August she returned to Boston to examine a few more institutions and concentrate on writing. She found the month-long visit home "peculiarly undesirable, inconvenient, and unpleasant," but her disdain for social rounds made for a productive sojourn.[35] In early September she published *Remarks on Prisons and Prison Discipline,* a one-hundred-page survey of penal institutions and issues relating to criminal punishment.

Compared to some of the bitter polemics inspired by the Boston Prison Discipline Society controversy, Dix's essay was well researched, thoughtfully designed, and evenhanded. She provided useful information about prison facilities and practices gathered from visits to all of the state penitentiaries and many other correctional institutions in the Northeast, as well as from her reading of American and European prison reports. She addressed a variety of penal issues in addition to "the two great *experimental* systems," most notably calling for restrictions on the executive pardoning power and elimination of the widespread practice of selling visitors tickets to see prisons. She aimed to present her conclusions with judicious restraint. "We claim too much for our present prisons, on whichever system established," she observed. She identified leading examples of the Auburn system as well as the Pennsylvania system, but she emphasized that widespread character reformation could only be achieved if teachers placed "*moral education* in the scale of instruction, from which it has so often been cast out."[36]

Dix's balanced tone did not prevent her from clearly indicating her preference between the rival systems. She endorsed the separate system as "a more direct application and exercise of Christian rule and precepts, than any other mode of prison-government." Her verdict partly reflected the standard indictment of the Auburn system. Although she readily agreed that some inmates could not be controlled without a whip, she called for milder punishments than the congregate imprisonment required. "Few have been attracted from an evil to a good life by the severity of their fellow men," she declared. "Many have been brought to a sense of that knowledge by the gracious influences of earnest piety, shining out in the life and conversation." Her proposals to "awaken and strengthen the *control* of the *conscience*" in penitentiaries closely followed her vision of the moral treatment of insanity and her methods as a schoolteacher. "*Steady, firm, and kind* government of prisoners is the truest humanity," she maintained, noting, "It is with convicts as with children."[37]

In addition to attacking Dwight's theories of punishment, Dix also signaled a more personal sympathy with the rebels against the Boston Prison Discipline Society. Her warm praise for the prison reform organizations in Philadelphia and New York was emphatically not extended to the more influential Boston organization. She suggested that Dwight's partiality left him "so warped in judgment as to be self-deceived" and deemed some of his charges against Pennsylvania system advocates "too unworthy to deserve comment." She urged international comparisons of penal systems, a pointed attack on Dwight's indifference to the European preference for the separate system. And of all the American prisons she described, she reserved her sharpest barbs for the Massachusetts State Prison at Charlestown, which had been organized under Dwight's guidance. Singling it out as the least competent implementation of the less effective prison system, she sardonically noted that the smug officials' "congratulations to each other and the public, as expressed in the last two annual reports, are based on their wishes and hopes, rather than on a knowledge of prison government and necessities."[38]

133

In some of the most striking passages of *Remarks on Prisons and Prison Discipline,* Dix moved beyond her criticisms of the congregate system and Dwight to endorse the total isolation of convicts under the Pennsylvania system. She dismissed as fantasy Charles Dickens's claim that the awesome stillness at the Eastern Penitentiary tortured prisoners' minds more insidiously than the congregate system could wrack their bodies. Solitary confinement tested the soul, Dix argued. The most wicked and incorrigible offenders would "dread solitude as the one great evil." But "convicts who have been betrayed into crime by sudden outbreaks of passion" would find isolation the path to spiritual renewal. When constantly alone, "the best faculties, feelings, and perceptions of the prisoner are called out and exercised, while the evil are for the most part left dormant."[39] Even more than her call for the reduced use of corporal punishment, Dix's commendation of solitude expressed a deep personal conviction. She would impose on prisoners a variation of the disciplinary regimen that she had found so beneficial for herself.

— 3 —

The reception of *Remarks on Prisons and Prison Discipline* confirmed Dix's emergence as one of the most widely admired women in America. The response from Boston was predictable enough. Sumner, who apparently shared the publication costs with Emerson and other friends, greeted it with enthusiastic admiration in the *Christian Examiner.* Promoting Dix to confound Dwight, he exclaimed that "she is in herself alone a whole Prison Discipline Society." Officials at the Charlestown prison denied her allegations, and a visiting committee divided between advocates of the separate and congregate systems found itself identically divided on the accuracy of Dix's description. But unlike Sumner and Howe, Dix made few enemies among Boston opponents who thought her admirably benevolent if somewhat misguided. When the principals in the Boston Prison Discipline Society dispute ran across her at the Eastern Penitentiary shortly after publication of the *Remarks,* Louis Dwight greeted her kindly and Samuel A. Eliot marveled at the "beautiful manner" in which Dix read a Psalm to the prisoners.[40]

More impressively, praise for Dix's prison reform effort transcended the parochial disputes of Boston. Chancellor Kent, the foremost jurist in the country, warmly praised her pamphlet. Another leading lawyer wrote that "there is a depth of research and a vein of profound reflection and manly sense in it which I hardly expected in an Enthusiastic Lady." Several reviews agreed with *The Harbinger,* the newspaper of the utopian retreat at Brook Farm, that Dix's "means of observation and clearness of judgment can not be inferior to those of any other person." Prison reform societies in the United States and Europe honored her. Civic leaders in several states promised to seek legislation in accordance with her views and invited her to assist their efforts.[41]

Dix's rapidly growing national reputation benefited immensely from the ready parallels between her efforts and the celebrated work of British prison reformers John Howard and, especially, Elizabeth Fry. During the last few years, Dix had come to be known widely as "the Elizabeth Fry of America."[42] The pairing of Dix and the Quaker she had angled to meet in England nine years before gave observers a useful shorthand with which to describe the two women's similar campaigns to promote moral instruction through custodial institutions like asylums, alms-houses, and penitentiaries. When Lydia Maria Child reprised her early magazine profile of Dix in her widely selling series, *Letters from New York,* she accordingly added a reference to her former housemate as "our American Mrs. Fry, the God-appointed missionary to prisons and alms-houses."[43]

Beyond this descriptive convenience, the parallel between Dix and Fry also reflected a more important assertion of American identity. In the United States and abroad, public institutions like prisons and asylums vividly symbolized the promise of the new republic. By inheriting the celebrity of Fry, who died in 1845, Dix became a representative of the American claim to moral leadership in the world. "Have you heard of Miss Dix?" one of Francis Lieber's correspondents asked in February 1845 while the legal and political commentator was overseas. "If you had not been abroad I would not have asked the question, but I think it highly probable that some accounts of her benevolent exertions in behalf of the Insane Poor must have reached Europe." When Lieber later met Dix, he would illustrate the competitive patriotism implicit in her reputation, observing that "she is far, far more than an American Mrs. Fry. She is actually a heroine."[44] Dix's intensely personal sense of vocation had become a vehicle for the American faith in a providential national mission. That stature opened new political opportunities as she returned her attention to the insane.

— 4 —

Arriving in Kentucky on the first day of November 1845, Dix again threw herself back into her travels. She began at the state capitol in Frankfort and the Kentucky Eastern Lunatic Asylum in Lexington, a twenty-year-old nontherapeutic facility for insane paupers that had recently appointed its first medical superintendent and initiated a program of moral treatment, as Edward Jarvis had urged four years earlier. To continue this trend in state policy, Dix took up the superintendent's request for a $20,000 appropriation for a new asylum building. She also proposed the construction of a second hospital in the western district near the Green River, a recognition of the regional competition for state institutions and a conclusive abandonment of her original view that public mental hospitals should be supplemented by nontherapeutic asylums for chronically insane paupers. After her brief visits to Frankfort and Lexington, Dix set off to research another of her now famous memorials, proceeding "without delay or repose from county to county, jail to jail, and poor-house to poor-house."[45]

The Kentucky countryside presented some of the most arduous traveling Dix had yet undertaken. She told Emerson she was plunging into "almost trackless forests, *over* mountains, and *through* rivers. Often the way has led through a wilderness, traced by slight cuts on the trees, and houses at intervals of fourteen and twenty miles—if those can be called houses which frequently consist only of a single room constructed of logs." At night she slept on chairs set before fireplaces, gazing out at the stars through the chinks in the logs or peering down at "the fierce Norway rats which swarm in the country."[46] The stagecoach she rode to Hopkinsville was once held up by a gunman, but the ex-convict relented upon remembering that he had heard Dix teach Bible classes in his former prison. "Oh, that voice!" he exclaimed, taking the five-dollar note she pushed at him over his protest, doubtless with an injunction to go forth and sin no more.[47] Summarizing her Kentucky adventures to Harriet Hare, Dix observed that an account of the journey "would make a very respectable novel—having enough of the marvelous, the dangerous, and the terrible to give vivacity to plain facts and daily movements."[48]

As with any "very respectable" novel, Dix emphasized the moral of the story: the adaptability and power of benevolent womanhood. Like her initial entry into politics, her peripatetic style created a tension between her aspirations as a moral crusader and her deference to social convention. She had been told on her arrival in Kentucky that "to travel here alone would certainly be to compromise my character as well as usefulness," for "it is almost unknown here for a lady to make a journey by herself." In a response that was more than a mere political gesture, she had openly hesitated before leaving Lexington and "resolved to try and be governed by the results." The reception she met now vindicated her course. "Every where I am treated with respect and my objects promptly and cheerfully advanced," she noted. Like the success of her lobbying, the gratifying welcomes and "preserving mercies" during her travels reinforced the central values of female conduct that she had feared overstepping. "I have full faith that after all a woman is her own best protector," Dix concluded. "Quiet manners and self-respect will command respect and sufficient attention from others. After this year's full proof and experience I shall not hesitate any where."[49]

Ironically, Dix was achieving this sense of freedom at the same time that her travels were becoming less central to her political strategy. The decline partly reflected local conditions. Dix found no insane paupers in Kentucky almshouses or jails, in part because the state supported a system of home-based care by providing a stipend to relatives who assumed responsibility for insane dependents.[50] Information on the condition of the insane under this "out of door" relief was more difficult to obtain and more sensitive to publish than a survey of almshouses.

No less important than these local considerations in Dix's changing strategy was the rise of her national reputation. Her views on the treatment of the insane and the administration of prison discipline were now assured of a respectful hearing in any state legislature without her having to conduct an extensive tour to collect information and publicize her cause. Standing to gain little from controversies over specific allegations of mistreatment, she retreated diplomatically when a Louisville newspaper printed her private criticism of a family that kept an insane relative in a log cabin rather than committing him to an asylum.[51]

Dix did not seriously try to repeat previous campaigns in which she had traversed entire states, although she did cover forty-four of the more than one hundred counties in Kentucky. Already thinking of writing an essay on southern and western prisons to expand on the success of *Remarks on Prisons and Prison Discipline,* she sometimes paused to advocate reforms at local jails. For the most part, however, she spent "much less time" in visiting county institutions than in her earlier surveys, asserting that "there has been no necessity for more."[52] She took advantage of her reduced itinerary to visit the Mammoth Cave, one of the great tourist attractions of nineteenth-century America. She also made a detour to examine the Indiana state penitentiary and "was gratified to learn that the Governor announced that his views of prisons, and of Prison discipline had undergone an entire change since reading 'the Remarks.' " The highlight of her autumn and winter travels was the week she spent in Nashville, where she investigated the state penitentiary and laid groundwork for a campaign to replace the Lunatic Asylum of Tennessee. The governor, legislators, and other state officials extended "the most flattering attentions," but Dix took the greatest pleasure in her recognition by Jane Erwin Yeatman Bell, the wealthy wife of prominent politician John Bell. Delighted by "my *social position* in the West," Dix promised to return for the next biennial meeting of the Tennessee legislature.[53]

Upon returning to Frankfort, Dix prepared two documents for the Kentucky legislature, a bifurcation of her comments on criminal punishment and the treatment of insanity that accommodated the constant efforts of asylum doctors to avoid any conflation of prisons and mental hospitals. The longer submission summarized Dix's observations at the state penitentiary and the local jails and poorhouses. Less a policy proposal than a step toward extending *Remarks on Prison and Prison Discipline,* which she excerpted in an appendix, this report mainly repeated her earlier recommendations to state and municipal officials. She hoped "to see the benefits of moral and mental culture more widely diffused" and the vigorous promotion of "more careful habits of self-discipline." Toward these ends, she called for improvements in prison ventilation, lighting, heating, cleanliness, and security. She urged the construction of jails that would "afford the means of separating or classing the prisoners," and she worried that "prisoners are without employment for mind or hands." The most important addition to the *Remarks* recommended construction of "work-houses, or *houses* of *correction*" in populous areas for "women-offenders" to avoid the expense of separating the few female convicts from men in the state penitentiary "under a system that the people will tolerate."[54]

Dix's second and nominally more important submission, the appeal on behalf of the Eastern Lunatic Asylum and the request for a new mental hospital, sharply underscored the changes in her political methods. Only about one-fourth the length of the memorials in New York and Pennsylvania, the fourteen-page document did not offer any information about the condition of the unhospitalized insane in Kentucky. The surplus of applications for admission to the Lexington asylum sufficed to show that "it is evident that much suffering exists, and many patients are annually becoming *hopelessly* insane through want of seasonable appropriate care." After echoing the Lexington superintendent's list of the flaws in his facility, Dix devoted most of the short paper to a summary of standard arguments about asylum medicine and economics. She emphasized that recovery depended on separating the insane from "the mistaken tenderness within the family circle," which was not only unable to provide therapy but likely to agitate the insane and exacerbate mental instability. "The solemn duty of the removal and non-intercourse of the insane, with their intimate friends and family, and their familiar homes" was crucial to the success of the moral therapy, much as separation from home had been essential to the transformation of her own character. She assured the Kentucky legislature that "all experience shows that insanity *seasonably treated is as certainly curable as a cold or a fever*," once again relying heavily on annual reports of asylum superintendents.[55]

Dix's perfunctory asylum memorial was now merely a prelude to her increasing reliance on personal persuasiveness in face-to-face lobbying. She remained in Frankfort through February 1846 while lawmakers considered a bill providing a $10,000 appropriation to the Lexington asylum and establishing a commission to select a site for a new hospital near the Green River. Although the legislature pared the budget request to $5,000, she declared herself "quite satisfied" that the state had committed itself to modernization of the Eastern Lunatic Asylum, and she was delighted that appointment of the Green River commission started momentum for another mental hospital.[56] Local observers agreed that her efforts had been decisive. "The impression made by her on our rulers will long be attested by its fruits," one Kentuckian predicted, correctly anticipating the full funding of the Lexington building program and the creation of an asylum at Hopkinsville within two years. The speaker of the state house of representatives later noted that "the celebrated Miss Dix" was responsible for the second facility.[57] "All my objects in Kentucky have been successfully accomplished," Dix concluded in her report to Harriet Hare. Two weeks after passage of the legislation she boarded an Ohio River steamboat to keep her triumphant procession rolling on.

— 5 —

When spring muds temporarily checked Dix's plan to continue westward from Kentucky, she turned south to work on her survey of prisons. Taking the river voyage from Louisville to New Orleans in March 1846, she wound her way back north through the state penitentiaries of Louisiana, Mississippi, Alabama, Georgia, South Carolina, Arkansas, and Missouri. Often traveling by stagecoach, she darted into local jails to conduct hasty additional inspections while the other stage passengers ate meals or the drivers changed horses.

The southern excursion provided Dix an ideal opportunity to vent her hostility toward her home. She compared the insanity ward of the Charity Hospital in New Orleans favorably with the Boston Lunatic Hospital, praised southern schools, prisons, and other public institutions, and told friends that traveling between Mobile and Columbia was at least as pleasant as between Boston and Providence. In the cultural juxtaposition of New England and the South, a contrast that was turning toward a deadly rivalry in 1846, Dix's admiration clearly expressed her antagonism to the world she had rejected. "At the north we do *great* injustice to the Southerners as I think," she concluded with keener sensitivity to the injustices of Boston than to the conditions in southern institutions. Finding "much less to blame and reform than I left at the north," she satisfied her meliorative impulses by donating collections of uplifting literature to the state prisons.[58]

Steaming up the Mississippi River, however, Dix revealed clearly that she still carried her Boston outlook with her. Shortly after her boat passed Vicksburg she met a fellow passenger named J. O. King from Jacksonville, Illinois, a town settled in the 1820s by a band of evangelical New England clergymen attempting to transplant their culture to the frontier. Styling itself "the Athens of the West" in echo of Boston's claim to be "the Athens of America," Jacksonville continued to reflect its Yankee origins in 1846. Town boosters had promoted it as the capital of state philanthropic institutions, including Illinois College and the Illinois Institution for the Education of the Deaf and Dumb. Similarly, a local physician had recently led an effort to establish a state mental hospital in the town. Impressed by this civic ambition, Dix changed her itinerary to work next in Illinois rather than Indiana.[59]

Dix launched her Illinois campaign from J. O. King's parlor, where she met the leading citizens of Jacksonville and outlined her "method of proceeding." Through the spring, King's brother drove her around the central part of the state in his one-horse buggy, stopping at the county seats to inquire about local cases of insanity. As in Kentucky, she found few insane paupers in county institutions, but she gathered anecdotal evidence about instances of insane men and women "in 'cabins,' in 'pens,' and wandering at large." She also continued her prison research by inspecting the local jails and conducting a thorough examination of the state penitentiary at Alton.[60]

Dix temporarily left Illinois in August 1846 to sweep through Indiana, but she soon found the prairie sun too debilitating to permit her to go on. After a few weeks she collapsed at the Ohio Lunatic Asylum while on a detour to Columbus to reexamine the state penitentiary and local institutions. William Awl diagnosed her malady as "congestive fever," a classification that included bronchitis and pneumonia. She remained at Awl's hospital for eight weeks, bedridden with exhaustion, a persistent cough, and an inflammation of her stomach and lungs. In early November she had herself moved to the Cincinnati home of financier Charles Stetson. Not yet fully recovered in December, she nevertheless felt "decided by imperative claims of duty, as seem to me, to renew my usual labors." She headed to Springfield for the opening of the legislative session, visiting additional Illinois institutions on her way.[61]

In the state capital, Dix teamed with Morgan County senator William Thomas and the medical community centered on Illinois College to complete the carefully orchestrated Jacksonville asylum campaign. The legislature printed 2,000 copies of the ten-page memorial she submitted in January 1847, which generated valuable publicity even as the lobbying device continued to deteriorate as a source of information. Dix also published a series of reports on Illinois jails in the Sangamo *Journal*, the Whig newspaper in Springfield. Most important, Thomas arranged for small groups of legislators to meet Dix privately in her hotel to discuss the need for a public mental hospital and the advantages of Jacksonville as a site.[62]

As in New Jersey, Pennsylvania, and Kentucky, Dix's contributions helped the Illinois coalition of asylum supporters achieve a breakthrough success. The Springfield legislature established the Illinois State Hospital for the Insane and, despite a strong rival effort from Peoria, selected Jacksonville as the location of the important institution. On March 27, Thomas, named secretary of the hospital's board of trustees, sent Dix the first resolution enacted by the governing body, an expression of gratitude for her humanitarian efforts. He added his own personal thanks for her "disinterested action" in furthering the dreams of Jacksonville to become the Boston of the West. "We can never compensate you, for your efforts, and success, in securing the location of the Hospital for the Insane," he later told her.[63]

As in Kentucky, Dix devoted her efforts in Illinois to prison reform as well as the asylum campaign. Her legislative memorial on the Alton penitentiary, longer and more informative than her asylum memorial, argued that *"no outlay of money can convert this prison into a secure, commodious, or durable establishment."* Joining other prison reform advocates in calling for the construction of "a *new prison,* on an approved plan, and under a correct system," Dix pointed to the Eastern Penitentiary as the model institution in the country. The Illinois legislature rejected her proposal and voted instead to apply rental income from the leased state penitentiary to its repair. Dix had specifically opposed that stopgap measure in her memorial, but she nevertheless joyously celebrated "the passage of both my principal bills" for the mental hospital and the penitentiary.[64]

This increasingly proprietary attitude toward reform legislation obscured the limits of Dix's achievements. Although she gloated from the west that "Mr. Dwight has I think no influence in these States, *if* he possesses it in any," the congregate system promoted by the Boston Prison Discipline Society continued to win more supporters in the

United States than the separate system. When Illinois eventually erected a new penitentiary at Joliet, the facility became a national model of the Auburn system. Moreover, beyond the defeat of Dix's chief policy, public interest in the entire subject of prison discipline was declining rapidly. Dix's correspondence with wardens around the country often affirmed the report of one administrator that "the people of this State manifest little or no interest in the well-being or well-doing of the men they send to their state-prison." As the controversy within the Boston Discipline Society faded, Dix too would turn her efforts away from prison reform as an application of her vision of moral education. Her easy contentment with the Illinois penitentiary legislation marked her last major initiative in the field. She would never write her projected essay on southern and western penitentiaries.[65]

Similarly, Dix's recent triumphs in asylum campaigns tended to be overstated. Distinctively personal as her efforts were, her success remained part of a nationwide trend toward the proliferation of mental hospitals providing the moral treatment. Although she merely agreed with others that she deserved personal credit for the passage of legislation, the establishment of new institutions reflected not only her influence but also the support of medical interests and the civic boosterism that she herself credited with *"setting the ball in motion"* in Illinois.[66] Significantly, in several states the asylum movement advanced without Dix. Indiana organized a public mental hospital before she could reach the state, and Louisiana established an asylum in the same month as Illinois.

But if prison discipline and the asylum movement proceeded on courses largely beyond Dix's control, her public stature had transcended its origin in those humanitarian causes. A national symbol of benevolence, she saw herself not only as a proponent of the moral treatment of insanity or the separate system of prison discipline but as a leader of a broader movement to redeem American society. Appalled by "the present political state of the Country" as unsavory ambitions for the conquest of Mexico began to dominate national affairs, she declared that "I see no redemption but in action—action which shall by the diffusion of true knowledge, and the cultivation of *principle,* qualify citizens to conduct the government more righteously."[67] She told George B. Emerson to advise "intelligent, devoted, pious men and women" with "true missionary spirit" to go not to China or the South Sea islands, for "here in each and all of these United States is enough and more than enough for them to do." Drawing on her own experience, she added, "If they are fond of roving and wish for more distant fields of labour than our New-England opens—let them come to the middle or the Western States."[68]

Dix felt a new sense of inner peace as success partly replaced isolation in sustaining her faith that she was pursuing a sacred mission. The pathetic tone faded from her letters to Emerson, and she lashed out less often at the spiritual dangers of society. Touring the West, she found that "the people are hospitable and attentive to strangers, and one cannot but feel a lively regard for most who become frequent associates."[69] Anne Heath shrewdly recognized the inward transformation that accompanied her old friend's triumphs. "You wear an armour," she observed, "and tho' it was wrought in disappointment labour & tears, it at length gives you safety." As Dix rejoiced in state after state that "for the Insane a home shall soon rise," her own yearning for a home was ending. She told Heath that "I grow more content with my own lot" as she observed the dis-satisfaction of those who led a more settled life. The asylums now open-ing fulfilled her dreams for a home literally as well as metaphorically; hospitals run by friendly superintendents would soon become her favor-ite resting places. From the quietude of Brookline, Heath congratulated Dix: "You are the only person I know, who is not in some respects to be pitied . . . you, my dear, dear friend have created for yourself a hap-piness *which goes with* you."[70]

— 6 —

By the summer of 1847, however, Dix was thoroughly road-weary. She calculated in August that she had traveled 32,470 miles since beginning her Pennsylvania campaign three years earlier. A list of the towns she had visited in the twenty-two months since she left Boston for Kentucky covered three closely written pages.[71] She briefly considered taking an ocean voyage to escape from "the temptation to visit and examine public institutions." Eventually she decided to spend much of the summer at Newport for the first time in years, resting in the company of Sarah Gibbs, Ruth Channing, the Hares, and the Emersons. She also spent several weeks in Boston, where Unitarian preachers lionized her in ser-mons and friends urged her to linger. But as Heath recognized in qualifying her own lonely plea, "I well know nothing will keep you, but wanting the power to go."[72]

Although Dix sighed that "travelling has become very tiresome to me," in October she set off with excitement for Tennessee.[73] She had looked forward to working in the state since her brief visit to Nashville almost two years earlier. Her eagerness partly anticipated another triumph. Efforts to organize a state mental hospital had made slow but steady progress in Tennessee for more than fifteen years. The first fruits of this movement, the opening in 1840 of the small, underfunded Lunatic Asylum of Tennessee, never satisfied physicians and other interested citizens who sought an asylum that provided the moral treatment. Newspapers, pamphlets, and politicians continued to discuss the issue over the next several years. In September 1847, shortly before Dix headed south, the Nashville *Republican Banner* urged Tennessee to "do something worthy of her character and the age in which we live." Governor Neill S. Brown's message to the legislature echoed that there was "no argument" against the establishment of a modern facility.[74]

In addition to these favorable legislative prospects, Dix took pleasure in the renewal of her friendly relations with the leaders of Nashville society, most notably Jane and John Bell. Establishing herself at the Sewanee House, she declared that she had "never found myself settled for a *winter's laborious* Legislative business so well before; so far as personal affairs are considered."[75] She quickly decided that she would conduct this campaign without traveling to any almshouses or jails outside of Nashville. The atmosphere of a working holiday suffered only the most delightful interruption when the legislature began its session by electing John Bell to the United States Senate. In December he returned with his wife to Washington, where he had previously served in Congress and in the Whig cabinet that resigned in mass protest following John Tyler's veto of party banking and public land legislation.

Dix followed the Bells to Washington temporarily in the winter and went on to Philadelphia to rest, but not before she had generated fresh momentum for the asylum measure in Nashville. Urged by key legislators to submit a memorial, contrary to her original plan, she spent four days writing an appeal to crystallize the campaign. As she had conducted little research in the state, she dwelled only briefly on the insane paupers she asserted were "pining in cells and dungeons . . . cast out, cast off, like the Pariah of the Hindoos." Most of the petition summarized the shortcomings of the existing asylum and presented an overview of the moral treatment based on her previous memorials and the annual reports of medical superintendents. "Anticipating the results of your legislation," Dix described the ideal hospital in detail. The legislature should locate it on a farm, near the conveniences of a city. Buildings should be designed inexpensively, taking care to avoid "every thing giving the *appearance* of a prison." Her close attention to "rules of hygiene" illustrated the interrelation she saw between physical and mental health and her understanding of the moral treatment as a purifying process. Wholesome rural air, nearby streams or springs, effective ventilation, and windows receiving abundant sunlight were crucial to her notion of asylum therapy.[76]

The memorial was greeted with endorsements and applause. The legislature ordered that 4,000 copies be printed in pamphlet form, and the document circulated widely in Tennessee and beyond. The Nashville *Republican Banner* called for the assembly to show "sufficient state pride" to follow the recommendations of this "most distinguished philanthropist." The Nashville *Whig* similarly pressed Tennesseeans to follow the national asylum trend by reprinting out-of-state praise for Dix's memorial. Stirred by "admiration of her disinterested, and persevering philanthropy, so honorable to their sex," twenty-five society matrons asked Dix to permit a sculptor to portray "in a permanent and pleasing form a countenance expressive at once, of feminine delicacy, and heroic firmness, sensibility and strength, compassion and courage."[77] Dix declined the honor in terms that echoed the ideals of female benevolence she shared with her admirers. "To us, women, it peculiarly belongs to reveal in its holiest aspects the *spirituality* of Religion," she noted, assuring the subscribers that "though our paths may conduct to various and different objects—our *aims are alike* directed to lessen the woes of suffering humanity, and to soften the trials which are so often the severe discipline by which the soul acquires that heavenly knowledge which causeth not to err."[78]

Surmounting the sectional divisions within Tennessee politics over the benefits of state expenditures, in February 1848 the legislature authorized construction of a new mental institution on "the most recent and accepted plans." The new institution was to be called a "hospital

for the insane," following a shift in usage away from the existing custodial "asylum." The legislature appropriated only $40,000 for the facil-
ity—half the amount Dix had requested—but the likelihood of further
funding contests like those she had seen elsewhere did not diminish the
luster of another success. Immediately after creating the Tennessee Hospital for the Insane, the legislature unanimously passed a resolution
declaring that Dix's "disinterested benevolence, sublime charity, and
unmixed philanthropy, challenge alike the gratitude and admiration of
our State."[79]

With affairs well in hand in Tennessee, Dix turned to Louisiana to
urge that the asylum under construction in Jackson comply with the
standards of the Association of Medical Superintendents. Her trip uncovered another state ripe for an asylum campaign. In New Orleans and
Mobile she met "many influential citizens of Alabama" interested in the
establishment of a state mental hospital, including "medical men, ministers, and Judges." She was introduced to Mrs. Clement Claiborne Clay
of Huntsville as "a perfect lady" who "seems to seek only the acquaintance of the most enlightened and highly respectable." Looking toward
the next biennial legislative session in 1849, she coordinated plans with
the president of the state medical society to collect information about
the insane and promised to supply newspapers with material "that facts
may be presented to the people, and the subject kept before the public."[80]

As she completed her circuit through Tennessee, Louisiana, and Alabama, Dix again found that "I can no longer endure fatigue as formerly"
and again felt torn by urgent requests to be in several states at once. But
she now had a plan to solve these problems while continuing to expand
her mission, a plan she had evidently formulated over the past several
months. In April 1848 she told Heath she would soon join the Bells in
Washington for "business which claims my attention there."[81] Turning
north in time for the opening of her beloved Trenton asylum on May
15, she arrived at the federal capital a few days later to begin a new and
different legislative campaign.

7

The Property of the People

"MY OBJECTS and aims now reach the length and breadth of the union," Dix declared in late May 1848 as she settled into Mrs. Birth's boardinghouse on Capitol Hill with the Bells. She predicted that "I may be here some weeks, possibly a long time." Provided free shipping privileges by the Adams Express company shortly before her arrival, she gathered supplies for her siege of Congress. She sent for a new muslin dress for the Washington summer, and she asked leading asylum superintendents to send her estimates of the incidence of insanity in the United States. Luther Bell of the McLean Asylum concluded his detailed analysis of the federal census with amazement at the grandeur of his friend's new project: "My dear Miss Dix, you have got work enough before you for twenty lives instead of one!"[1]

— 1 —

Dix's campaign for federal endowment of state mental hospitals was not only the most far-reaching but the most original effort of her lobbying career. Her state campaigns had complemented—and usually brought success to—local efforts by physicians, town boosters, and philanthropists. These appeals for the establishment of public mental hospitals sought fulfillment of government functions already widely recognized when Dix first became interested in insanity. Her federal undertaking, in contrast, was remarkably innovative. Although amenable to entrepreneurial and humanitarian arguments for the construction of hospitals and other charitable institutions, state legislatures had proven far less willing to provide continuing funding to sustain them. In most states, towns and counties remained primarily responsible for the expenses of their indigent residents who entered state asylums, a system that induced municipalities to prefer cheaper almshouse accommodations for the insane. The unreliability of municipal payments also intensified the demand of asylum superintendents for a significant proportion of privately supported patients, who ensured a dependable income for the hospital but reduced the room available for paupers.[2]

Dix proposed to solve this difficult problem by tapping a vast source of national wealth, the public domain. According to a well-publicized report by the General Land Office in April 1848, the federal government held legal title to 352,000,774 acres of land located in the states; the western territories still unorganized since the Louisiana Purchase comprised another 697,186,028 acres of federal property.[3] The value of this billion acres could not be so precisely calculated. The land in the territories would remain unavailable for sale until placed under government, and Congress was presently considering bills to open the fertile Oregon and Minnesota regions, which had already attracted large numbers of settlers. The rest of the public domain—scattered unevenly through all thirty states except the original thirteen plus Vermont, Maine, Kentucky, Tennessee, and Texas—varied widely in market value. Especially in older southwestern states like Missouri and Alabama, the failure of federal lands to command the minimum price of $1.25 per acre had long prompted calls for "graduation" of the price in proportion to the years that tracts remained unsold. Whatever its exact aggregate worth, however, the public domain was rapidly becoming more available for disposition by Congress without regard to revenue, for tariff income over the past decade had sharply reduced federal dependence on the proceeds from land sales.

More obvious and more far-reaching was another fundamental change taking place in the premises of federal land policy as Dix settled into Washington. Two months earlier, the Senate had ratified the Treaty of

149

Guadalupe Hidalgo, ending the war with vanquished Mexico and adding more than a half-million square miles of southwestern land to the public domain. The immense, controversial acquisition quickly altered the economic outlook as well as the map of the United States. Proposals for use of the federal wealth multiplied. The graduation movement revived; railroad promoters demanded land subsidies; advocates of homestead legislation intensified their call for a grant of free farms to settlers on the public lands. The federal domain seemed to offer a limitless resource for American development.[4]

Joining this land rush, Dix planned to ask Congress for a large donation to be divided among the states to endow public mental hospitals, thereby freeing the asylums from dependence on the appropriations of state legislatures and the patronage of municipalities. After considering a petition for three million acres, she decided to request five million acres, a small fraction of the national domain but approximately equal to the total of all federal land dispositions during the past two years.[5] Each state would sell its land grant to the public and establish a perpetual fund for the care of insane paupers. The federal grants would be conditioned on application of the funds to public hospitals with resident physicians; Dix would prohibit any use of the subsidies to maintain the insane in jails, poorhouses, or private hospitals.[6]

Similar to the later land-grant system of colleges, Dix's proposal adapted to insane asylums the long-standing policy for funding schools through the sale of federal lands. Since the beginning of the republic, Congress had reserved every sixteenth square mile of the public lands for educational purposes. Beginning with the admission of Ohio into the union in 1802, Congress had also dedicated a portion of each new state to the establishment of universities. Dix also found more closely comparable precedents for her plan in two of the many individual land grants passed by Congress, the small donations of land in 1819 and 1826 to benefit institutions for deaf-mutes in Connecticut and Kentucky.[7] But all of these models differed significantly from her idea for the financing of state mental hospitals. Congress had never considered a systematic set of land grants to promote welfare institutions throughout the country.

Dix was presenting her new version of an old policy to a Congress that was itself in the midst of a historic generational transition. Henry

Clay was temporarily out of the Senate for another unsuccessful presidential campaign, but the towering figures of Daniel Webster, John C. Calhoun, and Thomas Hart Benton remained active. Meanwhile, newcomers like Stephen A. Douglas, Jefferson Davis, and John J. Crittenden were building national reputations. Memorable members of the House of Representatives included David Wilmot of Pennsylvania, whose proposal to ban slavery in all territory acquired from Mexico had convulsed Congress for much of the past two years, and the chief combatants in the Wilmot Proviso debate, Joshua Giddings of Ohio and Robert Barnwell Rhett of South Carolina. Andrew Johnson of Tennessee had charted a new legislative direction as the sponsor of the homestead bill. Less prominent but hardly unnoticed was a single-term representative from Illinois, Abraham Lincoln.

Dix's own considerable celebrity had preceded her to Washington. Three weeks before she arrived, John P. Hale of New Hampshire ended a Senate debate over commissioning a portrait of General Zachary Taylor, an early sally in the 1848 presidential campaign, by declaring that Congress should instead decorate the Capitol with a portrait of Dix, "who has done more for humanity, Christianity, and the elevation of man above all that afflicts and degrades him, than a thousand so-called heroes."[8] Dix also knew several current congressmen as a result of her state campaigns. Aside from Bell, the most familiar faces were from her home state. John Davis and John G. Palfrey, her allies in the expansion of the Worcester State Lunatic Hospital, were now members of the Senate and the House, respectively. Only one month earlier, Horace Mann had also joined the House to fill the seat vacated by the death of John Quincy Adams.

As she surveyed Congress and assessed the prospects for her legislation, Dix assumed that politics would mirror the map on which she viewed her personal life. "I look for my chief opposition from the New England delegations," she predicted, adding that "I would as willingly anchor under lee of an ice-berg as have much to accomplish through our real Yankees."[9] Her analysis not only disregarded her earnest friends in the Massachusetts contingent; it also ignored the obvious sectional implications of her proposal. She had designed the plan mainly to benefit the populous Northeast, where her surveys of the insane had discovered "more actual suffering at present than in all other states beside" although the region had pioneered the establishment of asylums.[10] Reinforcing this northeastern interest in additional asylum funding, moreover, were the traditional sectional interests in the public domain. With no federal property in any of its states, New England had consistently demanded a division of the national wealth among all states rather than a graduation of land prices to stimulate westward migration or a cession of the federal property to the states in which the public lands were located.[11] Dix's native region would undoubtedly welcome her request far more enthusiastically than the representatives of the landed western states.

Dix's preliminary view of the partisan alignment on her proposal similarly reflected her personal disdain for organized politics rather than the realities of the situation. Although she expected to "share the good-will pretty equally of Democrats and Whigs," her plan was clearly more congenial to the latter.[12] As her state campaigns had indicated, Whigs more pervasively shared her ideals of moral reform and her view of government as an instrument for active benevolence.[13] Furthermore, ever since Henry Clay founded the party in the 1830s, Whig leaders had favored "distribution," or the use of public land sale proceeds to fund roads, canals, and other construction projects within the boundaries of the states. Parrying the Jacksonian argument that Congress lacked authority to spend money for these "internal improvements," the Whigs pointed to the provision of the Constitution that established federal power to "dispose of, and make all needful Rules and Regulations respecting the Territory or other Property belonging to the United States." Under the Territories Clause, the Whigs argued, Congress enjoyed full latitude to donate public lands to the states for directed sales even if the Constitution precluded the use of tariff income and other Treasury receipts for state purposes.[14]

Dix could be confident that Whigs would support her modification of Clay's program for the distribution of proceeds from federal land sales. Her challenge was to win a significant block of Democratic votes in the Senate, where President James K. Polk's party had established a commanding majority, and to tip the approximately even balance of party strength in the House. Characteristically, she depended on her personal connections and the power of female influence to override partisanship if Congress sent her bill to the president. "Fortunately I bask in *Court* favor," she confided to a friend. "Mrs. Polk is all attention."[15]

Dix launched her campaign with a memorial written while the flu confined her to Mrs. Birth's boardinghouse in June 1848. "I can only say it
embodies *facts*," she told Harriet Hare. "As a literary effort it is open I
suspect to severe criticism, but I was too ill to make much effort."[16]
Patched together in large part from Dix's previous memorials to state
legislatures, the thirty-two-page document reflected the diminished
importance of written appeals in her lobbying tactics. At the same time,
the national stage offered by Congress and the issues of federalism posed
by her legislation prompted her to address the subject of public responsibility for the insane in broader terms than she ever had before.

The memorial to Congress presented Dix's most powerful statement
of the commonplace idea that the political and moral freedom of American life tended to cause insanity. Drawing from annual asylum reports
and other standard authorities, she argued that "free civil and religious
institutions create constantly various and multiplying sources of mental
excitement." Insanity, she echoed, was inevitable "where, in effect, every
individual, however obscure, is free to enter upon the race for the highest
honors and most exalted stations." She reported a high incidence of
insanity among politicians and noted the dangers of "protracted attendance upon excited public assemblies." Writing shortly after the Democratic national convention nominated Lewis Cass and the Whigs chose
Taylor for the presidency, she warned that "the last presidential elections
throughout the country levied heavily on the mental health of its citizens."[17]

Dix derived from this stock analysis the novel inference that the federal government shared a duty to address the problem that it helped to
create. She appealed not only to the compassion of Congress, but also to
its "civil and social obligation" to restore the usefulness of the insane
"as citizens of the republic." Contrasting asylums with the public schools
funded by federal land grants, she observed that "comparatively but little
care is given in cultivating the moral affections in proportion with the
intellectual development of the people." The insane were *"wards of the
nation,"* she argued, and could not be relieved solely by state governments that already collected unpopular taxes to support mental hospitals.[18]

Reporting that she had traveled more than sixty thousand miles to investigate the condition of the insane in every state except North Carolina, Florida, and Texas, Dix estimated that eleven-twelfths of the rapidly increasing insane population lacked adequate accommodations. "I have myself seen *more than nine thousand idiots, epileptics, and insane, in these United States, destitute of appropriate care and protection,*" she calculated. Her state-by-state overview of the insane incorporated some of the most vivid descriptions in her previous memorials. The summary concentrated heavily on the Northeast, emphasizing the burden imposed on urban institutions by "a vast population of uneducated foreigners," but Dix stressed that she sought equal benefits for all sections of the United States. "I ask for the people that which is already the property of the people," she wrote in a stirring peroration. Implicitly comparing her objective to the recent war against Mexico, she declared that true national greatness would not be found in armies, aggrandizement, or vainglory; the grandeur of the country depended on "those God-like attributes which sanctify private life."[19]

The final step of Dix's preparation was the selection of a sponsor for her measure. Deciding to begin in the upper house, she boldly asked Thomas Hart Benton of Missouri to introduce her memorial and take charge of the legislation. The dean of the Democratic party in the Senate and chief spokesman of the West, Benton was the foremost opponent of public land revenue distribution. Dix's bid for his support attempted to establish her proposal as a nonpartisan, intersectional measure removed from ordinary congressional politics. Their interview was a classic match between determined lobbyist and nimble politician:

"Sir, I have not come to ask any favor for myself—not the smallest," Dix told him. "I ask for *yourself, your State, your people.* Sir, you are a Democrat, and profess above all others to *support the interests of the people,* the multitudes, the poor. This Sir is the opportunity of showing the country how far *profession* and *practice correspond.* Reject this measure, you trample on the rights of the poor; you crush them; sustain it and their blessings shall echo round your pillow when the Angel of the last hour comes to call you to the other life of action and of progress."

"My dear Miss Dix, I will do all I can," Benton replied evasively.

"Then sir, the Bill and the measure are safe."

Although Dix informed her friends that Benton "promised me all his influence," she was hardly surprised that he pleaded illness when the time came to present her memorial in Congress.[20]

Dix turned next to a congenial Capitol Hill neighbor, John Adams Dix. She was not related to the New York business leader, but in amused deference to the common error they soon playfully adopted each other, encouraging the public misimpression of their family tie and addressing each other in private correspondence as sister and brother. Like Benton, Dix was a prominent spokesman for Martin Van Buren's followers in the Democratic party, the wing that had promoted the Wilmot Proviso as a factional maneuver against the Polk administration rather than an expression of moral repugnance to slavery. In May he had led a New York delegation of "Barnburners" in withdrawing from the Democratic national convention because it failed to endorse the exclusion of slavery from the Mexican Cession. Against his preliminary counsel and much to the surprise of his newly adopted sister, who considered the Democrats "too sagacious partisans" to undercut Cass, the Barnburner secession quickly hardened. On June 22 a gathering of Barnburners in New York nominated Van Buren for president. Four days later, Senator Dix joined the independent movement in a speech calling for a ban on slavery in the organization of the Oregon Territory. Meanwhile, preparations began throughout the North to transform the movement into a broader Free Soil party.[21]

One day after his Oregon speech, on the morning of June 27, 1848, John Adams Dix rose in the Senate to present Dorothea Dix's memorial. He offered a short tribute to the author, emphasizing that as a lady she hesitated to address Congress, and he read the dramatic closing passages of her petition to his colleagues and the crowded gallery. As she had insisted, he moved for the referral of the subject to a select committee rather than to the standing Senate Committee on Public Lands. He assumed the chair of the committee, which as she had designated also included Benton, Bell, and John Davis, and he arranged for the printing of 5,000 copies of the memorial. Ironically, when Dix resumed his seat, the next speaker presented a request for a land grant submitted by another social visionary, Asa Whitney, who wanted the federal government to provide him a swath of land from Lake Michigan to the Pacific Ocean for the construction of a transcontinental railroad. The scramble for the public domain was under way.[22]

— 3 —

"Through God's good Providence, myself and my cause are now rather popular," Dix exulted one week after the presentation of her memorial, predicting that Congress would soon approve the land grant.[23] The response to her proposal was indeed gratifying. Charles Sumner wrote from Boston to say "how much higher I regard your triumphs than any in this Mexican war" and urged her to "shame them [at Washington] for their unholy purposes." From the other end of the political spectrum in New Orleans, J. D. B. DeBow's *Commercial Review* also commended her philanthropic goals, praising the memorial for its "most interesting, but touching and melancholy character." Reading the accounts of her proposal in major newspapers, Dix was disappointed only by the frequently reprinted telegraph dispatch identifying her as a citizen of Massachusetts. "I scarcely think that I can be called of Massachusetts," she protested, asking a friend to correct the article.[24]

Dix's optimism redoubled in two weeks when the select Senate committee reported a bill based on her memorial. The legislation provided for a grant of five million acres to be divided among the states according to a compound ratio of population and area, with a limitation providing in effect that no state would be considered larger in area than New York. Each state was to sell its land grant at no less than the standing federal minimum price for public lands, $1.25 per acre, and deposit all receipts in a perpetual fund for the care of the insane. States with federal lands of suitable quality would locate their shares in those tracts; other states would receive rights to lands in the territories, presumably in Minnesota or Oregon. Delighted that "even the unpredictable Colonel Benton concurred in my 5,000,000 bill," Dix rejoiced that "the greatest difficulty in the Senate is already surmounted."[25]

But although John Adams Dix gave notice that he would soon call up the land bill for Senate consideration, the measure stalled after the select committee reported it. The daily competition among hundreds of bills for congressional attention was a ferocious, complex struggle in which shrewd parliamentarians and ruthless party disciplinarians vied for control of the legislative agenda. Although well-regarded in Washington, John Adams Dix could expect little cooperation from the Polk administration or the Democratic majority in the Senate while he embraced the Free Soil opposition in the pivotal New York campaign. Moreover, as the organization of the Oregon Territory reopened the Wilmot Proviso controversy, the sharpening of sectional hostilities and profusion of speeches during the presidential election season left little time for consideration of Dix's bill.

Dix recognized that "the new Democratic movement in the northern States has threatened the safety of the whole measure."[26] The conflict over the extension of slavery affected the substance as well as the scheduling of her bill. Congressional power to bar slavery from the territories depended on the fiercely disputed interpretation of the Territories Clause, the same constitutional ground she claimed for her proposed division of the public lands. Indeed, the Senate gallery was crowded when John Adams Dix presented the memorial for the insane because spectators had come to hear John C. Calhoun respond to the Barnburner's lengthy argument on the previous day that the Territories Clause vested Congress with plenary government authority. Summarizing his contrary "common-property" interpretation, Calhoun answered that the Territories Clause "confers not a particle of governmental power." Instead, Congress acted merely as a fiduciary agent for the joint landholdings of the individual states. The assertion of broader federal authority, he warned, would lead to the destruction of the union.[27]

By the end of July, Dix grew more apprehensive about the opposition her proposal faced from southern Democrats and landed western states. Stunned by the defeat of Whitney's railroad proposal, she noted that "every Land Bill thus far has failed—both great and small, private and public."[28] She remained in Washington until the August adjournment of Congress, which ended with the organization of Oregon as a free territory on the final day, and resolved to return for the second session of the Thirtieth Congress in the winter.[29]

— 4 —

Dix turned south after the sectional conflict stymied her land bill. Following an itinerary planned before she went to Washington, she set off for North Carolina in September 1848. The journey offered her a striking opportunity to reexamine slavery in light of her close observation of the Free Soil controversy. It was not the first time that her lobbying activities had provided an occasion to reconsider the conservative view of the anti-slavery movement she had taken since her visit to St. Croix. In her New York campaign, as when her efforts in Massachusetts coincided with the Latimer controversy, she urged northern activists who focused on slaves rather than the insane that "having plucked the beam from our own eye, we can with a less pharisaical spirit, direct our efforts to clearing the mental vision of neighbor."[30] Now, after winding her way south to North Carolina, she affirmed that she attached little urgency to the problem of slavery. "The negros are gay, obliging, and anything but miserable," she reported shortly after her arrival in Raleigh. Neither on this trip nor on any of her other travels to the South did she express concern about the bondage of a people who were "of course thoughtless and irresponsible."[31]

Dedicating herself solely to the moral treatment of insanity, Dix canvassed local jails and almshouses throughout much of North Carolina during the autumn. Upon her return to Raleigh in November she established headquarters at the Mansion House hotel and drafted a memorial calling for a new hospital. Despite her most extensive survey and detailed memorial in the last few years, the prospect for asylum legislation seemed bleak. Organized efforts to establish a state mental institution had faltered for twenty years. With a total average annual revenue of $200,000—less than the construction cost for a modern asylum—North Carolina avoided the expenditure and relied on jails, poorhouses, home care, and out-of-state hospitals to accommodate the insane. For the past four years the Whig party platform had included a hospital proposal, without effect. The only new dimension of the deadlocked issue, as Governor William A. Graham noted in renewing his support for an asylum at the opening of the legislative session, was that "a most distinguished person of the gentler sex" had surveyed the state and would now lead the campaign.[32]

"They say '*nothing can be done here,*'" Dix told Harriet Hare. "I reply I know no such phrase in the vocabulary I adopt." After she completed a petition for hospital legislation, a delegation of Whig leaders came to her at the Mansion House and advised her that the Democratic majority was planning to "unite and silently vote down the Bill." Dix promptly called two Democratic leaders to her hotel suite, showed them the manuscript of her memorial, and announced: "Gentlemen, here is the document I have prepared for your Assembly." Handing it to Senator John W. Ellis, she charged, "I desire you, sir, to present it." She then turned to her astounded Whig allies and told them, "You I expect will sustain the motion this gentleman will make to print the same." Ellis not only introduced the memorial and moved for its printing; he assumed the chairmanship of the select Senate committee that reported a hospital bill in early December.[33]

The measure met stiffer resistance in the House, but Dix in turn responded more dramatically. Also staying at the Mansion House in Raleigh were Democratic leader James C. Dobbin and his wife, Louisa, who was critically ill. Dix nursed her devotedly. In a dying request, Louisa asked her husband to support Dix's bill. Dobbin returned to his House seat a few days after he and Dix accompanied his wife's body home for burial, and on December 23 he delivered a touching appeal for the asylum. "All opposition appeared to vanish into thin air," the *North Carolina Standard* declared. The House almost unanimously passed the measure, now amended to fund the hospital through a special land and poll tax rather than a direct appropriation. The Senate immediately concurred, and after a sober-minded motion to reconsider narrowly failed the next day, Governor Graham signed legislation establishing the Insane Asylum of North Carolina on January 1, 1849.[34]

Dix hastened back to Washington for the congressional session that had begun in early December, but she soon learned that the lame-duck meeting of Congress was a difficult time to promote new measures. Uncertainty about the incoming Whig administration under Zachary Taylor brought to a standstill the already leisurely pace of legislation. Moreover, the California gold rush, derided by Dix as a perfect example of the undisciplined American character, had suddenly enhanced the importance of organizing the Mexican Cession. The status of slavery in the western territories dominated the session and escalated sectional tensions to unprecedented levels. John Adams Dix's efforts to call up the land grant for the insane failed with little notice.[35]

Dix tried to remain patient by settling more thoroughly into the capital. She boarded at Mrs. Birth's house on Third Street once again with the Bells and the family of St. Louis merchant James E. Yeatman, Jane Bell's son by her first marriage, and she also strengthened her ties to John Adams Dix and Horace Mann. Her friends secured headquarters for her in a committee room adjoining the Library of Congress, then on the second floor of the Capitol. She went to her office daily to meet with members of Congress and maintain her voluminous correspondence. Often she wrote several letters simultaneously, rapidly scrawling each first page while the ink dried on her previous letters and continuing in succession until she completed the stack. Bell, Mann, and other friends sent and received her mail under their congressional franking privileges, grateful to serve as "the wire thro' which your electricity runs." On Sundays she frequently visited the prisoners in the District of Columbia penitentiary, to which she characteristically donated a collection of uplifting literature during the winter.[36]

But although she acknowledged that "I certainly enjoy all the advantages any one can possess here in relation to social position and public favor," Dix complained that "life in Washington is very tedious and very annoying." She was furious when the Democratic leadership again thwarted consideration of her bill in the final days of the Thirtieth Congress. "I have never seen so much that illustrates the life of sin," she seethed in March 1849. The only consolation was that she found "no substantial cause for discouragement." By her estimate, fifty of the sixty senators supported the land grant for the insane.[37]

Following the pattern she had set at the end of the previous session of Congress, Dix sought to make up for lost time in Washington by throwing herself into a series of local campaigns. She left the capital quickly in March and traveled through the Middle Atlantic states and Nova Scotia for most of the next seven months. In November she launched the Alabama asylum campaign she had helped to coordinate more than a year earlier with state medical leaders. Despite those preparations, the proposed expenditure faced some entrenched opposition. After Dix arranged for her brief memorial to be read to the legislature and printed, the *Alabama Journal* predicted that "tho' she writes with a quill from the wing of the pitying angel, her prayer will hardly be granted." The challenge excited her. "I turn now more quickly to work my way up the Hill Difficulty here," she wrote on November 15. "The summit is cloud capt, but I have passed amidst dark and rough ways before and shall not now give out." She pleaded her cause personally to the governor, the speaker of the House, the president of the Senate, and twenty-five members of the legislature. By mid-December, one of her few remaining opponents conceded that "it seems like an attempt to stem the torrent, to say any thing against this bill." A few days later, however, a fire destroyed the Alabama capitol building. The state government suspended operations with Dix's measure on the verge of success; when the legislature resumed in January 1850, the need to reconstruct the capitol forestalled the appropriation for a state mental hospital.[38]

During the hiatus in Alabama, Dix went to neighboring Mississippi to meet asylum supporters who had repeatedly requested her aid. When she concluded that the Montgomery legislature would not act on her bill, she repeated the trip to Jackson and drafted a memorial for funds to build a mental hospital authorized two years earlier. The Mississippi legislature hesitated over the petition until the end of the session, a common frustration in Dix's requests for major appropriations, but in March 1850 it voted to provide $50,000 for the construction of the asylum. Observers agreed that the appropriation "may be justly ascribed" to her memorial and her "unwearied personal exertions" in lobbying individual legislators. Local allies began a movement to name the state mental hospital for her, but she headed off legislative interest in the idea by firmly declining the honor.[39]

Dix's travels through the deep South during the winter of 1849–50 revealed the deepening of "sectional and political discords" as the organization of the Mexican Cession mounted to a crisis. The debate over the status of slavery in the federal territories often distracted state legislators from her hospital bills in Alabama and Mississippi. Horace Mann offered dismal relief for her anxiety about missing the December 1849 opening of the Thirty-First Congress when he reported on the ominous first days of the session. The land grant for the insane, he assured her, was unlikely to advance for several months. Hearing in New Orleans that a bill would be introduced to cede the public lands to the states in which they were located, a strategy for uniting southern and western interests in the divided Congress, Dix instructed Mann to double her land request to ten million acres in response to any movement for cession.[40]

Dix belittled the sectional conflict as a sordid fight for political power. "I do not feel sure that I shall not become quite willing to expatriate myself if a summer sky does not displace the dark clouds which now threaten our peace," she lashed out in February 1850. "I have *no* patience

and no sympathy either with northern Abolitionists or southern agitators. I am quite sure that neither the one nor the other party would
willingly see the question of Slavery determined as in that case they
would lose the whole political capital which they possess, or are likely
to command."[41] She followed a roundabout course to Washington while
Calhoun's grim valedictory, Webster's Seventh of March address, and
William Henry Seward's assertion of a higher law than the Constitution
echoed throughout the capital and the Union. Mann advised her on May
14 that "it cannot be of the least service for you to be here until this
all-absorbing question of the Territories is [resolved] unless you can work
miracles. If you can bring that power, come any time." She arrived a few
days later, eager to press her land bill in one of the most historic sessions
of Congress.[42]

— 5 —

The Compromise of 1850 bored Dix. "It seems impossible to hope that
any important or desirable Bills will be passed for the advantage of the
country," she grumbled after surveying the situation in Washington.[43]
Her frustration intensified while Congress debated and modified Henry
Clay's "omnibus" proposal to admit California into the union as a free
state, organize New Mexico and Utah as territories without determining
the legal status of slavery, adjust the boundaries and public debt of Texas,
abolish slave auctions in the District of Columbia, and enact a more
aggressive fugitive slave law. Dix could not hope to divert Congress from
the crisis. "The great question which alike divides and agitates the north
and the south absorbs all other claims," she sighed in June. "How, if at
all, this will be settled is now doubtful. Meanwhile, I still watch and
wait."[44]

Dix scarcely deigned to notice the scramble for the public domain
that continued in the back rooms of the Capitol during the great debate.
She expressed amazement when the Senate voted in May to contribute
three million acres of land for the construction of the Illinois Central
Railroad after Stephen A. Douglas shrewdly extended the proposed line
to Mobile, Alabama.[45] Her own bill offered an excellent basis for similar
bargaining because it offered grants to the land-hungry East that might
be paired with a donation for development of the West, but Dix guarded

vigilantly against the intrusion of politics into her measure. Her insistence on the referral of her memorial to select congressional committees insulated the asylum bill from the deals negotiated in the standing committees on the public lands.

Dix also bypassed other opportunities to advance her legislation while she watched and waited. Instead of revising the bill to accommodate reservations expressed by western and southern delegations about the procedures for selection of the donated lands, she began working on a petition to support institutions for the blind, deaf, and mute, although she recognized that the request for an additional two million acres of land would likely undercut her efforts on behalf of the insane.[46] Similarly, she emphatically rejected a suggestion that she urge state legislatures to instruct their congressional delegations to support the intergovernmental land grant for mental hospitals, a traditional tactic that retained considerable vitality, especially among states-rights Democrats who might otherwise oppose her bill.[47] She intended to win passage of the measure without any leverage other than her own moral influence, convinced that "the might, the sway of individual virtue exceeds all other powers."[48]

Dix did try a few new political tactics during the tedious summer, but they did not significantly vary her approach to lobbying. Chagrined by the opposition of the *American Journal of Insanity* to her proposal, she asked Thomas Kirkbride to call on the Association of Medical Superintendents to support her efforts. Kirkbride obtained a tepid endorsement of the bill, reporting "a prevailing sentiment, that it must be yourself, and your own Christian weapons that were to carry it." Dix also solicited letters to congressmen from a few of her more distinguished but not necessarily influential correspondents, such as Francis Lieber and Benjamin Silliman.[49]

For the most part, Dix continued to rely on inviting politicians to her office in the Library of Congress and appealing to them, as Mann marveled to his wife, "with her divine magnetism."[50] Her configuration of contacts had changed in the new Congress. John Adams Dix had left the Senate, but she gained two stalwart Whig friends in the House through the elections of Edward Stanly, an important ally in her North Carolina hospital campaign, and financier James Gore King of New Jersey, whose brother John A. King joined the New York delegation.

Concentrating for the first time on the presentation of her bill in the House, she chose as her sponsor Democrat William Bissell of Illinois, a Mexican War hero best known in Washington for disparaging remarks about the battle performance of a Mississippi regiment that had recently prompted its colonel, Jefferson Davis, to challenge him to a duel. In the Senate, Dix again tried to obtain a sponsor from a landed western state, Free Soil leader Salmon P. Chase of Ohio. When the illness of Chase's wife kept him from the capital for several weeks, however, Dix turned the management of her bill over to James A. Pearce of Maryland, an unobtrusive but effective Whig.[51]

Advised by Mann to "*retouch* your Memorial," Dix altered it only by confirming her plan to seek ten million acres of land after a conference with Daniel Webster. "Mr. Webster says one may as well ask for 10,000,000 as one or five," she noted.[52] In late June and early July, Pearce and Bissell presented the updated petition and took charge of the select committees to which it was referred.[53] But although Dix believed that "no clouds obscure the sunlight of my prospects," the slavery controversy continued to block almost all other legislation. She confessed to Mann in late July 1850 that "I find it hard, my friend, to possess my soul in patience—very hard." The hot, tense summer seemed to drain her life away. She began to suffer heart palpitations that made her climb to the library an exhausting ordeal. Alarmed, Mann warned that "I should not be surprised if she were to die suddenly, & on any day." When the watching and waiting continued into August upon the collapse of Clay's omnibus strategy for compromise, she groaned that she "never was so tired of any place."[54]

The slavery crisis finally turned toward resolution in August, in large part because the advocates of compromise gained a crucial ally when Millard Fillmore became president upon the death of Zachary Taylor in July. For Dix, the accession of Fillmore was important not only in breaking the legislative impasse; it also placed a potential personal supporter in the White House. The new president was a devout Unitarian, and Dix had obtained a letter of introduction from his pastor in Buffalo while winding her way toward Washington in April. She easily cultivated an earnest friendship during the summer. Their shared piety suffused a deep mutual respect and merged imperceptibly with Fillmore's ingrained deference to the social elite that Dix represented.[55] Their politics were equally compatible. Dix's proposal for the public lands reinvigorated the Whig platform that Fillmore had championed in Congress during the early 1840s. Her first letter to the new president, a warning against Henry Clay's plans to dominate the Cabinet, similarly paralleled his own assessment of party factions. Alert to Dix's national popularity, Fillmore soon considered her "the guardian angel of his administration."[56]

The acceleration of the compromise provided the opportunity that Dix had long awaited. On September 6, the day of the last pivotal House vote on the slavery legislation, she commented sardonically that "the National affairs are recorded historically in two brief syllables—*Delay.*" Within two weeks, however, Fillmore signed the compromise bills adapted from Clay's original proposals. As Washington celebrated the survival of the union in a jubilee of fireworks, serenades, speeches, and revelry, Congress attempted to forget the sectional conflict in a shared feast on the public domain. The second half of September 1850 inaugurated a new era of federal land policy. Douglas secured the passage of his bill for the Illinois Central Railroad, the first federal land subsidy for railroad construction. Veterans of the War of 1812 and Indian wars since 1790 received bonus grants of public lands that initiated a series of military land bounties. Congress approved a bill offering free land to settlers in the Oregon territory, an important precedent for the national homestead movement, and the federal government agreed to a vast cession of public swamplands to the states in which they were located.[57]

Dix's proposal shared in this momentum for land grants, although her plan had languished during the summer while the promoters of other bills had negotiated deals and attempted to associate their projects with the sectional compromise. On September 17 her select Senate committee finally reported its bill, a duplicate of the measure introduced in the previous Congress except in doubling the size of the proposed land grant.[58] Within a few days, Dix urged Fillmore to spur Pearce, his key lieutenant in the compromise legislation, to obtain passage of her proposal before the imminent adjournment of Congress.[59] After Bissell tried unsuccessfully to push the measure through the House, Bell brought the bill up in the Senate on September 26.[60]

The Senate debate was a tantalizing disappointment for Dix. Her memorial had anticipated the initial opposition to the bill raised by Jefferson Davis, who declared the proposed land grant unconstitutional under the common-property doctrine he had inherited from Calhoun during the long struggle over federal power to ban slavery in the territories. Congress acted in the public lands as a trustee for the states that jointly owned the federal property, he repeated, not as a government with legislative authority. Accordingly, the Territories Clause of the Constitution permitted Congress to dispose of the public lands only as prudent proprietor, in grants that increased the value of the remaining trust property. But Davis's painfully familiar argument carried less force in the aftermath of the compromise, and the majority of the Senate voted to consider the bill despite his preliminary attack on its constitutionality.[61]

Less dogmatic resistance from the landed states proved a more difficult obstacle. After several senators answered Davis, Salmon P. Chase turned the tide against passage. Chase endorsed the overall plan of the legislation but criticized its procedures for land sales and urged his fellow westerners to hold the measure back for technical modifications. The ensuing debate centered on ambiguities in the bill and clarifying amendments that were fully consistent with Dix's goals. Even ardent states-rights Democrats David Rice Atchison of Missouri and David Yulee of Florida, representatives of states with extensive public lands, concentrated their opposition on this ground rather than on Davis's constitutional objections. Atchison voiced the principal western fear that the bill provided the unlanded states with grants from the fertile lands of new territories while consigning the landed states to shares taken from the inferior public lands within their jurisdictions that had long failed to sell for $1.25 per acre. Advocating the same amendment offered by Williamson R. W. Cobb of Alabama in the brief House discussion, Atchison called for the landed states to receive grants from the territories if their own public lands could not command the federal minimum sale price.[62]

The avoidable snag resulted mainly from Dix's failure to involve potential western allies like Chase in the design of her proposal and her disregard for the politics of the public lands. Bell and Pearce, nominally responsible for the bill, answered weakly that the present text already provided for Atchison's remedy in less clear language. But Benton, another member of Dix's select committee, sealed the defeat of her proposal. Compounding confusion about a different provision of the bill and complaining incredibly of a lack of time to study the measure, he blustered, "I did not expect that any one would be serious in taking up such a bill." With strategic retreat clearly in order, Pearce secured an early position for the legislation on the Senate agenda in the upcoming winter session.[63]

"Pray that my patience do[es] not fail utterly," Dix snapped after the surprising setback. Despite the clear sectional alignment of the debate on her bill, she again looked homeward in her exasperation. "As usual the Massachusetts Delegation gave me no aid except Davis & Horace Mann," she complained. "I do not seem likely to be burthened with obligations to my own State."[64] She left Washington within a week, heartily sick of politics.

— 6 —

Expressing condolences to Dix after her defeat, several of her distinguished male friends instinctively commented on her paradoxical stature as the most politically prominent woman in the United States. President Fillmore, inviting her to a consolatory tea at the White House, apologized for the lack of formal hospitality during the absence of his family by awkwardly teasing that Dix might "see how a bachelor lives and it may induce you hereafter to take pity on some lonely gentleman and concentrate that affectionate tenderness upon one object that now circles in its embrace a suffering world." Francis Lieber agreed that Dix had transformed customary social roles. "How oddly the usual state of things is reversed in our two cases!" he exclaimed from his study in South Carolina. "You, a woman, are in action, up and doing everywhere; I, a man and carved out by nature for action, have been obliged to contract a morganatic marriage with literature." At the same time, Lieber recognized that Dix was "where you ought to be," a conclusion ably explained by Benjamin Silliman. "Neither Webster nor Clay nor Calhoun could have accomplished what you have done," the eminent Yale scientist assured Dix. "The undertaking arduous & appalling demanded the peculiar tact of a *gifted woman* who preserving perfectly the delicacy and refinement of her sex and combining perseverance and energy and resource with woman's gentleness sways the hearts of *men* and especially of *American men*."[65]

These paeans underscored the ambiguities in the ideals of womanhood that Dix embodied. As the preeminent exemplar of feminine benevolence, she vividly illustrated the tensions in the conventional contrast between a private, female world of domesticity and a public, male realm of politics. Impressing observers as both a housewife writ large and a rival to the titans of Congress, Dix inspired interpretations of her activities as both conservative and subversive. As a crusader for the moral treatment of insanity, she extended customary solicitude for the neighborhood poor and sick to the entire country. Conversely, she plunged into the very heart of masculine politics as a lobbyist in the grasping, scheming contest for the public domain.

This apparent double life partly reflected the sheer inadequacy of contemporary rhetoric to describe the principles by which women actually lived. Although ineligible to vote or hold public office, nineteenth-century women participated in political decision-making in many ways. In addition to the private moral influence traditionally regarded as the mainspring of female authority, women often signed petitions and joined in the parades and other mass demonstrations so vital to Jacksonian politics. Although on a less spectacular scale than Dix, other elite women also exchanged information and social patronage for access to officeholders. Like her, even the staunchest proponents of the ideals of domesticity sometimes found it necessary to address legislators openly as lobbyists.[66]

Although Dix thus personified social and political realities at odds with the dominant rhetoric about womanhood, she nonetheless continued to defend her activities in terms of popular attitudes about the appropriate conduct of the sexes. As a practical matter, she relied on this conformity with conventional social standards to enhance her political influence. Privately as well, however, she firmly maintained that "no woman who has a proper sense of self-respect will defy public opinion and established usage."[67] Internalizing the proscriptive distinction between private and public life, she absorbed the inconsistencies that riddled the separation of female and male spheres. The contradictions of her culture became the routine stress points of her career, in which she attempted to reconcile femininity and power.

A long series of perplexities constantly challenged Dix to mediate between her conflicting impulses as a woman reformer. A decade after she declared the Library of Congress "too public for ladies," she was one of the most familiar figures in its alcoves. Although she maintained that propriety required "a close rule of never receiving gifts" to defray her expenses, she relied heavily on free postage and railroad passes arranged by her friends. During her ceaseless journeys across the country, she remained sensitive about her position as a solitary woman traveler; in Washington, she recognized the opportunities for persuasion opened by her social position, but she declined to attend political soirées alone and disliked seeking an escort. Occasionally, she explicitly worried that lobbying was undermining her virtue. "I think after this year I shall certainly not suffer myself to engage in any Legislative affairs for a year," she mused after heady success suddenly turned to disappointment upon the burning of the Alabama capitol building. "I can conceive the state of mind which this induces to be like nothing save the influences of the gambling table."[68]

Dix responded to most of these dilemmas by asserting a rigid standard of ladylike propriety. In her political methods as in the ultimate goals of her asylum legislation, she championed "those God-like attributes which sanctify private life." She did not enter into Washington society except to visit with the Fillmores and attend a few parties hosted by personal friends. She invited congressmen to meet with her in the library or at the home of Smithsonian Institution director Joseph Henry, whose household she joined in May 1850, but she insisted that etiquette would not permit her "to visit the 'Fathers of the land' " if they failed to call upon her. She would not deliver public speeches.[69]

Dix's approach to politics contrasted sharply with the women's rights movement launched in Seneca Falls, New York, at precisely the same time that she started her land grant campaign. She regretted the drive for women's legal equality as a surrender of women's moral superiority, an admission of defeat in the contest between politics and femininity. "I do not think that women are oppressed in this country," she later explained, "and if they are intelligently educated, they will do themselves and the country I think, a truer & nobler service by influencing men in right directions than in attending the polls, and attempting to share abroad, in all masculine pursuits." The clash between paradigms of female political participation figured prominently in her appeal to legislators. "I am for 'Woman's Rights' in the highest sense of the word," rhapsodized Horace Mann, one of Dix's closest allies and most fervent admirers, after seeing her at work in the Library of Congress. "Not for her being made a politician, a soldier, a judge, or a President; but for her entering the glorious sphere of Benevolence, which Nature has opened, but which the selfishness & short sightedness of men have hitherto closed up."[70]

To Dix, the most troublesome obstacle as a woman reformer was not the burden of legal discrimination but the dilemmas of fame. Her emphasis on the authority of her female virtue had succeeded phenomenally in merging her causes into her own public identity. Newspapers and congressmen generally referred to the proposed land grant for state mental hospitals as "Miss Dix's bill," an unusual tribute to a lobbyist but a fitting reflection of her significance. The steadily increasing acclaim for her benevolence offered an obvious means to stimulate further support for the moral treatment of insanity. But if her fame was one of her greatest political assets, widespread publicity also contravened her notions of feminine modesty. Although "well pleased to be beloved by my country," Dix recoiled from the celebrity that her political style had created.[71]

Before coming to Washington, Dix already felt a discomfort with her fame that resembled the emotions of comparably prominent women authors.[72] Declining the request of Nashville matrons to commission a marble bust of her, Dix asked "rather *to dwell in your hearts,* affectionately and kindly remembered as a fellow-laborer in the world's wide-harvest fields."[73] Her ambivalence deepened under the national spotlight. Although eager for more favorable notice at home, she urged William Bentley Fowle to persuade a Boston publisher to refrain from writing about her. She similarly rejected the offer of *Appleton's Encyclopedia* to correct inaccurate information about her as "a great impertinence." Only hesitantly did she acquiesce in the promotional efforts of Mann, a popular lecturer whose repertory included an address that contrasted Dix with John Jacob Astor as the altruistic and avaricious spirits of the age. Agreeing to newspaper publication of one of the many commendations she received from state legislatures, she doubtfully questioned him: "but is it *best* that my name should be before the public so much?"[74]

Even Dix's staid older women friends Anne Heath, Mary Torrey, and Harriet Hare considered her distaste for publicity excessive. Disregarding Dix's stern, repeated instructions to burn the memorabilia of their youth and the letters she now received, Heath launched a lengthy campaign to convince Dix to write an autobiography. More aware than any-one else of her friend's sensitive points, she both pointed out the potential for the narrative to inspire readers and appealed to Dix's vanity and her resentment toward her family. "Some quack will seize the pen," she once warned, unless an authentic memoir preempted the field. "How enthusiastically the world will fall to, and read it," Heath goaded, "remarking at the close—'What kind relations to give her such powerful help at starting.' "[75]

Torn by conflicting impulses, Dix manipulated some opportunities to enhance her public image and reinforce her theatrical self-perception. Her encounter with best-selling novelist Fredrika Bremer during the summer of 1850 provided the basis for many subsequent accounts of her life. Meeting the Swedish traveler several times in Washington during the Compromise debates, Dix captured Bremer's imagination with the idea that her vigil in the Capitol was a foil to the protracted sectional wrangling. After a summer sail along the Chesapeake Bay, she agreed to sit for a drawing by Bremer, an amateur artist who used such sessions "to squeeze out of the orange-sitters she is painting, all the juice of information and opinion she is in want of." The model contributed much of the creativity to the resulting written portrait. Dix recounted her career in a powerful if not entirely accurate narrative. Waving aside the long chain of circumstance that had led into her mission, she dramatically traced her sense of vocation to a sudden revelation upon overhearing a casual remark about the plight of the insane in East Cambridge while on her way home from church. Her work since then, she explained, had been "merely an act of simple obedience to the voice of God."[76]

A few months later, however, Dix received an important opportunity to broaden her political appeal through further autobiographical reflection when Sarah Josepha Hale decided to include her in a compendium of the great women of history. Hale had risen to the summit of journalism in the quarter-century since she had reviewed Dix's children's tales in Boston. As the editor of the influential *Godey's Lady's Book,* she was one of the arbiters of American femininity and a leading exponent of the doctrines of benevolence. The opening of communication with Hale offered Dix a chance to form an alliance with one the most powerful and sympathetic shapers of public opinion in the country.

Dix spurned the invitation. In one of the most deliberate letters she ever composed, she objected that Hale's proposed biographical sketch was "an aggression I could not excuse." Neither her personal standards nor her political interests could permit such exposure. "Nothing in fact could more certainly wound my sensibilities, nor interefere more seriously with the real usefulness of my *mission,*" Dix wrote. Most remarkably, she argued that the lady of *Godey's* failed to respect the distinctive social role of women. Pressed by the editor, Dix readily conceded that Hale's intent "to assist women to educate themselves to perform their own women's part in life" was "a beautiful thought." But she nevertheless maintained that "giving unnecessary publicity to women while they yet live, and to their works—however unblemished their lives, noble their aims, or successful their deeds, seems to me singularly at variance with the delicacy and modesty which are the most attractive ornaments of their sex." Her campaign for the insane would not encompass an appeal to national opinion through magazines and other popular literature.[77]

Dix circulated her letter to Hale widely and adopted it as a policy statement governing similar situations. Her friends expressed a variety of opinions about her attempt to cut through the knotty issue of publicity. The priggish George Hillard agreed that Dix's stance was essential to distinguish herself from the hucksterism of P. T. Barnum and "the common herd of notorieties male & female—the Hungarian Amazon, the knocking girls, and the fat damsel now on exhibition in the Museum." But John Adams Dix, an impeccable Wall Street conservative, urged his political sister to reverse herself. "You are public property," he argued. "The world has a right to know where you were born, how old you are, and what you were doing in early life." Mary Turner Torrey laughed sympathetically at Dix's confidential description of Hale as a "literary hyena" but warned that "the public will claim a right in you, whether you give your consent or not."[78]

Torrey's prediction of course proved accurate. Although Dix shrank from systematically directing the growth of her reputation and turning it to full advantage, she did not prevent its continued expansion. Despite her objections, Hale included her in the monumental *Women's Record.* As if to demonstrate the resource that Dix had failed to exploit, the editor devoted much of the essay to attacking the federal bill for the insane— and promoting a rival appeal she launched in *Godey's* for a land grant to establish normal schools for women teachers.[79]

— 7 —

The extraordinary length of the Compromise session left Dix only a short wait before the Thirty-First Congress reassembled in December 1850. Missing the opening of the session to nurse a sore throat in Trenton, she arrived in Washington in the middle of the month, a few days after Pearce postponed further Senate consideration of the land bill. The delay lengthened, and when the short session dragged into February 1851 without action on her bill, friends prepared her for another disappointment. Francis Lieber, predicting that the legislation could not succeed during the notoriously uneventful winter term, emphasized that her effort was important even if the bill never passed. "Striving, working, persevering in a noble cause is one of the things worthy of our exertion on their own account," he wrote to Dix, "just as the fervent love of lovers is not lost though they may never be united."[80]

With the endorsement of Fillmore and the sponsorship of his most trusted Senate supporter, however, Dix's bill enjoyed some of the advantages of an administration measure. Taking up the legislation on February 11, Pearce demonstrated a firm grasp of the sectional and partisan dynamics of the proposed land grant. When Jefferson Davis renewed his argument that the Territories Clause did not authorize a land grant for charitable purposes, Pearce shrugged that "after the free, and I may say the lavish appropriations of public lands during a long series of years, it seems to me to be almost too late to inquire into the constitutional power of Congress over them." More ominously for Davis, states-rights Democrat Solon Borland of Arkansas replied in detail that Calhoun himself would have found Dix's proposal an acceptable application of the proprietorship principle because the land sales would stimulate economic development in the states and increase the value of adjoining federal lands. After surmounting the constitutional attack, Dix's supporters moved to accommodate the more pragmatic concerns of the landed states by adopting a clarifying amendment offered by Chase.[81]

With almost every Whig in attendance, the Senate easily approved the bill by a vote of 35–16. Ten Democrats and the Free Soilers Chase and Hale joined the unanimous Whigs in the majority. Receiving votes from every section of the country, Dix's proposal carried New England without dissent and attracted considerable Democratic support in the

Southwest. Opposition was divided evenly between Democrats from the South and the landed Northwest. Struggling to remain "perfectly calm and as cold as ice" while she waited in the Library of Congress, Dix received the long-awaited word of triumph midway through the proceeding from one of her friendly adversaries, the ostentatiously chivalrous James Mason of Virginia.[82]

Other congratulations soon anticipated her success in the House of Representatives, where the Whigs and Democrats were more evenly matched and the populous, unlanded northeastern states enjoyed a commanding majority. A surprised Lieber told Dix that "were I a Pope I would canonize you as Sancta Perseverentia."[83] On the night of February 28, Bissell moved to speed the legislation to Fillmore for approval, obtaining a two-thirds majority to take up the Senate bill out of turn and calling for an immediate vote on its passage.

Opponents of Dix's measure responded with a barrage of parliamentary obstacles, testing the determination of the obvious majority. Thomas Bayly of Virginia, one of the most prominent states-rights Democrats, moved that the House resolve itself into a committee of the whole on the state of the union for debate, which would have ruined the bill at this late stage of the session. When that maneuver failed, he demanded a roll call vote on the motion. Successive time-consuming votes next defeated motions to lay the bill on the Speaker's table in favor of other matters, to adjourn the House for the evening, and again to go into a committee of the whole.[84]

The rejection of these delaying tactics by steady margins held out hope for the passage of the bill if its supporters maintained their ranks. But after the overwhelming defeat of a motion to go into a committee of the whole on the private calendar of the House, Massachusetts Whig George Ashmun threw up his hands in surrender. "I have voted as long as I think it expedient for Miss Dix," he announced, "and I desire the bill to pass; but I think that we ought first to attend to more important public business." Ashmun's suggestion prevailed, and the House passed over Dix's bill. A final effort on the last day of the session to return to the land grant for the insane fell short of the two-thirds vote needed to suspend the schedule of business.[85]

The betrayal of Dix's hopes by a representative of her erstwhile home state was a devastating realization of her forebodings. "I put away thought of Massachusetts generally," she fumed to Anne Heath, reluctantly forgiving Ashmun. "When I *do* think of that quarter I have not much reason to dwell serenely upon facts and associations."[86] Nor did she see any reason to ponder her own decisions that had contributed to the defeat—her indifference to other interests in the public lands, her refusal to ask the state legislatures to instruct their congressional delegations, her failure to relieve the qualms of potential supporters by revising the bill, her contempt for party discipline, her ambivalence about publicizing her efforts. As Ashmun noted, she had asked the members of Congress to vote for herself as much as for a land grant to endow state mental hospitals.

Agonizingly close to success, Dix vowed to continue her legislative campaign. As Lieber wrote her, the fortunes of the land-grant bill now traced "the flood and ebb tide of your soul." She assured President Fillmore that she was "defeated not conquered; disappointed not discouraged." Belatedly, she asked Mann to plant a newspaper article emphasizing the clear majority support for her bill and denying rumors that she was despondent and dangerously ill. "I certainly am not cheerful," she acknowledged. "But I should very poorly illustrate my sense of duty by abandoning a cause of such importance because trial and disappointment interpose."[87] With nine months to wait before the opening of the Thirty-Second Congress, she prepared herself to begin again.

8

A National Work

Dix turned her back on Congress and her home state to embark on another reinvigorating tour after the failure of her land bill in March 1851. "I don't think I need fold my hands in indolent inaction," she snapped as she left Washington a few days later. Her mail bulged with requests for her assistance from asylum advocates throughout the country. The Massachusetts legislature was embroiled in a struggle over the establishment of a second public asylum to complement the Worcester State Hospital, but Dix decisively ruled out any participation in that effort. "Travelling this year in New England except as a *positive duty,* cannot be expected of me," she declared. Her "just aversion" to her native region outweighed the situation of Massachusetts's insane paupers and her own desire to spend the coming warm months in a mild climate. Perhaps aware that her popularity in Boston made her charges of "vulgar treatment and misconstruction" seem implausible, she firmly maintained that "I do not imagine myself a martyr." "I need health and mental strength . . . when I am in the New England states beyond what is required elsewhere," she explained to Heath, "and now the former at least is sadly deficient."[1]

— 1 —

Once again Dix headed south. She chose Alabama as her destination, assured by state medical leaders that her guidance was "indispensable" to the completion of the asylum initiative that the fire at the Montgomery capitol had frustrated in December 1849.[2] With eight months left before the state legislature assembled, she planned to work her way to Alabama through South Carolina, Georgia, and Florida in anticipation of future campaigns.

The proposed route enabled her to gather valuable political information for her friend President Fillmore. After the railroad trip from Richmond to South Carolina, Dix stopped to rest for two weeks in Charleston as the secession movement of 1850–51 neared its climax. She was astounded and appalled by "the hot-headed politicians here, who shout secession at the corners of the streets." At times she felt as if she was examining an asylum. "Here in South Carolina the delusion of the citizens seems fairly to entitle them to be classed with the insane," she concluded after hearing predictions that the state could sustain independence and expect the aid of England. Secessionism not only challenged the union; the demagoguery of the fire-eaters threatened the moral order of society.[3]

Dix summarized her observations in two obsequious but useful reports to the president. Meeting "few except Unionists" in the cradle of southern nationalism, she correctly foresaw that the crisis would soon dissipate. "All the bombast, declamation and legislation touching secession [is] just the passing ebullition of passionate politicians and excitable men who had really no great influence," she wrote to the White House. Even apparent radicals like United States senator Andrew Pickens Butler, now voicing "ultra opinions" at home after praising Fillmore's administration while in Washington, wore "the wolf's coat . . . to secure by an adroit movement, by and by, some saving influence." Disappointed but not surprised to see her Washington acquaintance bend to popular enthusiasm, Dix placed her greatest confidence in "the noble, manly spirit" exemplified by a high-spirited Charleston woman who denounced Robert Barnwell Rhett as "false to every principle and sentiment of honor." "If there are South Carolina women to speak out boldly in such ringing tones, and that amongst the highest circles of their proudest aristocracy," Dix concluded, "we may not doubt that the wordy boasted chivalry will be silenced."[4]

Dix's hosts in Charleston, Unitarian minister Samuel Gilman and popular author Caroline Howard Gilman, aptly illustrated her ideals of sectional peace and subtle social influence. She told Anne Heath that the transplanted Bostonians presented "that most beautiful of all pictures, the representation of entire domestic confidence, harmony, and cultivated thoughts." Unlike her onetime idol William Henry Furness, who had plummeted in her esteem upon embracing Transcendentalism and abolitionism, Samuel Gilman made pious self-discipline the center of his missionary efforts. Dix wished that his example would inspire emulation by "common sense northern ministers" to counterbalance the "young sentimentalists" and *"ultra-abolitionists"* in the clergy.[5]

After she left the drawing rooms of Charleston to begin her survey of the insane, however, Dix found few congenial refuges from the passions of politics. In Columbia to inspect the South Carolina Lunatic Asylum, she wrote that "nearly every person I have met is really or ostensibly a secessionist."[6] Her shift in impressions partly reflected the discontent of her Unionist host in the state capitol, the exile Francis Lieber. As she headed into the upcountry, though, her experience confirmed Lieber's views of his neighbors. Proud as she was to be received admiringly "notwithstanding I am 'from the North,' " she admitted that she won less support than she previously had in her travels through Mississippi, Alabama, and other southern states. "Everyone has been civil," she observed after a circuit of small towns, "but not one person has called" except Lieber's personal friends. At her hotel in Abbeville, where rumors had recently spread through the district of an abolitionist-led slave revolt, she sensed that *"every person avoided even looking towards me. It was really odd."*[7]

Dix's extraordinary exposure to these sectional tensions did not cloud her recognition that Unionist sentiment was in fact stabilizing. "The *furor* of political fanaticism is on the whole I think rather declining here . . . ," she maintained. "The fact is that we Americans do like to talk loudly and very extravagantly."[8] But the cool reception sharply increased her distaste for the "vicious machinations of Abolitionists" and added to her grievances against her native New England. Infuriated that southerners associated her reform crusade with the antislavery movement, she criticized the radicals more openly in her letters. "That the people have serious ground of complaint against the unjustifiable proceedings of northern unprincipalled abolitionists is quite clear," she told Philadelphia merchant William Hacker, who was not ordinarily one of her confidantes on sensitive matters.[9] Most likely, she also began to state her conservative views on slavery more plainly in conversations with southerners.

Looking ahead to Georgia, Dix prepared her way with favorable publicity. At her request, Lieber wrote an anonymous newspaper tribute to Dix "as a pass-port" to be published in Columbia and dispatched for reprinting in the Milledgeville capitol newspapers. "For shame, that such a thing should be considered necessary!" Lieber exclaimed, aghast at the commingling of female benevolence and political strategy.[10] When Dix skipped over Georgia to wait for the editorial to introduce her, an unexpected reunion with Fredrika Bremer on the way to Florida attracted additional newspaper attention. The two icons of womanhood met several times while Dix trekked 1,500 miles to examine the jails and poorhouses on the desolate peninsula, the last state in the Union she had not yet visited except for Texas and California. Bremer was finally completing her own highly publicized tour of the United States, but Dix privately noted that the Swedish novelist had "missed some of the finest portions of our country" and, most regrettably, "as yet has seen very little of New England."[11]

Dix's ambivalent feelings about public recognition and her home city were temporarily put to rest when her mail caught up with her in remote Anza, Florida. She learned that at the request of the Lee family of Boston, munificent benefactors of the exclusive McLean Asylum, the trustees of the Massachusetts General Hospital had recently voted to name its building for male patients the Dix Ward. Although she had steadfastly declined similar gestures, most recently in Mississippi, Dix hastened to accept the honor and express "my gratification for these sentiments of respectful consideration from citizens of *Massachusetts*." She confessed to the Lees that although she preferred to "avoid all distinctions of a personal character and retreat from notoriety," she was "profoundly moved" by this sign of the appreciation for her in Boston.[12]

Dix's strength to continue her southern travels gave out a few days later. She attributed the change of plans to "the heat and the necessary fatigue to which my special business exposed me," but the wary greeting she had received in South Carolina and the welcome honor she had received in Boston reinforced her decision by temporarily reversing the pattern that helped to sustain her southern travels. Alabama medical leaders would have to proceed without her to obtain legislative approval for a state asylum. In June 1851 she headed back to the New Jersey State Lunatic Asylum, where she regained strength while casting about for a new project in the vicinity of Trenton.[13]

— 2 —

After contemplating the preparation of a hymnal for use in insane asylums, Dix decided in September 1851 to undertake a reform campaign at the Bloomingdale Asylum of New York Hospital. The second hospital founded in the United States, New York Hospital was one of the most prestigious medical institutions in the country. The establishment of its rural asylum in upper Manhattan in 1821 had been a landmark in the development of the moral treatment. The pioneering Bloomingdale Asylum differed in several respects from the model that achieved dominance among American mental hospitals during the next three decades, however, and specialists in the Association of Medical Superintendents grumbled about the institution for many years without openly challenging its reputation.

The criticism of Bloomingdale stemmed from the related architectural and administrative principles of asylum therapy. Almost as soon as the facility opened, observers complained that its design prevented the classification of patients "by rank in life and form of disease," which was central to the moral treatment. Affluent, paying patients lived in crowded, dank quarters like the dormitories for paupers supported by state subsidies, and despite a series of modifications, little separated noisy, violent patients from the quiet and harmless. Chief physician Charles H. Nichols complained in June 1851 that the pandemonium prevented anyone from sleeping in the asylum on most summer nights.[14] Apart from the resulting difficulty in attracting paying patients, the primary constituency of the corporate hospital, the lack of differentiation blocked the aim of the moral treatment to modify patients' behavior by offering the incentive of life on a comfortable ward or the punishment of a downward transfer in the social order of the asylum.

Scarcely less irritating to Nichols and other asylum doctors was the organizational structure of Bloomingdale. Unlike other asylums at which trustees delegated full control to a medical superintendent, the New York Hospital board of governors divided operating authority among a board committee that was responsible for most admissions and employment decisions, a resident physician who was charged with treatment of the patients, and a superintendent who directed the staff and the daily maintenance of the institution. "You have no idea how queerly things are managed here," Nichols complained to a sympathetic Thomas Kirkbride, who ran his Pennsylvania Hospital for the Insane with little direction from the governing board of the Pennsylvania Hospital.[15]

Dix's decision to take up this long-standing dissatisfaction with Bloomingdale demonstrated her position as the foremost lay advocate of the principles endorsed by the Association of Medical Superintendents. Over the past six years, she had assumed an important role in advising hospital officials and trustees as well as in lobbying legislatures. Institutions for the insane widely acknowledged her expertise and cultivated her connections with potential benefactors. She played an active part in the competition among assistant asylum physicians for the few openings as a medical superintendent. The leading specialists, who called themselves "the brethren," depended on her "great influence" to strengthen solidarity among superintendents and encourage uniform standards of treatment around the country.[16] In her exercise of this influence as much as in the establishment of new mental hospitals, Dix was one of the most important forces of cohesion in an emerging medical profession.

After conducting a quick review of the Bloomingdale Asylum, Dix presented the New York Hospital trustees in October 1851 with a caustic memorandum outlining her criticisms. Her first set of objections, echoing and amplifying the report filed by Nichols in June, emphasized the "inconvenience resulting from architectural defects" in the asylum. She pointed out the inadequate facilities for the classification of patients, noting particularly the "wholly unsuitable accommodations for [the] highest class of patients," and stressed the failure to provide a pure and tranquil environment for moral therapy. In addition to the noise caused by agitated patients, she detailed flaws in the ventilation, heating, security, and sanitation procedures of the asylum.[17]

In her second and sharper thrust, Dix maintained that the asylum "*must* for the most part remain defective under the present defective organization." She deplored the division of power among the board's asylum committee, the resident physician, and the superintendent. "Three commanders in chief leading an army; three captains commanding a ship; three magistrates ruling a city; three presidents governing the union, might well lead respectively to defeat, to loss, to contest, to confusion, to anarchy and overthrow," she argued. Dix strenuously maintained that the chief physician alone should govern the asylum. Noting that the relatively short tenure of doctors at Bloomingdale revealed their frustration, she predicted that the hospital would never be able to retain competent medical specialists or provide effective treatment unless the board and the superintendent ceded full control to the chief physician. She closed with a rhetorical apology for her severe candor and a biting accusation that the trustees had failed the community in their administration of the asylum. "The Institution they direct should do honor to their City, to their State, to their Country," she charged. "It now does neither."[18]

For the next two months, Dix continued to lobby for a reorganization of the Bloomingdale Asylum. She met formally with the asylum committee and informally with individual trustees, establishing headquarters at the New York City home of prominent humanitarian Sarah Platt Haines Doremus and the New Jersey estate of James Gore King, a friend of several trustees. Mixing veiled threats and incentives, she disclaimed any intent to publicize her criticisms and intimated that she would aid a fund-raising campaign for the expansion that she recommended.[19] She solicited assistance from the superintendents of comparable corporate hospitals, including Kirkbride, and she tried unsuccessfully to enlist the aid of Pliny Earle, the distinguished expert on insanity who had previously served as the chief physician at Bloomingdale. These efforts received the enthusiastic endorsement of Nichols. Gradually, her campaign became intertwined with his continued tenure at the Manhattan asylum.[20]

The New York Hospital trustees rejected Dix's recommendations in December 1851, uniting against a consolidation of authority in the chief physician and showing limited support for a building campaign.[21] Around the same time, moreover, the board also formalized its long-standing policy that the chief physician should be married, a commonplace prerequisite under the psuedo-familial principles of moral therapy. The trustees' resolution presented a considerable embarrassment to Nichols, who had been jilted by his fiancée shortly after he was hired in expectation of his marriage. He soon resigned, asserting that the board would have retained him but that he could no longer tolerate the divided authority that Dix had protested.[22]

Dix pressed her arguments to several trustees, but a few acrimonious exchanges only hardened the view of the asylum committee that her imperiousness undermined her credibility. With Congress now in session, she had pursued the Bloomingdale project long enough at the expense of her land bill. "I cannot doubt something will be effected," assured King, who correctly anticipated the launching of a building campaign in predicting that "any alteration or improvement adopted will appear the result of their own motion—not of your suggestion."[23] Buoyed by his informed confidence and by reports of success in the Alabama hospital appeal, she headed back to Washington in January 1852, resolving to remain in close contact with Charles Nichols.

— 3 —

The Thirty-Second Congress began inauspiciously for Dix in December 1851 with a fire in the Capitol library. John Bell quickly provided another room for her office, but the incident foreshadowed a difficult session ahead. The rival proposals for grants of public lands had swollen to a flood. Scores of railroad promoters sought subsidies for construction projects; military veterans returned to Washington for additional land bonuses; a coalition across sections, classes, and parties caused the homestead movement to surge forward. Meanwhile, the Whig core of Dix's support was disintegrating. In a slight minority during the Thirty-First Congress, the party now could count on only 93 Whigs against 139 Democrats and a handful of third-party members in the new House of Representatives, and the already large margin in the Senate had widened further.[24]

Following Fillmore's counsel, Dix chose two Democratic sponsors for her bill. She left William Bissell in command of her efforts in the House, and she designated his Illinois colleague James Shields as her Senate spokesman. In addition to representing a landed western state, both war heroes were energetic and personable in a bluff manner, but neither was an effective legislative captain. In February Shields reintroduced the successful Senate measure of the previous session and took charge of a select committee that immediately reported the bill without amendment. The House blocked Bissell's attempt to pursue the same familiar strategy, referring the bill instead to the standing committee on public lands. Without any personal friends on the committee, Dix uneasily watched her legislation borne along the capricious current of the land rush.[25]

Dix devoted much of her attention to the other end of Pennsylvania Avenue while she waited for Congress to act on her bill. During the previous session her congenial relations with Fillmore had deepened into a steady position in the president's social circle. To be sure, she joined only selectively in the gala events of the administration. Protesting that "I am not greatly dazzled by the attractions of the gay Life in Washington," Dix told Anne Heath defensively in January 1851 that she had attended but three public gatherings in the past six weeks: a dinner at the White House; a grand reception at the home of her former North Carolina supporter William A. Graham, now the Secretary of the Navy; and "a very select party" given by Representative John A. King for the Cabinet members, the commanding officers of the Army and Navy, and the leading foreign ministers. "Probably if I remain here I shall not find myself consenting to be again in public," Dix noted. When the Fillmores, the Bells, and almost all of official Washington thronged to a recital by the celebrated Jenny Lind, Dix scoffed that disappointment about the rainy weather was "incomparably more fully expressed than for the loss or gain of any Bill of National Concern." She preferred to stay home and sew or read or keep up with her correspondence.[26]

Dix's reserved habits fused her moral intensity, her emotional isolation, and her social position as a single woman. She explained that "I do not like to visit attended by gentlemen who are my friends and I cannot properly refuse attentions when in public, nor go unattended."[27] Most of all, however, her lifestyle in Washington reflected a sense of social exclusivity that would reach full height in her relations with the president, his earnest wife, Abigail Powers Fillmore, and their vivacious young daughter, Abby.

Dix's friendship with the Fillmores blossomed during the Thirty-Second Congress. Moving upon her arrival into the home of the Titian Peale family near the corner of 15th and G Streets, she immediately sought to resume informal access to the White House a few blocks away. "I am a little exclusive in my tastes and habits, and do not court what is indiscriminate and general," she told the president. When he invited her to "come without ceremony," she promptly began to visit the White House for dinner, tea, or evening conversations. She came, she insisted, "not as a visitor, but quietly as a family friend."[28] She recommended dressmakers and doctors for the First Lady, while she and the president regularly exchanged effusive personal regards, solicitude for each other's health, warm religious sympathies, and commiseration in the difficulties of each other's work.

Although Dix repeatedly asserted that Fillmore's office was irrelevant to their friendship, politics remained the principal currency of their relationship. Dix's constant travels and wide circle of correspondents exposed her to public opinion throughout the country, and she relayed her decidedly partial perspective. "Thousands are added to your list of friends; the bad alone, if any, are enemies," she assured him in late March 1852, ten weeks before the Whig party declined to nominate him for re-election. In addition to these reports, Dix offered her own views on a variety of national affairs. She firmly endorsed the central goal of the administration, the establishment of the Compromise of 1850 as a final resolution of the sectional conflict. Just as she had been quick to find Unionist sentiment in South Carolina, she maintained that "the thinking and reliable portions" of New England supported the enforcement of the Fugitive Slave Act notwithstanding the uproar over the rendition of Thomas Sims. The sensational American reception of Hungarian revolutionary Lajos Kossuth appalled her. She expected "the *Kossuth Mania*" to prove itself "a self-curing disease," but she called on Fillmore to issue a stern warning that the United States would not "get up a new Crusade" of democratic liberation in Europe. She also hesitantly suggested several patronage appointments, including a diplomatic mission for Francis Lieber and a post in the Patent office for Titian Peale.[29]

Dix's assiduous cultivation of the president caused some awkwardness in her relations with other Washington leaders. She made conspicuous efforts, for example, to keep up her long-time connection with Fillmore's arch-rival in the New York Whig party, Senator William H. Seward.[30] But even more delicate was her relationship with her oldest and newest friend in Congress, Charles Sumner. Her important ally in the Massachusetts asylum and prison campaigns had entered the Senate as the most vociferous spokesman for the Free Soil coalition, determined to forestall the attempt to turn the country from slavery issues. Dix welcomed him gingerly. In an ingratiating report on public reaction to his maiden address, a dull endorsement of a proposed land grant for Iowa railroads, she called on him to redeem the nation from "noisy wordism and mean partizanship." She did not fail to note that she expected him to provide more assistance to her own land bill than she had received from other representatives of Massachusetts. "You and my efficient Chairman must carry the Bill through with the *largest* possible majority," she wrote in February 1852, challenging Sumner to surpass the vote by which the Senate had approved the measure in the Thirty-First Congress.[31] Privately, however, she confided that the Free Soiler knew nothing of statesmanship and was blinded by a "fog of self-esteem."[32]

Dix joined hesitantly in Sumner's main effort of the session, a campaign for the presidential pardon of Daniel Drayton and Edward Sayres, who had been convicted for aiding an attempted slave escape in the District of Columbia. Sumner urged Dix to "take advantage of the familiar access, which you enjoy to his [Fillmore's] house. Plead their care with him & with his family." At times, the mutual exhortations of the two Boston reformers sounded remarkably like a political bargain. Extending to Dix the liberal use of his congressional franking privileges, Sumner reminded her to "Remember the prisoners!" Dix acquiesced after a delaying quibble about Fillmore's power to pardon the federal prisoners, and in return she admonished Sumner to "Remember *my bill!*"[33]

During the late winter and spring, Dix detoured from her activities in Washington to assist an asylum campaign in Maryland that she had helped to prepare after the last session of Congress. "To fill up time while your *deliberative* body are considering whether you will do or not the wish of the country," she teased Horace Mann, "I thought that Maryland needing a State Hospital for the Insane, I would see if I could not get an appropriation, (and *superintend* the Building while detained at Washington!)."[34] As even sympathetic observers doubted that the state could afford to replace and expand the accommodations for the insane at the old Maryland Hospital, Dix focused her brief legislative memorial on asylum economics. "It is *cheaper to cure than it is to support,*" she argued, promising that almost all recently afflicted patients would recover and calculating that chronic patients would partly offset the costs of their care through the revenues from the asylum farm and the handicrafts produced in the course of moral treatment.[35] She shuttled between Washington and Annapolis until late May 1852, when the Maryland legislature appropriated modest funding for a new state mental hospital and appointed a commission to select the site. Local newspapers expressed surprise at the adoption of the long-discussed project and attributed its success to "the noble benefactress of suffering humanity, through whose instrumentality it has been originated and passed."[36]

In the same week as Dix's success in Maryland, the House Committee on Public Lands reported a revision of her federal land bill that clarified several aspects of the proposed grant without changing its basic design. The most important modification adopted the suggestion that William-son R. W. Cobb had urged since the first discussions of the measure, explicitly authorizing grants from the territories to any landed state if its governor determined that its federal lands were worth less than $1.25 per acre. Dix consented reluctantly to the amendment, maintaining that "it really is of *no* importance, except that it *opens debate,* which one would wish to avoid." To the contrary, however, the revisions silenced Cobb and several other western critics of her proposal. Public Lands Committee chairman Willard Hall of Missouri now expressed valuable support for the bill, reversing his opposition in the Thirty-First Congress.[37]

When Dix's bill advanced to the full House, Edward Stanly maintained its momentum by gradually supplanting Bissell to provide more effective floor management. Stanly succeeded in calling up the measure in August 1852, and the House further amended it to avoid conflict with sales of public lands in the settlement of Minnesota. In this form, Dix's bill easily prevailed in the House on August 17. Cohesive Whig support remained the heart of the 98–54 margin of passage; the party vote was 60–1 for the measure. Democrats now divided evenly on the issue. With the landed states partly mollified by the amendments, opposition was increasingly concentrated in southern delegations that objected to the measure on constitutional grounds. Stanly, whose resourcefulness had been crucial in securing a vote to demonstrate this majority, exclaimed that "I shall thank Heaven if it passes the Senate that my public life has not been spent altogether in vain" when he notified Dix in the library of the House result.[38]

As the Senate remained essentially the same group that had overwhelmingly approved the land bill in the last Congress, Dix could eagerly look forward to its passage. A few days after informing her that he had pardoned Drayton and Sayres, Fillmore confidently anticipated signing her legislation. " 'Patience has done her perfect work,' and you have triumphed," he congratulated Dix.[39] With similar optimism, the Philadelphia *North American* published a tribute suggesting that "even her gratification might be urged as a reasonable inducement to support such a measure."[40]

Dix strove to avoid any slips as her allies maneuvered against states-rights opposition to bring up the bill in the Senate. " 'Be constant in season and out of season' to pass my *Land Bill now* . . . ," she implored Seward. "*Please,* please, rouse *all your friends* to finish the work now *wisely* and *well.* Please pass it *at once.*"[41] She urged Sumner to help by casting his vote but otherwise keeping his distance. Enjoining the Free Soiler to refrain from debate shortly after he delivered a provocative demand for repeal of the Fugitive Slave Law, she insisted, "*Above all, do not you my good friend name me* in the Senate chamber: I have a keen sense of feeling on this point."[42]

The Senate consideration of Dix's bill on the last evening of the session fulfilled neither her hopes for a larger majority nor her request for anonymity. Although several former opponents joined the clear preponderance in favor of the bill, the dedication of Dix's supporters paled alongside their commitment to competing land legislation. Emphasizing that the grant for state asylums was "a portion of the land system," they seized the last-minute opportunity to offer germane amendments for railroad subsidies. William Gwin of California, the foremost congressional proponent of a transcontinental railroad, introduced his plan for twin lines to the Pacific Ocean from St. Louis and Memphis. Solon Borland submitted a sweeping proposal for construction projects in all but two public land states. In the final hours of the session, Dix's legislation could hardly withstand the conflicts over the transcontinental railroad that had already driven Asa Whitney to abandon his campaign in the United States and try his luck in Canada.[43]

Dix's suggestion that she would not figure in the debate was as futile as her dreams of an easy passage. Her bill was inseparable from her fame, and the Senate readily cast her name into the fray. Shields argued that her character was the factor that distinguished the asylum bill from other land grants and entitled the measure to priority over the transcontinental railroad. "This bill has been prepared by the only agent I respect about this Capitol—by Miss Dix," he declared. "All your other agents come here as the agents of selfish and sordid objects. But here is a lady, who is a voluntary agent for the unfortunate—for those who have no friends." Gwin's allies were quick to respond that his amendment complemented the asylum bill, "which generally bears the name of one of the most estimable females of our country," because the transcontinental railroad would ensure prosperity to consolidate the achievements of "the celebrated Miss Dix." Borland echoed the same striking pairing of Dix and railroad grants, to be countered in turn by John P. Hale, who delivered an impassioned speech for a vote solely on the asylum measure. The Free Soil candidate for president based his appeal for a vote almost wholly on a plea for deference to Dix. "This bill emanates from a lady whose history is well known to the country," he emphasized. Her career, more than any issues of welfare policy, made the asylum proposal stand out "from the ordinary objects of legislation."[44]

But Hale's eulogy could not beat back the railroad amendments, and the Senate refused to vote on the bill. To her frustration, Dix's personal identification with her measure remained its ultimate significance.

— 4 —

Dix found some consolation for the defeat of her land bill in the passage of a congressional appropriation to establish a public mental hospital for District of Columbia residents and military personnel. Although she had lived in Washington for much of the past four years, only in the past few weeks had she shown an interest in the asylum proposals that District physicians had urged sporadically since the 1830s and that Thomas Miller, head of the city Board of Health, had promoted intensively for the past seven months. Critics later claimed that Dix initially opposed Miller's efforts because she believed that the District measure would distract Congress from her land bill. Her main contribution to the project was certainly indirect. In establishing the new mental hospital that Dix advocated in May 1852, Maryland had mandated the removal of all District residents from the state asylum before the first day of 1853. The Washington campaign soon gained momentum. Dix began to lobby on its behalf by August, but Miller remained its chief advocate. Edward Stanly relied on Miller's correspondence in endorsing the asylum bill in the House, and it was Miller's friend Robert M. T. Hunter of Virginia, chairman of the Senate Finance Committee and one of the most powerful floor leaders in Congress, who added the $100,000 appropriation to a comprehensive budget measure. Dix nevertheless expressed pride in the passage of "my District Hospital Bill."[45]

The new federal asylum particularly mitigated the disappointment of the land bill because, as Dix's closest ally in Maryland observed, it not only added more local facilities for the insane but constituted "a national work."[46] In promoting the District asylum, Miller had sought to create "the Model Insane Hospital of America," to be imitated by the mental institutions that were rapidly proliferating throughout the country.[47] Dix now shared the same ambition, if not in all respects the same model.

As Dix had demonstrated at Bloomingdale, her vision of the model asylum rested on the design principles recently codified by the Association of Medical Superintendents. These intended professional standards, formulated primarily by Thomas Kirkbride, provided for rural asylums of no more than 250 patients. The key considerations in selecting a location were to be the availability of pure water and an abundance of cultivated land for the patients to contemplate and farm. In the construction of the hospital buildings, the superintendents emphasized the importance of fresh air, sunlight, unobtrusive security, and the classification of patients in separate wards for a regimen of moral therapy.[48] Like many superintendents, Dix saw the new Government Hospital for the Insane as an opportunity to establish the Association's standards by the force of a national example.

Beyond its influence on the development of mental institutions, moreover, the Government Hospital would also express a deeper relationship between the aims of the asylum and the values of the republic. The symbol of American scientific and humanitarian progress would be an important addition to the barren civic landscape of the capital, which still consisted mostly of flimsy wood buildings interspersed with a few substantial brick residences and a small handful of mismatched public structures. Fillmore, who made the reshaping of Washington one of the priorities of his administration, devoted several days to looking through the city with his Secretary of the Interior for an appropriate site for the asylum.[49]

Finally, and most important to Dix and the Association of Medical

Superintendents, the creation of the Government Hospital presented a dramatic reminder that the heart of the moral treatment was a program of governance. The asylum symbolized not only American compassion for the afflicted but also, and more fundamentally, the patterns of leadership and discipline on which the republic depended. Kirkbride declared that "the national hospital, located, as it is, at the seat of Government, should be a model, not only in its buildings, but, what is of still more importance, in its plan of government and system of management."[50]

From the outset, Dix fused these goals with a personal objective in the development of the Government Hospital. She had maintained a correspondence with Charles Nichols since his departure from the Bloomingdale Asylum, preserving the young physician's ties to his former specialty while he investigated the copper mines of Michigan and decided "which to serve—myself or *the* cause."[51] His theatricality poorly masked a fear that he had no choice. The competition among doctors for asylum jobs remained keen despite the increasing number of institutions, and although Nichols enjoyed a fine reputation he faced additional obstacles as a bachelor who had left Bloomingdale after an open clash with its trustees. During the summer, he asked Dix to keep him in mind for a position that commanded "the whole executive authority" at a mental hospital, noting that "I have tried the plan of divided responsibility to my heart's content."[52] Not surprisingly, his letter of inquiry about the Government Hospital and Dix's letter alerting him to the opportunity crossed in the mail in the first days of September 1852.[53]

Dix quickly persuaded Fillmore to make Nichols the superintendent of the federal mental hospital. Echoing an argument that the Association of Medical Superintendents had often advanced but never sustained, she urged that the asylum needed medical direction long before it opened. The emergence of hospitals as specialized facilities suggested that physicians should direct planning and construction as well as later administration and treatment. Nichols made the same point in a letter outlining his strategy for "a *model* institution," which Dix showed to Fillmore. Long before the appointment was made final, she gleefully wrote from the White House to notify Nichols of his selection, styling herself the "Ex Officio Member of the Board of Council for the Army & Navy Hospital for the Insane and Secretary pro tem."[54]

Dix's exultation in this triumph irritated even friendly admirers. Jane

Erwin Yeatman Bell, temporarily boarding at the Peales' house with Dix and the Henrys, wrote privately in October 1852 that she was "truly sorry I have been thrown with her in such a way as to have to see her as she is, more like the rest of the human family, actuated more by a desire to distinguish herself than to benefit the suffering portion of the community whose cause she so ably pleads. Her ambition is only equaled by her will . . . by which she accomplishes everything." Snubbed while her old friend basked in confidential access to the president, the aristocratic Bell reported that Dix was "more carried away by it than anyone you ever saw." She concluded a few weeks later: "To admire her much it is necessary to live in separate houses. You see *into* her motives too plainly when you are with her all the time. I find her possessing as many of the frailties of our nature as most of us, for which she is not to blame but for the assumption of so much superiority."[55]

If Dix's gloating irked Bell, the president's designation of Nichols prompted a more open confrontation with Miller, who vigorously protested that he deserved the superintendency of the Government Hospital as a reward for his lobbying efforts. Apprised by Fillmore of the attack, Dix obtained supporting recommendations for Nichols from Kirkbride and Isaac Ray, and the appointment was made final in November.[56] Privately, she savaged Miller as "a violent and undisciplined aspirant for official place."[57] The District physician continued to solicit support for his candidacy in the Washington medical community, however, as the victory of Franklin Pierce in the presidential election raised the prospect of a patronage shift in the incoming Democratic administration.

Apart from the struggle for federal spoils, Dix strenuously opposed Miller's alternative suggestion that he receive an appointment as an independent consulting physician. Common in Great Britain and adopted in some southern states, the division of medical responsibility squarely violated her insistence on the unified authority of the asylum superintendent. In an intermittent series of political skirmishes over the next few years, she and Nichols continued to fend off Miller and uphold the structure of asylum governance endorsed by the Association of Medical Superintendents.[58]

While the contest simmered, Dix and her superintendent made the crucial decisions that shaped the Government Hospital for the Insane. She reviewed the preliminary plans for the asylum drawn by Thomas

Ustick Walter, the architect directing the renovation of the Capitol, and Nichols kept her closely informed while he worked with Walter to develop the final design, a modification of the plan that Kirkbride had introduced at Trenton.[59] Dix and Nichols scoured Washington together for two weeks to find the best location for the institution. Although observers of Miller's legislation expected the asylum to cover 10 or 15 acres, Dix and Nichols settled on a 185-acre tract of land known as St. Elizabeths. About two and a half miles southeast of the Capitol, the site commanded a splendid view of Washington and the surrounding area, and its combination of farm and woodland offered a perfect natural setting for moral therapy. Fillmore and Interior Secretary Alexander H. H. Stuart, who had not considered St. Elizabeths in their search, soon agreed that it was "incomparably the best location."[60]

Dix personally took charge of subduing "the ill temper of a few disappointed Landed Proprietors" in negotiations over the purchase price for St. Elizabeths and a small adjacent farm.[61] She patently distrusted the hesitancy of lumber merchant Thomas Blagden, the owner of the principal tract, who told Nichols that he was content with the price offered by the federal government but that "as he comes to realize the loss of his pet place, he feels as though he were selling a member of his family." Although Blagden said he saw no purpose to Nichols's suggestion that he discuss his qualms with Dix, she nevertheless called on the merchant at Willard's Hotel on the day he had promised a decision. She emerged from the meeting in control of St. Elizabeths. "Since seeing you to-day," Blagden told her, "I have had no other opinion (and Mrs. B. also,) than that I must not stand between you and the beloved farm— regarding you, as we do, as the instrument in the hands of God to secure this very spot for the unfortunates whose best earthly friend you are."[62]

The organization of the Government Hospital for the Insane and the appointment of Nichols marked a resounding vindication of Dix's arguments one year earlier at the Bloomingdale Asylum. The new facility, eventually completed at approximately five times the cost anticipated by Congress, exemplified the moral architecture promoted by the Association of Medical Superintendents. The exclusive authority vested in Nichols ensured that the asylum management as well as its buildings would be a showcase for the coalescing professional standards. Aligned to face the Capitol, the Government Hospital for the Insane realized

Dix's vision of the asylum as not merely a medical institution but a model for the government of the country.

Dix's collaboration with Nichols soon blossomed into the closest of her relationships with "the brethren" of asylum superintendents. Nichols personified her belief that physicians should be moral guardians rather than mere scientists. As he told his patron, he "never attended to pills & general practice but as a necessity."[63] Nichols also shared the stiff manner and arch righteousness of his fellow Maine native. He fit easily into the Washington circle of the Fillmores, the Henrys, and the Bells. Adopting the same conservative stance as Dix on the most emotional social issue in the capital, he quickly decided to build separate accommodations for black patients and after several months even bought a slave.[64]

Nichols called Dix "my dear, good Mentor Sister," but her friendship with her protégé alternated in tone between maternal and flirtatious.[65] He addressed her in his letters as Christiana and Angelina before adopting Sandora as the counterpart to her nickname for him, St. Nicholas. The superintendent served as Dix's personal physician and financial aide in Washington, and in turn he half-teasingly looked to her to help him find a wife.[66] The conflated roles mirrored Dix's remarkably youthful appearance. Almost fifty-one, she was seventeen years older than Nichols, but she guarded the secret of her age jealously and observers guessed that she was still in her thirties. Her slender frame, elegant posture, and fine voice added to the impression that goodness kept her forever young, as did the twinkle that prompted one school of deaf-mute students to nickname her "smile of the eyes."[67] She had almost everything she wanted as construction began on the national asylum that would soon furnish her with a grand home in Washington, almost everything except for what she wanted most, the passage of her land bill.

— 5 —

For Dix, the lame-duck session of the Thirty-Second Congress from December 1852 to March 1853 was a dreary anticlimax to the Fillmore administration. Legislation virtually halted while Washington awaited the inauguration of Pierce and the arrival of an even larger Democratic majority in Congress. The Whigs would hold less than one-third of the seats in both the next Senate and the House. The Free Soil party, also a reliable source of votes for her land grant, appeared to be altogether spent. Several of Dix's closest personal allies were preparing to leave Congress, including Horace Mann and Edward Stanly. Devoting most of the first two months of the session to visits to the Washington penitentiary, a lobbying project in Pennsylvania, and a petition for a supplemental appropriation for the new Maryland asylum, Dix grumbled in February 1853 that "Congress is doing *literally* nothing."[68]

Her Senate supporters rallied in February, however, to bring up the amended bill that the House had approved during the previous session. Heartened by the determination of John Davis and "others of the wise and prudent," she begged her friends to make a final effort. She conferred almost daily with John Bell despite the cooling of their personal relations. She implored Sumner to promote the measure "which seems strangely engrafted upon my life" and to prove that he was no less sympathetic to "the most wretched of all God's creatures" than to "those who sigh in servile bondage."[69] Shields and Hannibal Hamlin moved for a vote on the measure, only to be thwarted by threats of protracted debate and Robert M. T. Hunter's insistence on the priority of appropriations bills.[70] Dix tried to maintain a stoic composure in the face of this opposition, but as the session drew to a close, she succumbed at last to a weary, desperate hope that caused her to sweat through the nights with anxiety.[71]

When the Senate finally took up Dix's legislation during the midnight hours of March 3–4, in the last gasp of the Thirty-Second Congress and the Fillmore administration, the debate repeated that of the previous session with mocking exaggeration. Now the bill was saddled not only with the stalemate on the transcontinental railroad but with the full array of conflicts over the public domain. Supporters of the homestead bill, which had also passed the House during the previous session, immediately moved to add it to the asylum grant, hoping either to enact both measures or to prevent speculators from buying up the lands to be sold under Dix's bill. "It is very evident that the gentlemen intend to make a mere demonstration in favor of benevolence," sneered Andrew Pickens Butler after an avowed supporter of Dix's bill tried to link it to the far more controversial donation of free farms to settlers in the public domain. Other amendments soon followed for additional military land bounties and for graduation of the price of public lands that remained unpurchased after years on the market.[72]

Salmon P. Chase assumed the role played by John P. Hale in the previous session, urging his homestead allies not to thwart Dix once again. The asylum proposal and the homestead movement, the Ohio Free Soiler observed, "claim a sort of precedence over all others, and seem, in some degree, to conflict with each other." Determined as he was to arrange a vote on the favorite land measure of the western states, Chase was willing to dispose of Dix's legislation first. "Who is the lady in behalf of whose measure we are appealed to to-night?" he asked. "She has no power or patronage. She controls no vast money claims with which to approach Congress . . . Shall we deny a simple vote upon her bill?" But the deepening entanglements of federal land politics could not be waved away by appeals that another senator called "considerations of mere personal respect to an accomplished and humane lady." The Senate extinguished Dix's hopes shortly before sunrise, shifting in its last hours to consideration of Stephen A. Douglas's plan to organize the Nebraska Territory for settlement.[73]

"The last thing they did in the Senate was to kill Miss Dix's bill," Jane Erwin Yeatman Bell recorded. "I expect it will almost kill her." Bell saw a certain justice in the failure, arguing that "she helped to kill it herself by being a little too much carried away by her success" in the establishment of the Government Hospital.[74] Other acquaintances were relieved to learn that the disappointment had failed to break Dix's determination and that she would return to Washington for the Thirty-Third Congress. "It is very sad for your friends to receive almost periodically such letters from you," Lieber wrote when he heard of her latest defeat. Offering his highest praise, he commented that her "heroic calmness" and "indomitable perseverance" personified the ideal he had described in an essay on political ethics.[75]

James Gore King more perceptively discerned a note of despair beneath Dix's resilience. Sympathizing with her "anxiety, deferred hope, and . . . *heart-sickness,*" he noted that she must be haunted by the loss of an excellent opportunity for passage of the bill. "As all agree, it might have been saved except by great mismanagement," he mourned, perhaps not stopping to remember that Dix had demanded full control of its management for the past four years. King's wistful diagnosis, especially persuasive for the previous Congress in which he had served, now seemed less and less accurate amid a dwindling core of Whig supporters and a bottleneck of land legislation. Faced with the changed situation of national politics, Dix apparently intended to persist in her effort for its own sake. "Your decision as to looking to the cause of suffering humanity, as the plan, purpose and *solace* of your life is couched in words of wisdom," King noted. "But there lurks through all your phrases a seeming consciousness, that the end may not be attained."[76]

As if by condensation of the gloom surrounding Dix's interests at the end of the Whig administration, Abigail Powers Fillmore contracted pneumonia during the inauguration of Pierce and died a few weeks later. "It belongs to friendship to be silent, and grieve with the wounded spirit," Dix wrote to her fellow Unitarian in a characteristically terse note of religious condolence on the loss of his wife.[77] After two heady years as the president's most prominent female political partner, she might have seen a grim parallel between her defeat and the death of the First Lady. Not for a decade had the providential superintendence of her mission seemed more obscure.

9

The Moral Horizon of a Unitarian Minister

EAGER FOR A RESPITE from the dismal state of affairs in Washington, Dix traveled to Nova Scotia in the summer of 1853 to help local officials choose the site for a new mental hospital. The seaside tour refreshed her health and presented a charitable diversion that further raised her spirits. As soon as she arrived in Halifax she took an interest in shipwrecks at nearby Sable Island, a treacherous barrier sandbank known since the sixteenth century as the graveyard of the Atlantic. A vessel sank during Dix's brief visit to the island, confirming her judgment that British and provincial officials had neglected their duty by failing to provide lighthouses, fog bells, or rescue boats to help reduce the frequent catastrophes. Upon returning to the United States, she solicited the donation of four rescue boats and a stock of lifesaving apparatus from prominent merchants in Boston, New York, and Philadelphia. The select roll of subscribers included Jonathan Phillips, Abbot Lawrence, Thomas H. Perkins, William Astor, and James Lenox; John Adams Dix contributed an expensive lifeboat.[1]

Dix completed the philanthropic project shortly before she turned back to politics for the winter. She named one boat the *Samaritan* as a rebuke to the derelict government authorities, and she christened another the *Grace Darling* in honor of the English lighthouse keeper's daughter who had become a national heroine by saving steamboat passengers wrecked on the Farne Islands. She formally presented the gift to Nova Scotia officials in November 1853. But the cargo ship transporting it foundered in a tempest near Cape Cod, and Dix's rescue fleet was devastated. Necessary repairs delayed the project for the next several months, adding an unexpected annoyance to one of the most tumultuous periods of her life.[2]

— 1 —

The pivotal phase of the Pierce administration, for Dix's land bill as for the nation, was the formation of the Cabinet. The youngest and one of the least experienced men yet elected to the presidency, Pierce won the office after Democratic rivals Stephen A. Douglas, Lewis Cass, and James Buchanan thwarted each other's ambitions. Pierce's weak position in the party reinforced a temperamental inclination to rely heavily on his inner circle, which became the only Cabinet in American history to remain intact for a full presidential term. As his biographer has observed, he "functioned merely as a member of an executive committee, not as a chief executive."[3]

In choosing this powerful council, Pierce hoped to restore a Jacksonian unity in the Democratic party that he half-remembered and half-imagined from his brief career in Congress more than a decade earlier. The cornerstone of his plan was the appointment of John Adams Dix to a key Cabinet post as a counterbalance to Robert M. T. Hunter, the campaign manager of John C. Calhoun's final bid for the presidency. But Hunter preferred to remain in the Senate, and his states-rights wing of the party joined Cass's supporters in objecting vociferously to the inclusion of any Barnburners who had undermined the national ticket in 1848 by bolting with Van Buren. Pierce retreated, eliminating Dix from his tentative Cabinet and asking him to accept a subordinate position as assistant treasurer until the president could bridge the intense party factionalism. Dix invited his adopted sister to "a family cabinet council" to consider these machinations, which were scarcely less ominous for her than for him.[4] Pierce's final slate left her with no proven allies in the executive branch except James C. Dobbin of North Carolina, and he wielded little influence beyond his duties as Secretary of the Navy. Even more alarming, one of the most outspoken congressional opponents of her land bill, Pierce's personal friend and forceful advisor Jefferson Davis, filled the states-rights vacancy in the Cabinet as Secretary of War.

After visiting John Adams Dix and Millard Fillmore in New York,

Dix returned to Washington in December 1853 for the opening of the Thirty-Third Congress. Despite her dwindling base of Whig supporters in Congress and the disappointing turn by the administration, she braced to press her land bill until it succeeded. "God, I think, will surely give me strength for *His* work so long as he directs my line of duty," she wrote resolutely at the outset of the session. She stayed in the capital for only a few days while Congress organized, meeting with her previous sponsors, William Bissell and James Shields, to arrange an early start for her bill. Shortly after she left town, Bissell submitted the proposal in the House of Representatives on December 14. But as in the last Congress, other Democrats rejected his request for a select committee and referred the bill to the House Committee on Public Lands. One week later Solomon Foot of Vermont, a respected parliamentarian and a Whig member of the Senate Committee on Public Lands, introduced the proposal in the Senate, accepting the referral of the bill to that committee without objection. For the first time, and apparently against her instructions, Dix's bill would bow to the standard procedures of Congress.[5]

Dix's attempt to win Pierce's support while in Washington was similarly inauspicious. She returned to the White House on December 7 with a bittersweet sense of nostalgia and foreboding. The familiar greetings of the doorkeeper, she reported to Fillmore, sounded both reassuring and disconcerting amid the remodeling that had completely transformed the old mansion. The new president, "his manner wavering and hurried," extended his sympathy but offered no commitments. When Dix asked whether she could tell congressmen that the measure enjoyed his "interest and good will," Pierce replied with forlorn equivocation. "More than that, Miss Dix," he said, "I sincerely regretted that it had not passed the last session. I shall be glad if it passes now, but I really have not gone into the subject." Even the hopeful Dix could place little confidence in "that air of restless, half uncertainty which he wears." She privately agreed with Fillmore that Pierce shared in the widespread admiration of her motives but doubted the constitutionality of her bill. The former president warned that his successor would "seek to avoid the veto by having his friends defeat the measure in Congress."[6]

Fillmore's prediction reflected sound, straightforward political reasoning for ordinary times. Pierce's advisor Hunter had skillfully blocked

Dix's bill before, and now he was better positioned to do so again. But the first session of the Thirty-Third Congress soon proved to a most extraordinary time in American politics. The pell-mell disposition of the public domain, which had preoccupied Congress since the Compromise of 1850, had at last circled back into a titanic collision with the controversy over slavery.

On the same day that Bissell presented Dix's measure, Senator Augustus Dodge of Iowa re-introduced the bill to organize the Nebraska Territory that Congress had almost passed in the last session. Stephen A. Douglas rewrote the legislation in his Committee on Territories, appealing for the southern votes that had previously defeated the bill in the Senate and responding particularly to the pressure exerted by David Rice Atchison of Missouri, who had staked his difficult re-election campaign on a promise to expand slavery into the neighboring territory. The bill that Douglas reported on January 4 ignored the historic Missouri Compromise bar against the establishment of slavery above the 36° 30′ latitude. Instead, it applied language taken from the Compromise of 1850 to the Nebraska Territory and provided that states would be admitted into the Union from the territory with or without slavery as their constitutions prescribed. A subsequent addition clarified that settlers would vote to determine the status of slavery.[7]

Archibald Dixon of Kentucky quickly outflanked Douglas's bill by proposing an explicit repeal of the Missouri Compromise bar, hoping to show that southern Whigs represented slaveholders' interests more zealously than Democrats. Douglas agreed to work Dixon's amendment into the bill as a partial appeasement of states-rights Democrats, who took the more extreme position that Congress had no authority whatsoever to prohibit slavery in the territories, by popular sovereignty or any other means. Foreseeing that the repeal of the Compromise "would raise a hell of a storm" in the North, Douglas sought to make the principle of popular sovereignty a strict test of Democratic party loyalty.

Through the intercession of Jefferson Davis, Douglas arranged an extraordinary Sunday meeting with Pierce, who ordinarily conducted no business on the Sabbath, and several states-rights congressional leaders who had the leverage and experience to block the president's policies as well as Douglas's initiative. The delegation included three members of the famous "F Street Mess"—Senate president Atchison, Finance Committee chairman Hunter, and Foreign Relations Committee chairman James Mason of Virginia—who shared their Washington boardinghouse with Senate Judiciary Committee chairman Andrew Pickens Butler of South Carolina. The highly charged meeting persuaded the hesitant Pierce to endorse the Missouri Compromise repeal as an administration measure. On Monday, January 23, Douglas presented a substitute bill declaring the ban against slavery "inoperative" in the territory that he now proposed to divide into Kansas and Nebraska.

Settled by early January 1854 into her old post in the Library of Congress, where she was delighted with Thomas Ustick Walter's restorations after the fire, Dix could see firsthand that "the land question is taking new phases." She took little interest in other aspects of the brewing Kansas-Nebraska imbroglio. Although she continued to receive her mail through Sumner, she ignored his efforts to fan public outrage against the bill in the North. She expressed no concern about the possible expansion of slavery and sheer contempt for the partisan maneuvering that surrounded the legislation. Douglas, she scoffed, "already sees himself in the *White House,* and demeans himself like the tom-tit, which fancied itself an Eagle."[8] The implications of the controversy for the disposition of the public lands, however, provided ample grounds for further anxiety about the prospects of her bill.

Intended by Douglas to be part of a comprehensive program for the development of the West, the Kansas-Nebraska bill portended a sweeping shift in land policy. The opening of the Great Plains territories for settlement, together with the pending Senate review of the Gadsden Treaty for the purchase of more land from Mexico, suggested a host of new railroad projects. Pierce added to this pressure by urging Congress in his first annual message to dedicate itself more intensively to the construction of a transcontinental railroad. At the same time, however, his warnings against reckless grants and his emphasis on the subordinate role of the federal government in the transcontinental enterprise raised widespread uncertainty about the direction of land policy.[9]

Even more disturbing to Dix than the competition of railroads for congressional attention, Douglas's plan to establish popular sovereignty in the territories created a surge of momentum for the homestead bill. Northern congressmen opposed to the extension of slavery increasingly argued that a policy of free farms for settlers would attract a tide of foreign emigrants and native yeomen to the West and preserve free soil principles. Moreover, for independent reasons, the homestead bill continued to maintain strong support from the Southwest. Many commentators predicted the ultimate consolidation of the Nebraska and homestead components of Douglas's program. The complementary support for the Nebraska bill in the Senate and the homestead bill in the House of Representatives reinforced this speculation, although once again, Pierce's position on the homestead bill was unknown.[10]

For Dix, the acceleration of the homestead movement promised another frustrating session. Her measure now faced not only the increased leverage of states-rights opponents like Hunter but also a separate strengthening of the demand that federal lands be donated to settlers rather than sold for revenue. "Either the whole public domain will be disposed of at *random*," she speculated gloomily in mid-January, "or all Land Bills, my own included, will be crushed."[11]

— 2 —

Contrary to Dix's fears, however, her bill soon began to advance more rapidly than it had in the past six sessions of Congress. The first step forward resulted from the integration of the measure into the bargaining in the Senate Committee on Public Lands, which revised the allocation of the land grant to favor the less populous states that all members of the committee represented. Foot reported the measure to the Senate on January 23, a few minutes before Douglas presented his amended Kansas-Nebraska proposal. But though placed in a favorable calendar position, Dix's legislation was completely blocked by the upheaval over the extension of slavery. Foot advised her on February 3 that "nothing will be done with that or any other bill till the Nebraska bill is disposed of, which is the all-absorbing question for the present." Fillmore soon echoed this prediction, warning Dix that "little or nothing will be done for the good of the country" during the slavery crisis.[12]

The legislative thicket seemed to grow more dense when Foot asked the Senate to take up Dix's measure on February 9. John Pettit of Indiana offered a hostile amendment that would limit the grant for the insane to states with public lands. His attempt to stir western opposition against Dix's proposal further strained her confidence. Foot assured her that the bill would eventually pass the Senate and Bissell echoed that optimistic forecast in the House, but she soberly noted that "this opinion has often been expressed before." She saw no encouragement in the familiar Washington patterns that the Kansas-Nebraska turmoil had intensified, "the usual assembling and dispersion of the Senate and House . . . , the usual amount of gossip, and the usual measure of vapid conversation and idle talk."[13]

When Dix's bill came up for consideration again on February 21, Foot responded bluntly to Pettit's amendment during the brief period that the Senate reserved for matters other than the Kansas-Nebraska question. Noting that the bill was the only measure likely to give a share of the public domain to the states without public lands, he warned that eastern congressmen would hold up railroad bills and other western demands for land grants unless the new states recognized intersectional equity in the territories. He also addressed the constitutional objections to the legislation, comparing the proposal with numerous charitable appropriations and pointedly arguing that Dix's proposal for the insane poor rested on the same constitutional basis as the homestead bill for the landless poor. Foot concluded with another florid congressional tribute to Dix. "With the vigilance and devotion of a patron saint, she has sought out the stricken maniac," he declaimed, reminding his colleagues that Dix was "fitted by rare endowments to have attained popular eminence and applause in the higher and more inviting departments of life; to have moved among the more attractive and admired scenes of its proudest and gayest circles." Cut short by the daily standing order for consideration of the Kansas-Nebraska bill, he proposed to make the question on Pettit's amendment a test vote on the legislation.[14]

On February 28, however, Pettit withdrew his amendment, glibly explaining that because "there is more insanity and lunacy, not to say idiocy, in the old northern free States than in the western and southern States, it may be a matter of philanthropy and justice to pass the bill as a remedy for that afflicted class." His quip illustrated the sharp sectional tensions of the past month but obscured a significant change in strategy by Dix's opponents. Although Pettit pledged to vote against passage of the measure, he indicated that he would not try to block it through standard parliamentary maneuvers. Assisted by further modification of the land allocation formula, the bill suddenly rushed forward against less tenacious opposition than it had previously faced in Congress. Legislative time was more precious and delaying tactics more powerful than at any point in recent years, but Dix's opponents in the Senate introduced no more additional hostile amendments and offered no motions to lay the bill aside in favor of other business. When discussion of the land grant conflicted with the hours set aside for the Kansas-Nebraska debate, Hunter suggested that the Senate return to Dix's bill on the next day rather than repeating the usually successful minority strategy of postponing it for as long as possible.[15]

The surprising course of Pettit and Hunter, contradicting Fillmore's prediction that Pierce's allies would try to stop Dix's bill in Congress, revealed the important position that her measure was quietly assuming in the complex politics of the Thirty-Third Congress. Rumors swirled about Capitol Hill that Pierce would veto the legislation if it passed through Congress.[16] As a result, the bill presented a opportunity to determine the president's position on related land issues, most notably the homestead measure, which was speeding through the House of Representatives while the Senate prepared to approve the Kansas-Nebraska bill. Moreover, the prospect of a veto promised to serve the dominant goal of the overwhelming Democratic majority, the reassertion of a clear party identity to reverse the schismatic tendencies illustrated by the patronage contests at the outset of the administration. The first major attempt to achieve this end, the Kansas-Nebraska bill, had backfired disastrously. Passage was certain in the Senate, but a desperate struggle was clearly looming in the House of Representatives as many northern Democrats placed section before party and spoke out in opposition to the administration measure. By rejecting Whig-sponsored legislation at this crucial juncture, a veto could rally Democrats around the party standard.[17]

As a result of these calculations, Dix's western opponents, such as Pettit, prudently sidestepped a clash over the asylum bill to preview Pierce's attitude toward their legislative priority, the homestead bill. Meanwhile, her more doctrinaire southern adversaries, such as Hunter, diffident allies of Douglas's popular-sovereignty proposal and proslavery opponents of the homestead bill, used Dix's bill to sharpen their constitutional critique of federal initiatives in the public domain. Too shrewd to believe that mere talk would dissuade the Senate majority that had consistently supported the land grant for the insane, they outlined their analysis in speeches that served as draft veto messages for Pierce.

James Mason, the author of the Fugitive Slave Law, opened the discussion of Dix's measure on March 1 with a warning that "this bill is an entering wedge" that would ultimately lead to federal domination of all state institutions. Specifically anticipating the impending homestead struggle, he argued that Dix's bill even more clearly treated the federal government as the owner of the public domain, empowered to dispose of the lands at the discretion of Congress, rather than as a trustee that only administered the lands in the fiscal interests of the states. If the federal government could provide states with land grants in exchange for asylum treatment of the insane, he asked, "what department in the police of the States is there which this Government may not invade, and take from the control of the States?"[18]

The answer to Mason's rhetorical question was evident in the current context. Unrestricted congressional authority to control the public domain implied power to regulate slavery in the territories, and even to influence the states through the manipulation of land grants. Directly linking the asylum measure to the antislavery attack against the Missouri Compromise repeal, Mason sneered that Dix's proposal reflected the same "sickly sentimentality" that Butler had recently denounced in Sumner's call for free soil in the territories.[19]

Hunter and Butler followed with similar speeches during the next week. Although the three messmates had voted against Dix's bill for years without commenting on it, they hastened to articulate their position amid the furor over slavery and federal power in the public domain. Butler predicted that Dix's plan "will be the most dangerous bill, so far as regards the disposition of the public lands, ever passed" because it recognized no restrictions on congressional authority except the limits of "legislative benevolence." On the other side of the issue, Dix's supporters among the western Democrats similarly looked ahead to the homestead debate in arguing for a broader interpretation of federal power to dispose of the public lands.[20]

The Senate approved Dix's bill on March 8 by a vote of 25–12. Fourteen Whigs maintained the party's record of solidarity on the land grant for the insane, joined by nine Democrats and the Free Soilers Chase and Sumner.[21] Twenty-five senators were absent, and the event went almost unnoticed by newspapers in the uproar that surrounded the Senate passage of the Kansas-Nebraska bill on March 4 and the House passage of the homestead bill on March 6. Anticipating a veto struggle, Dix noted that she had prevailed by more than a two-thirds margin and asserted that a vote of the full Senate would produce the same ratio. "I in my heart think the very opponents are glad," she exulted, not understanding why her states-rights opponents were indeed glad that her bill would be vetoed rather than stalemated. She struggled to restrain the budding sense that providence had ordained the success of her bill in the least promising congressional session. "I hope to have a good House vote," she speculated after the lower chamber approved the homestead bill, "but can't tell what to hope or to expect, when such Bills pass as we have just now seen forced upon the Country."[22]

Dix waited anxiously for the next five weeks. On March 29, the House tabled Bissell's version of her bill following the unfavorable report of the House Committee on Public Lands. By now, though, her hopes rested on the Senate bill. She calculated that "it will pass if voted in a full House, and fail otherwise," admitting that "this uncertainty keeps me *rather* unsettled."[23]

As Dix feared, the House barely managed a quorum when it considered her bill on April 19, but the poor attendance worked to her advantage. Several of her most formidable adversaries were absent, including Public Lands Committee chairman David Disney of Ohio and states-rights strategists Alexander Stephens of Georgia, Thomas Bayly of Virginia, and James Orr of South Carolina. In a few hours, Bissell guided his majority through a series of hostile motions to adjourn the House, lay the bill on the table, and bury it in committee. Although the parliamentary skirmish permitted little debate, Thomas Clingman of North Carolina found an opportunity to summarize the conjunction of Dix's bill, the homestead bill, and the Kansas-Nebraska bill. "This Government has no authority, under the powers given to it as a Federal and limited Government, to legislate in this way for either the lunatics, paupers, negroes, or anybody else," he declared. The final 81–53 vote to pass Dix's bill generally followed the usual distribution of votes on her

measure. Unanimous Whigs provided the nucleus of the majority, southern Democrats overwhelmingly opposed the bill, and northern Democrats divided almost evenly.[24]

"Thus have the labors of Miss Dix, the preserving patron of this beneficent act, been crowned with triumphant success," exclaimed the Whig
National Intelligencer after the House vote. Other newspapers similarly
saw a distinctly personal victory in the only significant legislation to
pass both houses of Congress during the Kansas-Nebraska crisis. The
Baltimore *American* crowed that the state asylums funded by the land
grant would stand as a monument to Dix's benevolence "when the last
remembrance of the disputatious women who thrust themselves into the
arena of public life and contend with loud-mouthed volubility for rights
that would unsex and disgrace them shall have passed away, and the
world has forgotten even to contemn them." Across town, the pro-
homestead Baltimore *Sun* fretted that "as regards the land bills now
before Congress, none but the *insane* ones seem to have a chance of
passing—*ipse* Dix-*it.*" The Richmond *Enquirer,* a prominent states-rights
organ, warned that the federal menace had assumed the guise of legislation "originating in the crotchet of a crazy old woman."[25]

Whether with relief or regret, observers widely expected Pierce to veto
Dix's bill. Anne Heath relayed to her friend a telegraph rumor that the
president had returned the bill to Congress on the same day he received
it, adding her own detail that "he was undoubtedly drunk."[26] When several days passed without a veto, however, some commentators began to
wonder whether they had correctly gauged the little-known, indecisive
chief executive. Rumors circulated through Washington that Pierce had
personally promised Dix his support, and reports of an animated Cabinet
debate on the bill surfaced in the press. One Democratic newspaper worried that Pierce would try to avoid controversy by holding the bill for ten
days and allowing it to become law without his signature.[27]

Dix's calm readiness for the president's action astonished her friends.
Charles Nichols wrote admiringly that she rested content in the conviction that she had " 'done *her* duty' & leaves the responsibility which in
no wise belongs to her, where it *does* belong & where it must remain."[28]
Inwardly, however, Dix trusted that Congress would sustain her cheerful
disposition. "As yet the President has not put his Veto upon my Bill,"
she told Heath in response to her premature condolences, "but I fully

expect it today or in a few days—and poor, weak man, it will be a bad day's work for him." In a full vote on its merits, she expected her land grant for the insane to crush the hapless president. "A storm impends which *he* little dreams of," she sympathized. "It will shake his very life."[29] On May 3, Pierce returned her bill to the Senate with a statement of his objections.

— 3 —

Pierce's veto message elaborated the arguments that Dix had anticipated six years earlier in her memorial to Congress. Reasoning that the insane were not "exclusively worthy of benevolent regard," the president broadly addressed federal authority under the Constitution to enter into "the novel and vast field of legislation" introduced by the charitable land grant. The issue resolved into an analysis of congressional power under the Territories Clause "to dispose of, and make all needful rules and regulations respecting, the territory or other property belonging to the United States," as Pierce correctly noted that Jackson had established a consensus that Congress could spend money only for the purposes specifically enumerated in the Constitution. In this first presidential veto of an appropriation from the public lands, "the Young Hickory" now attempted to imitate the bold leadership that Jackson had exercised in striking down congressional appropriations from the federal treasury.[30]

As in the formation of his Cabinet, Pierce strained to accommodate conflicting Democratic factions in his constitutional interpretation. Echoing the arguments of the F Street Mess, he concluded that the distinction between appropriations of land and money was "wholly immaterial." He sternly warned that the arrogation of federal power to pursue any national objective "confounds all meaning of language," and he emphasized that the congressional trusteeship over the public lands did not confer plenary legislative authority. But Pierce also appealed to northern and western Democrats by detouring from Dix's bill to acknowledge that land grants for railroads and other development projects were often legitimate investments that prudently enhanced the value of the states' common property. The president distinguished the asylum grant from the reservation of public lands for schools on both this proprietary principle and the contractual theory favored by strict states-rights Democrats. Perhaps recognizing that his position hardly reconciled the patchwork of federal land legislation, he discussed few other grants from the public domain. Most important, he tried to remain uncommitted on the homestead bill. He specifically repudiated only two congressional precedents, the small land grants for deaf-mute asylums that Dix had pointed out in her memorial.[31]

These arguments were painfully familiar to Dix, and she soon confirmed her suspicions about their origin when a friend heard Pierce's indiscreet private secretary recount the Cabinet meeting on the veto. "The poor President!" she reported sarcastically to Fillmore. "His *'conscience'* would not suffer him to make that bill a law! So he said—but all here know it was Jefferson Davis who would not suffer it." As she undoubtedly expected, the Massachusetts member of the administration, the influential Attorney General Caleb Cushing, had sided firmly with Davis, ridiculing Dix's objectives during the Cabinet discussion.[32]

Dix remained confident that her divinely appointed mission would surmount this last obstacle. Two days after the veto, an acquaintance wrote that her blissful reaction showed that "there is some great truth in the ancients always representing the fates & destiny as female." Of course, Dix did not rely entirely on destiny. She urged her allies to repulse the president's challenge to Congress, and she was probably behind the newspaper reports that Pierce had contemptibly violated a personal pledge to sign her bill. Although she denied any part in the rumors to a friend of the administration, she told John Bell and other Whigs that the president "gave to *me* his *positive assurance* that the Bill for the relief of the Indigent Insane *had* his *approval* and sympathy and *would not be vetoed!*"[33] Her distorted recollection of her meeting with Pierce, contradicted by her correspondence with Fillmore, demonstrated the vision through which she saw the issue.

In addition to Pierce's weakness, Dix counted on the pattern of increasing congressional support for her bill. Davis's identical objections to the measure while he was in the Senate had failed to sway several other admirers of Calhoun, let alone the northern wings of the Democratic party. Her land grant had enjoyed the support of approximately half of the Senate Democrats and the dependable enthusiasm of all the Whigs. The coalition had twice produced Senate approval by more than a two-thirds margin. Shortly after the veto she concluded that "in the abstract game of Chess I am waging with the President thus far I hold all the advantage."[34]

Plausible as these hopes seemed to Dix, there was no chance that the Senate would override Pierce's veto. Her disdain for partisan politics blinded her to the loyalty commanded by the president. In sixty-five years, Congress had defeated only one veto, and that in the uniquely vulnerable administration of John Tyler.[35] Knowledgeable Washington observers quickly agreed that Dix's measure was doomed. Pierce hardly lacked critics: a barrage of editorialists assailed his rejection of human-itarian expenditures and approval of donations to profit-seeking enter-prises.[36] But commentators nonetheless recognized that few Democrats would oppose the president's attempt to rally his party. Horace Greeley's New York *Tribune* judged that "if Miss Dix will devise a hospital for inebriates or an asylum for idiots there may be a chance of its escaping the Veto," but otherwise she could only wait until Pierce's term expired in 1857. Even the Association of Medical Superintendents, holding its annual meeting in Washington in May 1854 to celebrate the inaugu-ration of the Government Hospital for the Insane, cautiously replaced its annual endorsement of Dix's legislation with a resolution vaguely commending her work.[37]

The immediate Senate reaction to Pierce's veto message on May 3 sealed the fate of the measure and indicated the course of the override debate. Hunter signaled that the veto would be a test of Democratic fidelity, rejoicing that "we have an issue made upon principle." Robert Toombs of Georgia followed by breaking Whig ranks to applaud Pierce's states-rights stand, which he deemed "a matter of more consequence than any which we have had before us at this session." Arrangements for printing the veto message opened a wide-ranging discussion of land grants. When Butler remarked that the veto would at last permit an overdue reassessment of federal policy, John Bell pressed the South Car-olinian and his messmate Hunter to act as administration spokesmen and reveal the full scope of Pierce's veto. Douglas interceded to pro-nounce the message consistent with western demands for land grants, and the debate reached its sticking point in his attempts to parry fellow westerners who challenged him to reconcile opposition to Dix's measure and support for the homestead bill. "I wait in painful anxiety," said Albert Gallatin Brown, "as the whole country will wait, for the distinction between granting land to sane people and granting land to the insane."[38]

To almost everyone except Dix, the chief importance of her bill had become its relationship to the Kansas-Nebraska struggle and the homestead bill. As the administration scrambled to hold northern Democrats in line on the House vote over the repeal of the Missouri Compromise bar, Pierce's summons to loyalty ensured that further debate on Dix's bill would serve more as a partisan touchstone than as an exchange of ideas. Commentators anticipated "a sort of prompt general Democratic rally" behind a veto that was "destined to become a fixed land mark . . . of the Democratic party, being as Jeffersonian and Jacksonish as can be desired." Placing the land grant for the insane in a context that eluded Dix, the Richmond *Enquirer* observed that the veto "enunciates a principle which the Democratic party will approve and support" and predicted that "in battling for it they will lose the recollection of their discreditable feuds."[39]

Most immediate was the implication of the veto for the long-awaited homestead battle. Many observers reasoned that Pierce's arguments applied to the homestead proposal, but the Washington *Union,* a pro-homestead newspaper with close ties to the administration, soon reasserted that the veto was limited to Dix's measure.[40] In the Senate, the scheduling of the override debate became a crucial pawn in the fierce competition for control of the legislative agenda. Dix's allies recognized that her measure was lost and that "no discussion can take place upon it which will change a single vote here."[41] Supporters of the homestead bill accordingly sought to vote promptly on the veto or to combine consideration of their bill with the survey of land policy that Pierce had invited. Opponents of the homestead bill attempted to ward it off by first debating the veto message at length. "I am no parliamentary tactician," Butler pleaded disingenuously on May 8, "but I think I may assume to myself this much of parliamentary tactics, to say that the taking up of this homestead bill will be but making a masked battery, from which gentlemen intend to assail the veto of the President." As most of the Senate surely knew, the situation was exactly the opposite.[42]

After the opponents of the homestead bill established the priority of the veto on the Senate calendar, they led a far more protracted review of Dix's bill than any vetoed measure had ever received. The debate continued for two months in a halting succession of postponements and elaborate addresses delivered to a half-empty Senate chamber.[43] Administration supporters praised Pierce's message as a forceful complement to the Kansas-Nebraska disclaimer of federal authority over slavery in the territories. Isaac Toucey argued that Dix had opened "the Pandora's box of the Constitution" in her appeal for benevolent legislation under the Territories Clause, condemning her bill as "a grand scheme for regulating the public lands by a Wilmot proviso, based upon this same clause, and the same broad construction of it." Dix's allies retorted that Pierce's reasoning was "desultory, illogical, and confused" and challenged their opponents to distinguish the land grant for the insane from a variety of precedents in the 130 million acres of public land that Congress had previously appropriated.[44]

Few speakers attempted to draw the crucial distinction between Dix's measure and the homestead bill, however, because the discussion was dominated by opponents of the homestead coalition. Most of its supporters, including previously eloquent allies of Dix's bill and previously impassioned opponents, pressed the Senate for an early vote to end the needless veto debate. Only the notoriously longwinded Cass responded in detail to Hunter's lengthy argument that Pierce had foreclosed a policy of free farms for settlers on the public domain. Bemused by the Democratic disagreement over the ramifications of Pierce's veto, John M. Clayton of Delaware asked mockingly, "Who is the dupe in this play?"[45]

The elaborate maneuvers in the Senate cruelly sustained Dix's faith that she would eventually prevail. Oblivious to the political machinations that made her bill a valuable waste of congressional time, she understood the veto only as a direct confrontation between herself and Pierce. The first few rounds of disquisitions satisfied her that "the debates are sustained by my friends with great spirit and ability." After one postponement of the discussion, she characterized the vote as "on my side 34, that of the Administration 13," although senators' views on the scheduling issues did not correspond with their opinions about the veto. Fearing only absenteeism and that Pierce would resort to bribery, she declared that "I would certainly not exchange either mental, moral, nor social states with the President, poor man!" She told Fillmore on May 20 that "my friends stand fast in the ranks," prompting him to warn her that "I see no hope during this administration." But she could not so easily surrender the legislation in which she had put so much of herself. She remained in unbearable suspense through the early summer of 1854. "How gently for you moves the step of time," she sighed enviously to Heath in mid-June, confessing to "the least touch of impatience" with the congressional debates.[46]

The Senate ended her ordeal on July 6, voting 27–24 to sustain the veto. Far from its earlier two-thirds margin of approval, Dix's bill failed to carry a majority. Only four Democrats voted against the president. Dix's other previous supporters in the party switched or abstained, and eleven Democrats who were absent at the passage of the bill voted unanimously to defeat the override. The solid support of seventeen Whigs was a final flicker of that party's cohesion on an issue at the heart of its platform.[47]

Dix's greatest humanitarian effort had shattered in a heartbreaking failure. Her attempt to secure a permanent endowment for the moral treatment of insanity had provoked a federal renunciation of all philanthropic legislation. Despite her contempt for partisanship, her bill had become a vehicle for mobilizing Democratic loyalty behind the effort to repeal the ban on slavery in the public domain. The deliberations on the measure had also helped proslavery strategists break the hinge between the Kansas-Nebraska bill and the homestead bill, a fragile opportunity for compromise in the sectional conflict. She had come to Washington ready to use the political system selectively and transcend it, to sanctify the nation with benevolence; instead, her reform crusade had been manipulated by party strategists and had unwittingly contributed to the framing of the crisis that would bring the country to civil war.

— 4 —

Dix struggled to understand her defeat with a sense of numbed comprehension similar to that of another American heroine who abruptly confronted sophistication from "the moral horizon of a Unitarian minister." Like Isabel Archer of Henry James's *Portrait of a Lady*, Dix vented "a scorn that kept its freshness in a very tainted air."[48] She scrutinized the Senate roll calls on her bill and, in an apt metaphor for the increasing sectionalization of politics, she lashed out against congressmen who could be "so false to their own *previously declared opinions* and *principles* as to vote within one month *four times,* alternating on each occasion as the Vane on the neighboring Engine House."[49] She bitterly castigated "renegades" like her erstwhile sponsor Shields, who skipped the override vote. "The *price* of their forfeited honour is not shown," she seethed. "Probably the bid for so poor a commodity was not high." Nothing remained for her in Washington. The affirmation of Pierce's veto prompted little public reaction. Within a few days, the Senate turned to a graduation bill introduced by Hunter to continue his successful efforts to deflect the homestead legislation. Dix soon abandoned the capital, entrusting Charles Nichols with the "time & occasion-honored inkstand and sand-box" from her office in the Library of Congress.[50]

For the first time since she left Boston in 1843, Dix felt a strong urge to go home. "I really *pine* for *settledness,*" she wrote from the Trenton asylum in a somber meditation on her "rather *vagrant* life." After spending the past decade in almost every other part of the United States, she briefly contemplated a tour of New England poorhouses. But Boston remained impossible, and her remarkable ability to create a home through her work gave way to inertia upon the veto defeat. "I betake myself to the do-nothing class," she despaired, lamenting that "the poor weak President has by an unprecedented extremity of folly lacerated my life." Through July she searched for an occupation that would divert her mind from the wrenching disappointment. In an echo of her thoughts on leaving Washington Street sixteen years earlier, she vowed that "if I say little on this subject, it is rather a characteristic evidence of more abiding and profound impression. May God forgive [Pierce]—and *I* will *try* to forgive and to forget him also."[51]

The calamity of a friend soon provided Dix a chance to regain some of her vitality. At the end of July, twenty-two-year-old Abby Fillmore died suddenly of cholera. Dix entered more fully into bereavement for the young woman than on any other occasion in her vast experience of sorrow. After immediately extending her usual brief words of commiseration to the former president, as she had upon the death of his wife one year earlier, Dix surrendered herself completely to grief for her friend and her own misery. "I cannot be silent," she mourned. "Bear with me at least; I find comfort in writing, though all my words will fail to infuse any balm of consolation into your heart." For three weeks, she sent lengthy letters almost every other day to Fillmore. Aware that her lamentations were uncharacteristically "forgetful of the common usages of social intercourse" and likely an intrusive annoyance, she pleaded for indulgence in assuming "the office of consoler and friend to those whose sorrows are known to me."[52]

Dix gradually gathered strength as the theme of her unanswered letters turned from Fillmore's desolation to Abby's eternal happiness and the renewed consecration of the survivors. "When we lose what has been, as it were, the moving principle of the best part of our affections," she wrote six weeks after the Senate sustained Pierce's veto of her land bill, "a new epoch of life begins." She suggested that Fillmore and his son visit Europe in the autumn "as an object of action of sufficient consequence to stimulate your minds."[53]

The idea assumed a more immediate significance for Dix when she learned that John Adams Dix planned to leave shortly for Italy after trying unsuccessfully for eighteen months to re-establish himself within the Democratic party. Dix suddenly decided to follow her own advice and join her adopted brother in exile from the Pierce administration.[54] Greenbank had once welcomed her more warmly than her family home, and she had vaguely dreamed of a reform campaign in Europe since meeting Fredrika Bremer.[55] Hastily she sent Elizabeth Rathbone a warning of her imminent arrival in Liverpool, along with apologies for the interruptions in their erratic correspondence.[56] Her spirits chastened but unvanquished, Dix set sail in early September 1854 for a new epoch of life.

Twenty-two-year-old Dix
and her seventy-eight-year-
old grandmother, Dorothy
Dix, in May 1824, on the
eve of publication of
*Conversations on Common
Things.* (By permission of the
Houghton Library, Harvard
University)

Thaddeus Mason Harris, portrait by Chester Harding from about 1820. (Boston Athenæum)

Dix considered this daguerreotype, taken around 1850, "the only picture that seems to me a good likeness, and to convey something of the *tone* and *type* of character." (By permission of the Houghton Library, Harvard University)

The New Jersey State Lunatic Asylum in 1848, Dix's beloved "first-born child." (By permission of the Trenton Psychiatric Hospital)

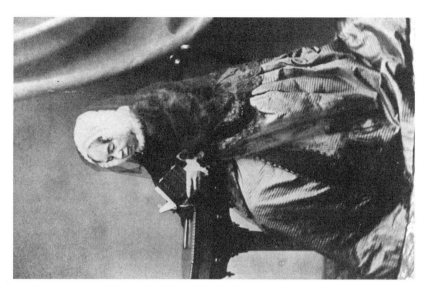

Anne Heath in 1864. (By permission of the Massachusetts Historical Society)

Elizabeth Rathbone in 1862. (Courtesy of the University of Liverpool Library, Rathbone Papers)

Godey's Lady's Book, January 1861. Firmament of benevolent womanhood, featuring Dix at the top left, Elizabeth Gurney Fry in the center, Florence Nightingale at the lower right, Grace Darling at the lower left, and Mary DuBois (founder of the New York Nursery and Child Hospital) at the top right. (By permission of the Houghton Library, Harvard University)

⊷ 10 ⊷

The American Invader

Dix's passage to Europe in September 1854 illustrated both the transportation revolution and the personal transformation that had taken place since her flight across the Atlantic eighteen years earlier. She traveled aboard the Collins steamship *Arctic,* one of the new federally subsidized ocean liners that had reduced the sailing voyage to a ten-day crossing. Line president E. K. Collins personally presented his distinguished passenger a complimentary berth with a private stateroom, but Dix trumped his publicity gesture by announcing that she would use the fare to buy herself a life insurance policy for the benefit of the Trenton asylum. The widely reported incident signaled that her second European trip would not be another timid retreat from calamity.

Although Dix enjoyed the company of several friends on board the *Arctic* and spoke eagerly of resting again at Greenbank, she aggressively began to pursue benevolent conquests even before the ship docked at Liverpool. Learning that some passengers had formed a gambling pool on the duration of the steamer's run, she prevailed on the winners to give the fund to charity. The next day, she collected a *"thank offering* for preservation thus far on our voyage," a solicitation that her shipmates may have thought less officious after the *Arctic* sank during its return to New York with a loss of almost four hundred lives. Dix interpreted the disaster as proof of the need for more lifeboats like her Sable Island fleet, which demonstrated its value in a dramatic Atlantic rescue immediately after the gift arrived in Nova Scotia in October. Once settled in Europe, she sought an equally vivid affirmation of her crusade on behalf of the insane.[1]

— 1 —

Weighing various plans while she visited the Rathbones during her first weeks abroad, Dix immediately repudiated her preliminary hints that she would make a leisurely trip to the Continent. "I have not the *slightest interest* in going into France, nor even Italy," she declared. "In contrast with the aim of my accustomed pursuits it seems the most trivial use of time."[2] As she spoke no foreign languages except the ruins of her forgotten French, she could hardly expect to lead a reform campaign outside of Britain. Inspections of European prisons and asylums would be pointless, she argued, if she could not act on her observations. "What should I gain or what would others gain by my passage through those dreary dungeons under the Piombino," she asked when Heath suggested that she could find both benevolent opportunities and artistic recreation in papal Rome.[3] She also refused to tie herself to any fellow travelers, including cherished friends like the family of John Adams Dix, who repeatedly urged her to join them in Italy. Defending her preference for a cold, damp autumn in Britain, she emphasized that "I can travel *alone* too without difficulty, which would be out of the question to attempt *on the Continent*."[4]

Dix had prepared effectively for a British campaign while characterizing her trip as an excursion for needed relaxation. Through Abbott Lawrence, the American minister to London during the Fillmore administration, she obtained letters of introduction to the brother of Elizabeth Fry and to Anthony Ashley Cooper, the seventh Earl of Shaftesbury.[5] The leader of the evangelical party in the Anglican church and a powerful force in Victorian reform politics, Shaftesbury was the most prominent statesman in the development of British policy toward the insane. He had sponsored the seminal Parliamentary legislation of 1845 that required every county in England and Wales to establish a public mental hospital and created a national Commission in Lunacy to supervise all insane asylums, and he had served as chairman of the commission since its inception. Looking forward to meeting his American counterpart in the promotion of mental hospitals, he foresaw a fruitful collaboration.

"We have some labour before us in the 'Reformatory way,' " he commented to a friend upon Dix's arrival, "but God be praised our prospects are better."[6]

In October 1854 Dix launched her first canvass of reform opportunities in Ireland, which had established a separate network of district asylums that were not regulated by the legislation of 1845. She took great satisfaction in pocketing her letters of introduction from Shaftesbury and other dignitaries in order to make her own way among the Irish hospitals, poorhouses, schools, and prisons. After one month she reported that she had "*compassed Ireland,* in a way few travellers have done before." The chief effect of this tour was to reinforce her disapproval of the vast migration from Ireland to the United States during recent years. Irish peasants were "sorely degraded by a thousand causes," she concluded, "and *we* reap the curse of a vicious population sent over to people our now fast corrupted and overburthened country." Although she thought the Irish asylums much worse than American institutions, she decided that they were sufficiently clean and well directed without her further attention.[7]

After resting at Greenbank for the last two months of the year, Dix turned her attention to Scotland, which like Ireland was beyond the jurisdiction of Shaftesbury's reforms. She organized her itinerary around visits to the prestigious Royal Asylums, which closely resembled the leading American mental institutions. She spent a week in Dumfries at the Crichton Royal Institution for Lunatics and another week in Glasgow, then continued north through the other Royal Asylums at Perth, Dundee, Montrose, and Aberdeen before turning south again toward Edinburgh. As in England and Ireland, she saw "nothing that satisfies me of Hospital treatment *this* side of the Atlantic so well as that on ours."[8]

On the main issue dividing American and British asylum practice, however, Dix's patriotic conclusion belied a deeper sympathy with the foreign approach to moral treatment. For the past decade, the most spectacular development in the British treatment of insanity had been the widespread abandonment of straitjackets, muffs, coercion chairs, and other mechanisms for the physical restraint of asylum patients. American superintendents regarded this movement cautiously, recognizing that self-discipline epitomized the ideal of the moral treatment but declining with a minimum of publicity to forswear altogether the use of restraints in the management of patients. Dix initially echoed this skepticism about "the great doctrine of *non-restraint.*" Gradually, however, her defense of American practices gave way to her view of asylum therapy as a method of internalizing standards of behavior. She began to "*strongly* advocate the largest possible *liberty* for patients," although she conceded to her friends in the United States that "I do not think that it is as easy to *direct* the poorer classes in *our* country as it is in Great Britain, where they are accustomed to being ruled both by their superiors and by *necessity.*"[9]

As usual, though, Dix remained less interested in the development than in the expansion of the moral treatment. Her ambivalent reaction to Scottish mental hospitals paled in comparison to her horror at the numerous private asylums for the insane poor. Licensed and nominally supervised by local magistrates, these commercial institutions scrambled to profit from meager parish outlays for the support of insane paupers. The asylum proprietors avoided costly attention to the residents, including routine medical treatment, and often shackled them to maintain order in the overcrowded warehouses. The rapacity of the "trade in lunacy," as contemporaries called the system, was notorious. A series of scandalous revelations about English private asylums, culminating in the appointment of a Parliamentary investigatory commission, had contributed significantly to the establishment of the permanent Commission in Lunacy and the county asylums of England and Wales. Shaftesbury and other reformers had proposed similar measures for Scotland, but their legislation had twice failed.[10]

Dix quickly made the problem of the Scottish private asylums her cause. She resolved in February 1855 that "I really cannot with a quiet conscience leave Great Britain till these abominable places are broken up or controlled." Of the various deficiencies in the licensed institutions, she identified the crucial flaw as nonmedical administration. "Miss Dix attaches much less importance to occasional improper means of restraint resorted to in some Houses, than to the want of qualification of persons conducting those for the right discharge of daily duties," she noted in a letter to Lord Advocate James Moncrieff. As in her American efforts, she would link her humanitarian appeal to the expansion of physicians' authority.[11]

Dix found a congenial circle of allies for her Scottish campaign. She felt especially comfortable in Edinburgh, a city that strikingly shared the cold climate, stern Calvinist heritage, and provincial outlook of Boston.[12] She settled into the city for several weeks and became friendly with physicians and professors in the distinguished medical community. Led by David Skae, the superintendent of the Edinburgh Royal Lunatic Asylum, several prominent doctors supported her determination to replace the private asylums with mental hospitals. Some other Scots, however, greeted her intervention less warmly. William Rathbone warned that she was treading on a resistance to London authority that she did not understand, but Dix was nonetheless disappointed by the opposition of W. A. F. Browne of the Crichton Royal Institution, one of the foremost European specialists in the treatment of insanity, who dubbed her "the American invader."[13] Concerned that similar antagonism might undermine her efforts, she asked a prominent society physician "to check the idea that some might naturally adopt that I *came here* to take up this measure—than which nothing was ever farther from my thoughts."[14]

In addition to resenting Dix as a meddlesome American, Browne also expressed a wariness about her intentions similar to the suspicions that doctors in the United States had long ago abandoned. He worried that her initiative, clearly tending toward the creation of a government regulatory board like Shaftesbury's Commission in Lunacy, might not only suppress the private asylums but weaken the independence of the medical Royal Asylums. Dix tried to reassure him that her goal was to secure medical control of institutions for the insane, noting that her plan was backed by other physicians interested in insanity. She anticipated that her work would duplicate Shaftesbury's reforms in England by establishing a system of public mental hospitals and a supervisory panel dominated by the medical profession.[15]

On February 26 Dix learned that one of her leading critics in Edinburgh planned to set off for London the next day to forestall her anticipated petition to the British government. She swiftly telegraphed a request to Shaftesbury for a conference and obtained a letter of introduction to the Duke of Argyll. Gathering her carpetbag, she jumped ahead of her opposition by taking the overnight mail train for London.[16]

Upon arriving in the metropolis for the first time, she learned that Shaftesbury had granted her an appointment despite his preoccupation with the Cabinet crisis of the Crimean War, which had elevated his father-in-law, Viscount Palmerston, to the office of Prime Minister three weeks earlier. From the train station Dix went to Argyll Lodge and asked the Duke to express the Scottish desire for reform to the Home Secretary, Sir George Grey. Satisfied that "an hour and a half conference settled matters," she next met with Shaftesbury, who joined enthusiastically in her new effort to secure the reforms that he had previously sought. Argyll and Shaftesbury agreed that she should immediately urge Grey to form an investigatory commission, but the plan was interrupted by an emergency council at Buckingham Palace. Exhausted by her train ride and the rapid developments of the day, she retired to the care of her banker, Junius Spencer Morgan, the husband of her former student Juliet Pierpont.[17]

Dix resumed her charge during the next few days, as Grey questioned his constitutional authority to establish the proposed commission without either parliamentary sanction or the concurrence of Lord Advocate Moncrieff. She appealed personally to the Home Secretary, and she cultivated some additional allies, most notably Queen Victoria's physician Sir James Clark. She also placed herself in Clark's care "as a sort of patient" to relieve an intense pain in her arm, which she diagnosed as inflammatory rheumatism and attributed to the exposure of her brief visits to Westminster Abbey and St. Paul's church.[18]

When Moncrieff endorsed her proposal within the week, clearing the way for Grey to appoint an investigatory commission, Clark prescribed a large celebratory dinner party as an antidote to Dix's current ailment. She took her medicine, viewing it as an opportunity to lobby for the parliamentary legislation that she correctly expected to emerge from the Scottish commission. "I have yet some things to ask and gain of her Majesties' Ministers and Her Majesty," she noted. She was not yet ready, though, for the honor of a royal presentation. Reinvigorated by success, she would wait to meet Victoria on her own terms. She wrote home to the United States: "I wish to see the Queen [but] when I do see her to *ask* for something for the good of others."[19]

— 2 —

Dix returned to Edinburgh with "a sort of half feeling that *I have done my part* and that the Commissioners must do theirs—without my aid."[20]

She remained vigilant against last-minute attempts to thwart the Scottish investigation and nominated the two physicians that Grey named to the four-member commission, but she was beginning to look ahead to new projects. She canceled her plans to return to the United States in the autumn because Britain seemed to offer more opportunities for usefulness. In April 1855 she confided to Elizabeth Rathbone that "I am considering the *chances* of my strength lasting if I undertake a Crusade against the *Private Houses* in England," which had been checked but not wholly eliminated by the competing public asylums and the Commission in Lunacy.[21]

Dix combined rest and preparation for an English campaign by spending part of the spring at the famous York Retreat with Daniel Hack Tuke, the great-grandson of William Tuke. The preliminary response to her plans, however, discouraged any more active steps. Clark pointed out that Shaftesbury's commission monopolized reform authority in England and that Dix could do little more than supplement its inspections of private asylums.[22]

Stymied in England, she concentrated on the Channel island of Jersey. Local physician D. H. van Leeuwen had urged her to visit the island and to agitate for government oversight of the Channel insane after he learned that an unscrupulous private asylum proprietor planned to escape from Shaftesbury's Commission in Lunacy by moving to Jersey. Dix's anticipation of the project illustrated her sense of exaltation in the overseas renewal of her vocation. She vowed to Heath that "I shall see their chains off. I shall take them into the green fields and show them the lovely little flowers and the blue sky, and they shall play with the lambs and listen to the song of the birds, 'and a little child shall lead them.'" "This is no romance," she assured solemnly, "this all will be if I get to the Channel Islands."[23] Ignoring Tuke's suggestion that she simply refer the problem to Shaftesbury, she left Liverpool for the Channel in early July 1855.

On her way, Dix paused in London for a reunion with Millard Fillmore, who had recently arrived in England for a European tour calculated to enhance his prospects for regaining the presidency in 1856. After several attempts to coordinate their schedules, they arranged a meeting at Dix's hotel in Piccadilly on July 3. The next day, Fillmore was the guest of honor at a gala Fourth of July dinner hosted by American financier George Peabody. Dix also attended the festivities, although like the other invited ladies she listened to the proceedings from behind a screen. She thoroughly enjoyed the patriotic occasion and the tribute to her friend, whom she thought "honored not less in the retirement of private life than he was honorable and valued as the Chief Magistrate." Apparently unaware that the two customers of his bank knew each other, Peabody relayed to Fillmore the complimentary remarks of "the celebrated Miss Dix."[24]

Upon arriving in Jersey, Dix immediately urged local officials to detain the private asylum proprietor contemplating flight to the Channel islands, and he was arrested soon afterward. As she had expected, she found the insane in the Jersey general hospital deplorably treated by unqualified attendants. She met with the governor and other leading citizens to call for the construction of a modern mental hospital, announcing that she would not seek government action in London if the people of Jersey moved forward independently. She toured the island with van Leeuwen to find a suitable site for the asylum, which she planned to call La Maison de l'Espérance, an echo of her old Hope-well school in Boston. Within two weeks local expressions of commitment to the asylum project satisfied her that she had achieved her purposes, although she worried that "I must *push* these people, or the building will not be finished till next century."[25]

Returning to a chorus of congratulations from her friends in England, Dix was at last willing to consider a visit to the Continent. The Rathbones invited her to meet them in Antwerp for a trip to Switzerland, the European country that she most wanted to see. Predicting that the home of Calvin would perfectly suit Dix, Elizabeth Rathbone urged that "I shall not feel able to enjoy Geneva myself unless I can think of you there it seems so exactly the place for you."[26] Dix pondered the invitation for several weeks, soliciting medical opinions from Clark, Tuke, and van Leeuwen about her ability to travel and recoiling from the Rathbones' suggestion that she bring a maid for assistance and companionship on the way to Antwerp. She assured her Liverpool friends that "I never felt desolate in my life, and I have been *much alone* in both populous and in thinly settled countries; for months, day after day, have met strangers, *never* seeing a person seen or known before."[27] Eventually she decided to take the vacation. She left London on August 6, promising to "forswear all hospitals & hospital thoughts" and "glide up & down the Rhine lazily."[28] In her trunk, however, she carried a request from van Leeuwen that she seek reforms in his home country, a set of directions to the worst Dutch asylums and the leading physicians, and a letter of introduction to the King of Holland.[29]

— 3 —

Contrary to the Rathbones' suspicions that Dix might forsake relaxation and launch another asylum campaign upon reaching the Continent, she joined the family on a leisurely journey to Switzerland. The eight-member party started by traveling from Antwerp to Cologne, where they toured the cathedral and boarded a steamer headed up the Rhine. After cruising slowly to Heidelberg, they completed the trip along the river in a train to Basel and then drove toward the Alps in a carriage. On August 20 they arrived in Geneva. Establishing their headquarters a few days later across the lake in Vevey, they explored the mountains for the next six weeks in sorties to Chamonix and the Bernese Oberland.[30]

For Dix, this excursion was "the great pleasure of my life." Her strength improved markedly under the influence of "the finest weather possible in the most magnificent country imaginable." The holiday was equally invigorating to her religious sensibility. She found that the Alps offered "the highest most spiritual happiness I ever enjoyed." "One felt that almost a new life of the soul had been attained," she later reflected, "through the contemplation of the sublime and glorious sky clearing heights which silently Praise the Creator from all time, through all time."[31]

Dix accompanied the Rathbones back to Liverpool in October 1855, but she decided to remain abroad through the winter. The calamity of the *Arctic* still haunted her, and although she had no specific plans in Europe, her future course was equally unclear in the United States, where new efforts for her land bill seemed pointless during the Pierce administration.[32] She knew only that her vacation was over. She had "outlived the period of mere *amusement*," she insisted, "and time must have a distinct use to be enjoyed."[33] At the end of the month, she formed a traveling party with Philadelphia physician Joseph Parrish and his wife to visit the public institutions of France, Germany, and Holland. By the first week of November she had arrived in Paris and settled into the Hôtel de Lille et Albion, a hotel popular among American tourists.

Through French asylum doctors friendly with her British medical connections, Dix soon obtained admission to the famous institutions for the insane in and around Paris. She began an ambitious schedule of visits to the Bicêtre and Salpêtrière, where Pinel had originated his version of the moral treatment, and to the vast national asylum at Charenton. She also visited many schools, and she examined a number of general hospitals and other specialized treatment centers to study French methods of nursing and hospital administration. Although impressed by the liberal government support that had helped to make Paris the acknowledged medical capital of the world, she found several "radical universal defects" in the hospitals of the city. She was shocked by the lack of ventilation, "which quite explains the amazing mortality," and sharply critical of "the well-known *experimental* methods of treatment by the *Internes,*—resident students." She also confirmed the dislike she had developed in the United States for Catholic nuns who worked as nurses in hospitals. "Some of them are very self denying, *not many,*" she reported to Trenton medical superintendent Horace Buttolph.[34]

Although she devoted most of her time to the study of charitable institutions, Dix also sampled the more typical activities of an American in Paris. She grumbled that her hotel was "thronged with English & Americans, none of them very attractive," but she was pleased to receive a call from Fillmore and the banker William Wilson Corcoran shortly after she arrived. A few days later, she had a more unexpected pleasure when she discovered that George B. Emerson and his wife were in Paris on a tour of Europe. Annoyed by Joseph Parrish's requests to join in her inspections, she gladly attached herself to her old Boston friends. She insisted that they move to her hotel, and for six weeks they met regularly for dinner or an evening glass of wine at the end of her daily work. She enjoyed the arrangement thoroughly, accompanying the Emersons to attractions ranging from Versailles to the Gaiétes. She particularly admired the Universal Exposition of 1855, in which thirty-four nations displayed contemporary arts and industries "in the most striking forms and modes" on the Champs Elysées.

For the Emersons, however, the renewed acquaintance with Dix almost spoiled the holiday of a lifetime. The recently retired schoolmaster had surrendered himself passionately to the experience of Europe, and he could scarcely bear Dix's stridently self-assured opinions. After they attended a performance of *Les Demoiselles de Saint Cyr* at the Théâtre Français, he sarcastically wrote home to his daughter that "We have the advantage of seeing Dolly every day, who knows every thing. You may conceive of her penetration. She was able to criticize the play last evening, though she certainly did not properly understand one sentence that was uttered, & had never heard of it before." On Christmas, he reported that "Your mother and I have come to the conclusion that saints are far less agreeable, at least in this world, than sinners, and that it would be pleasant to be left to the folly of our ways."[35]

Dix shared none of Emerson's enthusiasm for Paris. "I cannot imagine *what* constitute its so binding attractions to the many who resort thither," she wrote after two weeks. "I am quite ready to leave it as soon as I have seen all the Hospitals & Prisons." At its best, she decided, Paris was "as pleasant as any large noisy crowded city." To make matters worse, the constant November rains gave her a nagging cold, although she "invested myself with flannel as with a sort of armor."[36]

But Dix's principal complaint was neither the urban density nor the weather of Paris. She disliked the city as "*the heart* and *soul* and source of power" in France. "It is Government embodied," she objected. "The people are mere abstractions so far as vital will operating on society is considered." The subordination of personal independence under the Second Empire appalled her. She rebelled against the surveillance of the French police, nervously ridiculed the crowds at military reviews, and condemned the consolidation of state power through the charitable institutions that most interested her. "Hospitals, Hospices, Convents, Schools etc. gather in all who will relinquish their liberty and be subject to rules," she told Mary Torrey, "while those who neither will do this nor work must keep out of sight." The Catholic church seemed to her to present no hope for a regeneration of the French people, the only means by which she could imagine a reformation of society. The "strange basis" of French society was the opposite of her political and moral ideals. Dix concluded that "Americans do not know the blessing they possess—they *need* a little European experience."[37]

Dix's work also disenchanted her. Five weeks of studying French institutions left her "*very* impatient to see some thing *done*."[38] Suddenly changing her plan to go next to Holland, she decided to spend the winter in Italy. She turned south after Christmas, visiting hospitals on her way through Fontainbleau, Auxerre, Dijon, and Marseilles. The Emersons followed her, but not before her former mentor sent her a severely critical letter of advice about their six weeks together in Paris. Reunited on an excursion to Avignon, Dix was visibly wounded by the rupture in their friendship, although Emerson noted curiously that she was "sad and grieved, not irritated and hurt as I had expected."[39] She left Marseilles abruptly in the second week of January and sailed to Naples, alone once again.

— 4 —

After two weeks in Naples, where she examined the insane asylums with the aid of American chargé d'affaires Robert Dale Owen, Dix at last headed to Rome in February 1856. She had contemplated and resisted this step since crossing the Atlantic with John Adams Dix. Upon her arrival in Europe she had imagined herself confronting the pope over humanitarian reform of the Eternal City, a Protestant fantasy further stimulated by the historic stature of the present Catholic sovereign, Pius IX.[40] Since the restoration of his temporal administration after the revolutionary uprising of 1848, Pius had boldly sought to strengthen his besieged office. Through his chief advisor, Cardinal Giacomo Antonelli, he had undertaken a major civic construction program to pacify benighted, restless Rome. Seeking to expand his authority elsewhere, he had re-established the Catholic hierarchy in England, touching off religious strife that Dix called "a spiritual war."[41] And most dramatically, in the eyes of many critics he had asserted a claim to papal infallibility in December 1854 by proclaiming the dogma of the immaculate conception of the Virgin Mary, an absolute authority that his Vatican Council subsequently codified.[42]

Dix lost no time in concluding that Pius's policy toward the insane was conspicuously fallible. Visiting the insanity wards at the ancient Santo Spirito hospital on the day after her arrival in Rome, Dix quickly determined that "6000 priests, 300 monks, 3000 nuns, and a spiritual sovereign joined with the temporal Power had not assured for the miserable insane a decent much less intelligent care." She promptly called for a new asylum, launching "an appeal to the Pope which involved care, patience, time & negotiation."[43] She did not describe the details of that appeal in her letters, but it subsequently became one of her favorite reminiscences. Friends later repeated with relish that Antonelli had arranged a private audience in which Dix stunned Pius with her account of the suffering insane in the Roman asylum. The pope reportedly verified her description in an unannounced inspection, then thanked her profusely in a second interview and promised to build a new mental hospital immediately.[44]

Whether this dramatic tale accurately recounted Dix's appeal to Pius, or even faithfully related her version of events, the story clearly expressed the impulses animating her initiative. She argued that "the *very shame* of Foreign & Protestant interposition quickened them to action or *promise* rather than humanity."[45] By the middle of February, she told friends that she had received "Papal promises and *Cardinal* assurances of immediate action in remedying abuses and supplying deficiencies" and that the Vatican had purchased land and proposed plans for an asylum. "Poor man!" exclaimed George Emerson when she told him of her siege of the pope.[46]

Dix left Rome after two weeks, triumphant in her reforms. But reasoning that "nobody trusts *the word* of the Roman Priests *as a body,*" she warned that if the plans were not carried out she would "go to Rome and stay till they *do* what is needed." For the present she went to Florence, where again she was shocked by the treatment of the insane. Reporting "mountains of difficulties in the way of remedy for serious ills," she declared that "I have the idea of *mining these mountains*—and seeing if Protestant energy cannot work what Catholic power fails to undertake." To her disappointment, however, she soon learned that the fiscal drain of Florentine military defenses against Austria precluded the construction of a new asylum. As in Naples and Rome, she devoted little attention to the masterpieces of art and only slightly more time to the colonies of Americans, but she did meet Mary Turner Torrey's newest cousin, six-week-old John Singer Sargent, and wrote back to Boston that the baby was "already a darling pet & idol."[47]

Dix's pace quickened as she became more comfortable in moving through Europe without attaching herself temporarily to a touring party. After ten days in Florence, she continued north to Genoa and Turin. "It is just as easy travelling alone here as it is England or America," she concluded by early March. "I now regret I had not sooner tried the practicality of what I so lately have proved." Despite this sense of freedom, she passed rapidly across the region of Italy that she most enjoyed. Although she had recently promised to stay on the Continent through May to monitor the progress of the new Roman mental hospital and expected to remain abroad until autumn, she felt that "I have not time for long pauses anywhere."[48] She turned quickly from Turin to Milan and after three days left for Venice.

Dix expressed no concern that her travels had accelerated without evident purpose in the wake of her grand encounter with the pope. Although she had arranged her trip to lead through Austria and Germany into Holland, she continued to express faith that divine revelation would spontaneously direct her course. "I *seek* no work," she maintained, "but the will of God is made clear to me as I walk in the devious roads of this world." As her tour of Italy reached its end at the sea, she looked to that guidance at a new turning point in her journey.[49]

— 5 —

Even while Dix was observing that "my plans appear to be about as stable as firm breezes," an exhilarating new vision of her next destination was racing through her mind. "You need not be much surprised to hear of me in Constantinople," she warned Mary Torrey in the first week of March 1856. She explained that "I have for a long time felt distressed at the horrid histories of suffering in the Prisons & Hospitals there, yet, till quite lately have not had a thought of personally undertaking any thing in that quarter." The situation had changed with the February opening of the Congress of Paris for final resolution of the suspended Crimean hostilities between Russia and the alliance of Britain, France, and Turkey. Dix now suggested that "something might be *commenced* in the way of reform" to ameliorate the gruesome treatment of the insane that Samuel Gridley Howe and Pliny Earle had described after their visits to Turkey.[50]

To some observers, Dix's response to the Crimean peace seemed like a new military assault. Matilda Lieber described her plan as a charge into single combat. "She found the hospitals in Rome in a sad condition and got the promise from the Pope to build a new one for the insane," Lieber told Fanny Longfellow. "She goes to Turkey to see what the Sultan is doing with his mad people. What a woman!"[51] Boston reformer Franklin Benjamin Sanborn later agreed that Dix "rejoiced in a trial of strength with the Sultan."[52] But although they rightly recognized Dix's zest for dramatic personal confrontation, Lieber and Sanborn misunderstood the inspiration for this abrupt change of itinerary. Her sudden concern for the insane of Turkey was not spurred by any desire to challenge the ruler of the Ottoman Empire. She turned her crusade to Constantinople mainly to meet the great heroine of the subsiding war, Florence Nightingale.

Dix had inevitably followed Nightingale's spectacular career during the critical phases of the dismal military expedition against Russia. Arriving in England as the allied troops were crossing the Black Sea to invade the Crimean peninsula, Dix soon found that "little is talked of here beside the horrible war in the Crimea." The distant suffering came home to the English public in shocking vividness through an important innovation in journalism, the dispatches of a special correspondent to the *Times.* Dix tried unsuccessfully to avoid the accounts of such battle-field disasters as the suicidal charge of the Light Brigade. "I am sick of the details of these miseries and *never* read the Bulletins," she told Buttolph, "but one must hear conversation on these subjects except one turns hermit at once."[53]

Dix took a strong interest, however, in the crucible of war on the home front. "Trouble is on all sides," she observed after the collapse of the Aberdeen ministry during the protracted siege of Sevastopol. She predicted that increased economic pressures would intensify the bitter class divisions of Britain and that wartime anxiety and grief would lead to a sharp increase in the incidence of insanity. "There is little prospect of the soon coming of the kingdom of heaven on earth," she lamented, "and the peace which is of Christ and his doctrines."[54]

Like admirers throughout the world, Dix saw Nightingale as a beacon of hope in the Crimean quagmire. After leaving London in October 1854 with a small band of women to serve in the British hospitals at Scutari, the thirty-four-year-old Superintendent of Nurses had quickly become one of the most celebrated figures of the century. The *Times* frequently applauded her administrative reform of the disorganized, undersupplied military hospitals and her vigilant ministrations to soldiers, and the newspaper sent a correspondent to Turkey to help her disburse a large relief fund that it had collected for the troops. Dix followed the medical stories with interest and suggested that Buttolph and Kirkbride might benefit from them. Apart from her special attention to issues of hospital administration, moreover, she saw Nightingale's example as a powerful source for the moral redemption of the nation during the wartime crisis. "All the women in England who have not gone out as nurses, are making flannel shirts and knitting socks & mitts for the soldiers in the acting army," Dix observed in December 1854. "Thus the virtues and the Charities have something positive to hinder their gaddings and falling into idle ways." Similarly, Nightingale's work had sparked an outpouring of financial donations from citizens across the country to complement the *Times* fund, an inspiration of charity that climaxed in her designation as the almoner of Queen Victoria's gifts to the soldiers.[55]

Thus when Dix set off for Constantinople at the end of March 1856, her most astute friends were only surprised that she had not made the journey earlier. As Francis Lieber recognized, the meeting seemed to be ordained by the artistic logic of her career if not by a higher power. "Florence Nightingale is the *pendant* in my mind to your picture," he told Dix when he learned her destination. "I love her, too. I think myself happy that I have lived in a period which produced these two types of noble, truly feminine yet persevering and single hearted woman as Dix and Nightingale."[56]

Steaming from Venice to Constantinople, Dix made most of the landings to examine hospitals and prisons. From Corfu she reported that she found "travelling *alone* perfectly easy and attended *substantially* with no greater difficulties than in the United States." Proud of her self-reliance, she noted that "I take no refusals, and yet I speak neither Italian, German, Greek or Slavonic. I have *no* letters of Introduction, and know no persons en route."[57]

While in Athens, she learned that the Congress of Paris had adopted terms to end the Crimean War. Her immediate reaction to "the blessed news of peace" was subdued. "We give devout thanks that the horrors of warfare are arrested," she reflected to William Rathbone, "but how long it must be before the wounds which have been inflicted on social and domestic happiness are healed or forgotten." She continued to look forward to a spiritual rehabilitation of the combatants more thorough-going than a diplomatic treaty. "I feel that Miss Nightingale will have a *great work* still in the East," she predicted. "God bless her exertions!"[58]

The primary purpose of Dix's journey became clear immediately after she arrived in the Bosporus on April 10. Landing on the European shore of the strait at Pera, north of Constantinople, she stepped into a caïque and said two words to the ferrymen: "Hospital! Scutari!" Within a half-hour they rowed her across the Bosporus to Scutari, where Dix asked an English sailor for directions to the nurses' quarters.[59] She then strode to the army hospital, as she had so often appeared unannounced at prisons, almshouses, and asylums, to present herself to Nightingale.

Unfortunately, however, Nightingale had left Scutari a few weeks earlier to work at the main British base on the Crimea at Balaclava. Dix's eagerly anticipated encounter frustrated, she examined the Barrack Hospital, the principal site of the nurses' operations. Finding it in excellent order, she returned across the Bosporus to Constantinople to start the next day on her investigation of Turkish insane asylums.

Dix was not surprised by the impressive organization of Nightingale's famous hospital at Scutari, but she hastened to profess that the facilities for the insane in Constantinople "quite astonished me." The medical superintendent of the principal mental hospital had trained in Paris and implemented a Western program of moral treatment. Dix gratefully determined that "I *had substantially* little to suggest, and *nothing* to urge!!!" In her visits to other Turkish hospitals and prisons in the area, she similarly "failed to discover . . . any examples of abuse and barbarous usage." She directed most of her criticisms to the nearby Greek and American hospitals, concluding after two weeks in Constantinople that "the Mahometans have *now* at least, there, quite the advance of the *Christians,* in *Christian* practices."[60]

As Nightingale remained across the Black Sea indefinitely, Dix decided to leave Constantinople without meeting the Superintendent of Nurses. By continuing east she could now fulfill her lifelong dream of visiting the Holy Land, which she said she "desired more than any thing beside" in her foreign travels. But she "resisted the very great temptation" and refused to divert her personal crusade. "*As yet I have confined my journies* to those places where *Hospitals,* and the *want* of them has called me," she explained. Instead she prepared to turn west again. During her inspection of Trieste she had met a physician in the service of Archduke Maximilian who promised to provide her with access to Austrian public institutions. Although she foresaw little prospect for a reform campaign, she reasoned that "if I do not see much to amend, I may discover something to copy for application at home." On April 22, she took passage on the steamer *Ferdinando* to investigate the treatment of mental illness in Vienna.[61]

— 6 —

Her European goals satisfied by her successes in Britain and Rome, and her desire to meet Nightingale temporarily checked, Dix gave free rein to her taste for wandering after she left Turkey. Because the Greek and Italian ports along the Mediterranean route to Austria were closed for quarantine to ships from Constantinople, she decided to take "the more novel and to me more interesting route" of crossing the Black Sea and then steaming up the Danube. After foul weather kept her on board until the ship had entered the river, she made her first landing at Galatz. She toured "the Hospital which was neat and clean, and the Prison which was neither," in this "mean poor looking place," and she curiously watched the Greek Orthodox observance of Good Friday. She declared that she was "strongly tempted" to make a detour to Jassy, the capital of Moldavia, to protest the common practice of placing the insane in monasteries, where they were "subject to the most mistaken treatment which sometimes results in death (mercifully), and oftenest in incurable insanity." She quickly rejected this idea, however, because of the daunting language barrier, the instability of the provincial government, and the unpleasant prospect of a lengthy stay in Moldavia.[62]

Dix's trip through Moldavia, Walachia, and Serbia was one of the most exotic passages in her many years of travel. Not even the American consul in Galatz spoke English, and Dix reported that "Babel is not illy illustrated" by the astonishing host of nations represented aboard her boat, on which she was the only passenger from the United States or England. "I am afraid I shall be *obliged* to write a Book, a sort of Narrative of what I have seen during my long absence," she sighed in May 1856, reflecting on her unconventional European tour. At the same time, however, she recognized that her correspondents must "wonder that I give so meager descriptions of persons & places." Too occupied by public institutions to study foreign manners or scenes, she spent even less time forming her impressions in writing. Moreover, the constant refrain of her dispatches indicated that her most vivid journey was once again inward. Her voyage up the Danube tended toward the same conviction of self-sufficiency she had achieved long ago in the United States. "I find travelling here alone *no more difficult* than I should do in any part of America," she declared to Heath from Ossora, Hungary.[63]

Shortly before Dix arrived in Vienna, she received word that "the Pope has listened to my remonstrance & intercession" and restored the physician she supported to the superintendency of the asylum at Santo Spirito. She concluded that the appointment adequately proved Pius's commitment to reform and "augurs well for the residue of my petition & the fulfillment of the distinct assurances I received before I left Rome." Happy to free herself from her threat to return to the Vatican, she announced in Belgrade that she felt "so earnestly desirous to get again to England, that I shall allow no ordinary obstacles to interfere with my direct route, via Holland."[64] After studying the institutions of Vienna for a few weeks, she proceeded to Germany. There she passed rapidly through the hospitals of Dresden, Gounesteria, Hubersenberg, Leipzig, Stetteria, Halle, and Berlin. She made a rare detour from her course on May 23 to see Wittenberg, where she enjoyed a "very satisfactory visit to all the places of *pilgrim* resort" connected with the life of Martin Luther.[65]

Her determination to return directly to England was short-lived. Not wanting to arrive in the United States during the oppressive heat of summer, she determined that she could travel in Europe for several more weeks before making a leisurely final visit to Liverpool. After a conversation with the American minister in Berlin, she decided to go north to Russia and Scandanavia. In late May 1856 she took the three-day trip across the Baltic to St. Petersburg, where winter clothing remained in order.[66]

Dix saw "much to approve and appreciate" in Russia and concluded that "as for the Insane in the Hospitals in St. Petersburg and at Moscow, I really had nothing to ask. Every comfort and all needed care was possessed, and much recreation secured." Her holistic conception of moral treatment now in ascendancy over her national pride, she observed contentedly that "very little restraint was used."[67] She tried to nudge asylum physicians at home in the same direction. "I have long felt that our friends who direct American Institutions mistake in not giving all the totally tranquil patients, much more exercise and liberty abroad & within doors than is their usage,—also more employment," she suggested to Kirkbride and Buttolph. "I know how difficult this is, but I see it accompanied with excellent results *here* in Europe."[68]

The asylums of Denmark seemed less satisfactory to Dix than Russian mental hospitals and she was "inexpressibly pained" by the condition of the insane in Sweden, but she was pleased to learn that both countries were building new institutions. As elsewhere in her travels, she found time in Scandanavia to see the other attractions that she valued. She particularly enjoyed a visit to Upsala, Sweden, undertaken "with the double object of seeing there a small Hospital, and of visiting the scenes of the gentle life of Linnaeus . . . to whose system I still adhere with partiality of early interests." In July 1856, after almost six weeks in Russia and Scandanavia, she pronounced her northern excursion a success in her usual terms. "I find no difficulty in travelling alone, and see all that is important," she concluded.[69]

Summer finally caught up with Dix when she arrived in Holland. Severely fatigued by the first hot weather she had experienced in Europe, she curtailed the reform efforts that she had anticipated since leaving England exactly one year earlier. On the urging of physicians in Rotterdam and Utrecht she met with regulatory commissioners to discuss the treatment of the insane, but she was too exhausted for any strenuous work. She asked the Rathbones to book her return passage to the United States at the end of August or the beginning of September and headed back toward England.[70]

She stopped in Belgium, however, to see the famous Geel colony for the insane that she had long ago urged New York to imitate as an alternative to mental hospitals for incurable patients. She reached the medieval religious shrine shortly after it had again become a focus of conflict among Americans interested in insanity. John Galt of the Eastern State Lunatic Asylum in Williamsburg, Virginia, an iconoclast in the Association of Medical Superintendents, had published an article in the *American Journal of Insanity* in April 1855 charging that the Association's dogmatic promotion of hospitals was ineffective and oppressive. As Dix had suggested eleven years earlier, he pointed to Geel as a model for the inexpensive, unrestrictive management of chronically insane paupers through active employment.[71]

The superintendents lashed out against Galt as Amariah Brigham had previously attacked Dix, but she now followed the dispute as the foremost advocate of mental hospitals and an insider among the professional elite. Kirkbride seethed privately to her that Galt "never comes to the meetings, makes no improvements himself, but sits in his armchair criticizing whatever is done by his more active brethren." Buttolph sent her the minutes of the convention at which the Association had lambasted Galt; at the same meeting, the superintendents had also heard a paper from Buttolph and Nichols excerpting Dix's letters from Europe and had formally asked her to deliver her comments on foreign institutions at the next annual convention. She offered Buttolph an evaluation of the controversial Belgian colony in the same letter that acknowledged these tributes. Despite her enhanced appreciation for the principle of nonrestraint, her view of the controversial colony contrasted sharply with her earlier idyllic vision of Geel. "I see benefit for a portion of them," she concluded, "but much ill for the majority, especially the curative cases."[72]

Dix ended her Continental tour traveling with the popular British author Anna Jameson. She formed a fast friendship with the venerable literary socialite, and if she had not read Jameson's best-selling books about Shakespearean heroines, historic female sovereigns, and Christian iconography, she quickly recognized a moral and aesthetic sensibility much like her own. Returning from Belgium through Paris, she was delighted when Jameson took her to meet Elizabeth Barrett Browning.[73]

Jameson's most recent work was of special interest to Dix. Attentive throughout her career to the social position of women and keenly alert to the tides of popular interest, Jameson had become a leading promoter of nursing as a vocation for women, a cause that Nightingale's adventures in the Crimea had made one of the most often discussed movements of the day. Eighteen months earlier, Jameson had issued a widely read proposal for the founding of a Protestant sisterhood comparable to the Catholic nuns who served in hospitals, and she had lately elaborated her ideas after conducting an extensive survey of French, German, and Italian hospitals to study methods of training and organizing nurses. She and Dix undoubtedly compared their notes on medical institutions and their visions of a female Protestant vocation. In the convergence of these subjects, the rise of nursing presented Dix with a development that mirrored her own life's mission.

— 7 —

Back in London by the middle of August 1856, Dix resumed her efforts to meet Florence Nightingale. The heroine of the Crimean War had returned to England one week earlier, slipping past a gauntlet of newspapers and welcoming festivities to enter directly into the embrace of an adoring nation. While Nightingale rested at Lea Hurst, her family's estate in Derbyshire, Dix mentioned her desire for an interview to Charles and Selina Bracebridge, the Superintendent's chief lieutenants at Scutari. Charles Bracebridge answered that Nightingale had not yet received anyone but that they were anxious for a meeting of the benevolent paragons and that the encounter could easily be arranged. Nightingale, whose relations with her family were scarcely less strained than Dix's, would soon be leaving Lea Hurst to visit Atherstone Hall, the Bracebridges' estate near Coventry. As the Rathbones had booked Dix's return passage for September 17, wishing to see her off to America after the excitement of a new grandchild subsided at Greenbank, Dix and Bracebridge planned for her to meet Nightingale immediately after Dix traveled for two additional weeks in England and France.[74]

While waiting to see Nightingale, Dix went to Bristol to meet the distinguished reformatory school founder Mary Carpenter, who welcomed her as "a sister labourer."[75] She then proceeded to Salisbury to inspect the hospital and cathedral, and on August 30 she again crossed the Channel. In the following week she saw many of the important hospitals that she had not examined during her previous stay in France. "Alas the shortening days!" she sighed as she whirled through institutions in Rouen, Orleans, Blois, Tours, and Nantes, pausing only to visit the cathedral in Orleans and see the statues commemorating Joan of Arc. She ended her trip at Paris to inspect two communities for juvenile offenders and make a final visit to Salpêtrière.[76]

Dix returned to England on September 5 and spent the next few days at hospitals in Oxford and Birmingham before notifying the Bracebridges that she was near Atherstone Hall. On the day after her meeting with Nightingale had been arranged, however, Sir James Clark had invited the national idol to visit his Scottish estate in mid-September as a prelude to a momentous conference with Queen Victoria at nearby Balmoral Castle. Nightingale had gone as expected to visit the Brace-bridges at Atherstone Hall, but she had left with them for her parents' home on September 7. The Bracebridges accordingly did not receive Dix's letter until they returned home on September 10, the day before Nightingale's departure for Scotland. Hastily, Charles Bracebridge wrote back that Nightingale hoped Dix would come to Derbyshire.

Dix considered following Bracebridge's detailed directions to Lea Hurst, but she decided under the awkward circumstances to forego the eagerly anticipated meeting. She settled for a closely written twelve-page letter from Charles Bracebridge that attempted to satisfy her desire for more information about Nightingale's philosophy of nursing and her plans for a campaign to reform military hospitals.[77]

Dix was soon irked by her *"then indolent* feelings" in failing to meet Nightingale, but she was otherwise jubilant about her sojourn in Europe when she embarked for the United States on September 17. Two years of triumph had diverted if it could not erase the bitter frustration of Franklin Pierce's veto. Her Scottish commission had completed a comprehensive survey of facilities for the insane and prepared a report to Parliament urging the establishment of a public asylum system and a permanent regulatory commission to implement medical control of all mental institutions. She had received word that the island of Jersey was beginning construction on a new asylum, and a Paris meeting with the physician appointed by Pius IX confirmed her satisfaction in her intercession with the pope. She had studied countless hospitals and other public institutions, urged administrative improvements to government officials throughout Europe, and established personal friendships with some of the most eminent Victorian social reformers. Sailing wistfully from England, she promised that she would return to Greenbank to help the Rathbones celebrate their golden wedding anniversary, if they should all still be alive in March 1862.[78]

11

Our People Need to Suffer

Dix's triumphant tour of Europe not only renewed her spirits but expanded her range of interests in social reform. She had always conceived of her asylum campaign in the broadest terms, as a moral education for the sane as well as a therapeutic advance for the insane. But in contrast to her many contemporaries who promoted several different causes, she had maintained a sharp focus in her political efforts. Now, after returning to the United States at the end of September 1856, she increasingly saw her work as part of a common crusade for the regeneration of humanity. She began to ask Elizabeth Rathbone regularly for news about the activities of Florence Nightingale, Anna Jameson, and Mary Carpenter, as well as reports about Rathbone's own benevolent exertions in Liverpool. "Our work of *Reforms* seems gigantic and most discouraging if the whole field is taken in at one view," Dix reflected, "but if each does his or her part we may hope for final success."[1]

— 1 —

While Dix's reform sympathies were widening, however, the focus of American public life was rapidly contracting. In the two years since the veto of her land bill and the passage of the Kansas-Nebraska Act, the chronic conflict over slavery had turned into an unprecedented crisis. In the Kansas territory, civil war between proslavery and antislavery factions had fused a host of personal, economic, and political rivalries. Throughout the North and the South, the prospect of a violent sectional clash

240

had crystallized four months before Dix's return when her old friend Charles Sumner was beaten senseless in the Senate by a South Carolina congressman.

Dix had distanced herself from this excitement as much as possible while in Europe. "The slavery question I positively ignore," she declared firmly. She read no American newspapers, maintaining that "ignorance is the best discretion" in the crisis, and she frustrated some of her hosts by refusing to discuss the riveting situation despite her personal familiarity with the principal actors. The occasional lapses of her reticence underscored her hostility toward agitation by either section. She deplored "the outrages of the Missourians" who streamed across the state border to impose a proslavery government on Kansas, but she was no less critical of Harriet Beecher Stowe, whose antislavery stance had received enthusiastic acclaim during the novelist's recent tour of Britain. *Uncle Tom's Cabin,* Dix protested, had "produced the most mistaken and often absurd notions of America and American life." Overhearing a fellow train passenger remark that Stowe deserved more appreciation at home, Dix acidly interjected that "if she ever rendered any services to her country or to any section of it more than tens of thousands of other respectable wives and mothers had done—it has not been as yet known in the United States."[2]

Dix's antipathy toward the slavery controversy was strengthened by her hopes that the country would address other issues. Specifically, she dreamed that "some wholesome change in our National Government" would revive the prospects of her bill for a federal land grant to endow state mental hospitals. More generally, her travels through Ireland and the Catholic countries of Europe had reinforced her nativist leanings. Appalled by the massive immigration she had seen before she left Boston, for years she had quietly supported restrictions on the voting rights of new citizens and doubted that foreign-born physicians could succeed as asylum superintendents. In the expansion of her goals while abroad, she moved more openly toward the political nativism that had crested in the United States around the time of her departure. Her only significant attempt to lobby Congress from Europe was a letter urging Sumner to seek legislation that would check the continuing influx of immigrants.[3]

Uneasy about the direction of the country and uncertain about her own next project, Dix spent much of the month after her return absorbed in the most bitterly polarized presidential election in two decades. She knew each of the three candidates, but she could recognize none of the political parties that had emerged from the last two years of tumult. The Whig party, the former bulwark of support for her legislation, had utterly disintegrated. The Democratic party nominally endured, but the devastation of its northern wing after the passage of the Kansas-Nebraska Act had placed the states-rights opponents of her land bill firmly in control. Presidential nominee James Buchanan, with whom she had recently dined while he was the American minister to England, stood squarely on the party platform opposing any distribution of the proceeds from public land sales.

Dix enjoyed much closer ties with the new Republican party. Among its founders and leaders were most of her staunchest former Whig, Democratic, and Free Soil allies in Congress, including William H. Seward, Solomon Foot, Hannibal Hamlin, William Bissell, Salmon P. Chase, and Charles Sumner. The Republican nominee for president was John C. Frémont, whose wife and chief advisor, Jessie Benton Frémont, had admired Dix since they met in the home of her father, Thomas Hart Benton, during the debates over the Compromise of 1850. Despite these connections, however, Dix saw mostly reckless opportunism in the party that was rallying around an insistence on the exclusion of slavery from all federal territories. "What *strange* political misdoings disgrace our country!" she exclaimed shortly after the Republican convention. "I am ashamed of and for my fellow citizens who forget their true dignity in petty trials and party discords." Apart from the dangers of antislavery agitation, moreover, her loyalties depended above all on her judgment of each candidate's personal character, and she thought the Pathfinder of the West not only too impetuous but "vague and silly" as well.[4]

Dix's sympathies were with the new American party, a group of former Whigs and xenophobic Know Nothings who sought to restore the political order of the years before the Kansas-Nebraska crisis. The nebulous American platform of national harmony and nativism aptly matched Dix's views, but her support was shaped primarily by the party's nomination of Fillmore for a new term in Washington. She even wished that her closest political friend had declined the American nomination, hoping that the Republican movement would collapse and open a better opportunity. Failing any such stroke of luck, she exchanged letters weekly with the candidate in October 1856 and exerted as much private influence as she could. "I am not a declamatory politician," she commented to the former president on her self-appointed role as his informal spokeswoman, "but many discussions occur in my presence and a quiet word or two now and then might not be useless." She set firm limits on her commitment, however, pointedly declining his invitation to pay a public visit to his campaign headquarters in Buffalo during the race.[5]

Dix was disappointed but not surprised that Buchanan won the election. The more remarkable result was the strong Republican showing in the North. If the realignment of parties had confirmed her dim regard for politicians, the support for Frémont ratified her contempt for the general public. "The masses are too ignorant, the educated too busy, too self-seeking or too procrastinating to heed the real facts of our National position," she told Fillmore a few days after he lost. Naively certain that the overwhelming majority of Republican voters shared her preference for Fillmore over Frémont, she expressed amazement that they had not sacrificed the party's antislavery platform to support the better man. "One cannot but wonder how little men do to accomplish the idea of their own highest perception," she lamented.[6]

Even more discouraging to Dix, she saw no signs that the electoral upheaval educated the country. Three weeks later, she complained that "our busy, money-making, and excitable people, from the hour of casting their votes seem to forget that greedy politicians, and wordy demagogues have ruled *them* and made them *their* tools for selfish and narrow ends." The nation would improve, she predicted, only after a deeper crisis had instilled Americans with self-discipline. "I have not attempted to plunge into the turbid stream of circumstances out of which the *present* has emerged, and which was at its full height during my absence," she concluded, "but I have learned enough to convince me that our people need to *suffer* in order to bring them to . . . regulate national affairs with such prudence as shall assure security."[7]

— 2 —

Unable to see a congenial role for herself in national affairs, Dix resumed her work in the states for the first time in five years. The context of her mission had changed significantly since her celebrated campaigns of the late 1840s and early 1850s. Her own spectacular success and the broader advance of the asylum movement now limited the opportunities available to her. All but the smallest and the newest states had founded institutions providing the moral treatment of insanity. Several states had established second mental hospitals, and other states were considering the expansion of their facilities for the insane, but Dix could no longer win the precedent-setting victories of helping to create the first public asylums.

Paradoxically, moreover, Dix faced a grave erosion in the asylum movement as well as the consequences of its triumph. Her favorite cause shared in the broad decline of American enthusiasm for social reform during the 1850s. As the continued building of new hospitals indicated, the moral treatment of insanity did not abruptly collapse, as did the parallel interest in prison discipline, but John Galt's recent criticisms of asylums reflected a spreading sense of disillusionment among informed observers. Contrary to the asylum advocates' vision of a well-ordered therapeutic community, most state mental hospitals had become overcrowded custodial institutions for chronic cases. Asylums designed to accommodate approximately 250 patients now often housed almost twice as many, a frightening percentage of whom would spend the rest of their lives in mental institutions. From hospital to hospital, the regimen of labor and spiritual reformation was giving way to a torpid monotony and the more frequent use of mechanical restraints.[8]

Like most asylum physicians, Dix disregarded evidence that the moral treatment had not fulfilled its promise to cure insanity. She and her allies instead blamed the deterioration of asylums on the rapid increase and changing character of the American population. The building of mental hospitals had not kept pace with the growth of the country, and moral therapy seemed to be lost on the immigrant Irish paupers who now dominated the public asylums of the Northeast. Rather than joining the slowly gathering reappraisal of the asylum system upon her return to American public life, therefore, Dix merely added a nativist tinge to the renewal of her previous goal: the establishment of more state mental hospitals.

She resumed her crusade in New York, the state that most clearly illustrated the sources of support for the asylum movement and the undercurrent of doubt threatening it. The Albany legislature had not established any new facilities for insane paupers since adding a wing to the New York State Lunatic Asylum in 1844, and the crowded Utica hospital was sending scores of applicants to the county almshouses each year. Seeking relief from this burden, the county Superintendents of the Poor began in 1855 to lobby for the establishment of two more public mental hospitals, one in the eastern and one in the western region of the state. The Association of Medical Superintendents and the New York State Medical Society strongly backed the effort to advance their program for the treatment of insanity. Some physicians also candidly welcomed the drive as a valuable professional opportunity; D. Tilden Brown of the Bloomingdale Asylum, exasperated by the New York Hospital trustees, confessed unabashedly to Dix that he wanted her to establish a hospital under his control as she had for his predecessor, Charles Nichols. At the same time, however, Utica assistant physician John B. Chaplin pointed out in the *American Journal of Insanity* that the proposed new hospitals would still leave almost 2,000 chronic cases in county almshouses. Anticipating the corollary argument that the state should build a custodial, nontherapeutic institution instead of one of the proposed hospitals, the asylum advocates adopted a resolution affirming the Association of Medical Superintendents' position that separate facilities should not be created for curable and incurable patients.[9]

Dix showed no sign that she saw any relationship between the current situation in New York and her unsuccessful 1843–1844 campaign in which the superintendents had defined their opposition to asylums for chronically insane paupers. Without attempting to re-examine the policy of building more hospitals, she devoted herself to recapturing the sense of determination that had sustained her through the numerous state campaigns she had waged before concentrating her energies on Washington. She arrived in New York in early December 1856 and set out to inspect its public institutions. As the county Superintendents of the Poor had recently conducted a thorough survey of the insane, she traveled selectively to the most notorious almshouses in western and central New York and to some other hospitals, prisons, and public institutions in and around the state. The bitter winter of 1856–1857, the coldest in decades, made the journey a brutal ordeal. Characteristically, she sought to channel her suffering into a more powerful benevolent

245

will. "In proportion as my own discomforts have increased," she wrote at the end of the year, "my conviction of the necessity to search into the wants of the friendless and afflicted has deepened. If I am cold they are colder—if I am weary they are distressed—if I am alone they are abandoned and cast out."[10]

Upon arriving in Albany in January for the start of the legislative session, however, Dix saw little place for herself in the well-organized asylum campaign. She could depend on a hearty welcome and political support from Governor Charles King, the brother of her former congressional ally and close friend James Gore King, but the asylum bill was clearly in the hands of its sponsor, Mark Spencer, and the county Superintendents of the Poor. Unneeded by the asylum advocates and increasingly interested in other issues, she devoted much of her attention to different public institutions. She called for the reorganization of several county almshouses, a revision of state poor laws, and improvements in prisons, reformatory schools, orphanages, and inebriate asylums.[11]

When she realized that she had no pressing reason to remain in Albany, Dix took up an invitation to try a somewhat different campaign. Joseph Parrish, her sometime traveling companion in France, had asked for her aid in his new position as superintendent of the Pennsylvania Training School for Idiotic and Feeble-Minded Children. The third public institution of its type in the United States, the Pennsylvania Training School exemplified a growing effort to apply principles of asylum therapy to the problem of congenital mental incapacity. The Germantown institution had been founded by the first instructor at Samuel Gridley Howe's pioneering school for the feeble-minded in South Boston, and it similarly implemented the ideas of French physician Edouard Seguin, a former student of one of Philippe Pinel's protégés. Seguin's vision of the training school closely imitated Pinel's plan for the insane asylum in its emphasis on an isolated, wholesome environment governed by a doctor whose strong personal relationship with his charges would complement a vigorous physical regimen and inspire the feeble-minded to improve their condition.[12]

Dix responded readily to Parrish's request. Her legislative memorials had often grouped "idiots, epileptics, and the insane poor" as a single population deserving attention, and her federal land bill had authorized states to apply its subsidies to public institutions for "the maintenance and education of idiots." She had personally inspected almost all of the modern training institutions to which Parrish looked for models, including seven in Europe. Moreover, Parrish's immediate problem was a familiar political challenge. Germantown was on the verge of overrunning the fledgling school's crowded and ill-adapted facilities; most alarmingly, the town had planned to build a public street through the supposedly secluded grounds. The institution could not afford to move to a new site, however, without substantial additional funding from the state government.[13]

Dix quickly established herself as the Harrisburg agent for the Pennsylvania Training School. The board of directors established a committee in February 1857 to help her seek funds for a new site, but she rejected the assistance, having already started her work auspiciously by winning the support of the pivotal Ways and Means committee in the state House of Representatives. Thereafter the board gladly entrusted its legislative petition to her sole direction.[14] At the same time, she continued to participate occasionally in the New York campaign. Returning to Harrisburg after she spent a week as King's guest at the Governor's Mansion in Albany, she told Anne Heath that she was "swinging as you see like a pendulum from one State Capitol to another." From the Bloomingdale Asylum, Brown ingratiatingly attributed the progress of the New York hospital bill to Dix's persuasiveness.[15]

Dix's impressions of the state legislatures paralleled her scorn for the partisan maneuvering in the recent presidential election. Ambition and venality seemed to control affairs in Albany and Harrisburg with little regard for disinterested ideals. Frustrated by the slow progress of the bill for the Pennsylvania Training School, she explained to board president Alonzo Potter, one of the leading Episcopal clergymen in the country, that "*sordid* influences govern to an extent I have never before seen so openly admitted—bribery and corruption stalk through the Capital unmasked and unabashed."[16] When Fillmore sent a pessimistic report from the New York legislature contradicting the earlier promises of state politicians, she exploded that "*Honesty* in political life is a *myth.*"[17]

As Fillmore anticipated, the bill for two new mental hospitals in New York was defeated in the lower house of the state assembly. Dix felt "unqualified surprise" at the setback and resolved that she would not again be lulled into accepting a secondary role in the legislative campaign. "I will next year take the subject up without *sharing* responsibility," she vowed. "This year it was Mr. Spenser's [*sic*] measure; next year I claim it for mine."[18]

Apart from that disappointment, however, Dix's return to lobbying concluded happily. In Albany, she found some consolation in the establishment of the New York State Asylum for Insane Criminals. Echoing the opinion of leading medical specialists that convicts should be removed from general mental hospitals, she noted that "the impropriety of associating criminal insane men with other classes is obvious even when insanity precedes the criminal act, as is perhaps oftener the fact than the yet uninstructed mind of the public admits."[19] And in Harrisburg, the legislature voted to fund the construction of a new home for the Pennsylvania Training School. During the late spring of 1857 Dix helped school officials obtain a suitable farm for the institution. Grateful for her influence in Harrisburg, Parrish and the board of directors depended heavily on her continued counsel and invited her to join in board meetings about the relocation. In the next few months they concurred in her advice to move the institution from Germantown to a rural tract near the village of Media and to begin building a compound that would double the capacity of the school.[20]

Dix was delighted to be exerting a decisive influence once again on state legislatures and boards of directors. Although she missed her more glamorous congressional campaign, she was promoting the moral treatment and shaping the national character in the most far-reaching projects she could find. She had picked up her mission exactly where she had left it, as if the chaotic political developments and grim asylum record of the past few years had left untouched the momentum of her career.

— 3 —

Although Dix maintained that her work left her little time to contemplate "the shaded facts of our political condition," she continued to follow national affairs more closely after the 1856 presidential election than she ever had before. "How cloudy is our political horizon! And how many difficulties impend which wear a present unpropitious aspect," she exclaimed to Fillmore, with whom she kept up an active correspondence.

Her commentary presented a running jeremiad about the evils of partisanship, ambition, and avarice. "It is most sad to see the vanishing integrity of those who occupy places of trust and represent the sovereignty of the Nation," she told the former president long before the Buchanan administration proved itself one of the most corrupt in American history.[21]

Occasionally Dix saw revealing glimmers of hope. Not surprisingly, she rejoiced in the departure of Franklin Pierce. When the city of Savannah presented the outgoing president with a commemorative plate, she quipped that "one seems to see inscribed on it Judas the Younger." More remarkably, she expressed an extraordinary if short-lived approval for the *Dred Scott* ruling that Congress lacked authority to ban slavery in the territories and that American citizenship did not extend to blacks. Hoping that the sectional conflict would now subside, she told Fillmore that "Mr. Buchanan's first stroke of policy has surprised many and gratified more, if indeed the judgment of the Supreme Court on the Dred Scott Case . . . shall prove as designed, a quietus to all political wranglers on the Slave question." To Anne Heath she conceded that "the Judges will not be allowed to pass as Infallible, and Mr. Buchanan's policy at the opening of the administration may find questioners," but the uproar in the North soon proved that tentative prediction to be an egregious understatement. Even the apolitical Heath was outraged by the ruling, and by the end of March 1857 Dix recognized with disappointment that Buchanan's manipulation of the *Dred Scott* decision was "a total failure."[22]

While Buchanan was plummeting in her judgment and the view of many other northern conservatives, the upward spiral of Dix's own reputation was once again accelerating. In May 1857, her Scottish investigatory commission sparked a brief sensation with the submission of a massive report to Parliament. The London and Scottish press and several members of Parliament promptly endorsed the commission's horrifying account of the nonmedical private asylums and demanded an improvement on the ineffective system of local supervision. Sir George Grey and Lord Advocate James Moncrieff responded with remedial legislation based on Lord Shaftesbury's renowned regulation of asylums in England. The Lunatic Asylums (Scotland) Act of 1857, passed by Parliament in August, created a permanent Board of Commissioners in Lunacy to regulate the treatment of the insane. As in England, the legislation also sought to displace the licensed private asylums by providing for a network of public mental hospitals throughout Scotland. Although the establishment of a new administrative agency in Edinburgh sparked considerable Scottish protest against the increasing centralization of government, praise for Dix's role in the reform was unanimous. The House of Commons cheered when a Scottish member stated that the investigation was "entirely due" to her exertions. Grey and Moncrieff were quick to add their testimonials and, as Dix and the press noted, to overstate their cooperation with her efforts. The triumph was soon rounded out when her critic W. A. F. Browne resigned his position at the Crichton Institute to take one of the two places reserved for physicians on the regulatory commission.[23]

As for so many nineteenth-century Americans, foreign praise for Dix translated into more expansive acclaim at home. The New York *Journal of Commerce* boasted that "Miss Dix deserves to be at least as much honored in the United States for her beneficent and arduous explorations in Europe, as Miss Nightingale is in Great Britain for her enterprise and hospital services in the Crimea."[24]

While she reaped the credit for the Scottish asylum reforms, moreover, Dix also continued to enjoy success in her American initiatives. Shortly after the submission of the parliamentary report she became active in the affairs of a new state asylum in western Pennsylvania. Opened in Pittsburgh in 1853 primarily to treat victims of industrial accidents, the Western Pennsylvania Hospital developed a department for the insane during its first four years and obtained a farm on the Monongahela River in order to establish an asylum as a separate institution. But Dix objected that inadequate rail connections made the proposed location unfit for an asylum, and she persuaded the board of trustees to sell the Monongahela River farm and buy a tract overlooking the Ohio River eight miles from Pittsburgh. Quickly winning the confidence of the board chairman, she assumed a key ongoing role in the affairs of the new hospital. Praise for her effort echoed previous transatlantic comparisons. The humanitarian achievements of John Howard and Florence Nightingale had brought them "the homage of mankind," one newspaper noted, but Dix "promises to surpass them all, both in the amount of her labors and sacrifices, and in the magnitude of their results."[25]

Dix's work at the Western Pennsylvania Hospital aptly illustrated her continued attention to the daily administration of insane asylums. Although less spectacular than her lobbying, these efforts were important not only as a result but as a source of her political influence. Her peripatetic visits to hospitals and her immense correspondence with superintendents and trustees made Dix a vital channel of information about events within the asylum movement. She provided material assistance as well as information, sending an endless stream of cheap prints, magic lanterns, kaleidoscopes, musical instruments, and other gifts to mental hospitals around the country. She especially liked to donate books, and furnished many mental institutions with the collected works of William Ellery Channing. These gifts were an integral contribution to the fading ideal of moral treatment; one superintendent noted after receiving a shipment of books that they were "just such as the insane would be pleased with."[26] At the Pennsylvania State Lunatic Hospital in Harrisburg, for which Dix still controlled the private endowment she had raised in 1845, she passed judgment on plans for an annex and authorized a variety of purchases from the fund.

By the middle of August 1857, Dix was eager for a brief release from her mission. She expressed her usual mixed feelings about visiting Anne Heath in Boston, qualifying her anticipation of rest and conversation with a blunt recognition that "the chief practical objection to such enjoyment is the cold hard *fact* that I am *not social.*" She decided to return to Newport, however, mainly because Ruth Channing, Sarah Gibbs, and Harriet Hare were all declining as they neared the age of eighty. Dix spent the final days of summer at Oakland with her old friends, awash in memories. Her holiday was sweetened by the sense that she had in some part succeeded to William Ellery Channing's position of religious leadership. With unmistakable pride, she reported to the Rathbones that she now sat by the window through which she had often watched Channing gaze, "wrapt in meditation, contemplat[ing] the glories of the lower world, types perhaps of the heavenly habitations for which we are we trust duly preparing."[27]

— 4 —

While Dix rested at Oakland, a devastating financial panic was engulfing the United States. On August 24 her friend Charles Stetson announced the failure of the Ohio Life Insurance and Trust Company's banking subsidiary in New York, one of the most important institutions on Wall Street. The nation's tenuous credit system soon crumbled. Businesses, jobs, and personal savings vanished. The instinctive fiscal retrenchment of all governments during the panic and the ensuing depression of 1857–1858 scuttled Dix's plans to take over the campaign for additional insane asylums in New York. She decided to turn her attention to the South, which she and most observers expected to withstand the financial crisis more steadily than the industrial North.[28]

During the first months of 1858, Dix concentrated primarily on an appeal to the Maryland legislature on behalf of the new state asylum she had helped to establish six years earlier. As in the aftermath of many of her campaigns, legislators were outraged when the construction costs for the hospital far exceeded the initial appropriation. Dix and her allies had anticipated the reckoning, and in a well-organized lobbying effort, they successfully urged the legislature to grant more funds rather than back away from its commitment to the new asylum.[29]

Immediately after the Maryland legislature approved the supplemental appropriation, the Pennsylvania Training School summoned her to Harrisburg to seek additional funding for the ambitious relocation plans she had helped to formulate. She represented the interests of the Pennsylvania Training School in "the factious legislature" during March 1858 and while in Harrisburg also supported budgetary requests from the Pennsylvania State Lunatic Hospital and the Western Pennsylvania Hospital. The session proved to be another gratifying success, as the legislature voted significant appropriations to all three institutions.[30]

After lingering in Pennsylvania to inspect local almshouses and attend Harriet Hare during the final illness of her husband, Dix resumed her plan to work in the states of the upper South. For the next four months she was "very busy and a good deal annoyed by the defects of many institutions" as she traveled through Virginia, North Carolina, Kentucky, and Tennessee. In addition to urging medical superintendents to avoid mechanical restraints and provide patients with more liberty to work out their own recovery, she especially worried that the corruption of national politics was endangering all public institutions. Partisan patronage at asylums, prisons, and almshouses—an influence intensified by massive unemployment—placed the institutions in the control of officials whose "subserviency and lack of sound principle" she found to be "the chief obstacle interrupting and retarding my endeavors."[31]

During her travels Dix watched with deep interest the wave of religious revivals sweeping across the United States amid the financial depression of 1857–1858. Prayer breakfasts, evangelical rallies, and mass conversions were achieving unprecedented popularity among traditionally staid churches and materialistic businessmen. "The multiplication of public and social meetings for prayer and exhortation," she observed, was "like an electric impulse quickening the various communities of the Western world North and South." But although she had looked toward a spiritual renewal of the country stimulated by widespread suffering, the panic-induced revivals were not the sort of national regeneration Dix sought. "I do not myself see in this any evidence of a purer and holier idea of religious obligation and elevating soul-sanctifying influence," she concluded. She firmly maintained her Unitarian conviction that "sober *thought, steady* self-discipline, and close meditation, are [the] agents of conversion and parents of godliness."[32]

The revival excitement thus seemed to her fundamentally similar to the temperamental weakness that she saw beneath the political unrest in the country. "This is peculiarly the age of impulse," Dix sighed. Far too often religious and secular leaders merely exploited and enhanced that weakness. She emphasized that "nearly all forensic speaking, pulpit teaching, popular Lecturing, and legislative utterances are in the main *declamatory,* and chiefly composed of appeals to the emotions and feelings."[33] The calmer, deeper improvement of the nation would require a different sort of exemplary leadership.

— 5 —

Concluding her travels through the upper South in late September 1858, Dix again contemplated a visit to Boston despite the indifferent reception she expected there. When she heard that typhoid fever had spread through Anne Heath's home and that Lydia Greene was rapidly declining, however, she hastened to Brookline to help nurse them. She arrived a few days before Greene died on October 25. As Heath seemed to be only mildly ill, Dix stayed nearby for only a few days. Eager to mend broken ties, she kept Anne talking late into the night. Susan Heath privately seethed that her sister's old friend "had no *mercy* on her—but would certainly kill her or drive her distracted." Shortly after Dix left, Anne collapsed in a feverish attack. She spent the next three weeks in grave peril, but Dix learned of her recovering friend's illness only by chance as she passed through town again at the end of November.[34]

The awkward reunion epitomized Dix's incomplete reconciliation with her Boston past. Her thoughts absorbed by her religious mission and political projects, she could not step back into the prosaic life she had renounced. When Dix complained that her friend did not understand her, Heath reminded her of the gulf between their worlds. "True, we do *not* comprehend your employment," Heath wrote on one occasion. "We cannot; the very alphabet we know nothing about. Occasionally, we read of widespread misery, & we do not doubt its existence. We sigh perhaps, & wish it were relieved, 'but it lies out of our track, like the desert of Sahara,' & we turn away, & wonder if the pudding is boiling for dinner . . . Breakfast & dinner are to me tremendous & complicated obstacles to perfect repose in this world."[35]

Despite her poignant self-deprecation, Heath also saw that she enjoyed experiences and wisdom unavailable to Dix. She, too, had overcome bouts of profound loneliness, especially since recently taking charge of her sixteen-year-old niece, Grace. The vivacious granddaughter of Joseph Tuckerman and her young friends like Clover Hooper and Robert Gould Shaw now animated life on Heath Hill. Dix, on the other hand, shared the enthusiasms of the rising generation no more than she had as a schoolteacher. When she urged the father of one of Grace's friends to prevent the youths from skating on the thin ice of the Charles River, Grace protested that the injunction was "real mean" and demanded of her aunt, "What does Miss Dix know about skating?"[36]

Moreover, although Dix's bitterness toward her home had faded somewhat, her sense of emotional distance remained central to her identity even as she felt that "the sentiment deepens and strengthens which allies me to early friends." She still maintained that "I do not feel disposed to abide long in New England unless I could see that it was a *duty.*"[37] As she once put it, the rest of America had instead become her home. She proudly observed that "there is not a Hospital hardly a place I can name in all the United States from the south boundary of New York to the Gulf of Mexico where I do not feel at ease and enough at home to ask for what I want and find contentment." Further north, she emphasized, she *"should not feel at ease* or free to rest as an invalid or delay as a guest— *except* in a Hotel." Happy with the place she had made for herself in the world, Dix had settled into a placid antipathy toward her native region that she expected to last for the rest of her life. "I am a good deal at ease in the main," she concluded, "but I should not like to find myself ill in the city of Boston, nor at more than three points in all New England I think. It is a fancy perhaps, but it is *reality* to me."[38]

Shortly after Dix left Brookline in December 1858, however, she received a remarkable testimonial to her continued personification of Boston ideals and her national stature. Upon leaving politics in 1852, Horace Mann had become the first president of Antioch College in Yellow Springs, Ohio, a school established by a small religious group as a nonsectarian Protestant alternative to the many colleges founded recently by Presbyterians, Congregationalists, Baptists, and Methodists. Under Mann, Antioch soon became one of the most important outposts of the Unitarian movement beyond Boston. Ezra Stiles Gannett, Samuel Gridley Howe, and Josiah Quincy were but a few of the leading Unitarians who worked to help Mann build a school that would educate its students' consciences as well their intellects and extend its influence throughout American society. But even the foremost educator in the country could not save this vision from the initial difficulties of a new college, and the depression of 1857–1858 had pushed Antioch into bankruptcy. Mann actually welcomed the financial reorganization, in which a coalition of his Boston friends planned to buy the college, as an opportunity to consolidate his control and realize the dream of a model academy that he had come to regard as the most important project of his illustrious career. As part of this plan, he now tried to bring Dix to Antioch.

Mann's invitation could scarcely have provided a sweeter vindication for one of Dix's most crucial disappointments in Boston. The great educational reformer who had rejected her application to join the Massachusetts State Normal School implored her to "come now into this higher moral sphere, & take into your own plastic hands the rude material which their skill can convert into ministers of blessedness for the earth." "After having *been* a Miss Dix, to the unspeakable blessing & joy of one great class of sufferers," Mann exhorted her, *"create* a hundred others to walk in yet untrodden paths of usefulness & honor, & to reveal the yet hidden glories that belong to humanity."[39]

Mary Peabody Mann's flattering elaboration of the proposal demonstrated how fully the Antioch offer resembled Dix's former proposal for a model boardinghouse as the complement of classroom education. She pointed out that schools were supplanting the home as the source of moral education in America and that Antioch needed to instill "domestic, heart culture, as much as intellectual culture." With that responsibility, the Manns had learned that "what is needed is a home-parlor with a mother (either real or ideal) in it." Mary Peabody Mann urged: "We wish you could be that ideal mother." Indeed, she added, "a School-mother is nearly, if not quite as essential here as a President-father." She confidently looked forward to Antioch's rise from bankruptcy, particularly with the added luster of Dix to attract students. Mann predicted that "your name & fame would bring them here in flocks, we think, and would obviate all the objections the most careful parents have to sending them."[40]

Tempting though it may have been to join her former political ally in a position that encapsulated her fundamental principles, Dix declined the offer. She had found elsewhere the vocation that had eluded her as a teacher, and she would not now leave the platform that made her a moral exemplar for the nation rather than a school. Persisting, the Manns begged her to establish headquarters at Antioch and train a surrogate to take her place during her travels. After the mortgage foreclosure they reported that the new board of trustees included many Unitarians and that "all we want now to make the matter complete is Miss Dix."[41] Their intensive recruitment effort ended only with the sudden death of Horace Mann in the summer of 1859. By that time, however, Dix was absorbed in a new expedition, an extraordinary effort to connect her mission more directly to the political upheaval shaking the country.

╌ 12 ╌

Downright Madness

DURING THE WINTER of 1858–59, Dix shifted from apprehensive monitoring of sectional tensions to a remarkable private campaign to repress the conflict. "Political questions are beginning again to agitate the popular mind," she worried in September, as the Lincoln-Douglas debates attracted widespread attention. Unlike increasing numbers of Americans, Dix still considered the divisive issues to be the chimerical inventions of northern and southern demagogues who directed public affairs "at strange hazards and with more than usual lack of discretion." Most citizens failed to appreciate the gravity of the situation, she maintained, for the return of prosperity after the depression of 1857–1858 "satisfie[d] the less reflecting that the Government is 'well enough.' " But if Dix's basic diagnosis of the sectional conflict had not changed much during the past decade, her sharpened sense of its urgency brought a new impetus to action. "It does not help our perplexity nor lessen our anxieties that this deadly canker is seen and traced," she declared. "*Cure* is what the whole body politic cries out for."[1]

Dix's proposed treatment for "our downward track as a *Nation*" required relatively little change in her work. She already considered her asylum crusade the antithesis of the forces that had wrought the crisis. Open denunciations of the country's "infirm principles of virtuous life" would accomplish little, and would violate the indirect, almost imperceptible process of moral influence that she pitted against the political upheaval. "The spasmodic rebuke, like spasmodic virtue, is ineffective to heal," she observed.[2] Instead she hoped to quicken the "*purifying* current" of benevolence that she saw running counter to "the course of events which sweep on at Washington; much like the turbid autumn floods of some wild bankless river . . . wasting and destroying more than it fertilizes and benefits."[3] Although she thus described her efforts as part of a spontaneous, unorganized movement, she eagerly sought to assume its leadership. Most obviously, as the New England reformer most warmly regarded in the South, she personified and was unusually positioned to advance intersectional harmony. Changing previous travel plans to make the most of this potential, she set out in January 1859 on an ambitious tour of the deep South.

— 1 —

Although Dix's immediate aim remained the promotion of the moral treatment, several aspects of her new campaign distinguished it from her previous efforts and revealed her broader objectives. Current issues in asylum policy contributed little to the development of her itinerary. Unlike most of her projects—including the southern tours of 1848–1851 in which she had helped to found asylums in Tennessee, North Carolina, Alabama, and Mississippi—she did not seek out local asylum initiatives that she could bring to fruition. Uncharacteristically, she turned away from the high-profile campaign to establish additional facilities for the insane in New York, a drive that she had vowed to lead after its failure in March 1857 and that the state Superintendents of Poor had resumed in the fall of 1858 as the northern economy improved. Until recently, the South had also seemed to Dix less of a priority than the Northwest, where she might have guided Michigan, Iowa, and Wisconsin in the organization of new state mental hospitals. In the South, she would be aiding less glamorous ongoing efforts as a means of participating in the overriding controversy of the era.

The redirection of Dix's goals also led to a modification of her methods. Seeking to influence popular attitudes, she concentrated less on legislative lobbying and more on cultivating private connections. After starting her journey at the state capitals and asylums in Raleigh, North Carolina, and Columbia, South Carolina, she spent almost two weeks at the Mills House in Charleston to develop personal contacts in the exclusive social circles of the city. For the first time since her early efforts in Pennsylvania, she raised a private subscription fund to support the state mental hospital. As she received callers and paid visits in the epicenter of radical agitation, she eagerly monitored opinion on national affairs. "The Abolition fever seems declining," she wrote optimistically in February 1859, "and Southern Citizens may have time to improve the condition of the Negro population, if not disturbed by indiscreet northern interference."[4]

Always flattered by public recognition, Dix was especially pleased by a warm South Carolina reception that augured well for her intersectional mission. Superintendent J. W. Parker immediately adopted many of her recommendations for the state asylum at Columbia. The South Carolina Medical Association welcomed her graciously to Charleston, where her visit appeared to make the inspirational impression she had intended. One resident who joined her local inspections told a friend that it was "a great privilege & a solemn lesson to be almost daily with one . . . justly described as 'a good woman upon an awful scale.' "[5] Concluding that the next session of the state legislature would support a major appropriation for the state asylum, Dix left Charleston in February 1859 with plans to return at the end of the year.

She spent the next month in Georgia and Alabama, where she was again delighted by the response she met. The Georgia State Asylum superintendent, like his colleagues around the country, assured her that his hospital had set apart "*our* 'Dix room,' in the sincere hope, that it might be often occupied by the lady, whom it will be our peculiar pleasure always to honor." As in South Carolina, she spent one week visiting the asylum and capital in Milledgeville and another three weeks circulating through Savannah, Augusta, and Macon. When the Savannah press praised her lavishly, Fillmore, noticing the story, dimly began to recognize Dix's national aspirations. Her asylum work in the South "appears like an *Oasis* in the desert of crime," the former president told her, expressing hope that "these green spots may recur more frequently."[6] For her own part, Dix remained hopeful that moral benevolence could conquer political strife. She concluded that the Georgia legislature "has grumbled a little while giving, yet on the whole has really been open-handed" in supporting public charities. She found even more cause for satisfaction in Alabama, where she assumed an active role in supporting the successful candidacy of the physician selected to be superintendent of the state mental hospital recently completed at Tuscaloosa.[7]

After leaving Alabama on March 14, Dix rested in New Orleans for several days before embarking on the climax of her tour, an excursion to Texas. Her swing through the South had already included some of the most arduous traveling of her career. Constant rains and overflowing rivers had "left the country one vast swamp." Dix often rode trains for several days and nights at a time, but she avoided the *"quite detestable"* sleeping cars recently introduced on some lines. When she later relented for one night, she quickly decided that the experiment "will suffice for *life.* I cannot suppose that persons of decent habits especially Ladies will occupy them unless some essential changes are made in the arrangements and regulations." She much preferred to crisscross the country in her hard chair.[8]

Even by Dix's standards, however, her journey to Texas was particularly harrowing. She steamed from New Orleans to Galveston, where her boat wandered among rocks and shoals in the foggy bay for six hours until the pilot found the winding channel to Houston. Arriving at dawn, she took a train for eighty miles, as far as the tracks penetrated the desolate prairie, and finally headed toward Austin in a stagecoach with nine passengers inside and six more outside. The trip lasted two days and nights with only brief stops, except for the night spent at the bottom of a gully after the lead horses broke loose and the coach became mired in the mud. "You ask perhaps what I did under this press of adverse circumstances," Dix crowed to one friend. "Why, meditated how poor sick insane people were to live, in being transported over such roads and such distances!" Back in Boston, Heath argued that Dix's errand into the wild Southwest had at last carried her pilgrimage too far. "I feel as if you were going among Cannibals, and would never return. How *can* you do so!" she objected. "I wish you would come home . . . I wish you would stay in civilized quarters!"[9]

Contrary to Heath's expectations, Texans proved eager to show their rapidly growing state to the famous humanitarian. As throughout the South, Dix was "constantly surprised by spontaneous demonstrations of the heartiest good-will" from private citizens and public officials. Deeply gratified to see "that I do in very truth dwell in the hearts of my countrymen," she noted with her customary irony that "when 3000 miles from New England, I was welcomed as an old and cherished friend." Several Texans assured her, "We have *known* you years and years." When she offered suggestions on the organization of public institutions, she found that her opinions were considered definitive judgments. One state official told her: "You are a moral Autocrat—you speak and your word is law."[10]

After three weeks in Texas, Dix concluded the first phase of her intersectional mission in Louisiana and Mississippi, offering to return to both states during the winter for the legislative sessions. In Mississippi, she again devoted her attention both to the capital and mental hospital at Jackson and to the wealthy cotton-growing district around Natchez, where she preached the virtues of the moral treatment and appealed to the planter aristocracy for contributions for the state asylum. The groundwork laid for a productive series of legislative campaigns during the upcoming winter, she finally headed upriver in May 1859 for a summer respite.[11]

— 2 —

On her way north, Dix stopped in St. Louis for a two-week visit that solidified one of the most important friendships she had formed in many years. She had briefly met William Greenleaf Eliot one year earlier, and she quickly recognized that the forty-eight-year-old Unitarian minister personified her ideals as fully as any man she ever knew. A member of a distinguished Boston family, he had been ordained at the Federal Street Church with his hero Channing in the pulpit before setting out as a Unitarian missionary with his wife, Abigail Adams Eliot. The pastor's zeal, like Dix's, included little interest in the institutional development of the church. He measured the progress of his St. Louis parish "not in a denominational direction, but through its individual members in all its various directions of philanthropy." He set a powerful example with his own tireless efforts, most famously as the chief founder of Washington University, which was to be named Eliot Seminary until he declined the honor. The minister and educator shared with Dix a fervent belief that "no social improvement is permanent except that which comes through individual virtue, and to elevate society you must regenerate the individuals of which it is composed." Also like Dix, he extended this principle to the most explosive issue in his border state, clinging to hopes that the slavery crisis might be resolved eventually through voluntary emancipation.[12]

Dix soon became closely attached to the Eliots and their children, Thomas Lamb Eliot, Henry Ware Eliot, and Christopher Rhodes Eliot. She ranked the minister, and later his oldest and youngest sons, with Channing, Gannett, and Henry Ware, Jr., as the ministers she most admired. Eliot agreed that "no new friendship has ever seemed so near as this which we have now formed with you." He soon began to address his letters to Dix as his sister.[13]

During the five months after she left St. Louis, Dix continued north to escape the summer heat. She passed through Springfield to call on her former congressional sponsor William Bissell, whose election as governor of Illinois had been an important victory for the growing Republican party, then went to visit the state mental hospital she had helped to found at Jacksonville a dozen years earlier. Asylum superintendent Andrew McFarland, recently elected president of the Association of Medical Superintendents, insisted that she stay for a week to meet with the board of trustees. Pleased with the condition of the facility, Dix invited Eliot to "visit this my Hospital at your first leisure. Do come: I am quite *proud* of it."[14]

Dix continued to correspond with southern allies about her plans for the upcoming legislative sessions as she traveled. "You can do more than folk such as I am," one supporter of the Mississippi asylum assured her.[15] Returning east by way of the Ohio Lunatic Asylum in Columbus and the Western Pennsylvania Hospital for the Insane near Pittsburgh, she rested for a month in and around the Trenton asylum. In July she left for Canada, where she spent the balance of the summer at institutions for the insane in Nova Scotia, Newfoundland, New Brunswick, and Prince Edward's Island. After dividing a final month between Boston and New York, she turned back toward Jackson in November 1859 to resume her campaign for national peace of mind.

She could hardly have chosen a less propitious moment for a Bostonian to enter the lower South. Sectional antagonisms had risen to a fever pitch in the wake of John Brown's October 16 attack on the federal arsenal at Harpers Ferry, Virginia, and the apotheosis of Brown that was already under way in some northern circles. Dix unequivocally condemned the attempt to incite a slave rebellion, calling it "the strangest illustration of mistaken feelings overruling judgment and practical common sense that I have heard or read of." She was stunned by newspaper reports that her sometime collaborator Samuel Gridley Howe, whom she had considered only mildly irresponsible, was one of the principal backers of the raid. Poised between disbelief and disgust, she commented that "if the conspiracy is as extensive as claimed, which I very much doubt, it only proves that there are more impulsive people than one could have supposed among our impulsive countrymen." Like other events in the breakdown of the Union, "this mad scheme of Brown's" strengthened her conviction that the heart of the crisis was the singular American susceptibility to uncontrolled passions.[16]

As befitted the clash she perceived between sanity and insanity, Dix's mission to Mississippi presented a striking contrast to Brown's raid on Harpers Ferry. She arrived in Jackson on November 9 and assumed a highly visible role in the capital. She visited not only the state penitentiary and asylum but also the state agricultural fair. With disarming modesty, Dix asked permission to enter several small examples of her sewing in the exhibition of ladies' handicrafts. Officials of the fair expressed their appreciation for her friendly gesture by waiving the rules that restricted competition to the daughters of Mississippi and awarding a prize to the former needlework instructor of the Boston Female Monitorial School.[17]

Dix's political efforts met an equally warm reception. State officials provided her a spacious alcove in the library of the capitol building, and she went there daily to "receive the Members of the legislature from the Senate and House and unfold to their respectful listening ear the wants of the State Hospital for the Insane." She enlisted politicians, physicians, and the local clergy in the appeal for an appropriation to expand the hospital and its grounds. The measure advanced rapidly, preceded by a unanimous resolution thanking Dix for her efforts in the state. The progress of her lobbying and the personal affection of numerous Mississippians encouraged her hopes for a widening tranquillity, and she was pleased to observe that "all in all the Southern people are as moderate in their opinions under such press of danger as could possibly be expected" in the aftermath of the attack on Harpers Ferry. Her quixotic campaign excited Dix beyond even her usual sense of satisfaction with her legislative accomplishments. "I do see the Sun, the Moon, and the Stars and the glory of them shines into my soul," she proclaimed.[18]

Dix left Mississippi at the end of November 1859 to aid a similar bill for expansion of the South Carolina Lunatic Asylum. Ominous secession debates ignited by Brown's raid consumed the legislature, and Dix found "all Hospital business not at a stand-still merely, but looking very unpromising." As Columbia asylum superintendent J. W. Parker had anticipated in urging her to come, however, the fire-eaters paused to welcome their celebrated northern guest. Lonely Unionist legislator Benjamin F. Perry observed that she "seems a great favorite with the Members." The warm greeting of politicians and citizens in South Carolina, following the effusive farewell in Mississippi, impressed Dix deeply. "I am very happy in _knowing_ I am much _beloved_ by my fellow citizens in this part of the Union," she reported to Heath.[19]

After the Palmetto State legislature set aside room in the capitol library for Dix's conferences, she was soon engaged in another lobbying effort. Within two weeks, the Senate and House both put aside their convulsions long enough to appropriate $85,000 for the asylum, which was almost as much as the legislature voted to spend on military preparations for the impending crisis. The triumph of moral benevolence amid the distractions of political agitation perfectly realized Dix's aspirations. "Indeed," she said, "I never had [a] more satisfactory experience of legislation for charitable purposes." Awed by the contrast between the fierce sectional strife and her friend's national popularity, Heath wrote that "surely the angels have charge concerning you. Would not any other northerner have been killed to bits, without Judge or Jury? And _you_ were welcomed, listened to, and commended!"[20]

"Providence seems leading me on," Dix agreed as she prepared to leave Columbia. Her safe travels and legislative achievements affirmed her faith in her sacred mission. "I feel _it is the Lord,_" she exclaimed, "and I am the instrument fashioned to do his Holy will." She spent the final weeks of the year in Charleston and Milledgeville attending to the private hospital subscriptions she had solicited during her last visits. After hurriedly pressing some asylum work on Alabama legislators while the state assembly was in recess, she marched through Atlanta, Dalton, and Chattanooga to Nashville, passing "over _bridgeless_ rivers by strange expedients on rafts." At Nashville she rested briefly in the apartment at the Tennessee Hospital for the Insane that the legislature had dedicated to her use several years earlier. Meeting with the House and Senate committees responsible for public charities, she was delighted when the delegates agreed to support a bill for a tax to improve the state asylum and establish a new mental hospital in Knoxville.[21]

Dix planned to turn next to Kentucky, but much to the disappointment of Lexington asylum superintendent W. S. Chipley she ended her southern tour in January 1860 in order to fulfill prior commitments to lobby once again in Pennsylvania. The past few months had been one of the most gratifying periods of her career. Never resting from her work for two days in a row, she felt "devoutly thankful for a series of successes as remarkable as they have been uniform."[22]

Her contentment was only partly diminished by the continued escalation of the sectional conflict. She readily conceded that moral education worked far more gradually than the violent disruptions stirred by madmen like John Brown. Looking back over 1859, she felt less frustration than a sense of vindication in the opinions with which she had begun her long southern travels. "The people at large let politicians and agitators quarrel & wrangle & disgrace the nation," she lamented, "considering that at any time it please the *Nation* to look to its public interests and its reputation, it can *quell the storm* at *will*." As a result, the country was more threatened than ever by polemicists "pampering the *popular* demand for *exciting* and *extreme* narratives, or *rabid* opinions based on false theories." Dix yearned for a statesman who would awaken "our busy people" that "there *is* danger in 'letting *fighting animals* fight *along*." But as the 1860 presidential election year opened, she saw no such conservative likely to restore national stability. "No one can even conjecture results," she concluded, "but one fact is quite certain. We lack strong *leading* minds, and a sort of fatality seems to sweep our Ship of State towards the Rocks of Destruction."[23]

— 3 —

Dix's return to the North reduced her sense of participation in the unfolding sectional drama, and "a very severe Influenza" soon relegated her temporarily to the role of a spectator. The illness was more unpleasant than dangerous, but it was enough to alarm the institutions for which she had again agreed to lobby the Harrisburg legislature. The Pennsylvania Training School for Feeble-Minded Children had asked her to seek additional funding for its relocation to Media "in such manner as her judgment may approve"; the Western Pennsylvania Hospital for the Insane had similarly named her its sole agent in the appeal for a large appropriation to build the asylum on the site she had chosen near Pittsburgh; and the Pennsylvania State Lunatic Hospital was counting on her to secure approval of its budget request. Shortly after a favorable committee report on these bills in February 1860, Dix temporarily halted her daily visits to the capitol in order to nurse herself back to full strength.[24]

She applied the same principles to her own health that she advocated in her lobbying for mental hospitals. Because illness expressed the intimate connection between body and soul, moral treatment was the best therapy for influenza as well as insanity. And consistent with her self-image as the embodiment of emotional equilibrium, Dix prided herself on her autonomous powers of rehabilitation. "In illness I require no great care and attention—self-reliant—and not anxious or nervous," she told Heath, who had recently complained of acute headaches. "I get on by myself quite satisfactorily." Professional medical attention seemed to her far more likely to be dangerous than useful. "I have no great faith in most Physicians," she explained to another friend. "Good nursing and attention to the laws of life are more health-restoring and health-giving than medicines or stereotyped prescriptions."[25]

Dix's generally vigorous condition affirmed her ideas about health. Her latest travels had been as grueling as any she had ever undertaken, but she seemed to grow stronger with the exertion. She had become quite stout, even plump, in recent years. Although ill-fitting false teeth caused her cheeks to sag into something of a permanent scowl, she looked significantly younger than her fifty-eight years, an age that she still guarded secretively. By the end of March 1860, her "usually elastic strength" was virtually renewed, and she was able to resume her lobbying efforts.[26]

Her spirits brightened further in early April when the Pennsylvania legislature granted approximately $100,000 to the three state institutions she represented. Dix calculated that in the last two years she had obtained more than $500,000 for hospitals in different states. The chairman of trustees for the Western Pennsylvania Hospital for the Insane firmly agreed that "*your individual* influence alone obtained so handsome an appropriation." Around the same time, the institution also indicated its appreciation for her efforts more openly. Evading Dix's request to select the name for the hospital's new home near Pittsburgh and overriding their expectation that she would object to their choice, the trustees christened the asylum the Dixmont Hospital. Superintendent J. A. Reed apologized that "I had thought of asking your permission, but finally concluded that we would *do it* anyhow."[27]

Despite the success she continued to enjoy, Dix admitted by the early spring that she was eager to "refresh myself by a *change* of employment." A winter of constant lobbying spurred her to resolve that "instead of exhorting people to do their duty, I shall talk less, and think & act more."[28] For the six weeks after the adjournment of the Harrisburg legislature she visited poorhouses and hospitals while resting at Harriet Hare's home in Philadelphia. But more than she missed direct contact with the intended beneficiaries of her efforts, her recent immersion in the affairs of Pennsylvania welfare institutions made her miss the grand scale of her previous ventures. She continued to follow closely the activities of Florence Nightingale and other British women reformers, and she looked forward to crossing the Atlantic again to take up her deferred campaign against nonmedical private insane asylums in England. Privately, she expressed blistering criticism of the vaunted Lord Shaftesbury and his "next to useless" Commission in Lunacy for failing to "crush the Hydra-headed monster." Until the Rathbones' golden wedding anniversary, however, she told her overseas friends and herself that she would find more than enough work to do in the United States.[29]

As Dix looked about for a suitable project, the accelerating downward spiral of the Union remained a prime focus of her attention. Shortly before the Republican and Democratic parties met to nominate presidential candidates, she worried that "the United States will be the arena of a great political strife during the coming elections. Already party-spirit rises and foams . . . , and [it] may be expected to overflow and spread abroad all the slime and refuse of base passions." Looking forward to the nomination of her original congressional ally, John Bell, on a Unionist ticket, she repaired her strained personal relationship with Jane

Erwin Yeatman Bell, who spent much of the spring with her daughter in Philadelphia and now found Dix "very much softened in manner and as gentle and affectionate as possible."[30] The reconciled friends agreed that the political situation seemed bleak and chaotic. Dix was "deeply mortified" by the prospect that the sections might come together to elect the coarse, aggressive Stephen A. Douglas, but she told a receptive Fillmore that "we have suffered so many humiliations as a Nation" that it was folly to expect much from the decision of the masses.[31]

Indeed, Dix looked to the moral weakness of the American people for the most likely resolution of the crisis. The whims of popular passions and the force of narrow personal concerns about money or health sustained her mordant hope "that the *wordy* demonstrations of reckless politicians will pass off like the stormy gusts which toss the waves into wild commotion but soon subdue to more moderate breezes."[32] After the Democratic party ruptured on sectional lines at the Charleston convention, she admitted that the political situation had never looked worse, but she still predicted that the hysteria would wane after the autumn elections. "At this exact time the Japanese Embassy seems to have turned the heads of our volatile people," she argued in the middle of May 1860, amid the burst of publicity surrounding the arrival of the first delegation from that country. "In a few weeks some new wonder will draw the multitude to other transient pursuits, and so the little life of not very well regulated minds will glide on."[33]

Meanwhile, Dix's survey of public institutions near Philadelphia did not produce the refreshing change of employment she sought. Her inspections mainly impressed upon her the overwhelming proportion of Irish immigrants in urban facilities for the insane. Drawing a sharp contrast between cases of insanity among native American citizens and those of recent immigrants, she noted that "mostly they [the immigrants] are incurable, especially the Catholics who seem singularly low in intellect or dulled by their religious creed and total want of education." She met with city officials to discuss the situation, but she proposed no new reforms and remained relatively inactive through the late spring and early summer. At the end of July, Fillmore even invited her to meet his second wife at Saratoga "during this vacation in your labors." Refusing to acknowledge her temporary lack of direction, Dix quickly shot back that "such periods do not find place in my notation of time."[34]

At the beginning of August 1860, Dix established headquarters in

Chicago to undertake the series of northwestern journeys she had earlier postponed in favor of her southern tour. After a sharply critical inspection of the new Illinois State Penitentiary in Joliet, she moved west into states that she had rarely or never visited. She stopped at as many public institutions as she could reach, meeting with the trustees of the new state mental hospital in Mount Pleasant, Iowa, and donating books to the Home of Industry and Farm School for the Homeless Orphans and Foundlings of Large Cities in Iowa City. She dipped briefly into Missouri and Kansas before spending most of August and early September in Wisconsin and Minnesota, where she traveled "day by day from Hospital to Hospital and Prison to Prison and Alms House to Alms House." Despite her relentless pace, she felt invigorated by "this wonderful country of vast Prairies, wide deep ocean-reaching rivers, and Lakes that deceive you into the idea that you are where the Atlantic rushes in upon the resisting shores of the eastern States." After touching base again in Chicago she made another sally through Michigan, Ontario, and western New York that lasted until mid-October.[35]

Throughout her summer circuit, Dix continued to follow the presidential campaign anxiously. Much to her regret, she saw little chance for John Bell's candidacy under the improvised banner of the Constitutional Union party. She had long ago lost her youthful admiration for his running mate, Edward Everett. She scorned the Boston orator's "very questionable" efforts to promote sectional harmony through a speaking tour about the preservation of Mount Vernon, a campaign not unlike her own southern mission. Although relieved by the collapse of Douglas's chances, she looked toward the probable election of Lincoln without enthusiasm. Alarmingly, the political convulsions now seemed increasingly likely to persist after the presidential election. In late August she reported gloomily to William Rathbone that "this country is just now agitated to its centre by the wild schemes of self-seeking politicians, that class of agitators who seem to live for no good and look never beyond their own interests which are mostly conflicting with the best interests of every community." She desperately wished that the fickle public imagination would shift from the slavery controversy and secessionist threats to a more edifying theme. "I am tired of such scenes and the *noise* of this brawling war of words and waste of energies," she complained in the final weeks of the campaign.[36]

The election of Lincoln realized Dix's fears that "our Southern friends seem to have enough to keep all their liveliest passions and prejudices in full exercise, and to disturb the quiet which is most in harmony with our free government." Three weeks later, the grim tendency of the times took a turn more immediately connected to her vocation when a fire destroyed the state mental hospital that she had helped to establish in Hopkinsville, Kentucky. Dix was promptly summoned to Frankfurt for a special legislative session expected to consider the crisis of the union and the replacement of the asylum.[37]

To Dix, the two topics were symbolically connected. "We now illustrate a National contagious phrenzy, culminating in downright madness," she wrote three days after South Carolina voted to secede from the Union. "The insane proceedings of the Palmetto State" and the prostration of the corrupt Buchanan administration demonstrated the fundamental principle on which she had based her career. Betrayed, plundered, teetering on anarchy, the United States now stood as "an example to present and future illustrating the fact that without religious education a people may plunge in a moment of hot-headed excitement to the verge of ruin."[38]

— 4 —

Dix tried in vain to help calm the secession crisis. She hurried to Washington, expecting to discover rampant public disorder. Instead she found an eerie stillness. "The seat of Government that was is all but a city of the Dead," she reported, ". . . . dead in action, intellectual force & resource." This "singular tranquillity" left her "rather hopeful that the *worst* is past and that we may trust a reflex movement is about to turn the waves of loss & destruction back." Crediting rumors that southerners in the Buchanan administration had emptied the federal treasury and arsenals, she conceded that the course of the next few months was utterly unpredictable, but she prayed that "the lessons people are now learning may be wholesome and permanently instructive."[39]

Dix's most direct response to the crisis was a much-belated attempt to influence the radical politician she knew best. Meeting with Charles Sumner immediately after South Carolina seceded, she implored him to adopt a moderate stance in his next scheduled public address. "If there was ever a time for wise reservation of expression on exciting subjects it is now," she urged the antislavery spokesman on December 21. In a calculated appeal to Sumner's vanity and his uncertain relations with the incoming administration she argued, "You may exercise a wide beneficent influence and hereafter bear a most honorable distinction with those who strive to spare calamity if you are prudent now." Three weeks later, Dix again pressed him to "exercise to the last point forbearance and forgiveness" and dissuade the southern secessionists by the force of moral example. "I would try to be generous," she grandly advised, "and by contrast of temper and act show them the superiority and dignity of a nobleness so immeasurably above them." Sumner politely ignored her counsel.[40]

Indirectly as well, Dix sought to promote compromise and peace. She suggested to Charles Nichols that the Association of Medical Superintendents move its upcoming annual meeting from Providence to Washington as the latter was a location "more likely to conciliate the southern members." Passing the proposal along to Thomas Kirkbride, Nichols saw little sign of "quarrel between northern & southern *mad* doctors," but he vaguely recognized that "our good friend has in view the spread of the leaven of a conciliated frame of mind on the part of the southern doctors among the southern people till the whole mass is leavened."[41] As in her southern tour of 1859–1860, Dix's asylum crusade seemed the most obvious vehicle for this diffusion of sectional harmony. An opportunity was available to pursue her joint interests in a state of critical importance, for she received repeated requests from Kentucky to aid in the reconstruction of the Hopkinsville asylum.

In her eagerness to be at the center of swirling events Dix was somewhat reluctant to leave Washington, and she promised that "if worse comes to worst and a general border War is declared, I shall get a military pass and return."[42] But she could see that the chances for a mediated solution were fading. Despite the addition of John Adams Dix as a prominent Unionist force in the interregnum Cabinet, she repeated that "passion and politicians rule the public mind," and she mourned that "one strong decided mind, one resolute will could have stayed all this mischief." Now, she predicted once more, "the only chance of making peace will be *after* a period of positive suffering and experience of *exceeding* distress." The fate of the nation apparently turning less on events in Washington than in the border states, Dix headed south in mid-January.[43]

Like her visit to South Carolina during the secession movement of 1851, Dix's decision to go to Kentucky was partly an effort to gather the local intelligence that she knew to be a valuable asset in national politics. In an important stopover she demonstrated her confidence in her ability to determine the southern mood. Certain that "the amazing quick succeeding revolutionary movements of plotting Secessionists" were nearing a climax, she presented her understanding of the threat to Samuel Morse Felton, president of the Philadelphia, Wilmington & Baltimore Railroad, in a private meeting. She warned Felton that there was "an extensive and organized conspiracy throughout the South" to seize the federal capital "and then declare the Southern conspirators *de facto* the Government of the United States." Troops were drilling alongside Felton's rail line in preparation for this *"coup d'état,"* she informed him; if Lincoln traveled to Washington before the southerners struck, "his life was to fall a sacrifice to the attempt at inauguration." With widespread rumor thus confirmed by a reliable source "familiar with the structure of Southern society, and also with the working of its political machinery," Felton ordered the Pinkerton investigation that culminated in Lincoln's secret midnight passage into Washington.[44]

Proceeding to the contested border in the same spirit of intrigue and suspense, Dix received a gracious welcome in Kentucky from secessionist Governor Beriah Magoffin, the state legislature, and "people in general who lose no opportunity of expressing regard and good-will." Her contacts and observations confirmed her belief that the national crisis was the work of a handful of agitators. "I *know* that quite 2/3 of the Southern vote is for the Union," she concluded within a week.[45] Coercion, misrepresentation, and intoxication explained most of the support for secession, she argued, intimating that prominent southern leaders were working through treacherous secret societies. "I have hope for the Union," she maintained, *"if the whole people* might vote on the question uninfluenced by self-seeking Secessionists and reckless Abolitionists." Her contentment with the progress of her own appeal contrasted sharply with her despair at the perversion of national politics. After she inspected the ruins of the Hopkinsville asylum and several other institutions in the state, friendly senators asked for her advice and introduced legislation to rebuild the mental hospital.[46]

When the Kentucky legislature recessed to monitor national developments, Dix took up a telegraph request for her intercession in Illinois on behalf of the Jacksonville hospital. She arrived in Springfield shortly after Lincoln left on the speaking tour that ended with his inauguration. If she missed a chance to meet the president-elect, she received a warm welcome from the state legislature. She bragged to Heath that after she drew up an asylum bill "the Senate courteously suspended the Rules and passed it without dissent saying I no doubt represented the right work for them to do." With the lower house equally amenable to her wishes, she accomplished her goals in little more than a week. But the uncompromising tenor of Lincoln's speeches and the continuing breakdown of the Union overwhelmed her sense of satisfaction. From the Springfield state library she lamented in letters to three different friends that "I have never before, save once, been so unhappy." The present calamity could be compared only to the land-bill veto that had "crushed the hopes of thousands, and the health-salvation of perhaps tens of thousands."[47]

From Illinois she headed back to the border states, where she remained for the last week of February and all of March. Lobbying for routine asylum measures in order to be near more momentous legislative decisions, she divided her time among Missouri, Tennessee, and Kentucky. As she had provided Fillmore with reports of public opinion in South Carolina ten years ago, she now tried to gather information about the pivotal upper South that might strengthen her ties to the new administration. Returning toward the capital along the Ohio River at the beginning of April 1861, she paused while in Cincinnati to send a lengthy summary of her findings to her old friend William H. Seward, who was now the Secretary of State and widely expected to be the most powerful figure in the government.[48] Continuing east, she had reached Trenton when Fort Sumter fell.

Dix was among the first northerners to respond when Lincoln called for volunteers to subdue the rebellion. Leaving the New Jersey asylum, she drove through Philadelphia in a carriage at breakneck speed in time to catch the last southbound train before the destruction of the Susquehanna River bridges cut off the road to Washington. She passed through Baltimore only three hours after the riot in which the Sixth Massachusetts Regiment suffered the first casualties of the war. Upon safely reaching Washington, she went directly from the train station to the White House, which was filled with soldiers in nervous anticipation of a southern invasion that night. There, on the evening of April 19, she volunteered "herself and an army of nurses gratuitously for hospital service."[49]

Dix's proposal followed naturally from her view of the sectional conflict, her understanding of hospital treatment, and her faith in the divine vocation of benevolent womanhood. Although many historians would later describe her wartime work as a reluctant interruption of her crusade for the insane, Dix hurried to volunteer precisely because she recognized that the Civil War presented a chance to bring her antebellum mission to a climax. As the commander of "an army of nurses," she could be—as she had always sought to become—a crucial link between the regeneration of individuals and the reform of American society. Saving the lives of the wounded and guiding the souls of the dying, she would personify the force of exemplary moral character in the ordeal of suffering she had long anticipated. She would not merely tend to soldiers; she would help to heal the nation.

The prominent role Dix sought in the Civil War reflected her conviction that the crisis of the Union presented the same struggle between self-control and passion to which she had dedicated her life. Many conservatives spoke of secessionism as a form of mania. But when the country's most famous commentator on mental disorders concluded that "the South is literally insane on the secession question," she extended the commonplace rhetoric beyond metaphor to a specific diagnosis and therapeutic program.[50] More emphatically and successfully than anyone else, Dix had argued that the cure for insanity was moral treatment, a process of conversion to inward discipline mediated by the stabilizing personal influence of the asylum superintendent. Now she would respond to fanatical agitation from the North as well as the South by representing a similar ideal of composed, nonpartisan benevolence amid the violent disruptions of the war-torn country.

Certainly ambitious, Dix's hopes might have seemed grandiose had not she and much of the English-speaking world been buzzing for the past five years about the comparable achievements of Florence Nightingale. "The Lady with the Lamp" was already an epic figure, celebrated in countless panegyrics for her midnight vigilance over the sick and wounded British troops in the Crimean War. Virtually synonymous with the idea of nursing by 1861, Nightingale was widely credited with opening the first major field of career opportunities for women since the transformation of schoolteaching a generation before. Moreover, though influential on both sides of the Atlantic she was a distinctly national heroine, so successful in rallying her bitterly divided country around a model of aristocratic leadership during the Crimean War that Queen Victoria had shrewdly linked the British crown to the heroine's popularity by naming her almoner of the royal gifts to the army. The omnipresent image of Nightingale ensured that countless women and men would share Dix's expansive sense of the cultural influence that might be achieved through Civil War nursing.

Like Dix's vision of the chief nurse's role in society, her conception of the individual nurse's role in a hospital simultaneously followed Nightingale's lead and drew on her own experience. For both women, the nurse was not merely an assistant to physicians but the coordinator of a different and more powerful form of holistic care. Nightingale's *Notes on Nursing,* an immense best-seller upon its publication in the United States in 1860, argued strenuously that illness represented the disturbance of a natural moral harmony. "Is it not living in a continual mistake to look upon diseases, as we do now, as separate entities, which *must* exist, like cats and dogs?" she asked in a typical attack on the scientific speculation that diseases resulted from specific germs. She maintained that diseases instead were "conditions, like a dirty and a clean condition, and just as much under our control." Consequently, the crucial instruments of recovery were not surgery or medications but a pure, tranquil environment and a nurse who would discipline and inspire her patients. Nurses embodied the curative power of the milieu—whether it was a home or a hospital—by supervising ventilation, light, noise, cleanliness, and diet for their patients and by filtering all other contact with the outside world. They were first and foremost moral guardians, consistent with Nightingale's own plan to dedicate herself to "the education of the bad" if she had not found her vocation in nursing.[51]

More than a dozen years earlier, Dix had expressed a similar conception of nursing in outlining the key qualifications for the work. Nurses "must possess correct principles and self control," she stressed. "They must be patient, enduring, and forbearing; firm but kind."[52] To be sure, nursing had been of subordinate importance in Dix's work, but mainly because she considered asylum therapy itself an essentially holistic process that happened to be administered by doctors. In the treatment of illnesses other than insanity, as she showed in caring for her own health, she considered "good nursing and attention to the laws of life" no less superior to aggressive intervention than in the treatment of mental diseases.[53]

The idea of nursing as a calling specifically for women was at the center of the connection drawn by Dix, Nightingale, and countless others between nurses' duties in hospitals and reformers' work in improving society as a whole. "Every woman is a nurse," Nightingale declared in the famous introduction to *Notes on Nursing*.[54] In the perfection of that role, social forms converged with a grander destiny. The advance of nursing would not only save lives and reform nations but would also fulfill the world-historical mission of womanhood. Linking that charge directly to the triumph of pietistic Christianity, Dix rose to the inspiration as enthusiastically as she had responded forty years earlier to Hannah More's conception of schoolteaching.

Not surprisingly, Dix endorsed *Notes on Nursing* but found little new in it. Reading the popular guide to home health care immediately upon its publication, she told Elizabeth Rathbone that "it did not meet my expectations, but it may be useful." She helped to spread Nightingale's ideas by sending a copy to of the book to the indefatigable William Greenleaf Eliot for implementation in St. Louis.[55]

Dix was in many ways favorably positioned to repeat Nightingale's success. For one thing, she had the advantage of her predecessor's experience, a saga she knew at least as well as almost any American. Although Dix had failed in her determined efforts to meet Nightingale, she had watched the growth of her influence firsthand while in Britain, visited the fabled hospitals at Scutari, and spoken at length with the nursing superintendent's chief lieutenants. She had undoubtedly discussed Nightingale and nursing with Anna Jameson while they traveled together in Europe, and she may have learned more in conversations at Greenbank, for William Rathbone, Jr., took a strong interest in nursing and was now beginning a long-term collaboration with Nightingale. Dix also owned several relevant books in addition to *Notes on Nursing,* including a narrative by one of the Scutari volunteers and a report by the deaconesses of the Protestant Institution of Kaiserwerth, which had trained Nightingale.[56]

Moreover, Dix could count on other important advantages that Nightingale had not enjoyed. Although she lacked the sophistication and wide-ranging intelligence of the younger woman, Dix had accumulated a vast fund of experience in hospital administration and national politics. For almost twenty years she had been visiting large-scale medical facilities in the United States and Europe, and in her close relations with many physicians she had immersed herself in the details of superintending complex mental hospitals. Her political record was potentially equally relevant to the government post she sought. Dix enjoyed no source of influence in Washington comparable to Nightingale's crucial personal tie with the British War Secretary, but she had many friends in high places and had proven herself one of the most successful lobbyists in American history.

Dix's reputation was in some respects her greatest asset in an initiative designed to display her personal character as a model for the nation in crisis. She was already the country's most famous benevolent heroine. For the past five years, Americans had readily compared her to Nightingale as they had previously associated her with Elizabeth Fry. When she encouraged the juxtaposition by sending a picture of her latest British counterpart to the Liebers, they aptly captioned the gift "Dix and Nightingale, the Double Star of Charity in the Meridian of the XIX Century."[57]

This parallel was dramatically affirmed by Sarah Josepha Hale, whose intrusions Dix had so vociferously resented a decade earlier. A lifelong conservative supporter of sectional harmony, Hale would address the political crisis only obliquely in her widely circulated *Godey's Lady's Book*. In a cover illustration that demonstrated her contempt for the military fever overtaking the country during the dark secession winter, *Godey's* featured idealized portraits of Dix, Nightingale, Elizabeth Fry, and Grace Darling. Hale pointedly argued that their female philanthropy had done more for humanity "than all the conquerers who have won the crown of everlasting fame from 'Macedonia's madman' to the Duke of Wellington." Dix characteristically scoffed at the publicity, laughing that "one cannot tell *which* [portrait] is intended for D. L. Dix. 'Tis too absurd!"[58] But it was the similarity of the simple engravings that expressed their most important message. The country would expect her to be, as she intended to become, the Florence Nightingale of the American Civil War.

Dix's appearance at the White House on the evening of April 19 met a warm reception. Lincoln's private secretary, John G. Nicolay, bracing for a Confederate assault with the Union soldiers billeted in the executive mansion, recorded at midnight that "we have been much impressed" by Dix's proposal, especially considering "the conditions surrounding us." Nicolay's young assistant, John Hay, concurred, writing in his diary that "she makes the most munificent and generous offers."[59]

Confident that providence was directing her career, Dix awaited an official appointment with a serenity that contrasted sharply with the tense uncertainty of Washington. "The sun shines fair today," she reported from the capital the next morning. "The innocent song-birds trill their melodies from the budding, leafing trees; the sky is blue and cloudless." The signs of nature offered portents of the nation's future. "The fresh northern breeze keeps us a little dependent on artificial warmth, but leaves one with more strength," she noted optimistically. "While the citizens pursue their accustomed peaceful callings, the soldiers are on drill and learning how to defend the perilled *National Capitol.*"[60]

After two days of waiting, however, she betrayed her eagerness for the position and sweetened her proposal. She sent a personal note to beleaguered Secretary of War Simon Cameron, one of several Cabinet members who had served in Congress during Dix's land-bill campaign, in which she repeated her "offer of *free service* in the Military Hospitals, for so long as shall be needed." Anticipating opposition from the Army Medical Bureau, she promised to work *"subject to the regulations* established by the Surgical Staff." And seeing the underfunded scramble to gather supplies for war, she emphasized to Cameron that she sought "that *authority* which you as head of the Department can alone give" in order to "call in such substantial aid as I can immediately effect" by soliciting the donation of needed hospital materials.[61]

Cameron accepted Dix's offer the next day. His brief announcement authorized her to "give at all times all necessary aid in organizing military hospitals," particularly by furnishing nurses and assisting in the collection and disbursement of Army supplies.[62] Only Florence Nightingale had ever undertaken a comparable responsibility, but Cameron took no time to define this position clearly or consider other possible candidates for it. The nation simply created the office for Dix, as destiny had evidently made her for the office.

⊱ 13 ⊰

A Huge Wild Beast Has Consumed My Life

DIX RECOGNIZED that the Civil War presented an extraordinary opportunity to realize her most expansive ambitions. As the first and foremost humanitarian to take the field, she enjoyed considerable latitude to choose the specific capacity in which she would symbolize the heroic ascendancy of female benevolence over passion and politics. Her vague mandate from the War Department enabled her to concentrate on gathering donations of supplies, recruiting nurses, organizing hospitals, or tending to soldiers. The shining example of Florence Nightingale similarly offered a powerful but imprecise precedent. Well aware that she was assuming the grandest public role ever undertaken by an American woman, Dix made the definition of her war duties the fullest expression of her lifelong mission.

— 1 —

Dix's first task in the tense, chaotic spring of 1861 was to clarify her relations with the War Department and the profusion of humanitarian initiatives springing up throughout the North. Her policies in this maneuvering both reaffirmed her long-standing ideas about moral reform and demonstrated the political skill she had developed over the past two decades.

Dix faced a difficult challenge in working with the Army Medical Department, headed on an interim basis by Colonel Robert C. Wood during the final illness of longtime Surgeon General Thomas Lawson.

Almost to a man, military physicians opposed the introduction of women nurses with a vehemence that far exceeded the ordinary contempt of career Army officers toward all volunteer relief efforts. Wood, a cautious administrator eager to advance within the Medical Department, expressed the doctors' hostility adroitly in discharging his obligation to work with Dix. He tried to use her appointment to minimize the number of women volunteers and isolate them from the medical bureau. Dix accepted much of the assignment that the Acting Surgeon General designed for her, partly because she did not foresee all of its difficulties but mostly because she believed the role would also serve her own goals.

In his first contacts with Dix, Wood emphasized the standard view of career officers that the best occupation for volunteers was to furnish additional supplies to the Army. If subordinate to the work of military professionals, the task certainly was urgent. The Medical Department, designed to care for a peacetime army of about 15,000 soldiers, was wholly unprepared for a conflict of the scale that the Civil War soon presented. Lint, bandages, clothing, and bedding were in short supply. "All sick & surgical Hospital stores are in all details insufficient," Dix concluded after her introductory meeting with the Acting Surgeon General.[1]

Recognizing this priority, Dix had emphasized her ability to tap private resources when she volunteered her services to the federal government. In fact, however, the solicitation of charitable contributions had played a minor part in her asylum crusades, and she had little experience in conducting a broad-based collection campaign. She was stunned when Wood asked her to supply 500 hospital gowns two days after Cameron's announcement that the government had accepted her services. Eager to pass this apparent test of her usefulness, she promptly spent all of her available cash to buy the gowns personally. In anticipation of the next calls for hospital supplies, she sent an almost desperate note to Thomas Kirkbride asking the asylum superintendent to help her find donors. A few days later, she added a suggestion that he put his patients at the Pennsylvania Hospital for the Insane to work scraping lint from table linen.[2]

But if Dix's instinctive reliance on a small personal supply network showed little inclination or ability to funnel large quantities of supplies into the Medical Department, she clearly saw that private contributions could play an important part in her plans for her role as well as Wood's view of it. Her well-publicized campaign to provide lifeboats at Sable Island had demonstrated her ability to combine fund-raising and self-promotion. Shrewd in stretching money, she had routinely obtained additional influence in mental institutions through her modest gifts and fund-raising efforts. She soon applied to military hospitals her asylum strategy of furnishing unbudgeted materials rather than building up basic supplies. "Government buys no *comforts* or *conveniences* for Hospitals," she explained to Kirkbride in her next request, for a set of institutional-sized coffee pots.[3]

More complex than Dix's role in plenishing hospital stores was her authority to recruit women nurses. Cameron had charged her with "aiding the Chief Surgeons by supplying nurses," but she soon assumed far broader duties. Like other observers, Wood realized that many northern women would not await a government commission to visit military hospitals. In hopes of forestalling this expected flood of volunteers, the Acting Surgeon General interpreted Cameron's directive as placing Dix in charge of all women nurses. On May 1, he issued an announcement instructing interested women to contact Dix at her residence on 12th Street "before entering upon their duties." Sounding a theme that would be manipulated constantly throughout the war, he emphasized that "efficient and well-directed service can only be rendered through a systematic arrangement."[4] To the Army Medical Department, efficiency and systematic arrangement meant the elimination of unsanctioned hospital attendants and the reduction of women's involvement to a minimum. If Dix took public responsibility for restraining as well as supplying women nurses, she might be made to serve, in the subsequent words of one critic, as "a break-water against which feminine sympathies could dash and splash without submerging the hospital service."[5]

Dix stepped readily into this prominent but precarious position between the government and the volunteers. She had already asserted her authority in opening relations with the most important of the soldiers' aid societies organizing throughout the North, the Woman's Central Association of Relief. Initially sponsored by Elizabeth Blackwell, the first woman to have graduated from an American medical school, the New York City group planned not only to collect bandages and other hospital supplies but also to train women nurses. At a preliminary organizational meeting on April 25 at the New York Infirmary for

Women she had founded several years before the war with her sister Emily and their fellow physician Maria Zakrzewska, Blackwell proposed to direct a program of instruction for volunteer nurses. Louisa Lee Schuyler, soon to be one of the chief officers of the Association, immediately wrote to sound out Dix on the subject.

On April 29, the day on which the Woman's Central Association of Relief formally organized in an immense public meeting attended by Vice-President Hannibal Hamlin, Dix answered the society from Washington with her fullest statement of her ideas about nursing. While cautioning that volunteers "should by no means come on now," she outlined "some of the many requirements of those who would propose themselves as nurses for the sick and wounded." Medical training was of secondary interest to her. Although she hazily endorsed "some suitable organized instruction in nursing duties," Dix devoted little attention to the content or administration of the program. "If a conflict ensues," she wrote, still hoping vainly for a sectional reconciliation, "let the leading surgeons of New York direct and decide the course which should be adopted."[6]

Far more important to Dix were the moral and spiritual qualifications of women nurses. She called for volunteers "who are sober, earnest, self-sacrificing, and self-sustained; who can bear the presence of suffering and exercise entire self-control, of speech and manner; who can be calm, gentle, quiet, active, and steadfast in duty, also who are willing to take and to execute the directions of the surgeons of the divisions in which they are stationed." Her profile of the ideal nurse, dominated by themes of self-reliance and self-discipline, epitomized Dix's religious values. Two additional requirements further reflected her eagerness to obtain nurses as much like herself as possible. Insistent on her own status as an unpaid volunteer, she expected nurses to be "women who can afford to give their services and time and meet part of their expenses or the whole." And to govern the nurses' mandatory independence, she looked for a practical test of each candidate's emotional maturity. "No young ladies should be sent at all," Dix declared, presumably unaware that her correspondent, Louisa Lee Schuyler, was only twenty-four years old.[7]

Dix repeated some of the same points in a press release issued after Wood referred all prospective women nurses to her. In one of the few statements to publicize nursing opportunities at the outset of the war,

283

she asked volunteers on May 4 not to leave home until notified that the Army wanted them. And although neither Secretary Cameron nor Congress had made any decisions about compensating women nurses, Dix again set forth her position that "this is a *free* service," for which the volunteers should expect no wages or reimbursement of expenses.[8] For her, as for the Acting Surgeon General, female benevolence and government authority were to preserve much of their antebellum separation during their wartime union. The terse statement and the lack of other publicity seemed designed to discourage rather than recruit women who wished to help the soldiers, but Dix was not troubled about limiting the number in her corps, for she expected nursing to influence the nation primarily through her personal example. Nightingale, after all, had achieved immortality by leading a few dozen volunteers.[9]

In the two weeks after Dix's May 4 press release, further developments in the Woman's Central Association of Relief increased the likelihood that she could establish a satisfactory relationship with her fellow humanitarian volunteers as she had with the Army Medical Department. Unitarian minister Henry Whitney Bellows, the presiding official at both organizing meetings of the Woman's Central Association, now moved forward with his own plans to create an organization that would seek far more wide-ranging influence. Working closely with several leading New York physicians, Bellows took charge of a committee appointed by the Woman's Central Association to go to Washington to obtain federal approval for the body that would soon come to be called the Sanitary Commission.[10]

As indicated by its name—taken from the Sanitary Commission created by Great Britain at the close of the Crimean War to investigate the appalling incidence of military deaths caused by disease—the new organization aimed not only to coordinate the donations from soldiers' aid societies throughout the North but also to mobilize the medical profession. Physicians Elisha Harris and William H. Van Buren proposed to inspect health conditions in Army installations and promote the use of current hygienic theories and surgical techniques. Moreover, Bellows also had more sweeping goals for the agency. The clergyman wanted his Sanitary Commission to assume leadership in the promotion of civilian and military morale as well as in solicitude for soldiers' physical well-being. As a model social institution and powerful propaganda machine, the Sanitary Commission would help to influence the conduct of the war and guide the expected redefinition of American character.

Bellows left New York with his delegation as soon as direct train service to Washington resumed upon the repair of connecting bridges and the reassuring concentration of troops in the Union capital. On the evening of May 16, he settled into Willard's hotel, headquarters for the circulation of war rumors and formulation of unofficial initiatives. The next morning at 9:00, he met with Dix to discuss the idea of a Sanitary Commission. The immediate conference suggested the similarity of the relief projects and the fair prospect for cooperation between them, although their animating principles were in some ways profoundly different.

Indeed, Bellows's conception of the Sanitary Commission had originated as a critique of the strain of Unitarianism that Dix personified. Alarmed that the Puritan roots of the church and the influence of William Ellery Channing had left Unitarianism without an adequate institutional framework, the fifty-two-year-old Bellows firmly advocated what he called "the doctrine of institutions." The stimulation of personal piety and benevolence—the hallmarks of Ezra Stiles Gannett, William Greenleaf Eliot, and other clergymen admired by Dix—formed a subordinate part of Bellows's ministry. He dedicated most of his career to the jurisdictional and financial affairs of parishes, the construction of church buildings, and the founding of denominational schools and newspapers. The Protestant vanguard had overemphasized "self-directing, self-asserting, self-developing, self-culturing faculties," Bellows argued in an important 1859 speech at the Harvard Divinity School designed to counterbalance Emerson's scandalous Divinity School Address of 1838. The Sanitary Commission brought this proposed reform of Unitarianism to a secular climax: the organization would forge national identity by disciplining the spontaneous patriotism and philanthropy of individual citizens.[11]

But although Bellows's ideas squarely contradicted Dix's understanding of reform as an expansion of personal self-governance, their wartime projects shared important grounds for mutual accommodation. Dix had long cooperated with a variety of political allies, and Bellows, as one of his closest wartime associates later observed, was markedly not "an *ideologue.*"[12] More particularly, their common Unitarianism established a

285

potentially powerful bond between them. The minister had developed his critique of individualism not merely to articulate an abstract social philosophy but to defend the church from a Transcendentalist fragmentation that Dix equally professed to abhor. Other forms of denominational loyalty further guaranteed goodwill between the relief organizers. Not the least of these sources of Unitarian identity was Dix's own reputation, energetically promoted by ministers like Bellows. His own first cousin, Frederick Newman Knapp, destined to be one of the principal agents of the Sanitary Commission, had illustrated this process while he was Anne Heath's pastor in Brookline, eulogizing Dix in a sermon on the text of "Jesus with us."[13]

In addition to the tie of Unitarianism, the complementary strengths of Dix and the Sanitary Commission raised hopes for a strong working relationship. Unlike Dix, Bellows and the physicians with whom he planned the Commission had little reputation outside of their professional circles and almost no personal connections in Washington. Conversely, the vast network of relief societies envisioned by Bellows promised to free Dix from the burdens of coordinating large donations of hospital supplies and recruiting nurses. In short, the proposed Sanitary Commission offered Dix an arrangement much like her relationship with the Association of Medical Superintendents, materially advancing her efforts to serve as a national symbol of benevolence.

Dix enthusiastically agreed to back the Sanitary Commission in her May 17 meeting with Bellows, and a few days later she joined in the New York delegation's presentation to the Acting Surgeon General. Wood quickly recommended to Cameron that the War Department adopt Bellows's formal proposal, including the employment of one hundred women nurses to receive training through the Woman's Central Association of Relief. Growing more optimistic about the work ahead in Washington, Dix decided that "I think Hospital organization here will gradually become fully satisfactory."[14] She had further reason to be pleased when Wood authorized her on May 20 to supervise the assignment of nurses to military hospitals in and around the capital, except at a few hospitals already served by Catholic nuns. Her authority over women volunteers in the Washington area was now virtually complete, "subject to the advisement and control of the Surgeon-General's Office in matters of detail, numbers, etc."[15] One month after proposing to command her new model army of women, Dix had turned Cameron's vague mandate into working relationships with the Medical Department and the ambitious Sanitary Commission, and she had assumed direction of an incoming corps of well-trained volunteers. Her expansive hopes for the Civil War were beginning to take definite shape.

— 2 —

If Dix's duties to solicit hospital supplies and recruit nurses resolved into a test of her political skills, her charge from Cameron to "give, at all times, all necessary aid in organizing Military Hospitals" also engaged her in the sort of administrative activities she had for so long conducted in mental hospitals, almshouses, prisons, and other public institutions. The Army Medical Department, which consisted of fewer than one hundred doctors at the outbreak of the war, had no general hospitals; its largest facility was a post hospital in Leavenworth, Kansas, with only forty beds.[16] Dix joined eagerly in the effort to improvise treatment centers in and around Washington. As the medical bureau hastily converted hotels, colleges, and even one District of Columbia jail, Dix demonstrated the shift of her own energies by asking Charles Nichols to make room for sick and wounded soldiers at the Government Hospital for the Insane.[17]

The primary tasks that Dix saw for herself in the establishment of hospitals—critical inspection of facilities and advocacy of improvements—followed not only from her prewar reform career but also from the conception of hospital nursing advanced by Florence Nightingale. As the popular *Notes on Nursing* made clear, Nightingale envisioned nurses as the managers of a moral environment that facilitated the recovery of patients. The hospital nurse, as sovereign in her domain as nineteenth-century rhetoric imagined the woman to be in her home, was responsible for protecting patients from all sources of potential harm, including incompetent physicians as well as inadequate light, unclean air, excessive noise, and poor food.[18] Dix assumed this duty with relish. When the governor of Massachusetts sent Samuel Gridley Howe to the capital in late May 1861 to examine medical preparations for the state's volunteers, the famous philanthropist reported in a public letter that "the ladies of Washington visit the infirmary frequently, and Miss Dix, who is the terror of all mere for-

malists, idlers, and evil-doers, goes there, as she goes everywhere, to prevent and remedy abuse and shortcomings."[19]

Dix's criticisms quickly antagonized further the Army doctors who
from the outset had strenuously opposed the introduction of women
nurses. Charles Nichols noted in early June that she was "thorning the
Army Surgeons immensely." "She seems to the surgeons, some of them
at least, impracticable & meddlesome," Nichols evenhandedly told Kirkbride, "and they seem to her inattentive, inefficient & unfeeling in their
intercourse with the sick, & grossly ignorant of nursing & cooking."[20]
The clash was ironic, for Dix's fame resulted in no small part from her
vigorous promotion of exclusive medical authority in mental hospitals,
but it was predictable. Nightingale's system maintained that "a patient
is much better cared for in an institution where there is the perpetual
rub between doctors and nurses." Collisions like those experienced by
Dix were "often disagreeable, but generally salutary."[21] The question was
whether she would emerge from the conflict, as in previous disputes over
the administration of public institutions, with her reputation and
authority enhanced.

Nichols, a perceptive observer, recognized that his patron was "getting the upper hand." The movement by leading physicians to create a
Sanitary Commission testified to the widespread public conviction that
the tradition-bound, seniority-dominated Medical Department was not
merely too small but pervasively inept, a judgment supported by memories of the Mexican War, in which disease killed seven American soldiers
for every one who died from battle wounds.[22] Nichols believed that Dix's
criticisms were "half right at least" and winning popular approval. "The
officers have cursed her & the men blessed her," he reported. He foresaw
that her awesome energies would be sustained indefinitely by "really
doing some good & fancying she does a great deal." And after almost a
decade of experience in Washington politics, he knew too that while
"many an army surgeon . . . has sent her to h-ll as far as his fiat could
do it," Dix enjoyed considerably more influence than her critics, "being
supported by both ends of the service, the Secretary of War & the soldiers." Like Acting Surgeon General Wood, the staff physicians would
have to learn to compromise with the foremost woman in the Union
war effort.

Despite this progress in her hospital inspections and occasional plaudits like Howe's letter, Dix longed to move closer to the central stage of the crisis and to nurse soldiers who had been wounded in battle. Like many other observers, she expected the war to begin in earnest near Fortress Monroe, the key Union outpost near the mouth of the James River, and at the end of May 1861 she obtained a pass from Cameron to help organize hospitals on the Virginia peninsula. "There is soon to be some active service there I fear, and our brave men must be provided for if wounded," she explained to Anne Heath. "I have but one difficulty which is [the] chance of being [there] longer than I desire; but it would be better to be there during the battle if there is one." Before she left she issued another announcement instructing women not to go to Washington or any other military installation. She still hoped that these volunteers would prove unnecessary and that a swift, glorious Union victory would strengthen the agitated and pointlessly divided country. Despite the intensifying martial fervor of the past six weeks, her battle cry remained "God grant us a solid peace!"[23]

During late May and June, Dix tried to turn the attention of northern women from nursing to a different patriotic service. She called on them to sew havelocks, cloth coverings for military caps that covered soldiers' necks to provide protection from the sun. "*Do* make *Havelocks for the Troops!*" Dix beseeched Heath. "*Any* quantity wanted from *1000* to *5000!*" She exhorted the Woman's Central Association of Relief to produce 20,000 more, and Philadelphia newspapers circulated her appeal that the Army "never can have too many of them." After she visited Fortress Monroe, she worried that "*thousands* of men are *suffering* for Havelocks."[24] Dix did not invent the northern craze for havelocks, used by British troops in India under Sir Henry Havelock, and it is not entirely clear why she considered this curious phase of war preparations so urgent. In part, at least, the conspicuous commitment to preventive medicine dramatized the impotence of her critics in the Army Medical Department. Havelocks were essential, she told one friend, because "the cases of sun stroke are almost always fatal through the ignorance of parties who ought to know how to treat the cases."[25]

Although Dix's havelock campaign did not succeed, the reallocation of military medical responsibilities in June 1861 amply indicated her ascendancy. On June 10, Cameron formally outlined her role in detail to the new Surgeon General, Clement A. Finley, who by the Medical

Department's seniority system had supplanted Wood upon the death of Thomas Lawson. The secretary explained that "public sentiment and the humanity of the age" dictated that "women nurses be adopted or substituted for men nurses in the General Hospitals, whenever it can be effected." He wrote that "in order to prevent embarrassing applications and to exclude persons unfitted by youth, inexperience and temperament" he was empowering Dix "to preside over the volunteer women nurses" and to exercise "sole authority to select and accept nurses." Perhaps reflecting discussions with Dix, the War Department required all nurses to be over thirty years old and to present "certificates of character and capacity" from two doctors and two clergymen.[26]

Beyond Dix's recruitment duties, Cameron also vested her with broader administrative powers. Ratifying the authority previously conferred by Wood to assign nurses in Washington hospitals, the Secretary of War now extended her jurisdiction across the country. He also charged her with "diligent oversight" of the nurses, although he noted that "it is of course, understood, that all women nurses are to be under the direction of the Surgeons in charge of the Hospitals." Finally, Cameron provided that Dix "will have the right and duty of visitor and inspector" in military hospitals, and he ordered that "her suggestions, wishes and counsels, will be respected and carried out as far as is compatible with the order of the Medical Bureau." Expressing his confidence in "the past services, the great experience, and the humane intentions of Miss D. L. Dix," the Secretary of War appointed her Superintendent of Women Nurses, the first position of federal executive authority to be held by a woman in American history.[27]

At the same time, the War Department also furnished Dix with a useful ally against the hostile Army medical bureau. On Cameron's recommendation, Lincoln approved formation of the Sanitary Commission on June 13 to conduct inquiries and advise the Medical Department on a broad range of topics, including "the proper provision of cooks, nurses, and hospitals." Especially promising for Dix, the six civilians named to the original panel included not only Henry Whitney Bellows but also, in an attempt to make the New York initiative into a national organization, her old associate and promoter Samuel Gridley Howe.[28]

Fittingly, four days after Dix assumed the title of Superintendent of Women Nurses, friends in England sent her a photograph of Florence

Nightingale. Dix's success in following the example of the transatlantic heroine was made clear by Cameron's widely publicized July 1 report to Lincoln on preparations for war in the six hectic weeks after the fall of Fort Sumter. The secretary's comprehensive survey of the situation left little space to describe the organization of military hospitals and ancillary medical topics. Cameron informed the president and the American people only of what seemed most vital: that "this important subject" had been wholly "intrusted to the charge of Miss D. L. Dix."[29] Thus recognized as a national personification of vast, complex relief preparations, Dix was on the way to winning her war before the first battle had been fought.

— 3 —

Even as Cameron saluted the Superintendent of Women Nurses, however, Dix faced challenges to her authority. Tensions emerged first between her and the Woman's Central Association of Relief. Stymied in her own aspirations to lead the wartime contributions of northern women, Elizabeth Blackwell grumbled that Dix had been appointed "meddler general" and was "without system, or any practical knowledge of the business."[30] The personal rivalry merged with a deeper generational and ideological conflict. Dix's preference for older nurses, codified by Cameron's directive that volunteers be over thirty years of age, seemed an insult to the young New York women who had quickly taken control of the Central Association. As Louisa Lee Schuyler and other leaders of the Central Association sought to forge personal identities in an age of national crisis, they pinpointed the Superintendent of Nurses as the foremost representative of the older generation to be overthrown.[31]

Dix's early encounters with the Central Association's representatives in Washington vividly illustrated this tension. Twenty-eight-year-old Georgeanna Woolsey, one of the first graduates of Blackwell's training program, arrived in the capital with her sister Eliza Howard on July 3 and began to report back to the Central Association leadership—including her sisters Abby and Jane Woolsey—on the management of Army hospitals and the assignments received by women nurses. As Dix fully recognized, these daughters of the New York elite represented the core constituency for her ideals of female benevolence. She warmly welcomed the Woolseys to Washington and furnished information about the progress of hospital organization.[32]

When Georgeanna stopped on one of her inspection visits to fan a dying soldier, however, the surgeon in charge of the hospital promptly protested her unauthorized solicitude, and the dispute exposed the dilemma of the Superintendent of Women Nurses. Establishing a pattern that would be repeated constantly, Woolsey's voluntarism forced Dix to choose between enforcing her government position and recognizing individual initiatives that resembled her own self-constituted mission to the insane. Fatefully, she upheld her office rather than her example. Together with the doctor, Woolsey later recalled, Dix "brought all the weight of professional indignation to bear upon me." But the real issue was not professionalism in nursing; the superintendent and the agent for the Central Association differed more fundamentally about the role of women in America. In sharp contrast to Dix's aims to represent the benevolent Christian ideals of women who mostly remained outside of public life, Woolsey claimed the right of women to participate directly in national affairs. She reasoned that "I was the Benevolent Public, and . . . the sick soldiers were, in some sort, the property of the B.P." She accordingly "informed the Bogies (how well that rhymes with Fogies) that I had ordered my carriage to return at such an hour, that the sun was hot, that I had no intention whatever of walking out in it, and that, in short, I had decided to remain."[33]

The Woman's Central Association firmly supported its agent's symbolic stand against the superintendent. "Your rebuff by Miss Dix has been the subject of great indignation," Jane Woolsey reported to her sister. She exhorted Georgeanna to "outflank the Dix by any and every means in your power . . . We shall be disappointed if you do not establish some sort of relations with the hospitals, at least enough to give you free access, and to make a reliable channel for such things as we can send."[34]

In addition to the frustrations posed by competing humanitarians and excluded volunteers, Dix also quickly faced conflict within the Office of Women Nurses, as she came to call her command. From the outset, she treated the nurses with the same affectionate condescension she had shown to her pupils throughout her schoolteaching career. Her rules of conduct for hospital nurses echoed her plans for a model boardinghouse at the Massachusetts State Normal School. One volunteer reported that the women "must be in their own room at taps, or nine o'clock, unless obliged to be with the sick; must not go to any place of amusement in the evening; must not walk out with any private officer; must not allow a private or officer in their own room except on business."[35] The superintendent's strict personal austerity set the standard for her general guideline that "a nurse will dress according to her work."[36] Yet Dix warmly welcomed every new nurse to Washington by taking her on a tour of the city. Perhaps imitating a famous habit of Nightingale's, she regularly gave money, food, clothes, tea, flowers, and other small gifts to her nurses to supplement the meager wages that Cameron had authorized. And unconsciously following a habit of her own grandmother's, she often addressed her charges as "my child," a tendency that startled some of the middle-aged volunteers who looked as old as Dix.[37]

Like her students long ago, nurses reacted sharply to Dix's commanding personality. Despite her maternal gestures, she struck many observers as cold and distant. She kept her own counsel, neither discussing her vision of the nursing initiative with her fellow women volunteers nor revealing to them the reasons for the orders she imperiously issued. Critics pronounced her "arbitrary & impudent," a reflection of her emotional isolation as well as her anti-institutional thinking and the haughty righteousness that tended to break through her formal manners. Her admirers—an easily neglected faction in Dix's wartime career as in her schoolteaching debacle on Washington Street—similarly felt frustrated by unexplained decisions and recognized that the superintendent was "very peculiar about every thing." They emphasized instead her dignified bearing, her awkward kindnesses, and her determination to give far more of herself to the war effort than she asked from anyone else.[38]

Regardless of their personal reactions to Dix, almost all new nurses arriving in Washington were initially shocked by the intensity of her clashes with Army doctors. Catharine Lawrence, an early graduate of Blackwell's training program, expressed astonishment and dismay when Dix assigned her to a Baltimore hospital despite a request for help from physicians at Fortress Monroe. "She heeds not the doctor's authority, and yet she wears no military badge," Lawrence aptly summarized.[39] Contrary to the popular ideal of patriotic relief efforts as the epitome of northern unity, Dix seemed to be waging a civil war that pitted women against men, moral treatment against medical science, and individual willpower against the government.

The belligerent attitude Dix adopted toward the only major group of women nurses beyond her jurisdiction, the various Catholic sisterhoods at work in Army hospitals, illustrated the confrontational style that surprised and disenchanted some of her early recruits. Although the services of the nuns generally helped to temper pervasive northern anti-Catholicism, Dix aggressively sharpened the division between her charges and her principal rivals. She instructed subordinates like Lawrence "not to speak to those Catholic nurses."[40] Beyond the main-stream religious prejudice Dix had developed before the war, her animosity reflected her recognition that Army doctors would seek to employ the nuns as widely as possible to limit her influence as Superintendent of Women Nurses.

Catherine Lawrence's experience revealed not only a typical reaction to Dix by an early recruit but also the availability of alternative arrangements for the disaffected. Unable to see why Dix had assigned her to Baltimore, Lawrence resigned from the nursing corps during the summer of 1861 and secured a nursing position at the Kalorama Hospital in Washington. She later claimed that Surgeon General Finley turned down Dix's appeal to remove her from this new post, although it is probable that at some point the superintendent simply let the matter drop.[41]

Dix's plan to cooperate with the Sanitary Commission offered a shrewd solution to the rifts that emerged in her early dealings with the Woman's Central Association of Relief and the first volunteer nurses. The Sanitary Commission continued to work closely with the Woman's Central Association and could be relied on to exert considerable influence in defining relations with the Superintendent of Women Nurses. And fully keeping pace with Dix in its contempt for the Medical Department, the Sanitary Commission actively sought to turn public opinion in a direction that would support her criticisms of Army surgeons. As the northern prop-aganda unit most concerned with military health, the commission offered a means to shape the expectations of incoming nurses and estab-lish a unified image of moral triumph from Dix's countless daily inter-actions with nurses, doctors, and soldiers.

Based less on a common philosophy than personal ties and mutual advantage, the marriage of opposites envisioned by Bellows and Dix became dramatically apparent when the commission first met in Washington in July 1861. Although Dix held an appointment from the War Department and her subordinates were Army employees, the Office of Women Nurses was plainly the lengthened shadow of one woman. Dix continued to work without pay and without an administrative hierarchy beneath her. Moving to a rented house at 430 15th Street, she maintained her headquarters in her home, which also served as a warehouse for donated supplies and a refuge for nurses who temporarily needed a place to stay. The Sanitary Commission, in contrast, missed no opportunity to emphasize that its activities had been sanctioned by the federal government. While in Washington, the commissioners met in the Treasury Department building across the street from Dix's house. Wall Street lawyer George Templeton Strong, added to the commission as treasurer in an earlier New York meeting, marveled at the "very grand official room in the Treasury Building, with its long, official, green-covered table and chairs ranged in official order around it, and official stationery in front of each chair." Strong observed that "one could not sit there a moment without official sensations of dignity and red-tapery."[42]

Dix's personal relations with the members of the Sanitary Commission opened without the full harmony she had had reason to anticipate. Samuel Gridley Howe failed to attend the meeting, foreshadowing his limited interest in the commission throughout the war. And perhaps in part because Dix had not bothered to introduce herself to the New York members through influential intermediaries like the family of John Adams Dix, the renowned humanitarian failed to impress some key figures whom she now met for the first time. With no haze of goodwill to obscure the ideological conflicts between the Sanitary Commission and the Superintendent of Women Nurses, Strong deemed the commissioners fortunate to have "extricated ourselves from an entanglement with that philanthropic lunatic." A few weeks later, he brilliantly summarized the admirable and exasperating qualities he saw in Dix. "She is energetic, benevolent, unselfish, and a mild case of monomania," Strong wrote in his famous diary. "Working on her own hook, she does good, but no one can cooperate with her, for she belongs to the class of comets and can be subdued into relations with no system whatever."[43]

One particularly unfavorable turn of events for Dix had taken place even before the Sanitary Commission came to the capital. On June 20, the commission appointed Frederick Law Olmsted its resident secretary in Washington, a position he swiftly made tantamount to that of chief executive officer. The thirty-nine-year-old Olmsted was impressively prepared to advance the commission's bureaucratic, political, and propaganda goals. As superintendent of Central Park in New York City, he had managed a large crew of construction workers and proven himself an adept infighter in a treacherous government, and he was also well known for a series of travel books in which he had surveyed the slave states from a free-labor perspective as rigid as the Whig Unionism through which Dix had seen the South. More than any other member of the Sanitary Commission, Olmsted invigorated the organization's parallel drives for scientific humanitarianism and national discipline with a relentless doctrinaire fervor, perhaps a remnant of the religious turmoil that had preceded his current agnosticism. From Dix's point of view, he was in all respects a less fortunate choice for the commission's executive post than the other major candidate, Unitarian minister Edward Everett Hale, a Bostonian linked to her by a host of loyalties, associations, and friendships.[44]

But if Dix's relations with the Woman's Central Association of Relief and the Sanitary Commission might have been more congenial, the Union humanitarian coalition nevertheless worked well together. Dix remained eager to cooperate. She tried to smooth over her flap with Georgeanna Woolsey in a series of gracious notes and assurances that "any requisition on my stores will always be met."[45] She appointed the most energetic promoters of the Sanitary Commission's branch in Chicago, Mary Livermore and Jane Hoge, her agents for the recruitment of nurses in the Northwest. When Blackwell tested the superintendent by sending underage volunteer Caroline Burghardt to Washington, Dix not only certified the recruit but made her a lifelong personal protégée. By the fall of 1861, she had assigned thirty-two graduates of Blackwell's training program to hospitals in Washington, Georgetown, and Alexandria.[46] She also made sure to meet with the Sanitary Commission when it convened in Washington, and Olmsted found that she "kept poking me up" with accounts of the government inefficiency they both deplored.[47] After the battle of Bull Run, Dix joined with Olmsted, Knapp, and other commission inspectors to assess the quickly overburdened hospital system. Her military pass from President Lincoln, directing "all persons in official charge of Hospitals, to render at all times every facility to Miss D. L. Dix," testified to her stature as a national exemplar of wartime philanthropy.[48]

On August 3, Congress ratified Cameron's order sanctioning women nurses and formalized the payment of wages and rations to the volunteers.[49] The Sanitary Commission, already preparing to lobby for a more comprehensive legislative overhaul of the Medical Department, planned to include a further consolidation of Dix's initiative in the reform proposal. The superintendent's mood remained buoyant, although like many Americans she had found herself suddenly working harder than ever before.[50] In mid-August, as the North regrouped after the shocking rout of Union troops at Manassas, Dix temporarily gave in to debility and retreated to the New Jersey State Lunatic Asylum for several days. The convalescence would prove to be her last peaceful respite of the war.

— 4 —

While Dix was resting at Trenton, the next major military engagement turned her Civil War toward its pivotal crisis. Disorganization and supply shortages at the battle of Wilson's Creek on August 10 led to a medical catastrophe in which hundreds of wounded Union soldiers suffered in the summer Missouri heat for a full week without rudimentary treatment. John C. Frémont, the federal commander of the Western Department, telegraphed a request to Dix to "come here and organize these hospitals." "You can do vast good by coming and you will be very welcome," the impetuous leader assured her shortly before his ill-fated proclamation of emancipation and martial law in Missouri. When Dix arrived at Frémont's headquarters in St. Louis on September 2, she found that local citizens led by William Greenleaf Eliot had already begun to organize an impressive relief network. Three days later, Frémont formally recognized the Western Sanitary Commission, to be headed by Dix's friend and former housemate James Yeatman, the son of Jane Erwin Yeatman Bell.[51]

The leaders of the existing Sanitary Commission were furious when they learned of the new organization, established without the involvement of the commission's regional secretary for the Western Department or its agent in St. Louis. To Bellows and Olmsted, the two humanitarian ventures exactly paralleled the central issue of the war. Local autonomy was undermining national unity, just as southern secession had ruptured the country. Olmsted added at the top of his lobbying agenda an urgent appeal to the War Department to overrule Frémont's order or subordinate the Western Sanitary Commission to its more ambitious counterpart. Underscoring the point, the New York–based Sanitary Commission soon began to call itself the United States Sanitary Commission.[52]

Dix's exact role in the founding of the Western Commission remained unclear, but her loyalties in the ensuing conflict were plain. Although she denied any responsibility and Eliot maintained that Frémont acted solely on his suggestion in establishing the new organization, Dix supported the initiative by delegating to James Yeatman her authority to assign nurses in the trans-Mississippi theater. She evidently did not urge affiliation with the United States Sanitary Commission or attempt to involve its regional agents in the creation of the western hospital system. In all probability, she simply deferred to the determination of her close friend Eliot, whose course seemed to be governed as much by personal ambition as by his claims that the unique wartime conditions in Missouri required a separate relief organization.

Whatever Dix's influence in St. Louis may have been, the leaders of the United States Sanitary Commission blamed her for the schism. "This has doubtless been got up by that indefatigable woman," Strong fumed when he heard of the new rival. Despite Dix's efforts to work harmoniously with both commissions, Strong speculated that "she is disgusted with us, because we do not leave everything else and rush off the instant she tells us of something that needs attention." In place of the mixed admiration and exasperation he had expressed six weeks earlier, he now lashed out against Dix as the stock negative stereotype of wartime philanthropy, a sentimental incompetent. Historians would later see the differences between Dix and the Sanitary Commission encapsulated in Strong's complaint that "the last time we were in Washington, she came upon us in breathless excitement to say that a cow in the Smithsonian grounds was dying of sunstroke, and she took it very ill that we did not adjourn instantly to look after the case." But more important than the incident itself was the fact that Strong only seized upon it as significant in the midst of a separate disagreement. The clash between Dix and the

Sanitary Commission involved no conflict between tender hearts and hard heads.[53]

Ultimately frustrated in its efforts to stop the Western Sanitary Commission, which remained a powerful fund-raising rival throughout the war, especially in the New England states, the United States Sanitary Commission made Dix the principal casualty of the humanitarians' battle of St. Louis. On September 27, Olmsted concluded that the commission should drop plans to cement her authority in the upcoming legislative campaign to reorganize the Medical Department. He told Bellows that another conversation with Dix about the continuing hostility of Army doctors had convinced him that "female nurses, in her, and our plan, are . . . not practicable." Although ordinarily not one to surrender easily to Medical Department resistance, Olmsted professed that abandonment of the superintendent simply reflected Dix's own conclusion that there was "but one doctor who really does well with the nurses, and he, she thinks, is a Secessionist." "Poor Miss Dix," Olmsted sympathized disingenuously. "I really am distressed for her, as well as on my own account."[54]

Shortly after he eliminated the women nurses from his efforts in Congress, Olmsted published a nationwide circular in October 1861 that similarly struck at Dix's supply of private donations for the troops. The Sanitary Commission, he emphasized, was the only reliable agent for the administration of charity. When Dix protested the undermining of her authorized collection efforts, the extraordinarily well-informed Olmsted claimed ignorance of her public solicitations. Perhaps because she stored the donations in her house just across 15th Street from the commission's official meeting room in the Treasury building, Dix found this excuse "strange."[55]

Most important, the Woman's Central Association of Relief announced that it would no longer supply nurses to Dix. Women serving in Army hospitals held "a very uncertain semi-legal position, with poor wages and little sympathy," the Central Association complained. The official explanation for the decision, that Blackwell's well-trained, dignified graduates were "the objects of continual evil speaking among coarse subordinates," closely echoed Olmsted's report that "there is not a woman in all the hospitals of Washington, unless she be of the Sisters, who is not constantly watched for evidences of favor to individuals and for grounds of scandalous suspicion."[56] The Central Association's reversal of policy left Dix to recruit and train her own nurses. This arrangement required that she devise a new organizational structure, a burden she was unprepared to meet. For the remainder of the war she would obtain nurses mainly through informal, inefficient personal contacts, and her hiring decisions would subject her to criticism from the acquaintances of every rejected applicant.

By the end of October, the Union humanitarian partnership had disintegrated. The dispute over the Western Sanitary Commission had broken the bonds of patriotic cooperation, benevolent voluntarism, political advantage, Unitarian denominationalism, and civilian distrust of the Army Medical Department. Dix and the United States Sanitary Commission now began to pursue their related missions with remarkably little interaction. One of her subordinates later wrote that the nurses "sometimes were repulsed like street beggars" when they asked commission officials for hospital supplies.[57] Without the support of the commission, moreover, Dix could no longer suppress the tensions between her ideals and the attitudes typified by the leadership of the Woman's Central Association of Relief.

But if unforeseeable circumstances played a key part in dashing Dix's hopes for cooperation with the Sanitary Commission, the collision also revealed the fundamental contrast between the two reform efforts. It was not by coincidence that Dix had developed a spiritual kinship with Eliot or that she had failed to anticipate the furor of Bellows and Olmsted. She revered the ethos of philanthropic self-cultivation that Ralph Waldo Emerson had recognized in saluting Eliot as "the Saint of the West," and her imaginative world of individual wills and personal relationships scarcely comprehended the bureaucratic reordering of American society endorsed by the Sanitary Commission. Through a combination of luck and logic, she now stood apart from the Sanitary Commission and the Army Medical Department, in the position from which she had for so long sought personal strength: alone.

— 5 —

The depression into which Dix fell after her clash with the Sanitary Commission was less predictable than the conflict itself. Along with her independence, her relentless tenacity was the aspect of her character in which she took the most pride. Throughout her life, she had combined the two traits to rebound repeatedly from personal rejection. Suppressing her anger toward her family, her home city of Boston, and other real or imagined adversaries, she had channeled her energies into a powerful sense of righteousness as a champion for the insane. Now, after her estrangement from the Sanitary Commission, Dix's position as Super-intendent of Women Nurses offered her an opportunity to continue established patterns of behavior and add to her fame and influence by caring for the Union soldiers who were beginning to fill the makeshift hospitals of Washington.

Instead, Dix concluded by November 1861 that "this dreadful civil war has as a huge wild beast consumed my whole of life."[58] Despite her original zeal to participate in the war, she felt none of the exhilaration reported by countless northern volunteers who thought the convulsive ordeal more invigorating than anything they had ever known before. To the contrary, Dix maintained wearily that "the afflictions of this most strange and unprecedented period corrode the forces of life."[59] The phe-nomenal vitality that had sustained her constant travels across the coun-try gave way to a numb despair. "I hardly think at all," she mourned at one point. "I only do day by day that which my heart finds for my hands to perform, or my experience suggests to direct for others."[60]

Dix's appearance reflected her deteriorating spirit. She lost forty pounds in the first seven months of the war, dwindling from a peak weight of 139 pounds to a mere 99 pounds that scarcely filled her five-foot-seven-inch frame. As the war continued she lost even more weight.[61] Although her hair retained most of its red-brown color, her gaunt form and need for eyeglasses ended the illusion that goodness kept her forever young. A few months short of her sixtieth birthday, she was for the first time beginning to look old. When she later acceded to the fad of giving friends a *carte de visite,* or wallet-sized picture card, she distributed copies of a daguerreotype made years before the war.[62]

The Civil War quickly lost for Dix the social and religious meanings that had sharpened her keen expectations. The contest of arms exploded her hopes for a dose of suffering that would teach the nation to quell political passions. "God grant us peace," she prayed in October 1861, "but I see *no* prospect of this, *none.*" The prospect of individual regeneration seemed even less promising than her related vision of national renewal. Significantly, Dix's lifelong religious habits lapsed early in the war. "There is no Sunday now," she told William Rathbone in November, noting that "I have been present in body, I can surely say not in mind, twice, at a religious service during six months."[63] She "doubt[ed] much the wisdom" of William Henry Channing's return from Liverpool to seek a Unitarian awakening in Washington, and she skipped the popular sermons by her former mentor's nephew. "I do not feel inclined to seek my place of prayer in public congregations any more, till peace shall come," she would later explain.[64]

Dix's iron will and her quest for national redemption were partly displaced by a bellicose sectionalism. Her prewar attachment to the South had distinguished her among northern reformers, revealed her antipathy toward her home, and given content to her contempt for political agitation. But after the fighting began she quickly concluded that southerners had been "transformed to demons."[65] Throughout the war she not only credited with absolute certitude almost every rumor of cruelty by rebel soldiers; she identified these incidents as the characteristic expression of an alien, hated people. "I am so amazed and shocked at the *atrocious* conduct of the Confederates," she wrote four months after the battle of Manassas. "No pitiless savages ever perpetrated more horrible atrocities: the acts of the Sepoys fall harmless in comparison. I really never wish to see these traitors and blood thirsty men again."[66]

This open hostility choked deep wellsprings of Dix's energy. No longer did she turn to heroic philanthropy to avenge and submerge her grievances; she released rather than redirected her aggression. After decades of inward struggle, she abandoned her effort to exemplify her religious ideals. "God forgive those savage wretches in the South: *I cannot,*" she blazed later in the war.[67] She told a friend: "If you are a Christian woman enough to pray for me, you may do so, for I can't *just now* 'forgive my enemies,' and do'nt know when I shall obtain that reach of Bible excellence from which I have declined."[68]

Without the public or private motives that had animated Dix's sympathy for the insane, her anticipated ministry to the soldiers devolved into a matter of patriotic duty and personal compassion. And the limits of that compassion, the heart of her prewar reputation, now became apparent. As one of her closest observers later noted, "the tenderness of a mother for a child, the pity that a deeply sympathetic person has for one in affliction, that whole-souled sympathy that goes out from the heart of some to those who are in sore trouble, she did not have."[69] Although Dix fervently appreciated the sacrifices of the Union soldiers, she chose not to devote much of her time to caring for the sick and wounded. She mentioned no individual patients in her letters, unlike so many hospital nurses whose lives became intertwined with the men they attended and whom they often saw die. After the war, a veteran who published several regimental histories as well as a profile of Dix noted that in his extensive researches he had never met a single soldier with any personal recollection of her.[70]

Dix's aimlessness may have contributed to her weak response to the barrage of public criticism that became sharper and more dangerous after her estrangement from the Sanitary Commission. Around the time that Olmsted issued his circular calling on northern civilians to donate supplies solely through the Sanitary Commission, rumors were already spreading that Dix "is *not* the most efficient or reliable agent . . . in many instances, stores have been suffered to remain unpacked, until quite spoiled."[71] The Medical Director of General George B. McClellan's Army of the Potomac simultaneously filed a comprehensive reorganization plan urging that Catholic nuns were "far preferable" to Dix's nurses.[72] In December 1861, her name was drawn into a prolonged newspaper debate between supporters of the Medical Department and the Sanitary Commission when a young female volunteer complained in the New York *Times* that the superintendent "does not live in the hospitals, but in her comfortable house in Washington, and has never nursed a sick soldier, nor folded a shroud over a dead one, since the war began."[73] Even among philanthropic matrons wary of wartime enthusiasm, Dix was fast becoming known as "a deaf and despotic maiden lady of uncertain age."[74]

Most seriously, the clash between Dix and the younger generation began to transform the antebellum heroine into an object of ridicule. Implementing the War Department policy on the age of volunteers and echoing Nightingale's scathing contempt for popular fashions in *Notes on Nursing,* Dix announced: "No woman under thirty years need apply to serve in the government hospitals. All nurses are required to be very plain-looking women. Their dresses must be brown or black, with no bows, no curls, or jewelry, and no hoop-skirts."[75] A derisive howl greeted her typically terse, poorly worded generalization of the informal dress code, and the public distorted her stipulation that women should be "very plain-looking women." In one of the most familiar comic legends to emerge from the Civil War, Dix was branded as a spinster who foolishly believed that the most important qualification for nursing was homeliness. Sanitary Commission leader Mary Livermore vividly summarized the widespread misinterpretation of the superintendent's policy when she later recalled that "women must be over thirty years of age, plain almost to repulsion in dress, and devoid of personal attractions, if they hoped to receive the approval of Miss Dix."[76]

Much of this legend was inaccurate. To be sure, like many observers Dix was acutely concerned about the sexual dynamics within Army hospitals. Along with the surgeons, she saw a troubling romanticization of wartime duty in the seemingly commonplace marriages of nurses to the soldiers they attended.[77] And as she had confided to Olmsted, she also worried that the few nurses to receive the approval of physicians seemed to be "women of bad character . . . in fact the mistresses of the doctors." She pointedly warned new recruits to beware of the surgeons' sexual traps.[78] Her commonplace desire to protect young women undoubtedly resulted in the rejection of many well-qualified applicants. In a decision that reflected not only enforcement of the age restriction but the distinction Dix drew between nursing and medicine, she even turned down a request for a nursing position submitted by one of the few women doctors in the country.[79] But her policies were thoroughly conventional, and she enforced them with more flexibility than her critics acknowledged. She repeatedly waived the War Department's age restriction, and she tolerated a variety of nursing attire, including fashions that appalled her. Contrary to the complaints of some underage applicants, she evidently never rejected a candidate on the basis of personal beauty.[80]

Nevertheless, Dix refused to defend herself against the misleading criticisms. "Mosquitos always will sting, reptiles hiss, and malignant animals attack," she shrugged disdainfully in January 1862 when a friend urged her to answer the newspaper articles about wartime relief efforts.[81] Although Dix recognized that unfavorable publicity caused her "present harm," she could not comprehend the vulnerability of her position. Her self-conception by now inseparable from her antebellum popularity, she never fully understood the extent to which she owed her reputation to the work of interested allies like the Association of Medical Superintendents, the Unitarian clergy, the Whig party, and a host of politicians who promoted her fame to advance their own projects. The Sanitary Commission's renunciation of a similar role threw back upon her the most troublesome dilemma of her career, how to cultivate an influential public image while remaining a paragon of the private virtues of womanhood. As ambivalent about that problem as she had been when she gave up her literary ambitions thirty years earlier, Dix remained silent and hoped to ride out the controversies.

Dix's deeply engrained sense of gender conventions also shaped her failure to respond to the political threat she now faced. Olmsted and the Sanitary Commission devoted much of the winter of 1861–62 to the legislative campaign for reorganization of the Medical Department, setting aside any plans to establish more firmly the position of women nurses in Army hospitals. During the complex series of amendments and compromises that continued until passage of a bill in April 1862, Dix made no effort to use her lobbying experience to secure her current office. Continuing to see herself as a volunteer who represented the authentic national will rather than a mere governmental sanction, she remained aloof from the Union efforts to organize the war.

Dix strikingly demonstrated her view of her independent status when Smithsonian Institution director Joseph Henry—shocked to find his old friend "feeble and exhausted," trudging through the Washington streets in December because her wartime work consumed all of her available income—secretly asked Secretary of War Cameron to provide the Superintendent of Women Nurses with a one-horse wagon and a driver. Although Congress had not authorized any expenditures for female nurses except for wages and rations, Cameron decided that "the law might be stretched a little to do an act of grace and kindness to so good a woman as Miss Dix." Lincoln agreed, but Dix declined the offer. "I give cheerfully my *whole* time, mind, *strength* and *income,* to the service of my country," she informed Cameron. "Indeed I have done this for 21 years, only transferring from Hospitals for the insane the means I now render to the Military service. I cannot now begin to receive any form of remuneration for what I cheerfully render as a loyal woman."[82]

While the Sanitary Commission lobbied for control of the Medical Department, Dix looked to protect her position through her customary strategy of keeping up personal ties with high-ranking officials. The fall of Cameron in January 1862 removed her most important ally, but his replacement, Edwin Stanton, regarded Dix with equally warm personal admiration if not with the same indifference to managerial irregularities in the War Department. Dix also maintained her friendship with William H. Seward, and she enjoyed fine relations with one of the Secretary of State's chief contacts in the Army, Quartermaster General Montgomery C. Meigs, the paragon of efficiency responsible for the construction of hospitals and the supply of provisions. Like many old Washington insiders, she barely knew the president, but she quickly offered to send one of her nurses when she learned that his young sons Willie and Tad were dangerously ill in February 1862. Lincoln accepted the offer after Willie died, and Dix detailed one of her favorite subordinates to the White House. Doubtless oblivious to any appearance of insensitivity, she answered Lincoln's request in early May for an extension of the courtesy with a note recommending candidates for several Medical Department posts created by the passage of the Sanitary Commission's reform legislation.[83]

Dix's isolation from the bureaucratic overhaul rendered her office a strange exception to the organization of Union medical relief. She was not alone, however, in thinking that the appointment of new leadership was the most important part of the commission's successful lobbying campaign. Dismantling the seniority system that had made Clement Finley the Surgeon General, the commission arranged for him to be replaced by thirty-three-year-old physician William A. Hammond, a forceful and efficient medical administrator, a distinguished research scientist, and a protégé of Sanitary Commission founder William H. Van Buren. With the appointment of Hammond in the spring of 1862, the war entered a new phase for the Superintendent of Women Nurses, precisely as the military conflict seemed likely to reach a climax in General George B. McClellan's plan to march his huge, painstakingly drilled Army of the Potomac up the Virginia peninsula between the James and York rivers to capture Richmond.

— 6 —

The Peninsula campaign provided northern women volunteers the sense of glorious triumph that eluded the Union military offensive. Under the direction of Olmsted, the Sanitary Commission assumed responsibility for operating steamships fitted out as "floating hospitals" to transport sick and wounded soldiers from the Virginia lines to hospitals at Fortress Monroe and in northern cities. The commission recruited a group of socially prominent women—including Henry Bellows's wife, Eliza; George Templeton Strong's wife, Ellen; Georgeanna Woolsey; and several other leaders of the Woman's Central Association of Relief—to serve on the ships as "superintendents of nursing." Eager to participate first-hand in the confrontation that many northerners expected to end the war, the women arrived in the final days of McClellan's prolonged siege of Yorktown. "We all know in our hearts that it is thorough enjoyment to be here," exclaimed Central Association officer Katharine Wormeley shortly after Union troops took control of the historic Revolutionary War battle site. *"It is life."*[84]

Dix scrambled to join in the decisive moment of the war and to repair her relations with the Sanitary Commission and the Woman's Central Association. Establishing headquarters in Yorktown at the old brick house that had been used as a command post by Lord Cornwallis, she greeted the arriving commission nurses with lilies of the valley and invited them to join her corps. One volunteer noted with some surprise that the superintendent's "appearance and manner pleased me. She is very ladylike in both, and seemed clear and decisive."[85]

But Dix's efforts did little to win over her fellow volunteers. Aside from the other obstacles to a reconciliation, the institutional links between the Sanitary Commission and the Office of Women Nurses were now too attenuated to allow for much interaction. The newcomers remained almost entirely aboard the transport ships; Dix's work on the Peninsula centered on the base hospital at Fortress Monroe, where her imperious manner and futile claim to full authority over women nurses continued to draw criticism from agents of the Sanitary Commission.[86] Although at least one commission volunteer eventually decided to join the Army nurses under Dix's direction, it was Olmsted who awed the women as an exemplar of efficient service and whose reputation they, especially Katharine Wormeley, would soon begin to promote actively. Olmsted's own reports of the transport initiative—an influential force in the public recognition of women nurses—similarly took no notice of Dix's unit further from the front lines. The most celebrated moment of wartime female benevolence simply passed her by. In somber contrast to the commission volunteers, she hoped only to endure. Even before the Seven Days' battles induced McClellan to abandon the offensive on the doorstep of Richmond, Dix sighed that her participation in the war was "eroding the forces of life." "In the midst of all that is most painful and distressing," she reflected that "the future is not clear: the present full of real anxieties, & the past year very sorrowful to recall:—so *I wait.*"[87]

While most of the commission volunteers wistfully returned to their homes during July 1862, Dix's war continued to plunge further into a chaotic nightmare. Her office initially seemed likely to gain importance after the Peninsula campaign, for the achievements of northern women and the appalling escalation of casualties intensified interest in the use of women nurses. On July 14, Surgeon General Hammond issued a circular order to "give greater utility to the acts of Miss D. L. Dix as 'Superintendent of Women Nurses,'" and Dix issued an order restating her requirements for volunteers.[88] Potentially the most promising provision of Hammond's guidelines concerned the ratio of female to male nurses. Cameron had ordered the substitution of women for convalescent soldiers and other men in the general hospitals "whenever it can be effected," even if no trained volunteers were available, but Congress had authorized the Surgeon General to determine the number of female nurses. Hammond now ordered that women should comprise one-third of the nurses in general hospitals. Although a substantial retreat from Cameron's position, the directive suggested a possible expansion of Dix's office, as she counted only about 250 nurses under her command in Washington and Virginia, less than one-fifth of the hospital staff authorized by Army regulations permitting one nurse for every ten patients.[89]

But Dix continued to see little connection between increasing the number of nurses and adding to the contribution made by her office. In June 1862, as the Union offensive against Richmond neared its climax, she told Hammond that no more nurses were needed on the Peninsula. Moreover, she lacked the recruiting mechanisms necessary to take full advantage of the opportunity provided by Hammond's order, and her reputation as an autocrat discouraged women who were eager to serve. When she asked one of her lieutenants to send to Massachusetts for one hundred nurses, the subordinate refused because she "knew they would not be treated decently when they came." Some women who were offered positions in Dix's corps chose instead to perform unpaid hospital work outside of her jurisdiction.[90] Hammond's proposed ratio remained unfulfilled.

Rather than enforcing the expansion of Dix's office, the new Surgeon General widened the loopholes to her authority. While he prohibited the employment of women nurses without the superintendent's approval, "except in cases of urgent need," he provided that Catholic nuns—originally limited to hospitals at which they had served before the war—would be available whenever doctors obtained their services "under special instructions from this office." When President Lincoln asked Hammond to justify the expanded use of nuns, the Surgeon General answered that Dix's nurses "cannot compare in efficiency and faithfulness with the Sisters of Charity." Similarly, Hammond halfheartedly enjoined his subordinate physicians to "receive [Dix's] suggestions and counsels with respect, and to carry them into effect if compatible with the hospital service." More important as a practical matter, he empowered the chief surgeons at Army hospitals to dismiss women nurses "if incompetent, insubordinate, or otherwise unfit for their vocation," requiring no explanation to Dix and providing for no appeal from the decision.[91]

The failure of Hammond's order to establish peace between Dix and the Army doctors immediately became apparent. Bringing new recruit Mary Phinney to the Mansion House hospital in Alexandria in August 1862, Dix warned that "the surgeon in charge was determined to give her no foothold in any hospital where he reigned, and that I was to take no notice of anything that might occur, and was to make no complaint whatever might happen." Despite the need for additional hospital assistance as the bloody battle of Cedar Mountain shifted the scene of Union frustration from the Peninsula to the Rappahanock River, Phinney found the prediction distressingly accurate. Two surgeons, "the most brutal men I ever saw," tried to "make the house so hot for me I would not stay long." When she complained repeatedly to the superintendent, Dix replied: "You can bear it awhile, my child; I have placed you here and you must stay."[92]

As she continued to battle the doctors, Dix also remained caught in embarrassing conflicts with unofficial nurses willing to forsake the wages paid by the government. Often these volunteers allied themselves with Army surgeons to circumvent Dix's authority. Anna Lowell, successfully looking for work at the Union Hotel Hospital in Georgetown after Dix had rejected her application on the basis of age, expressed a common view when she wrote that she "would prefer to be entirely under Dr. Bliss and have nothing to do with Miss Dix."[93] But neither the strategic protection of the physicians nor the personal determination of the volunteers fully explained the unofficial nurses' continued presence on the wards. For all of the hospital confrontations in which she was involved, Dix revealed an ambivalence about suppressing the self-controlled voluntarism that she identified as the only genuine authority for her own efforts. In the case of Anna Lowell and her friend Sarah Low, it was Dix who resolved the conflict by suggesting that the young volunteers remain in the Union Hotel Hospital as "guests of the house," which Low thought "a much better position than if I was nurse, as I could leave any time for home." The superintendent never seriously pressed the Surgeon General or his superiors in the War Department to close the hospitals to her civilian rivals. She later admired rather than resented the most celebrated freelance nurse of the war, Mary Ann Bickerdyke, known as the "cyclone in calico" for her attentions to Sherman's army in the West.[94]

As the organization of female nursing satisfied almost nobody, Hammond began to urge the adoption of "a different management system" in the fall of 1862, and rumors swept through the hospitals that Dix would be removed from office.[95] Her principal antagonist, however, was the best guarantor of her continued tenure. The Secretary of War, not the Surgeon General, was responsible for the administration of Dix's office, and Stanton despised Hammond. Disgusted that the meddlesome Sanitary Commission had forced its nominee upon him, Stanton remained content to ignore Hammond's complaints and indulge his warm feelings for Dix by remaining aloof from the tempest over women nurses. Stanton's policy of neutrality left Dix in a wearisome bureaucratic struggle in which Hammond slowly chipped away at her jurisdiction. "The *present* Surgeon General chooses to question *most* authority delegated by others," she concluded bitterly in a futile appeal for help from ex-secretary Cameron.[96]

Dix's spirits continued to sink further as she fought her increasingly lonely, aimless war like a soldier detached from his company. The restatement of Union purpose that followed the failure of the Peninsula campaign, climaxing in the commitment to emancipation, left little imprint on her. "It is difficult to look forth from the urgency of the passing hour and reach by a steadier vision to what final better results in human conditions this strife may bring this nation now rent and tossed," she noted in October 1862, shortly after she returned from the ghastly site of the battle of Antietam. She commented only sparingly on public affairs in her painfully nostalgic letters to the Rathbones in England. Her views on emancipation a few weeks after Lincoln's preliminary proclamation reflected her disillusionment. Unable to see a redeeming value in war, she emphasized to her merchant friends "the pleasant fact" that the rapid increase of cotton production in India would "promise the independence of slave labor in the Southern States" regardless of the present upheaval.[97]

Embattled and embittered, Dix continued to spiral downward in public standing through the winter of 1862–63. The most widely admired prewar exemplar of female benevolence was now scorned as "Dragon Dix," an arbitrary and querulous tyrant. "Dragon Dix . . . won't accept the services of any *pretty* nurses . . . ," one typical young woman jeered in January. "Just think of putting such an old thing over everyone else . . . Some fool man did it, so now . . . his sex must suffer from it."[98] Older women often agreed with the confident assertion of a volunteer who proudly claimed the nickname "Mother" that Dix "meant well, but she knew as little of the wants of a hospital as Queen Victoria."[99] Far more rare was the soldier who wrote home from Aquia Creek after an inspection by Dix that "a few such women as she is, are landmarks to show that God has not forsaken us entirely."[100] The superintendent's mixed reputation was better measured by a popular campfire anecdote in which she descended without introduction on a hospital and imperiously ordered sweeping changes in the wards. After a testy confrontation, as soon as she had left the hospital the head surgeon asked a subordinate the basis for Dix's authority. The sage private replied, "Why, she has the rank, pay, honors and emoluments of a major-general of volunteers, and if you have got her down on you, you might as well have all hell after you!"[101]

The notoriety fanned by private letters and conversations entered only occasionally into the exhaustive scrutiny of the war in newspapers, magazines, pamphlets, and books. Propriety ensured that Dix would be coolly ignored more often than openly criticized. The Woman's Central Association of Relief took no notice of her in its widely circulated pamphlet surveying the means to forward donations to the troops, and she similarly did not figure in a memoir of the Sanitary Commission's achievement on the Peninsula during the previous year.[102] Katharine Prescott Wormeley's semiofficial history of the commission, also published in 1863, passed by the original cooperative plan for women nurses in jabbing at Dix for her clashes with the Army surgeons. "It is hard to realize that even benevolence must be obedient," Wormeley admonished the volunteers in Washington, calling for women in the capital hospitals to be "in the service of the Government, yet allied to the Sanitary Commission."[103]

Within the bounds of contemporary manners, however, public criticism of Dix continued to intensify. She acquired a particularly virulent nemesis when the slashing western journalist Jane Grey Swisshelm moved to Washington and began to visit Army hospitals in the spring of 1863. Chilled by the superintendent's "tall, angular person" and "totally unsympathetic manner," Swisshelm created a national sensation in May after seeing Dix among the wounded soldiers, who had multiplied in number once more after the Union defeat at Chancellorsville. When one patient asked the visitor if he could drink something more flavorful than water and Dix declined to challenge the restrictions imposed by doctors, Swisshelm appealed to the country through the front page of the New York *Tribune* for the distribution of lemonade to the hospitalized troops.[104] She thereafter continued to assail Dix as the unfeeling personification of government bureaucracy. The Superintendent of Women Nurses, Swisshelm once declared, was "a self-sealing can of horror tied up with red tape."[105] The diametric opposite of the Sanitary Commission's charge that Dix could not work efficiently within a system, Swisshelm's attacks revealed the many fronts of public opinion collapsing around the former heroine.

A few weeks after Swisshelm launched her lemonade crusade, Olmsted astutely described Dix's diminished stature in a letter written in the morning darkness of July 4 as he anxiously awaited news about the fighting at Gettysburg. Whether the Union won or lost that portentous battle, he told Bellows, the Army and the country could no longer follow the national leadership respected at the outset of the war. McClellan had proven that he was "no more to be compared" to the rising western hero Grant in commanding an army "than Miss Dix is to be compared with Miss Nightingale in the work of reforming military hospitals." The vanquished general and the Superintendent of Women Nurses not only illustrated the humiliation of personal failure; they epitomized the displacement of antebellum American idols during the war. "Both are popular heroes," Olmsted pointed out; "both are great at beginnings and in promises and hopes."[106]

It was one of Dix's nurses, however, who most sensitively captured the significance of her ordeal. Thirty-year-old Louisa May Alcott joined the contingent of Massachusetts women at the Union Hotel Hospital in December 1862, immediately after the grisly battle of Fredericksburg again filled the wards with wounded soldiers. The fledgling writer thought Dix "a kind old soul, but very queer, fussy and arbitrary; no one likes her and I don't wonder."[107] Alcott remained in service for only about three weeks before an attack of typhoid pneumonia nearly took her life. Eventually acceding to the advice of Dix and other bedside attendants, she returned to Concord carrying a basket from the superintendent filled with tea, wine, toilet water, medicines, a pillow, a fan, and a Bible. As soon as she regained strength, she turned her experience into the springboard for her literary career. In her Dickensian comedy *Hospital Sketches,* published serially during the spring of 1863 and in book form in August, Alcott used Dix's character to counterpoint her own coming of age in the weeks before the Emancipation Proclamation.

Reassessing the value of her plans for righteous self-sacrifice alongside the dying soldiers, Alcott cast her fellow New Englander as a symbol of the youthful ideals that the author's alter ego, Nurse Periwinkle, leaves behind. In "that Washington defeat," as Alcott called her transformation, the most valued relic was "the little book which appeared on her pillow, one dreary day; for the D.D. written in it means to her far more than Doctor of Divinity." Her allusion to the maternal superintendent's unpopularity—"whatever others may think or say, Nurse Periwinkle is forever grateful"—made more poignant the observation that Dix's sympathy for her young women was as futile as the nurses' solicitude for the soldiers. Nothing diverted the superintendent from her doomed mission:

"Daily our Florence Nightingale climbed the stairs, stealing a moment from her busy life, to watch over the stranger, of whom she was as thoughtfully tender as any mother." Linking Dix and the changing nation in a sad tenderness of her own, Alcott sighed ironically, "Long may she wave!"[108]

— 7 —

The official repudiation of Dix came more abruptly than the erosion of her public image. After feuding with Hammond for sixteen months, Stanton exiled the Surgeon General to an inspection tour of western military hospitals in August 1863 while a patently biased investigatory commission concocted charges of financial impropriety in the Medical Department. Pending the proceedings that eventually culminated in the court-martial of Hammond, Stanton appointed his friend and personal physician Joseph K. Barnes to the post of Acting Surgeon General. Barnes lost little time in moving against the Superintendent of Women Nurses. Five weeks after he assumed his command, he called formally for a redefinition of Dix's office. Hammond's circular order of July 1862, issued without the cooperation of the War Department, "by no means meets the case," Barnes argued on October 13. Only a more thorough-going reallocation of authority could prevent "improper interference with Hospitals" and "frequent conflicts of opinion as to the powers of the Surgeons in charge."[109]

In North Carolina during early October 1863 to help organize a new hospital on the Outer Banks, Dix probably knew little of the maneuvers to undermine her. She could not have been surprised, however, had she known. Apart from the continued friction between her and the Medical Department, the war had obliterated her faith that the national crisis would forever end Washington intrigues. She now only occasionally expressed a doubtful hope that "so great national trouble will work out a great benefit to national character—that the fires of tribulation may act like the refiner's fire and purify from sin and wickedness—and elevate and spiritualize."[110] On her return from North Carolina, she noted that the rampant prostitution, alcoholism, and vice in the capital epitomized the failure of the war to regenerate the country. Contrary to her lifelong disdain for the masses, she could not blame the heroic soldiers for "this modern Gomorrah." The troops were "patient and long-suffering," she told her old friend Ezra Stiles Gannett on October 27. "I cannot say as much for Officials—or *Officers*—in general."[111]

The next day, Secretary of War Stanton summoned Dix to his office to notify her privately of the reorganization engineered by Barnes. The general order issued by the War Department on October 29 severely circumscribed her authority. She remained empowered to certify women for duty, but she could only assign nurses to hospitals when a surgeon in charge asked her to do so. All assignments, moreover, now required approval of the medical director for the appropriate Army department. The War Department also ratified Hammond's reduction of the number of nursing positions to be filled by women, and its order emphasized that nurses were "under the exclusive control of the senior medical officer" while on duty. Most important, the general order provided that applicants might circumvent Dix altogether in the processes of certification and assignment if they were "specially appointed by the Surgeon-General." The exception to Dix's authority over women nurses, previously limited to Catholic nuns, was now opened as wide as Barnes cared to make it.[112]

As Jane Woolsey recognized with approval, the War Department order of October 1863 "practically abolished the office of General Superintendent of Nurses."[113] The announcement did not even acknowledge that any such position existed, referring instead to the role of "Miss Dix." The shift was telling, for her connection to the War Department was henceforth mostly honorific. Dix's supporters claimed that the order added to her authority by requiring surgeons to state the reasons for the dismissal of women nurses, but the requirement was a hollow formality. Three weeks after issuance of the departmental order, Barnes affirmed that "appointments were made altogether [by] the Surgeon-in-charge." To a twenty-three-year-old volunteer who had attached herself to the medical bureau at Gettysburg and now sought a hospital appointment, the Surgeon General promised that "he both could and would appoint ladies at the request of a surgeon *irrespective* of *age, size, or looks.*" He had initiated the reorganization, he explained, "to allow Surgeons to choose their *own* nurses, as many objected to Miss Dix's."[114]

A series of new proposals to advance cooperation between surgeons and women nurses presented final proof of the titular superintendent's weakness. Encouraging one short-lived initiative, the New York *Times* declared in December 1863 that "the time has arrived when something practical should be done" to establish women nurses in Army hospitals. The newspaper passed over Dix's efforts without mention, except insofar as the editorial pointedly called for "some organized system of women nurses" and emphasized that "surgeons in charge will not call for woman's aid unless they know in what direction they are calling, and that the call will be responded to by skillful and responsible persons."[115] Dix's vitriolic critic Jane Grey Swisshelm later sponsored a similar reform venture, to be called the Surgeon's Aid Society. Swisshelm's proposal also faded quickly, however, and women nurses remained for the rest of the war under the administration devised by Barnes.[116]

— 8 —

Dix responded to the evisceration of her office in part by ignoring the calamity. Mary Peabody Mann, sympathetically remembering her husband's admiration for Dix, hinted to her old acquaintance in January 1864 that "your nerves must have suffered from this great tension" and urged that "it would be the part of wisdom in you to drop your mantle upon some younger sister."[117] But Dix refused to resign. To the contrary, she maintained with pride that she never took a day of furlough during the war. Still authorized to recruit nurses, she continued to investigate the moral qualifications of women who applied to her. Often, however, she was obliged to admit that she could not assign the candidates she approved for nursing duty because she did not control any vacant positions in Army hospitals. She tried to maintain an illusion of authority by ratifying the assignments issued by the Medical Department. When she needlessly endorsed the posting of Georgeanna Woolsey to a military hospital near Philadelphia, the younger woman exulted in "a good-natured laugh over a visit from Miss Dix, who, poor old lady, kept up the fiction of appointing all the army nurses."[118]

Recognizing that the reorganization of women nurses left Dix with little function in the Army, Stanton asked her to inspect the Virginia Eastern Lunatic Asylum and determine the supplies needed at the Williamsburg institution. She spent much of the first months of 1864 working on the affairs of the mental hospital, but her return to the care of the insane only sharpened her sense that she was fated to "measure out time" until the war ended.[119] She still longed to participate more directly in the epic drama unfolding around her. "My place is in nearness to the greatest trouble," she remarked at one point, "and I feel that where is the deepest distress there must my work be found."[120]

Dix soon found a sustaining sense of purpose in one of the most emotionally charged issues of the conflict, the plight of prisoners of war. With the collapse of the exchange cartel in 1863 and the continued escalation of hostilities, the number of prisoners held by both sides had multiplied rapidly. Conditions in military detention centers had deteriorated even faster. By the end of the year, northern prisons were dangerously overcrowded and inadequate. In the South, where the war had cut the civilian population close to the bone, the suffering of Union prisoners was appalling. Instead of exchanging prisoners, the two sides traded accusations of deliberate brutality and threats of retaliation.[121]

The controversy entered a new phase when General Benjamin F. Butler, now the Union commander at Fortress Monroe, made a widely publicized gesture toward the establishment of a new cartel by returning five hundred rebel soldiers from the federal prison at Point Lookout, Maryland, on Christmas Day 1863. Confederate authorities responded by releasing an equal number of men held at Libby Prison in Richmond and Belle Isle on the James River. This exchange and the subsequent negotiations for a new cartel offered the northern public its best opportunity to test the commonplace charge that the South had wantonly starved and mistreated Union prisoners.[122]

Dix was immediately attracted to the prisoners. She traveled to Annapolis to see the men as soon as they arrived at the principal Union facility for released captives. Their "wholesome horror of Confederate prisons" sharpened her previous notions of southern barbarism and confirmed her doubts that the North could ameliorate the situation by sending food and clothing to the prisoners of war. Her pity and anger intensified a few weeks later when she returned from a trip to the Virginia Eastern Lunatic Asylum in the company of twenty-five Army officers who had escaped from Libby Prison. She circulated word to Butler of her support for his efforts to negotiate a new exchange cartel, and on March 1 the general invited Dix to Fortress Monroe to discuss her role in the initiative.[123]

Dix recognized that the issue of prisoner exchanges was a "game of military-civil chess."[124] For Butler, the stakes included his hopes to position himself for the upcoming presidential election. Success depended not only on sorting out the strategic and humanitarian considerations of a prisoner exchange, but also on shaping impassioned public opinion on both sides and navigating the delicate relations on the issue between top government and Army authorities. As a celebrated witness to suffering and a discreet backchannel to Washington, Dix offered the general a useful ally. In March 1864 she inspected Point Lookout, the largest Union prison, and she also began to report "candidly and confidentially" to Butler on rumors she heard in Washington and through her contacts in the Army.[125]

But this tactical maneuvering was less important to Dix than her imaginative identification with the prisoners of war. Unlike the sick and wounded soldiers in the hospitals, the prisoners' suffering elicited an anguish reminiscent of her early legislative memorials on behalf of the insane. "Our poor dying returned prisoners," she mourned. "Language is faint to convey the least *idea* of their state." Her letters during the last year of the war almost invariably dwelled on this horror. Again and again, she cried that "our hearts are half broken over our *returned paroled Soldiers.*" The prisoners seemed to mirror her own wartime ordeal, their hopeless misery more immediate than the promise of personal and national recovery symbolized by the Army hospitals. "In my worn out condition I may be seen a type of our skeleton Belle Isle men," she acknowledged to one of her close friends.[126]

In addition to expressing her despair, Dix's pity for the prisoners differed from her earlier vicarious suffering in its open declaration of fierce hatred. Dix admitted no qualifications or excuses in her condemnation of the South. "I feel no placability toward the Rebels," she seethed. The emaciated prison survivors were "mere skeletons gasping out a *murdered* life." "It is *horrible*," she wrote after she saw some recent arrivals. "I have no heart to say much & am *too* indignant to be forgiving." When a party with which she was traveling "just escaped being made prisoner by Guerillas," Dix bitterly regretted that she had no guns with her. "I *surely surely* would have used them," she exclaimed, underscoring her words repeatedly. She beseeched a reporter for the Rochester *Democrat* to "stir up the Administration to some adequate retaliation for these awful crimes against humanity—and if that *can not* be, tell your people of Rochester to send their soldiers even more freely to conquer these savages."[127]

Dix's partisanship proved too unswerving to suit Butler's intricate purposes. The general had asked her to inspect Point Lookout because he expected a vivid report of its squalid conditions that he hoped would induce southerners to press for a new exchange cartel. But convinced that the North maintained exemplary prisons while the South committed unspeakable atrocities, Dix found that "there was nothing which could be objected to, and so much to commend that I sum up all in saying that there is no [change] called for."[128] Similarly, prison commissioner-general Ethan Allen Hitchcock later hesitated before granting Dix's request to visit the notorious compound at Elmira, New York, where one-quarter of all prisoners died during the war. There, too, however, Dix's loyalty to the Union guided her perceptions. Although Elmira officials reported one month before she arrived that the entire population of eight thousand prisoners would die within a year at the current rate, Dix reported to Hitchcock that the rebel soldiers were receiving all necessary care and that sickness was rare in the facility.[129]

Butler's attempt to arrange a new cartel failed dismally, but the prisoners remained Dix's central interest for the rest of the war. She frequently returned to Annapolis to see the sick prisoners sent home after prospects collapsed for further exchange of healthy soldiers. On one occasion, a local monument dealer recorded a haunting account of Dix inadvertently walking into the burial of a group of prisoners recently returned from Savannah. The funeral procession seemed to envelop the famous humanitarian, he observed. The sound of the dirge and the sight of the carriages heading toward the aging woman "overcame her so much that when we met her her eyes were red with weeping."[130]

Dix's absorption in the prison issue eventually led to a new cooperation with the Sanitary Commission that underscored the impact of the war on her ideas about the dangers of exciting the public. When negotiations for a new exchange cartel failed, the commission renewed the propaganda war on the subject by preparing an inflammatory pamphlet about prison conditions. Dix assisted in the gathering of information from returned Union soldiers in late May 1864, "glad this investigation is to be made, though it is late for all the facts and features of those horrible cases." The widely distributed commission pamphlet also included her testimony from Point Lookout as evidence of the moral superiority of the North.[131]

Dix's contributions to stirring the northern outcry over prisoners marked the full reversal of her hopes to bring to the sectional conflict the ethos of calming discipline she had promoted in her asylum crusade. Her changing political sympathies demonstrated the same transformation. Despite the increasing war weariness that pervaded the North during the summer of 1864, she broke with old Whig allies like Fillmore, who continued to blame self-interested politicians in the North as well as the South for manipulating public passions to prolong the conflict. While the former president advocated a policy of "Christian forgiveness" toward secessionists and openly supported George B. McClellan in the election of 1864, Dix denounced the Democratic candidate as "a traitor." Her contempt for political partisanship, elaborated throughout the antebellum sectional crisis, now crumbled under the wartime pressure of unconditional loyalty to the Union cause.[132]

As the war dragged on, moreover, Dix's long rebellion against her home ended not only in aggressive partisanship but also in debilitating nostalgia. After almost twenty years of leaving, avoiding, and criticizing Boston, she pined to return. Contrary to her previous assertions of self-reliance, she reminisced about her days as a schoolteacher, yearned to talk for hours in Anne Heath's familiar rooms, and even briefly contemplated a vacation to make a flying visit to Brookline. Eventually, however, she recognized with sadness that "this idea is *dreaming*."[133] For her, home had been a personal conception to defy and refashion. She could not simply turn around and take up the ties she had so long ago broken. "How life passes—how life changes—how strange is our *present*," Dix cried to Heath, warning that "this dreadful war will wear many out beside myself."[134]

Dix's spirits brightened somewhat when the war entered its final phase after the decisive Union victories at Atlanta and in the Shenandoah Valley. The value she saw in the national ordeal, however, contrasted sharply with her original expectations. Contrary to her initial vision that a small American elite might instill discipline in the masses, the plain people had revealed their independent power. The heroic soldiers offered numerous examples of "noble traits of character developed that ordinary

circumstances would never have quickened [to] visible expression . . . ,"
she acknowledged in October 1864. "And so all is not dreary & sorrowful."[135] Her celebration of the divine average showed that the war had
not only shattered her own national influence; it had undermined her
broader conservative conception of cultural leadership.

Determined to salvage some sense of personal victory alongside the
eventual Union triumph, Dix continued her wartime work through the
peace at Appomattox. One of the last patients she attended was Secretary
of State Seward, severely stabbed in the Lincoln assassination conspiracy.
Dix provided food and cologne for her longtime political friend. But as
throughout the war, her nursing efforts were at best a limited success.
When Seward's daughter asked whether he liked a "delicate preparation"
from the kitchen at 430 15th Street, the Secretary of State answered
wanly: "I like it because I like Miss Dix."[136]

— 9 —

"Those who threw their lives with the Armies those four years will _never_
be the same persons again," Dix reflected several years after the Civil
War ended. "_Life_ has for all time changed aspects."[137] Unlike so many
northern volunteers who strove to preserve their exciting sense of commitment to a glorious national cause, however, Dix regarded the war as
a nightmare that she could never fully escape. She remained "_within_ the
folds of the _Pall_" through the summer of 1865 as she watched over the
last of the sick and dying men, but she gladly referred the anxious
inquiries she received from the wives of missing soldiers to Clara Barton,
who specialized in handling such cases after winning fame as a freelance
nurse during the war. In August Dix at last surrendered her house in
Washington and, in an unnecessary gesture, submitted her resignation
as Superintendent of Women Nurses.[138]

Even before the end of the war, Dix had begun the struggle to envision
her ordeal as an accidental diversion in her career rather than a fitting
climax. "This is not the work I would have my life judged by!" she is
said to have declared repeatedly.[139] She tried in vain to avoid the authors
of popular books on wartime philanthropy, and she firmly repelled the
renewed solicitations of potential biographers.[140] After the war, she
destroyed many of her papers despite her ingrained habits of accumu-

lation and her awareness of the government's claim to documents about the women nurses.[141] Preparing many years later for an authorized posthumous biography, she emphasized that her experience as superintendent should be treated as a minor episode. She instructed the executor of her will to withhold much of her surviving wartime correspondence from publication.[142] But her efforts to minimize her stake in the war could never conceal that at the peak of her career, she had pursued the heroic role of an American Florence Nightingale as carefully as a hunter might stalk a beast in the jungle.

The shift in Dix's attitude toward nursing reflected her attempt to put the war behind her. Despite her admiration for Nightingale, her earlier friendship with Anna Jameson, and her intimate connection with William Rathbone, Jr., who became one of the most prominent organizers of nursing in Great Britain, Dix took no interest in the rapid postwar growth of this new field of work for women. Transparently trying to hide her disappointment, she maintained to Elizabeth Rathbone that the movement in the United States, led in part by the Woolsey sisters, would likely fail as a result of "the ease people have in finding other and usually more acceptable employment than nursing the sick, as a profession or vocation."[143] In an ironic manifestation of her hardearned recognition that hospital nursing would never become a holistic counterpart to treatment by doctors, Dix helped to pay for one of her wartime subordinates to attend medical school.[144] But although she treasured personal friendships with several of her former charges, she did not care to perpetuate the wartime community of women nurses. She declined to encourage the formation of the Army Nurses Association, which nevertheless elected her president for life, and she flatly refused to aid petitions by former nurses for a veterans' pension or women's suffrage.[145]

The awkward relationship between Dix and the Army Nurses Association typified her inability to avoid remembrances of the Civil War. When Secretary of War Stanton suggested that her nursing efforts should be honored by a grand public meeting or a congressional expression of gratitude, Dix asked to receive only an American flag. She kept the ceremonial stand of colors presented to her by the War Department in storage during her lifetime, arranging in her will for it to be displayed permanently at the Memorial Hall built by Harvard College to honor the students and alumni who had died in the Union Army. Her instinctive identification with the other New England victims of the war was eventually thwarted, however, for Harvard lost the flag.[146]

Dix's most remarkable attempt to bury the Civil War took place at Fortress Monroe, an important center of her nursing efforts. A committee of veterans asked her in May 1866 to aid in the erection of a monument to the six thousand soldiers interred at the cemetery on the James River. Dix assumed full direction of the tribute to the common soldiers whose fortitude in death she so deeply admired.[147] Within a few months, she collected $8,000, much of it from personal friends in Boston, Providence, New York, and Philadelphia, and began to design the monument.[148]

Constrained by a conventional artistic imagination as well as a limited budget, Dix made the centerpiece of the cemetery a traditional granite obelisk, tall enough to be seen from the Hampton Roads harbor. She expressed her mixed feelings about the war more strikingly in the fence that encircled the obelisk. With the Army's permission, she embedded in stone and tied together with iron bars one thousand muskets and bayonets, fifteen cannons, and a large amount of shot. The bristling barricade armed a fortress for the dead soldiers, as if like Dix they would remain forever besieged rather than released by the sacrifices of the war.[149]

Dix took singular pride in her work at Fortress Monroe. She circulated photographs of the monument widely to friends and dignitaries, including General Grant, and she presented the privately funded monument to Stanton with a quiet flourish. The Secretary of War welcomed it as typical of his friend's "arduous, patriotic, humane and benevolent labors."[150] He evidently did not see that her remembrance of the honored dead was also a characteristic attempt to repress her own wartime ordeal. "Thank Heaven the War is over," Dix sighed as construction began on the monument. "I would that its memories also could pass away."[151]

⇥ 14 ⇤

At Last

D IX WAS EAGER to resume her asylum crusade at the end of the war. Her frustrations as Superintendent of Women Nurses compounded her anxiety that "the insane are needing me long since," and upon resigning her position she immediately started to evaluate requests for her assistance.[1] The conditions that she had protested before the war had persisted and deepened during her absence. Throughout the country, the construction of insane asylums lagged far behind the growing population. "No State Hospital provision has been adequate to the needs of the insane," she noted in 1862. "*Old* cases are removed at present of a *hard necessity* to make place for *recent* and *probably curable* cases."[2] The renewed challenge promised to redeem and invigorate her in her mid-sixties. "It would seem that all my work is to be done over," she exclaimed after one tour of jails and almshouses.[3] But beneath this apparent continuity, the underpinnings of her triumphant antebellum career had changed profoundly. The consensus among professional specialists in support of the moral treatment, the reform impulse within Unitarianism, and the ideal of women's benevolence all faced devastating attacks in the aftermath of the Civil War.

— 1 —

Dix's long anticipated return to Boston opened her postwar life on a note of disappointment. As she had promised, after she finally left Washington in November 1865 she appeared without warning at the Heaths' home for the first time in five years. Her old friends were delighted by the surprise visit but shocked to see that she was so "terribly worn." Nor could they offer much rejuvenation, for the war years had also been harsh on the distant homefront. Grace Heath, the vivacious favorite of the family, had collapsed suddenly while visiting her friend Clover Hooper and died at the beginning of August 1864, three months after she announced her engagement and exactly one year after she learned that the romantic hero of her youthful social circle, Robert Gould Shaw, had died while leading the 54th Massachusetts infantry regiment of African-American soldiers in an assault on a Confederate fort. Dix had urged Anne Heath to seek consolation in the Union war effort, but she now saw that her longtime friend was permanently shattered. "That fearful tragedy took away a sustaining or rather impellent power," Heath later explained after another unsatisfying visit. "I hardly know what it was, or how. I only know I daily miss it—nothing now seems *worthwhile.*"[4]

Dix's first inquiries into recent developments in the treatment of the insane were equally discouraging. She examined several institutions, most notably the state almshouse for foreign-born paupers at Tewksbury, which featured a separate department for incurably insane immigrants. The purely custodial unit for chronically insane paupers departed significantly from the hospital program of moral treatment that Dix had promoted before the Civil War, an abandonment of therapeutic goals made more striking by the state's historic position at the vanguard of the asylum movement and by the notoriously deplorable living conditions at Tewksbury. Already convinced before the war that the plight of insane immigrants was an intractable problem, Dix frowned that the situation in Massachusetts presented "a good deal more in hand than I like to undertake" and demurred from seeking reforms.[5]

She turned her attention instead to the most important mental institution created in the United States during the war, the Willard Asylum for the Chronic Insane in Ovid, New York. The establishment of the Willard Asylum climaxed the campaign begun in the 1850s to expand state facilities for the insane in New York. John Chapin of the private Brigham Hall asylum in the west central part of the state, his colleague George Cook, and the State Medical Society had continued to press for a new asylum after Dix abandoned the project to concentrate on the sectional crisis. In 1864 the Albany legislature commissioned Sylvester

Willard, secretary of the State Medical Society, to survey the care of the insane in county almshouses. Willard's report one year later highlighted physicians' accounts of mistreatment in local institutions and urged the construction of a purely custodial state asylum for the incurable insane. The legislature soon moved to establish a comprehensive state asylum system by approving the new institution and rededicating the New York State Lunatic Asylum at Utica exclusively to recent cases. Led by Chapin, the Willard building commissioners obtained the Ovid site of the debt-ridden state agricultural college, which legislator Ezra Cornell arranged to move to his home district of Ithaca with federal funds provided by Morrill Act land grants. In January 1866, Chapin submitted final plans for an immense nontherapeutic institution for the chronic insane.[6]

Dix spent much of the winter in New York aiding an effort by prominent asylum superintendents to halt or modify Chapin's proposal. Utica superintendent John P. Gray led the opposition in his capacities as the chief state official responsible for the treatment of the insane, the editor of the *American Journal of Insanity,* and an influential member of the Association of Medical Superintendents. Gray pointed out that the distractions of the Civil War had prevented a thorough debate on the decision to establish a nontherapeutic institution rather than another center for moral treatment. Maintaining that the vast majority of patients would recover if the state built enough hospitals to treat every case quickly, he emphasized that there was "no subject connected with provision for the insane, upon which the verdict of the profession has been more unanimous than their condemnation of asylums for incurables." As a new legislature prepared to assemble in Albany in January 1866, he urged it to repudiate Chapin's plan and establish additional mental hospitals in the eastern and western regions of the state to relieve the overcrowding at his institution.[7]

After traveling to Utica to confer with Gray, Dix contributed to the campaign by soliciting testimonials against the Ovid facility from D. Tilden Brown, who remained the superintendent of the Bloomingdale Asylum of New York Hospital, and from his predecessor Charles Nichols. Further behind the scenes, she also circulated rumors of "the most monstrous swindling operations in connection with the *Willard* Asylum that I have ever been acquainted with." After conducting her own survey of the insane in poorhouses near Rochester, she settled into

Albany to "give light to the Members of the Legislature" about the need for additional hospitals providing moral treatment.[8]

As the proponents of the Willard Asylum hastened to point out, Dix's opposition to a separate institution for the incurable insane contradicted the policy she had urged during the 1844 legislative contest that resulted in the expansion of the Utica hospital. Ironically, Gray relied repeatedly on Amariah Brigham's condemnation of nontherapeutic asylums in the inaugural issue of the *American Journal of Insanity,* a manifesto originally written as an attack on Dix. George Cook, one of the most articulate advocates of the Willard plan, professed "sorrow, surprise & disappointment" at her hostility and sharply reminded her that "the views I now hold in regard to the paramount necessity of provision for the chronic insane, & the nature of that provision were once held by you." Certain that the legislature would never fund enough therapeutic hospitals to accommodate all recent and chronic cases, he reasoned that custodial facilities like the Willard Asylum provided the best hope for the elimination of the almshouse system that partisans on both sides of the Willard debate unanimously condemned.[9]

Inconsistent though Dix may have seemed, the similarity between her original program of asylum reform and the Willard proposal obscured the fundamental challenge that the innovation presented to her ideals. Her proposal for nonmedical institutions had expressed her faith that a wholesome moral environment, with or without physicians, could restore the spiritual stability of the insane. Even after she translated that religious conviction into an endorsement of the superintendents' promise to cure almost all of their patients, she continued to criticize medical aspects of asylum therapy, such as the extensive prescription of drugs. The Willard Asylum, in contrast, reflected the ascendancy of an opposite, research-oriented approach to mental illness. Younger physicians scoffed at unfulfilled predictions about the efficacy of the asylum therapy. Chapin, the first superintendent at Ovid, noted that most Utica patients either died in the hospital or were discharged without recovery. Disdaining the moral treatment as not only unsuccessful but unscientific, he preferred to await "the revelations which the microscope will furnish." Contrary to Dix's skeptical attitude toward medical expertise, the therapeutic agnosticism of the Willard Asylum illustrated the increasing prestige of experimental sciences, particularly the rise of neurology, in the years following the Civil War. Led by Dix's old nemesis William A. Hammond, who had rebounded from his court-martial as Surgeon General to achieve a phenomenal success as the first consulting neurologist in New York City, the proponents of a "physiological" view of insanity were poised to make a withering onslaught against the "metaphysical" interpretation that Dix and the Association of Medical Superintendents had long articulated.[10]

In addition to substituting newer scientific values for the ethos of self-governance represented by the moral treatment, the Willard proposal for the state to assume responsibility for all insane paupers also threatened Dix's vision of the asylum as a model of institutional governance. Chapin, Cook, and their allies sought to correct the "lack of comprehensiveness that characterizes the system everywhere."[11] Although it answered the demand of Dix and other antebellum reformers for displacement of the county almshouse system, the wartime Willard legislation expanded and unified state power in a manner unlike the previous multiplication of autonomous mental hospitals. In the creation of the Ovid institution and the parallel rededication of the Utica hospital, New York had moved decisively toward the integration of its welfare institutions under centralized government control. The growing state interest in bureaucratic supervision and coordination—corresponding to broad approval of the Sanitary Commission's efforts to organize wartime philanthropy—introduced new levels of asylum governance superior to the medical superintendents, a cardinal violation of the administrative model promoted by Dix and the superintendents of antebellum asylums.[12]

The conflicts between Dix's ideas and the new scientific and bureaucratic order represented by the Willard Asylum were ably expressed by Franklin B. Sanborn, secretary of the trendsetting Board of State Commissioners of Public Charities, which had been established by Massachusetts in 1863 to supervise mental hospitals, almshouses, and other public institutions. Meeting Dix shortly after the war, the thirty-four-year-old Sanborn echoed the frustration of the Willard advocates in New York. The crowded asylums for moral therapy inspired by Dix were "centres of intellectual indolence or of semi-political intrigue," he argued. She could not help to remedy "the situation which her own heroic activity had so largely created," partly because "age had lessened her activity and given even more rigidity to her opinions than they had by force of her positive and exacting nature." More important, Sanborn maintained, even if Dix had retained her energy and tact she lacked "the special knowledge and discrimination required" to lead modern reforms. His role in founding the American Social Science Association, an extension of his efforts to rationalize asylum management and apply recent medical theories of insanity, epitomized his rejection of the religious principles of moral treatment.[13]

Despite the efforts of Dix, Gray, and other antebellum leaders of the asylum movement, the opponents of the Willard project failed to prevent legislative approval of the design for the new institution and the beginning of construction at Ovid. Without backing away from the controversial project, the New York legislature attempted to mollify the advocates of additional therapeutic facilities. In April 1866 the legislature established a commission to select a site for another state mental hospital.[14]

As she so often had before, Dix tried to recover from her setback in New York by throwing herself immediately into new campaigns. In addition to taking up the erection of the monument for the Union dead at Fortress Monroe, she joined an effort already under way in Connecticut to establish a new public mental hospital. In early June 1866 she prepared a brief legislative memorial criticizing the state's reliance on county almshouses and subsidization of patients at the Hartford Retreat to accommodate its insane poor. With little opposition, the reform-minded legislature voted a few weeks later to create the Connecticut Hospital for the Insane. Governor Joseph R. Hawley, the husband of one of Dix's loyal Civil War nurses, signed the measure on June 29.[15]

The rapid success of the asylum campaign in Connecticut fleetingly recalled the spirit of Dix's antebellum crusade. The Hartford *Courant* urged the state to imitate New York by establishing a facility for chronically insane paupers like the Willard Asylum and relying on the Hartford Retreat for curable cases, but the proposal won few supporters. Dix's easy political task enabled her to spend much of her time in Connecticut at the home of Benjamin Silliman, Jr., reminiscing about his father and moving a second generation of the prominent New Haven family to applaud her benevolence. Hawley and other allies attributed the legislative success to her efforts, and the trustees of the new institution implored her to play a central role in its organization.[16]

But the familiar pattern of triumph could not entirely hide signs of Dix's dissatisfaction and weariness. After adding her voice to the selection of the hospital site, Dix surprised several trustees by declining to remain active in the early development of the institution.[17] She endorsed the choice of Abram M. Shew as medical superintendent, but she formed no meaningful personal relationship with him, choosing to follow events at the asylum more distantly, through correspondence with one of the trustees. The Connecticut Hospital for the Insane would never achieve the same place in her affections as the asylums that she had earlier helped to found.

As Dix participated with mixed success in asylum campaigns in Indiana, Pennsylvania, and Ohio during the next several months, the problem of accommodating chronic cases while preserving the structure of moral treatment remained the issue that most engaged her interest. Returning to Albany in January 1867 to support the bill for establishment of a mental hospital along the Hudson River, she renewed her attack on the Willard Asylum. Chapin exploded in fury when Ezra Cornell quoted Dix on the Senate floor as disapproving large expenditures at Ovid "because of the disfavor into which such enterprises are in future likely to be brought." Charging that Dix and Gray were conducting a malicious innuendo campaign, Chapin dared a full investigation of his management. No legislative examination followed, and construction continued at Ovid.[18]

Extending the result of the previous legislative session, Dix was forced to settle for passage of the anticipated funding to establish a new therapeutic institution at Poughkeepsie under the direction of Gray's assistant. Emphasizing a distinction that had become increasingly contentious, the legislature changed the name of the new facility from the Hudson River *Asylum* for the Insane to the Hudson River State *Hospital.* Although Gray declared that the Connecticut and Poughkeepsie mental hospitals marked decisive victories for the Association of Medical Superintendents, the Albany legislators continued to weaken the superintendents' authority by creating the New York Board of State Commissioners of Public Charities, the first of many state agencies across the country to follow the model of the Massachusetts regulatory board.[19]

The pervasive changes in asylum politics initiated in New York and Massachusetts effectively foreclosed Dix's hope to resume her antebellum crusade. She still lobbied for additional mental hospitals, evaluated possible asylum locations, and recommended candidates for job openings, but she would play little part in the controversies looming among asylum superintendents, neurologists, and state regulatory boards. And as she lost influence in the field she had once dominated, her sense of vocation was conversely becoming a less central force in her life. She suspended work altogether during the winter of 1867–68 to nurse eighty-seven-year-old Harriet Hare and care for her own persistent cough. After a series of hospital projects took her through the Middle Atlantic states in the spring, she concluded in June 1868 that "it is no longer needful to labor so incessantly for the insane." Notwithstanding the erosion of support for the moral treatment, she decided that "the public is widely instructed on that subject" and that "liberal acts by private individuals, with just Legislation in the States, keep pace with the necessities of a fast increasing population."[20] Her indifference to the mounting crisis of asylum therapy signaled the waning of her self-appointed mission.

— 2 —

As Dix became less active in asylum affairs, she became increasingly close to the family of William Greenleaf Eliot. Still accustomed to traveling, if no longer a solitary pilgrim, she gladly left Washington in April 1869 after a tedious winter at the Government Hospital for the Insane to join the minister and his wife for a journey to the Pacific coast. Their principal destination was Portland, Oregon, where Thomas Lamb Eliot was following his father's example as a Unitarian missionary and civic leader. The travelers crossed most of the country on the Union Pacific railroad, begun during the Civil War. Stopping amid the sagebrush in Promontory, Utah, at "a tent of fair proportions" called The New England House, they might have witnessed the ceremonial installation of the golden spike on May 10, 1869, marking the completion of the transcontinental railroad that antebellum politics had intertwined so vexatiously with the fate of Dix's land bill.[21]

The vacation tour through California, Oregon, and Washington Territory thrilled Dix. From the Yosemite Valley to Mount Ranier, she marveled at the majestic scenery and thriving agriculture. "Scenes that profoundly impress the least observing and serious, move the very inner-most depth of the devout soul," she told Elizabeth Rathbone, fondly recalling their holiday journey through the Alps. The passionate amateur naturalist recorded the varieties of birds, fish, mammals, insects, and flowers that she saw, noted the diameter of trees and length of pine cones, and pondered phenomena like mountain cascades and petrified forests. The progress of commerce and stabilization of the tumultuous mining communities also pleased her. Visiting prisons and asylums throughout the region, she found that "the humane and liberal Insti-tutions of those newly settled countries fill one with amazement in . . . their variety, their numbers, and the excellence they have already reached."[22]

Thomas Lamb Eliot and his wife, Henrietta, delighted Dix most of all. At sixty-seven, her social connections outside of asylum circles were beginning to center increasingly on her friends' children. After the death of Harriet Hare in March 1869, for example, the New York home of Hare's daughter, Lydia Prime, replaced Philadelphia as one of Dix's favorite rest-ing points. She now welcomed another bond with the Eliot family. Open-ing a prolific correspondence with the young couple soon after she left Portland, Dix asked the energetic minister to serve as her representative in seeking a public insane asylum in Washington Territory.[23]

Dix's pleasant excursion came to an abrupt end after she returned to Washington by way of the state mental hospitals of Kansas, Missouri, Illinois, and Iowa, for Congress had opened an investigation of the Gov-ernment Hospital for the Insane. Charles Nichols seethed to her that the inquiry was "the wickedest plot I ever heard of." A federal parallel to the rise of state commissions regulating public charities, the legislative review presented another example of the nationwide shift to central bureaucratic supervision of asylums. Dix's offer to assist her favorite superintendent proved unnecessary. The investigation criticized the hos-pital administration on several minor points, including the dedication of one guest room to Dix's exclusive use, but by December 1869 the controversy had abated. Nichols invited her to reoccupy her apartment for another winter and to help determine the proper location in the asylum for the hanging of her portrait.[24]

Dix decided to pass the season at a different scene of her prewar success, however, accepting with some uncertainty an invitation from the superintendent of the North Carolina state mental hospital to make her first trip to the South since the Civil War. During the previous five years, southern asylum officials had repeatedly sought her intervention to help them avoid dismissal by Republican governments. Dix had written letters on behalf of her old friends and urged her wartime associate Benjamin F. Butler, now a congressman from Massachusetts, to support the early removal of their civil disabilities. She had also raised small donations for public institutions and private suffering in the South. Now, in January 1870, she tried more fully to "put out of mind the terrible past, during the years of the Rebellion—and take up the line of work here where I left it in 1860."[25]

Dix found her warm reception in North Carolina gratifying but perplexing. Her sense of political identity now based almost wholly on her intense wartime loyalty to the Union, she could not easily recognize that she and many of her southern hosts still shared a chastened conservatism. "Strange to say," she reported, "none are heartier, in welcoming me '*home* to North Carolina,' than the Democrats & Confederates." She remained in Raleigh for most of the month, assisting an effort to expand the overcrowded Insane Asylum of North Carolina. Upon her departure, she consented to the renaming in her honor of the asylum that she had played a central role in founding.[26]

Pleased to be on familiar and hospitable grounds, Dix traveled from Raleigh to South Carolina, Georgia, Tennessee, and Kentucky, although the poverty of the postwar South precluded far-reaching political activities on behalf of the insane. Throughout her southern tour, moreover, her plans to work were hampered by "a cough & sore throat, my winter enemies." When she arrived in Columbus, Ohio, in early April 1870 for the legislative debate on a bill to finance a new state mental hospital, she complained that the persistent nuisance "finally seemed to unite Bronchitis and Pneumonia." William Peck, superintendent of the Central Ohio Asylum in Columbus, diagnosed her condition as malarial fever, complicated first by bronchial disease and subsequently by rheumatic neuralgia.[27]

For the rest of the year, Dix remained "captive to malarial fever." Indeed, she did not declare herself fully recovered from her April 1870 attack until December 1873, and she thereafter suffered frequent relapses of malarial symptoms that seemed "not easily driven off when once having had possession."[28] After spending a month bedridden in Columbus, she chartered an express railroad car to transport her to Trenton under the care of Peck and his wife. She rested at the New Jersey State Lunatic Asylum through the summer, the tedium relieved temporarily in July 1870 when Wells College in Aurora, New York, awarded her an honorary doctoral degree. In the autumn she sought to refresh herself in New England, overruling Nichols's advice that the care at the Trenton and Washington asylums "would be more than a match for the bracing airs of Newport & Nahant."[29]

While convalescing, Dix devoted much of her attention and a considerable part of her investment income to the Eliot family. Although she once wrote that William Greenleaf Eliot, Thomas Lamb Eliot, and John Taylor Gilman Nichols were "the *richest* persons I know, if wealth may be estimated by *goodness,* and *rare prospective usefulness,*" she was able to assist her western friends significantly under a more mundane definition of affluence. When Henry Ware Eliot disappointed his father by deciding not to enter the ministry, Dix supplied capital for his business enterprises. In 1870 she gave Thomas Lamb Eliot $1,000, approximately one-third of her annual income, to travel to New York for treatment of his failing eyes by former Sanitary Commission member Cornelius Rea Agnew. A year later, she provided the young minister another $500 to help salvage a real estate investment he had undertaken for a Portland charity. Dix disclaimed any repayment, but "taking the attitude of Mentor," she added sermons on Eliot's family financial responsibilities to her previous exhortations that he attend more prudently to his health and vision.[30]

Dix's attention to the tribulations of the Eliot family merged with her concern about the decline of the Unitarian impulse that she and her friends personified. Henry Bellows had sparked a bitter conflict at the close of the Civil War by attempting to translate his organizational success in the Sanitary Commission back to the religion for which he had developed his zeal for social institutions. In 1865 he led a major initiative toward the establishment of a comprehensive denominational structure by sponsoring the creation of the National Conference of Unitarian Churches. Dix remained wary both of this consolidation movement within Unitarianism and its most vocal critics, Transcendentalist advocates of unrestricted freedom for the individual consciousness. She disagreed with "our well meaning, but vague, weak-minded radical friends" like Octavius Brooks Frothingham, as she had earlier condemned Emerson and Theodore Parker, but she thought the Transcendentalists "too wholly destitute of plausibility to involve danger of harm to even the most credulous." To her, churchmen like Bellows and Edward Everett Hale posed a more subtle, menacing threat to Unitarianism. She objected to the introduction of "systems" into the faith and questioned "the sufficiency of church organizations for building up religious Institutions."[31]

Caught in the middle of the schism was Dix's version of Unitarianism, the faction that Bellows derided as *the elder men, old-fashioned Unitarians, very ethical* in their humor—preaching the doctrine of self-culture & personal righteousness." Concentrated heavily in Boston and loyal to the congregational polity of the Puritans, this group was represented most prominently in national councils by Ezra Stiles Gannett until he died in a train wreck in August 1871. Dix looked to the Eliot family as the best hope of a Unitarianism based on evangelical piety and active benevolence. She once listed her exemplars of the ministry as Channing, Gannett, Henry Ware, William Greenleaf Eliot, Thomas Lamb Eliot, and Tom's brother Christopher Rhodes Eliot, who became the pastor of her uncle Thaddeus Mason Harris's old church. Similarly, the Eliots regarded her as an ideal model for the female Unitarian laity. In February 1871, Henrietta and Thomas Lamb Eliot named their first daughter Dorothea Dix Eliot.[32]

In addition to enforcing a temporary retirement that strengthened her relationship with the Eliots, Dix's illness quickened her reconciliation with Boston. Shortly after the war, her brother Joseph built a new house in Dorchester and reserved a room in it for her. She soon became an annual visitor to New England, often prolonging her summer and fall sojourns in the early 1870s until Nichols insisted that she move to Washington for the winter. Meanwhile, a narrowly Bostonian perspective gradually supplanted the rebellious independence that had animated her antebellum career. On her seventieth birthday, she reflected that the time had apparently come to give up her national crusade for moral treatment and devote herself to "those neighborhood works & cares which always await the willing worker." She joined proudly in her brother's initiative to place a pure water fountain near the Boston customs house, and she reported that she "*never* had as much real satisfaction in relieving people" as she felt in aiding the victims of the fire that devastated the city in November 1872.[33] Starting to distribute her possessions during her illness, she demonstrated her renewed attachment by donating books to the Massachusetts Historical Society and the New England Historic Genealogical Society.

Dix's simultaneous religious anxiety and civic pride expressed a new discordance in her view of American society. Although she discerned "a strong tendency towards a superficial faith or positive unbelief," she repeatedly took a roseate view of current policies toward the insane and a variety of public institutions and reform movements. "Good in all and every thing predominates," she concluded. Notwithstanding her disappointment in "the *materialism* of the prominent scientific men" who espoused evolutionary theory, her own postwar thinking suggested a similar faith in secular progress.[34] In her separation of declining piety and advancing charity, she no longer defined genuine social reform as the spiritual regeneration of individuals.

"*We* and some others *have* outlived the sober times," Dix acknowledged to Anne Heath in December 1873, "and needs must be careful that we are not tossed on the waves of unbelief or swept away by the rushing tide that bears half the human world to wreck." After three and a half relatively unproductive years, she at last felt restored to "*full* working ability" and hoped to participate again in the advance of humanity that she had become eager to see around her. Freshly conscious that "life is drawing with me toward the sun-down," she resolved one final time that "I must not put aside what comes before me through the leading of Providence to do."[35]

— 3 —

After hesitating over several projects, Dix joined another defensive stand by her longtime asylum allies in the early months of 1874. Along with old friends Thomas Kirkbride, John Curwen, and several other asylum superintendents, she sought to block a proposal by the Pennsylvania State Board of Charities to move insane convicts from penitentiaries to state mental hospitals. The superintendents argued bitterly that the reversal of their extensive efforts to distinguish asylums from prisons would ruin the public standing of institutions for the insane. Dix echoed their call for the establishment of separate prison hospitals. The intermingling of respectable mental patients and "murderers, burglars, horse thieves &c," she argued, would undermine the efforts of moral therapy to instill a sense of self-respect in the insane.[36]

Dix's return to lobbying ended in another telling defeat. The State Board of Charities won legislative approval of its plan for insane convicts in May 1874, and the growing antagonism between her old friend John Curwen and his new superiors on the Board of Charities eventually cost the superintendent his position at the Harrisburg asylum that Dix had helped to found three decades earlier. She experienced similar frustration in her other important political effort during the first months of the year, an attempt to expand asylum facilities in neighboring Maryland. The Annapolis legislature "disgraced itself and dishonored Maryland" by declining to make the appropriation she had requested.[37]

Disappointed by these setbacks but pleased to be able to travel again, Dix headed west in the spring for a grand tour of mental hospitals. She left Trenton on a northern route through the asylums in Wisconsin, Minnesota, and Nebraska, returning two months later through Illinois and Indiana. Her inspection rounds prompted a variety of responses among asylum officials. Friendly observers maintained that her critical examinations "constitute, of themselves, a better 'lunacy commission' than would be likely to be appointed in many of our States." But young physicians often snickered or balked at her intrusion. Other rising doctors cultivated her aid in the advancement of their careers, mindful of her connections among hospital trustees and superintendents.[38]

At institutions that Dix had been instrumental in founding, her appearance often inspired a celebration of the original asylum ideals. "The hospitals are your children," trustee John Harper noted in one standard formulation, "and if Dixmont is not the first-born I know she is well-beloved, and we must try and make her worthy of her *alma mater.*" Adopting another common metaphor, Harper later wrote that "notwithstanding our Protestant and iconoclastic ideas," the managers of Dixmont "regard you as its *patron saint,* and time will only hallow the association."[39] Dix commemorated these bonds after the Civil War by acceding to requests for her portrait from several of her favorite asylums. Like the picture cards that she circulated while Superintendent of

Women Nurses, all of the paintings were based on her favorite daguerre-otype of herself taken before the war.

After lingering in Boston once again into the winter of 1874–75, Dix turned toward Washington for a confrontation that had long been gathering momentum, a collision with the rival asylum reform crusade of Elizabeth Packard. Dix had watched Packard's rise to national fame for almost a decade. Committed to the Illinois State Hospital for the Insane in 1860 by her husband, Packard spent three years in the Jacksonville asylum before obtaining a judicial declaration of her sanity. She then launched a spectacular campaign for legislation to expand the rights of the allegedly insane in involuntary commitment proceedings, and especially to provide further protection for married women. The Illinois legislature unanimously enacted her "personal liberty bill" in 1867 and ordered an investigation that spurred the establishment of the Illinois Board of Public Charities and the resignation of superintendent Andrew McFarland from the Jacksonville asylum, to which Dix had remained affectionately connected since playing an instrumental role in its founding.[40]

Urging other states to adopt similar restrictions on involuntary commitments, Packard also began to advocate legislation to bar superintendents from screening all letters written by their patients. She promoted these postal bills successfully in several states despite the vociferous insistence of asylum doctors that she was "a fascinating crazy woman, who managed to seduce partisan prejudice and ignorance for her allies." The superintendents denied that freer communication was a necessary safeguard against the abuse of patients and argued that the change would undermine their control over the moral environment of the asylum. In January 1875 Packard shifted her efforts to Congress, proposing that the Post Office place secure mailboxes in mental hospitals. Isaac Ray, former president of the Association of Medical Superintendents, summarized his colleagues' opposition in asserting that "the boxes themselves would be a standing proclamation to the patients that the officers were unworthy of their confidence."[41]

Apart from Packard's assault on the authority of superintendents, she and Dix represented clashing attitudes toward the role of women in American society. Although not affiliated with the women's suffrage movement, the younger lobbyist shared in the demand for equal rights that escalated sharply after the Civil War during the debates over the Fourteenth and Fifteenth Amendments to the Constitution.[42] She vigorously attacked the subordination of women in her criticisms of asylum superintendents and in her proposed reforms of involuntary commitment procedures. Financing her work by selling sensational narratives of her experience as an asylum inmate, she joined prominent suffragists Elizabeth Cady Stanton, Myra Bradwell, and Mary Livermore to obtain legislation in Illinois securing the power of married women to control their earnings independently.[43]

Dix was dismayed by this shift from a reform movement based on the moral superiority of womanhood to an assertion of legal parity. When a suffragist suggested that the former Civil War nurses petition Congress for the vote, Dix refused to provide a list of her nurses' names and answered that "their duties were based in religion & charity, not in civil & political obligations." She despaired during the 1870s that "with the wild confusion wrought by self-seeking restless women, on the suffrage question and the question of 'women's right,' society and domestic force seem passing into chaotic confusion." Continuing to urge "more correct training and suitable uses of time for young girls and women," she sponsored students at Vassar and Wellesley colleges, and she aided unmarried women friends in their careers as doctors or teachers. But she saw these educational and professional advances as a refinement rather than an elimination of the social division between the sexes. She still saluted "those domestic labors which are the crown & glory of a *true woman's* life and which need no *out*going from the dignified paths of feminine occupations to evidence worth or influence."[44]

The confrontation in Congress between Dix and Packard reflected the political implications of their different ideas about the proper public role of women. Packard collected signatures on a petition in behalf of her mailbox bill, which she drafted with prominent women's rights attorney Belva Ann Lockwood, and she delivered an address about her asylum ordeal to the House committee on postal affairs. Dix quietly sought to block the measure behind the scenes with Nichols, now the president of the Association of Medical Superintendents. When Packard's bill stalled, asylum directors thanked Dix warmly for "your labors to prevent mischief." Superintendent Mark Ranney, who had unsuccessfully opposed Packard's campaign in Iowa, exultantly added that Dix's influence had not only vanquished her rival in Washington but also driven her from New Jersey and Pennsylvania.[45]

The apparent triumph tarnished, however, shortly after Packard learned that Nichols had maintained that she truly was insane. Several District residents, including a prominent signer of Packard's petition, soon initiated another congressional investigation of Nichols's administration at the Government Hospital for the Insane. The exhaustive inquiry lasted for months while a House committee heard testimony from approximately 125 witnesses. Dix submitted an affidavit in support of her most eminent protégé, assuring the committee that the charges resulted from "misapprehension, misrepresentation, and in some instances, I fear, malicious assertion." The investigation finally exonerated Nichols in July 1876, but the demoralizing trial contributed significantly to his decision to resign one year later. Although it was not clear whether Packard was behind the congressional review, Nichols's former assistant sighed to Dix that the office of superintendent had lost its attractions through the attacks of "new lights, self conceited reformers, [and] boards of state charities."[46]

The attack against Nichols coincided with the fading of some of Dix's other closest remaining personal relationships. Anne Heath had continued to decline steadily since the wartime death of her niece, and by August 1876 she could recognize her old friend only intermittently. During the same summer, Joseph Dix declared bankruptcy after struggling for three years against the severe national depression. His ruin slowed his sister's return to Boston and sharpened her anxieties about the course of American society. She helped Joseph try to recover financially, but in February 1878 he suddenly died. Anne Heath followed two months later, while Dix was still in Dorchester winding up her brother's affairs.

At seventy-six, Dix had outlived her immediate family and all of the older women who had been her most intimate confidantes since her youth. The deaths of John Adams Dix, Joseph Henry, George B. Emerson, and other friends continued to shadow her life during the next few years. Although she wanted to resume her work, recurrent malarial symptoms relegated her to "one prolonged season of hindering experiences." Often her legs were too weak and swollen for her to walk.

She could only mail documents to oppose Packard's continuing state campaigns or watch helplessly when the Pennsylvania legislature fired Curwen, "a man of religious spirit & *good morals,* and good *intentions.*" Her attempts to arrange her personal papers and write an autobiography proved no less frustrating. She moved among her favorite asylums in a slow rotation, keenly aware that "I really have not an 'abiding place, nor any continuing City.' "[47]

At the beginning of October 1881, Dix traveled for the last time from the Government Hospital in Washington to the New Jersey State Lunatic Asylum in Trenton. Complaining of severe chill and a pain in her lung, she collapsed shortly after she arrived. Asylum superintendent John Ward notified the Eliot family that her condition was grave, and William Greenleaf Eliot hastened from St. Louis to visit her deathbed. Eliot's nephew Horace Lamb, a Boston merchant who had served in recent years as Dix's chief financial advisor, arrived to organize her estate. When she still remained in the asylum at the annual meeting of its trustees in early November, the board voted to authorize Ward to care for her indefinitely. After a journey of almost forty years, Dix had at last settled into a permanent home in the mental hospital that she regarded as her first-born child.

— 4 —

Anticipating her imminent death, Dix elaborated plans that she had begun to formulate several years earlier. She instructed Lamb and his co-executor, Henry Kidder, to consolidate almost all of her estate into a charitable trust fund to assist young men in learning a trade and young women in learning to become wives and mothers. Except for a few isolated bequests, most notably to the Meadville Theological Seminary and the Hampton Institute, she was "very much opposed to leaving money to be managed by Institutions." She asked that William Greenleaf Eliot conduct a simple funeral service but left her burial site to the judgment of her executors, preferring to regard herself as a citizen of the United States rather than any particular city.[48]

Contrary to the predictions of her doctors and friends, however, Dix's condition stabilized shortly after she moved to the Trenton asylum. She settled into the same top-floor suite that she had often occupied as a visitor and that she called her Beulah, the land of heavenly joy. Mountains of letters, books, clippings, and miscellaneous memorabilia dominated the small bedroom. When Dix was able to sit, an attendant wheeled her into the equally small parlor, which offered a picturesque view of the asylum grounds and the landscape composed by the Delaware River as it wandered past Trenton toward the domes and spires of neighboring towns.[49]

As the weeks slipped into months, however, Dix's residence in the hospital proved to be profoundly different from her previous visits. Although she wrote hopefully about resuming her work soon, she was unable to leave her bed during the day or sleep at night for much of the winter of 1881–82. More surprising and painful to her, she quickly developed "a *vivid* sense of *aloneness*" in the hospital. Ward ordered the women on the staff to sit with her, but they often avoided the assignment and Dix dismissed them at other times as improperly dressed. Her solitude was accentuated rather than relieved when Anne Callis became her full-time attendant. Callis infuriated Dix by refusing to follow her minutely detailed directions. After nine months, Lydia Prime observed that "these two people, utterly incapable of thinking alike upon any subject, are compelled to spend most of their days together and are utterly weary of the enforced association." Dix nonetheless retained her nurse because she thought Callis honest, in contrast to her suspicions that Ward planned to steal her possessions. Her hostility toward the superintendent became perceptible in the half-hour that he or his assistant physician spent with her every morning and evening, and Ward's wife soon reciprocated the antagonism.[50]

Despite her isolation, Dix declined to receive most visitors. She tried for a while to maintain her correspondence by dictation, but she disliked the intervention of an amanuensis. Instead she painfully scrawled a few broken sentences on barely legible postcards to Lamb, Prime, the Eliots, and other surviving friends. "I *am so alone, so truly alone*," she told Lamb in August 1882 after a downturn in her condition. She implored William Greenleaf Eliot to come to Trenton again, but she had passed the point at which the apprehension of her imminent death marked a crisis. "What can be done?" he wrote sadly to his nephew. "Nothing that I can see. She will grow weaker & become more anxious to see us, but neither of us could be there long, at a time, & to go back & forward takes more strength & money than either of us has to spare."[51]

Dix's summer relapse silenced her customary anticipation of a return to active life. When Ward informed her in September 1882 that she suffered from ossification of the arterial membranes, she acknowledged that his opinion *"may* be correct." She cautioned Lamb not to believe any reports of her health, however, and observed that "I still *think* Physicians are not infallible." Although Dix still had *"no* faith in *medicines,"* doctors ordered frequent stimulants to relieve her pain. Friends supplied her with madeira at a steady pace that left her noticeably embarrassed.[52]

Dix spent much of her time reading, usually alone but sometimes to fellow members of the asylum community. Ward later reported that she was the most expressive reader he had ever heard. She drew mostly from the Bible, devotional commentaries and exercises, and the hymns of Wesley, Watts, and Montgomery. Religious poetry loomed especially large in her imaginative life. She could not concentrate well enough to write verses again, but she exchanged her youthful pious effusions with William Greenleaf Eliot, who similarly "coveted the poet's gift, but have never been weak enough to think I had obtained it." She once told Lamb that she occupied herself by "trying to repair the One-Hoss Shay," the deacon's carriage that served as Oliver Wendell Holmes's metaphor for the breakdown of the New England church.[53]

Dix particularly absorbed herself in the poetry of John Greenleaf Whittier, whom she had met during the 1870s as a result of her visits to the state mental hospital near his sometime home in Danvers, Massachusetts. Fascinated by the transformation of life into didactic art, she joined warmly in the controversy over the accuracy of Whittier's "Barbara Freitchie," offering the poet her corroborative testimony and sending him a portrait of the aged Maryland woman who had reportedly defied Stonewall Jackson.[54] She kept a copy of Whittier's melancholy "At Last" by her bedside in the Trenton asylum and almost every night recited its prayer: "Be near me when all else is from me drifting / Earth, sky, home's picture, days of shade and shine." Despite their slight personal acquaintance, Dix assured the poet in May 1884 that he was her "friend in the abiding comprehensive meaning of the word, not in the sham & conventional interpretation in the heedless use it is so often employed by the thoughtless *many.*"[55]

Still ambivalent about transforming her own life into a moral tale, Dix finally authorized the writing of her biography but continued to grumble about "that class of *literary* tormentors."[56] She rarely talked about her experiences and shielded personal information like her birth date from the curiosity of her closest friends. In the top drawer of her desk she filed a package marked "Family papers to be destroyed unopened."[57] As she reached her mid-eighties, however, the long-resisted past slowly invaded the present in her mind. In February 1886 she drifted into a rare reminiscence about her childhood upon the birth of Henry Ware Eliot's daughter, Theodora Sterling Eliot, whom the family nicknamed Dorothy in honor of Dix. As her eyesight and hearing slowly failed she opened her asylum suite to more visitors, especially welcoming a former student from her school at Orange Court and a former Civil War nurse.[58]

Dix's deterioration accelerated in January 1887 on the death of William Greenleaf Eliot. Afraid to tell her the sad news but more afraid to withhold it, a friend reported to Lamb that she had never seen Dix so shaken. She became feebler and more oppressed by "a painful sense of isolation" after the passing of the minister whom she had considered almost a brother. Neither he nor she would see the birth of Henry Ware Eliot's next child, Thomas Stearns Eliot, whose initials commemorated the short life of his sister, Dorothy. Mercifully, they would not watch the poet repudiate their religion and embrace Anglo-Catholicism.[59]

Dix slipped from unconsciousness to death in the late afternoon of July 18, 1887. Lamb brought her body back to Boston with a box of white lilies from the pond beneath her window at the Trenton asylum. A small knot of remaining friends, no more than fifteen or twenty mourners, attended the brief funeral service conducted by Christopher Rhodes Eliot. They read Whittier's "At Last" and planted the lilies by a stone that bore only Dix's name, amid a myrtle grove cultivated for her.[60] She was buried less than twenty paces from the tomb of William Ellery Channing in Mount Auburn cemetery, the sylvan park built by nineteenth-century Boston Unitarians as a reform of the Puritan church graveyard, at home at last.

Notes   Acknowledgments   Index

Notes

Abbreviations

AEH	Anne Eliza Heath
AJI	*American Journal of Insanity*
BPL	Boston Public Library
DLD	Dorothea Dix
GBE	George B. Emerson
HCH	Harriet C. Hare
HLHU	Houghton Library, Harvard University
HM	Horace Mann
MF	Millard Fillmore
MHS	Massachusetts Historical Society, Boston
MTT	Mary Turner Torrey
PHA	Pennsylvania Hospital Archives, Philadelphia
SGH	Samuel Gridley Howe
SLRC	Schlesinger Library, Radcliffe College
TSK	Thomas S. Kirkbride

Unless otherwise indicated, all letters from Dorothea Dix to Anne Heath are in the Dorothea Lynde Dix Letters to the Heaths, HLHU (bMS Am59), and all other letters are in the Dorothea Lynde Dix MSS., HLHU (bMS Am1838). On many points, a more comprehensive citation of evidence is available in Thomas J. Brown, "Dorothea Dix: The Portrait of a Reformer" (Ph.D. diss., Harvard University, 1994).

Preface

1. Francis Tiffany, *Life of Dorothea Lynde Dix* (Boston: Houghton, Mifflin and Co., 1890), pp. 289–292.
2. George Eliot, *Middlemarch,* Chap. 5.
3. In addition to Tiffany, *Life of Dix,* the standard biographies are David Gollaher, *Voice for the Mad: The Life of Dorothea Dix* (New York: The Free Press, 1995), and Helen L. Marshall, *Dorothea Dix: Forgotten Samaritan* (Chapel Hill: University of North Carolina Press, 1937).
4. Gollaher, *Voice of the Mad,* pp. 13–14, 19–23, 103–107; Marshall, *Dorothea Dix,* pp. 29–30; Charles Schlaifer and Lucy Freeman, *Heart's Work: Civil War Heroine and Champion of the Mentally Ill, Dorothea Lynde Dix* (New York: Paragon House, 1991); William J. Browne, "A Psychiatric Study of the Life and Work of Dorothea Dix," *American Journal of Psychiatry* 3 (September 1969): 339.
5. John L. Thomas, "Romantic Reform in America," *American Quarterly* 17 (Winter 1965): 663.
6. Robert Penn Warren, *The Legacy of the Civil War: Meditations on the Centennial* (New York: Random House, 1961), pp. 83–84.

1. Almost Alone in This Wide World

1. DLD to Alexander Randall, Aug. 23, 1878; DLD to Mrs. Alexander Randall, July 2, 1878, Sept. 6, 1878; DLD to [Alexander Randall?], May 10, 1880.
2. Thomas Bellows Wyman, *The Genealogies and Estates of Charlestown, Massachusetts, 1629–1818* (1879; reprint ed., Somersworth, N.H.: New England History Press, 1982), pp. 637–640; *Sibley's Harvard Graduates,* 17 vols. (Boston: Massachusetts Historical Society, 1873–1975), 7: 143, 214–215; Caleb A. Wall, *Reminiscences of Worcester* (Worcester, Mass.: Tyler & Seagrave, 1877), pp. 254–259.
3. William Lincoln, *History of Worcester* (Worcester, Mass.: Moses D. Phillips, 1837), p. 263 n. 1, reprints Thaddeus Mason Harris's useful sketch of his father-in-law.
4. Samuel B. Woodward, "Worcester—Medical History," in *History of Worcester County, Massachusetts,* ed. D. Hamilton Hurd (Philadelphia: J. W. Lewis & Co., 1889), pp. 1555–56; "Worcester Tax List, 1789," *Proceedings of the Worcester Society of Antiquity* 16 (1899): 373–388; Elijah Dix et al., Broadside, Jan. 3, 1793, American Antiquarian Society. See John L. Brooke, *The Heart of the Commonwealth: Society and Political Culture in Worcester County, Massachusetts, 1713–1861* (New York: Cambridge University Press, 1989), p. 242.
5. Franklin P. Rice, ed., "Worcester Town Records, 1784–1800," in *Proceedings of the Worcester Society of Antiquity* 8 (1890): 56, 77, 95–105; Walter Donald Kring, *The Fruits of Our Labors* (Worcester, Mass.: First Unitarian Church of Worcester, 1985), p. 45.
6. Mary Dix to Ruth Haskins, Dec. 1, 1793, Ralph Waldo Emerson Memorial Association Collection, HLHU; *Columbian Centinel,* June 6, 1795; *22d Report of the*

*Record Commissioners of the City of Boston, Containing the Statistics of the United States'
Direct Tax of 1798, As Assessed on Boston* (Boston: Rockwell and Churchill, 1890),
pp. 48, 406; Andrew Johonnot, "The Johonnot Family," *New England Historical
and Genealogical Register* 7 (April 1853): 141–144; Walter Muir Whitehill, *Boston:
A Topographical History* (Cambridge: Harvard University Press, 1959); Tamara
Plakins Thornton, "The Moral Dimensions of Horticulture in Antebellum America," *New England Quarterly* 57 (March 1984): 3–24.

7. Nathaniel L. Frothingham, "Memoir of Rev. Thaddeus Mason Harris, D.D.," *Collections of the Massachusetts Historical Society,* 4th ser., 2 (1854): 130–155.

8. Faculty Records and Library Charge Records, 1794–1797, Harvard University
Archives; Sidney Willard, *Memories of Youth and Manhood,* 2 vols. (Cambridge,
Mass.: John Bartlett, 1855). R. Kent Newmyer, *Supreme Court Justice Joseph Story:
Statesman of the Old Republic* (Chapel Hill: University of North Carolina Press,
1985), pp. 3–4, 20–36, is the best description of this Harvard class.

9. William Dix to John Warren, n.d. [1795], J. C. Warren MSS., MHS.

10. Elizabeth L. Bond to Helen Marshall, July 20 [1932 or 1933?], Autograph File,
HLHU; Elizabeth Harris to Editor, *Harvard Graduate Magazine,* Feb. 7, 1915,
Quinquennial File, Harvard University Archives.

11. Charles Schlaifer and Lucy Freeman, *Heart's Work: Civil War Heroine and Champion
of the Mentally Ill, Dorothea Lynde Dix* (New York: Paragon House, 1991), p. 157,
proposes that Dix developed "a devastating fear of men" because "she had seen her
father attack her mother in an alcoholic fury." David Gollaher, *Voice for the Mad:
The Life of Dorothea Dix* (New York: The Free Press, 1995), pp. 21–22, suggests
that Dix's "bitter disavowal of her childhood fits the classic paradigm of physical
assault" and conjectures that alcoholism intensified her father's "penchant for
physical abuse."

12. Francis Lieber, "Miss D. L. Dix—After a Visit at Our House in April 1851," MS.
Memorandum, Lieber MSS., Huntington Library, San Marino, California.

13. Alfred S. Roe, *Dorothea Lynde Dix: A Paper Read before the Worcester Society of Antiquity, November 20th, 1888* (Worcester, Mass.: Franklin P. Rice, 1889), p. 6.

14. Helen L. Marshall, *Dorothea Dix: Forgotten Samaritan* (Chapel Hill: University of
North Carolina Press, 1937), p. 6, confuses Mary Biglow with a Mary Bigelow in
stating that Dorothea Dix's mother was eighteen years older than Joseph Dix; in
fact, she was one year younger. Gilman Bigelow Howe, *Genealogy of the Bigelow
Family of America* (Worcester, Mass.: Charles Hamilton, 1890), pp. 97–98. The
psychological speculations of Schlaifer and Freeman in their *Heart's Work* depend
heavily on this error. I have found no basis for the conjecture in Charles M. Snyder,
ed., *The Lady and the President: The Letters of Dorothea Dix and Millard Fillmore*
(Lexington: University Press of Kentucky, 1975), p. 54, that Mary Biglow Dix
was "possibly mentally retarded."

15. Joseph Blake to Peleg Coffin, Dec. 13, 1801, Eastern Lands Papers, Massachusetts

State Archives; Administration of Elijah Dix Estate, Suffolk County Probate Records, File No. 23353, Massachusetts State Archives, Boston.

16. Gollaher, *Voice for the Mad,* pp. 13–14, claims that Elijah Dix was "killed in cold blood" and that "his murder profoundly scarred the Dix family." The entire evidence for this conjecture is an anecdote recounted in Francis Tiffany, *Life of Dorothea Lynde Dix* (Boston: Houghton, Mifflin and Co., 1890), pp. 5–6, of a thwarted attempt to assault the overbearing entrepreneur and the statement in Levi Lincoln, *Reminiscences of the Original Associates of the Worcester Fire Society* (Worcester, Mass.: Edward R. Fiske, 1862), p. 20, that it was "more than suspected" that Dix was "foully dealt with . . . through a conspiracy of squatters and fraudulent contractors and debtors." These shreds of gossip decades after the fact are extremely weak evidence that any crime took place. No suggestion of a murder appears in contemporary newspaper coverage of Elijah Dix's death or in the record developed upon the administration of his estate. Rather, the contrary presumption that he died of natural causes is supported by the probate testimony that he "was laboring under severe sickness and disease" when he drafted his will three months before his death. "Elijah Dix—Objections to His Will," July 10, 1809, Suffolk County Probate Records, File No. 23353. Neither Thaddeus Mason Harris's sketch in Lincoln, *History of Worcester,* nor the profile in Henry Bond, *Family Memorials: Genealogies of the Families and Descendants of the Early Settlers of Watertown* (Boston: Little, Brown and Co., 1855), pp. 199–200, supports in any way the charge of murder. Finally, Alan Taylor's careful study of violence against Maine landowners in *Liberty Men and Great Proprietors: The Revolutionary Settlement on the Maine Frontier, 1760–1820* (Chapel Hill: University of North Carolina Press, 1990), has uncovered no evidence to support the melodramatic speculation about Elijah Dix's death.

17. Joseph Dix's youngest brother later created a similar trust, supporting the impression that the family considered Joseph irresponsible. As a result of the other claims on the estate, however, that bequest also produced no income for Dorothea Dix. Administration of Henry E. Dix Estate, Suffolk County Probate Records, File No. 22617, Massachusetts State Archives.

18. Tiffany, *Life of Dix,* p. 2; Benjamin Thomas Hill, ed., *The Diary of Isaiah Thomas, 1805–1828,* in *Transactions and Collections of the American Antiquarian Society* 9–10 (1909), 9: 172; William Monroe Newton, *History of Barnard, Vermont,* 2 vols. (n.p.: Vermont Historical Society, 1928), 1: 153–193, 235–237, 351–360. Joseph Dix's publications are catalogued in Marcus A. McCorison, comp., *Vermont Imprints, 1778–1820* (Worcester, Mass.: American Antiquarian Society, 1963). Marshall, *Dorothea Dix,* pp. 6–7, claims that Joseph Dix was a well-known itinerant Methodist preacher from the time of his daughter's birth, a description further embellished in Gollaher, *Voice for the Mad,* pp. 17–19. This story neatly foreshadows Dorothea Dix's peregrinations, but no evidence supports it. Gollaher relies on a supposed recollection that Joseph Dix was "a very ardent and zealous member,

and was a sort of lay preacher." This quotation does not appear in the cited source and moreover does not indicate that Joseph served as a minister. His name does not appear in the copious records of preachers, deacons, and elders in *Minutes of the Annual Conferences of the Methodist Episcopal Church, 1773–1828* (New York: T. Mason & G. Lane, 1840), or the lists of traveling Maine preachers and prominent Hampden laymen in Stephen Allen and W. H. Pillsbury, *History of Methodism in Maine, 1793–1886,* 2 vols. (Augusta: Charles E. Nash, 1887), 1: 84; 2: 83–89. The omission of any significant preaching career would also be highly unlikely in Newton's *History of Barnard,* which carefully details the development of Methodism in the town and documents Joseph's experience as a book dealer. It is worth noting that shortly before Joseph left Maine he accepted title to the pew formerly owned by Elijah Dix in the Congregational meetinghouse in Hampden.

19. See the excellent discussion in Randolph A. Roth, *The Democratic Dilemma: Religion, Reform, and the Social Order in the Connecticut River Valley of Vermont, 1791–1850* (Cambridge: Cambridge University Press, 1987), pp. 62–65.

20. [DLD], "The Pass of the Green Mountains," in *The Pearl; or Affection's Gift: A Christmas and New Year's Present* (Philadelphia: Thomas T. Ash, 1829), pp. 115–122.

21. Tiffany, *Life of Dix,* p. 2; Elizabeth L. Bond to Helen Marshall, July 20 [1932 or 1933?], Autograph File, HLHU; Anne M. Boylan, "Growing Up Female in Young America, 1800–1860," in *American Childhood: A Research Guide and Historical Handbook,* ed. Joseph M. Hawes and N. Ray Hiner (Westport, Conn.: Greenwood Press, 1985), pp. 153–184; Joseph F. Kett, *Rites of Passage: Adolescence in America, 1790 to the Present* (New York: Basic Books, 1977), pp. 11–37.

22. Roe, *Dorothea Lynde Dix,* pp. 9–11; Tiffany, *Life of Dix,* pp. 12–13.

23. John W. Ward to Alfred S. Roe, April 20, 1888, reprinted in Roe, *Dorothea Lynde Dix,* p. 5.

24. The deaths of Dix's parents are recorded in Bond, *Family Memorials . . . of Watertown,* pp. 200–201, and Howe, *Genealogy of the Bigelow Family,* pp. 97–98. On the insolvency of Joseph Dix, see Administration of Joseph Dix Estate, Suffolk County Probate Records, File No. 29659, Massachusetts State Archives. The extent to which Dix supported her mother is disputed. Marianna Davenport Trott to Francis Tiffany, Feb. 19, 1890, reports that she contributed significantly. Elizabeth L. Bond to Helen Marshall, July 20 [1932 or 1933?], Autograph File, HLHU, maintains that she left this burden to Dorothy Dix and Mary Harris. For Dix's affection toward the Biglows, see DLD to Joseph Dix, March [1?], [1837].

25. Patricia Carley Johnson, ed., "Sensitivity and Civil War: The Selected Diaries and Papers, 1858–1866, of Frances Adeline [Fanny] Seward" (Ph.D. diss., University of Rochester, 1963), p. 452. DLD, "On receiving a flower which in Childhood had been a dear favorite," MS. notebook no. 2, February 1837, is a rare sentimental reverie. More typical was the tone of DLD, "My *Natal* Day," MS. notebook no. 4, on the theme "My cradle was the couch of care." DLD MSS., HLHU (bMS Am1838).

26. DLD to AEH, n.d. (Sunday evening); DLD to [?], Sept. 5, [?] (draft). For excellent analyses of Unitarian preaching in Boston during the early 1820s, see Mary Kupiec Cayton, *Emerson's Emergence: Self and Society in the Transformation of New England, 1800–1845* (Chapel Hill: University of North Carolina Press, 1989), pp. 3–56; Daniel Walker Howe, *The Unitarian Conscience: Harvard Moral Philosophy, 1805–1861* (Cambridge: Harvard University Press, 1970); and Anne C. Rose, *Transcendentalism as a Social Movement, 1830–1850* (New Haven: Yale University Press, 1981), pp. 1–37.

27. DLD to AEH, n.d. (Sunday evening).

28. DLD to AEH, n.d. [January 1825?] (Sunday evening), n.d. (Tuesday eve.)(fragment), n.d. (Sunday morning), n.d. (Sunday evening), n.d. (Monday).

29. DLD to AEH, n.d. (Saturday evening) [spring 1825].

30. MTT to DLD, Dec. 7, 1830; Elizabeth Heath Howe, MS. diary, Sept. 1, 1827, Heath Family MSS., MHS; Marshall, *Dorothea Dix,* p. 254 n. 13.

31. DLD to AEH, n.d. (Tuesday evening) (fragment).

32. DLD to AEH, n.d. (Sunday in church).

33. DLD to AEH, n.d. [August 1824] (fragment).

34. DLD to Benjamin Silliman [?], Dec. 11, 1858, Notable American Women MSS., Historical Society of Pennsylvania, Philadelphia.

35. [DLD], "Letter II," in *The Pearl; or Affection's Gift: A Christmas and New Year's Present* (Philadelphia: Thomas T. Ash, 1829), p. 47.

36. Ibid.; Frothingham, "Memoir of Harris," pp. 138–139; DLD to AEH, Dec. 25 [1827].

37. Carroll Smith-Rosenberg, "The Female World of Love and Ritual: Relations between Women in Nineteenth-Century America," *Signs* 1 (Autumn 1975): 19.

38. Susan Heath, MS. diary, July 4, 1823; AEH, MS. diary, Aug. 26, 1826, both in Heath Family MSS., MHS.

39. DLD to AEH, n.d. (Sunday evening).

40. Susan Heath, MS. diary, March 2, 1824, Heath Family MSS., MHS; DLD to AEH, n.d. (Thursday evening); DLD to AEH, n.d. (Friday).

41. DLD to AEH, n.d. [1823–24] (fragment); DLD to AEH, n.d. (Sunday evening); DLD, "Addressed to A.E.H.," MS. poem, DLD-Heath MSS., HLHU.

42. DLD to AEH, Nov. 28 [1824].

43. Roe, *Dorothea Lynde Dix,* p. 11, reports memories of the town gossip, and Marshall, *Dorothea Dix,* pp. 15–16, 18, 29–30, speculates about a significant romance on the basis of Lynde family recollections. The Edward Bangs MS. diary, Bangs Family MSS., American Antiquarian Society, makes clear that no such relationship existed after the first surviving entry of March 27, 1823, although it is possible that Dix was the unnamed fiancée discussed in Edward D. Bangs to Nathaniel Howe, May 11, 1820. If any courtship took place, Marshall misdated its end in presenting the highly dubious conclusion that love for Bangs became "a secret shrine" for Dix.

44. DLD to AEH, n.d. (unsigned). Dix's letters do not articulate an ideological commitment to the "cult of single blessedness" described in Lee Virginia Chambers-Schiller, *Liberty, A Better Husband: Single Women in America: The Generations of 1780–1840* (New Haven: Yale University Press, 1984), pp. 10–28.

45. Susan Heath, MS. diary, Nov. 21, 1823, Heath Family MSS., MHS.

46. A. T. Perry to Alfred S. Roe, April 27, 1888, in Roe, *Dorothea Lynde Dix,* pp. 14–16.

47. Susan Heath, MS. diary, Nov. 21, 1823, Heath Family MSS., MHS.

48. Henry James, review of William Channing Gannett, *Ezra Stiles Gannett, Unitarian Minister in Boston, 1824–1871,* reprinted in *Henry James: Literary Criticism—Essays on Literature, American Writers, English Writers,* ed. Leon Edel (New York: Library of America, 1984), pp. 278–281.

49. Susan Heath, MS. diary, Nov. 30, 1823, Heath Family MSS., MHS; DLD to AEH, n.d.; DLD to MTT, Jan. 26, 1828.

50. Ezra Stiles Gannett MS. diary, Feb. 1, 1824, Gannett MSS., MHS; Susan Heath, MS. diary, May 5, 1824, Heath Family MSS., MHS; DLD to AEH, n.d. (Wednesday), n.d. (Sunday evening).

51. DLD to AEH, n.d. (Saturday morning).

52. DLD, "Pass of the Green Mountains"; DLD to AEH, Nov. 28 [1825].

53. Linda K. Kerber, *Women of the Republic: Intellect and Ideology in Revolutionary America* (Chapel Hill: University of North Carolina Press, 1980), pp. 185–231; Carl F. Kaestle and Maris A. Vinovskis, *Education and Social Change in Nineteenth-Century Massachusetts* (New York: Cambridge University Press, 1980), p. 287; Nancy Cott, *The Bonds of Womanhood: "Woman's Sphere" in New England, 1780–1835* (New Haven: Yale University Press, 1977), pp. 101–125.

54. DLD to Dorothy Dix, n.d.

55. DLD to AEH, n.d. (Sunday evening).

56. DLD to AEH, n.d. (Sunday in church).

57. DLD to AEH, n.d. (Tuesday evening) (unsigned). See Elizabeth B. Keeney, *The Botanizers: Amateur Scientists in Nineteenth-Century America* (Chapel Hill: University of North Carolina Press, 1992), pp. 38–46, on botany as a metaphor of self-improvement.

58. DLD to AEH, n.d. (Sunday).

59. Carl F. Kaestle, *Pillars of the Republic* (New York: Hill and Wang, 1983), pp. 40–42.

60. Elias Nason, "William Bentley Fowle," *New England Historical and Genealogical Register* 23 (April 1869): 110–117; John Pierpont to DLD, May 1 [1824?].

61. DLD to Joseph Dix, June 28 [1853]. On reprinting and revisions, see the different editions of *Conversations on Common Things* in HLHU, published from 1824 to 1864.

62. DLD to AEH, n.d. (Sunday evening).

63. Review of *Conversations on Common Things, American Journal of Education* 1 (February 1826): 126; review of *Conversations on Common Things,* 2d ed., *American Journal of Education* 2 (June 1827): 383.

64. DLD to AEH [August 1824] (fragment); DLD to AEH, Nov. 28 [1824].
65. DLD to AEH, n.d. (Wednesday) [Aug. 25/27, 1824].
66. DLD to AEH, n.d. (Monday).
67. DLD to AEH, n.d. (Friday evening) [September 1824].
68. Ibid. Dix was reading *Athaeneum, Spirit of the English Magazines* 1 (Sept. 15, 1824): 481–487. The review, with a plea for respect of Landon's copyright that was omitted from the American reprint, originally appeared in *The London Literary Gazette* (July 3, 1824), for which Landon wrote much anonymous criticism.
69. John Pierce, MS. memoirs, 4: 154 (December 1824), Pierce MSS., MHS; AEH, MS. diary, Heath Family MSS., MHS.
70. DLD to AEH, n.d. (Thursday) [Dec. 9/11, 1824]. Dix's use of a dash in this sentence is typical of her circumspect allusions to the absence of a close male attachment.
71. DLD to AEH, n.d. (Sunday).
72. DLD to AEH, n.d. (Sunday evening).
73. DLD to AEH, n.d. (Sunday).
74. DLD to AEH, n.d. (Saturday evening) [spring 1825].
75. DLD to AEH, n.d. (Sunday evening) [spring 1825].
76. AEH, MS. diary, March 25, 28–29, 1825, Heath Family MSS., MHS.
77. DLD to AEH, n.d. (Wednesday); DLD to AEH, n.d. (Sunday evening) [spring 1825]; DLD to AEH, n.d. (Sunday) [late spring 1825]; DLD to AEH, Nov. 7 [1825].
78. Susan Heath, MS. diary, May 15, 1825, Heath Family MSS., MHS.
79. DLD to AEH, June 26 [1825].
80. DLD to AEH, Jan. [?], 1826 (Sunday).
81. DLD, MS. journal, n.d., HLHU (bMS Am1274).
82. DLD to AEH, May 31 [13], [1826].
83. DLD to AEH, n.d. (Tuesday) [fall 1825].
84. Josephine Waters to DLD, Dec. 29, 1827.
85. DLD to AEH, n.d. (Wednesday evening) [fall 1825].
86. DLD to AEH, Nov. 7 [1825].
87. DLD to AEH, Dec. 29 [1825].
88. DLD to AEH, March 5, 1826.

2. Fixed as Fate

1. DLD to AEH, May 31 [13], [1826] (Sunday). Dix's date was plainly an inadvertent transposition.
2. DLD to AEH, n.d. (Saturday morning) [summer 1826]; Susan Heath, MS. diary, Nov. 11, 1826, Heath Family MSS., MHS.
3. DLD to AEH, March [?], [1826].
4. Daniel Walker Howe, *The Unitarian Conscience* (Cambridge: Harvard University

Press, 1970), p. 19; Andrew Delbanco, *William Ellery Channing: An Essay on the Liberal Spirit in America* (Cambridge: Harvard University Press, 1981), p. 1.

5. Elizabeth Palmer Peabody, *Reminiscences of Rev. Wm. Ellery Channing, D.D.* (Boston: Roberts Brothers, 1880), p. 165n.

6. DLD to AEH, n.d. (Thursday evening).

7. DLD to AEH, May 31 [13], [1826] (Sunday).

8. DLD to MTT, Jan. 26, 1828.

9. DLD to AEH, June 16, 1826.

10. DLD to AEH, May 31 [13], June 16, 1826.

11. DLD to AEH, March [?], [1826].

12. DLD to AEH, Dec. 25 [1827].

13. DLD to Joseph Dix, Jan. 30, 1849.

14. DLD to AEH, n.d. (Tuesday evening).

15. On Rowson's *Biblical Dialogues,* see David S. Reynolds, *Faith in Fiction: The Emergence of Religious Literature in America* (Cambridge: Harvard University Press, 1981), pp. 130–132.

16. DLD, "John Williams, or the Sailor Boy," in *American Moral Tales for Young Persons* (Boston: Leonard C. Bowles and B. H. Greene, 1832), pp. 10–13, 18, 21.

17. Review, "Books for Children," *Christian Examiner* 4 (March–April 1827): 180–181.

18. DLD to Elizabeth Davis Bliss, Feb. 2 [1827], Bancroft-Bliss MSS., Library of Congress.

19. DLD to AEH, n.d. [March 1824].

20. DLD to AEH, n.d. (Sunday).

21. Ibid.

22. *Third Report of the Instructer of the Female Monitorial School* (Boston: Munroe & Francis, 1830), p. 19; *Fifth Report of the Instructer of the Boston Female Monitorial School* (Boston: William W. Clapp, 1838), p. 10.

23. Susan Heath, MS. diary, April 9–10, June 5, 1827, Heath Family MSS., MHS.

24. George Gibbs, *The Gibbs Family of Rhode Island and Some Related Families* (New York: privately printed, 1933), p. 101.

25. Mary Channing Eustis to Francis Tiffany, n.d., quoted in Francis Tiffany, *Life of Dorothea Lynde Dix* (Boston: Houghton, Mifflin and Co., 1890), p. 34.

26. Ibid.

27. John Pierpont to DLD, Nov. 15, 1827.

28. William Ellery Channing to DLD, Dec. 3, 1827; DLD to MTT, Jan. 8, 1828.

29. DLD to MTT, Nov. 29, 1827; DLD to AEH, Dec. 25 [1827].

30. DLD to MTT, Nov. 29, 1827.

31. DLD to MTT, Jan. 8, 1828.

32. DLD to MTT, Dec. 17, 1827; Jan. 26, Feb. 19, 1828; March 3 [1828].

33. DLD, *Private Hours* (Boston: Munroe and Francis, 1828), pp. 10, 21–22, 45; DLD to MTT, Dec. 17, 1827.

34. On the evangelical vernacular, see Russell E. Richey, *Early American Methodism* (Bloomington: Indiana University Press, 1991), pp. 84–85.
35. DLD to MTT, Jan. 8, 1828; April 12 [1828].
36. DLD to AEH, June 23 [1827]; DLD to MTT, Feb. 19, 1828.
37. DLD to MTT, March 3, April 12 [1828]; MTT to DLD, March 30, April 24, 1828. On the infant school movement, see Carl F. Kaestle and Maris A. Vinovskis, *Education and Social Change in Nineteenth-Century Massachusetts* (New York: Cambridge University Press, 1980), pp. 53–60.
38. Amos Bronson Alcott, MS. diary, May 9, 20, 1828, Alcott MSS., HLHU (*59M-308).
39. DLD to AEH, July 27 [1828].
40. DLD to MTT, Jan. 26, 1828.
41. DLD to AEH, n.d. (Sunday evening).
42. DLD to AEH, n.d. (Sunday evening), n.d. (fragment), Jan. 28, 1826.
43. DLD to AEH, March 5, 1828.
44. Review of "The Storm," "John Williams," "Marion Wilder," *Ladies' Magazine* 1 (August 1828): 380; review of *Evening Hours* 1–6, *American Journal of Education* 3 (March 1828): 192.
45. DLD to MTT, April 12 [1828].
46. DLD, MS. journal, n.d. [1827?], HLHU (bMS Am1274).
47. [DLD], "Llerena de la Reyna; or the Developement [*sic*] of Firmness," in *The Pearl; or Affection's Gift: A Christmas and New Year's Present* (Philadelphia: Thomas T. Ash, 1829), p. 169.
48. DLD, "The Storm," in *American Moral Tales,* p. 254.
49. Review of "The Pearl," *Ladies' Magazine* 1 (December 1828): 574–575; review of "Thomas Mansfield—James Coleman," *Ladies' Magazine* 2 (March 1829): 96; review of *Original Moral Tales, intended for Children and Young Persons, Christian Examiner* 5 (September–October 1828): 407.
50. [DLD], *A Garland of Flora* (Boston: S. G. Goodrich & Co., 1829), preface.
51. Review of *The Garland of Flora* [sic], *Ladies' Magazine* 2 (June 1829): 295–296.
52. Sarah Josepha Hale, *Flora's Interpreter* (14th ed., Boston: Benjamin B. Mussey & Co., 1847; first published 1833), p. v.
53. DLD to AEH, June 27 [1828].
54. [DLD], *A Garland of Flora,* p. 1.
55. Mary Kelley, *Private Woman, Public Stage: Literary Domesticity in Nineteenth-Century America* (New York: Oxford University Press, 1984) provides an excellent analysis of the personal tensions confronted by women of Dix's generation who became professional writers. In works after *Conversations on Common Things,* which identified her as "A Teacher," Dix had identified herself by her publications in all works before *A Garland of Flora.*

56. DLD to AEH, July 8, 1829.

57. Ibid.; Helen C. Loring to DLD, Sept. 2, 1829; MTT to DLD, Aug. 16 [1829].

58. MTT to DLD, Aug. 5 [1829]; Josephine Waters to DLD, Aug. 10, 1829.

59. MTT to DLD, n.d. [1830]. On the significance of setting up housekeeping independently, see Kathryn Kish Sklar, *Catharine Beecher: A Study in American Domesticity* (New Haven: Yale University Press, 1973), p. 62.

60. Josephine Waters to DLD, Aug. 10, 1829.

61. DLD to AEH, July 8, 1829; MTT to DLD, Aug. 13, 1831.

62. DLD to Benjamin Silliman, June 3, 1830; Benjamin Silliman to DLD, Jan. 10, June 17, 1830; DLD, "Notice of the Aranea Aculeata, The Phaloena Antiqua and Some Species of the Papilio," *American Journal of Science and Arts* 19 (January 1831): 61–63.

63. DLD to Benjamin Silliman, June 3, 1830, Sept. 7 [1830].

64. DLD to MTT, n.d. [January 1831]; DLD, MS. journal, December 1830, DLD MSS., HLHU (bMS Am1274); William Ellery Channing, MS. Santa Cruz journal, Dec. 13, 1830, Channing MSS., MHS.

65. Channing, MS. Santa Cruz journal.

66. DLD to MTT, n.d. [January 1831].

67. Neville A. T. Hall, *Slave Society in the Danish West Indies* (Baltimore: Johns Hopkins University Press, 1992), pp. 5, 86, 180.

68. DLD to MTT, Jan. 27 [1831]; William Henry Channing, *Life of William Ellery Channing, D.D.* (reprint ed., Boston: American Unitarian Association, 1880), p. 522.

69. DLD, "The Storm," in *American Moral Tales,* pp. 260–263. On the antislavery perspective of comparable writers, see John C. Crandall, "Patriotism and Humanitarian Reform in Children's Literature, 1825–1860," *American Quarterly* 21 (Spring 1969): 12–17.

70. MTT to DLD, Dec. 7, 1830.

71. DLD to MTT, Jan. 27 [1831]; Hall, *Slave Society,* p. 73.

72. DLD to MTT, Jan. 27 [1831]; Hall, *Slave Society,* pp. 83–86.

73. DLD to MTT, Feb. [?], [1831].

74. DLD to MTT, Jan. 27 [1831], April [?], [1831].

75. DLD to MTT, Feb. 25 [1831], April [?], [1831]; John White Chadwick, *William Ellery Channing: Minister of Religion* (Boston: Houghton, Mifflin and Co., 1903), pp. 361–362.

76. MTT to DLD, March 3, 1831.

77. DLD to MTT, April 5 [1831].

78. Ibid.

79. Jack Mendelsohn, *Channing: The Reluctant Radical* (Boston: Little, Brown and Co., 1971), p. 237.

80. DLD to MTT, May 5 [1831].

3. Moral Power

1. Helen C. Loring to DLD, July 23, Sept. 8, 1831; MTT to DLD, Aug. 13, 1831.

2. George B. Emerson, *A Lecture on the Education of Females* (Boston: Hilliard, Gray, Little and Wilkins, 1831), pp. 25–26.

3. Elizabeth Alden Green, *Mary Lyon and Mount Holyoke: Opening the Gates* (Hanover: University Press of New England, 1979), p. 65.

4. DLD to Mrs. Dwight, n.d., Jared Sparks MSS., HLHU (MS. Sparks 153); *Order of Exercises at the Concert Given by the Pupils of the Female Monitorial School to Their Parents and Friends, Feb. 24, 1837* (Boston: Munroe and Francis, 1837).

5. DLD to Mrs. Dwight, n.d., Sparks MSS., HLHU; Jane Lathrop Loring, MS. composition book, SLRC.

6. Francis Tiffany, *Life of Dorothea Lynde Dix* (Boston: Houghton, Mifflin and Co., 1890), p. 41.

7. MTT to DLD, n.d. [1833?].

8. Marianna D. Trott to Horatio A. Lamb, July 27, 1887.

9. Mary Haven to DLD, Aug. 18, 1836. On the campaign for a Unitarian awakening, see Daniel Walker Howe, *The Unitarian Conscience: Harvard Moral Philosophy, 1805–1861* (Cambridge: Harvard University Press, 1970), Chap. 7.

10. Tiffany, *Life of Dix,* p. 39.

11. Ezra Abbot to DLD, Nov. 16, [?]; Arlington Street Church Records, membership list, Andover-Harvard Theological Library, Cambridge, Massachusetts.

12. DLD to Andrews Norton, n.d. [1833], Andrews Norton MSS., HLHU (bMS Am1089).

13. DLD to Thomas Wren Ward, March 12, 14, 1833, Thomas Wren Ward MSS., MHS; Jane H. Pease and William H. Pease, *Ladies, Women, and Wenches: Choice and Constraint in Antebellum Charleston and Boston* (Chapel Hill: University of North Carolina Press, 1990), pp. 69–70, 85–86.

14. Tiffany, *Life of Dix,* pp. 34, 40. See also Louisa Jane (Park) Hall to Francis Tiffany, May 17, 1889.

15. DLD to Anna M. Price, n.d.

16. Margaret Fuller to Caroline Sturgis, July 12, 1840, *The Letters of Margaret Fuller,* ed. Robert N. Hudspeth (Ithaca, N.Y.: Cornell University Press, 1983–), 2: 149.

17. Elizabeth Palmer Peabody to Mary T. Peabody, May 4, 1834, typescript, Olive Kettering Library, Antioch College.

18. Martha Saxton, *Louisa May* (Boston: Houghton Mifflin Company, 1977), pp. 82–83.

19. Mary Haven to DLD, Aug. 18, 1836.

20. DLD to MTT, Oct. 1, 1836.

21. Marianna D. Trott to Horatio A. Lamb, July 27, 1887.

22. DLD, MS. note, Jan. 1, 1835; DLD to Joseph Dix, Aug. 16, 1847.

23. Indenture of Mary Ann Smith, Dec. 4, 1833, records of the Boston Overseers of the Poor, MHS.
24. Helen C. Loring to DLD, July 23, Sept. 8, 1831.
25. For the date of death, see Gilman Bigelow Howe, *Genealogy of the Bigelow Family of America* (Worcester, Mass.: Charles Hamilton, 1890), pp. 97–98; and DLD, MS. journal no. 4, Dec. 22, 1835, DLD MSS., HLHU (bMS Am1838). Compare with Tiffany, *Life of Dix,* p. 48, which indicates that Mary Biglow Dix died in 1836; and David Gollaher, *Voice for the Mad: The Life of Dorothea Dix* (New York: The Free Press, 1995), p. 103, which guesses that she lived until May 1837 because Dorothea Dix had two months earlier urged her brother Joseph to write to Fitzwilliam, where many of their relatives continued to live after the death of their mother.
26. DLD, MS. journal no. 4, Dec. 22, 1835, DLD MSS., HLHU (bMS Am1838).
27. DLD to GBE, n.d. [March 1836], DLD MSS., BPL.
28. Marianna Davenport Trott to Francis Tiffany, Feb. 19, 1890.
29. Charles G. Loring to DLD, March 4, 1835; William I. Lawrence, ed., *Autobiography and Diary of Elizabeth Parsons Channing* (Boston: American Unitarian Association, 1907), pp. 6, 70.
30. DLD to AEH, April 20, 1835.
31. Lucy Ella Abbot to DLD, Aug. 8, 1835; Susan Heath, MS. diary, Aug. 10–13, Sept. 1, 1835, Heath Family MSS., MHS; GBE to DLD, Nov. 16, 1835.
32. DLD, MS. notebook no. 1, DLD MSS., HLHU (bMS Am1838).
33. DLD to GBE, n.d., DLD MSS., BPL.
34. Ibid.; MTT to DLD, March 31, 1836.
35. DLD to GBE, n.d., DLD MSS., BPL.
36. William Ellery Channing to Joanna Baillie, April 21, 1836, DLD MSS., HLHU (bMS Am1838).
37. AEH to DLD, April 14, 1836; DLD to AEH, [April] 16, [1836].
38. Cyrus Peirce to HM, Sept. 13, 1841, HM MSS., MHS.
39. DLD to Dorothy Dix, June 2 [1836].
40. Andrew Buchanan to DLD, n.d.
41. On the Rathbones, see Sheila Marriner, *Rathbones of Liverpool, 1845–1873* (Liverpool: Liverpool University Press, 1961); Eleanor F. Rathbone, *William Rathbone: A Memoir* (London: Macmillan and Co., 1905); Emily A. Rathbone, *Records of the Rathbone Family* (Edinburgh: R. & R. Clark, 1913).
42. DLD to Dorothy Dix, June 2 [1836].
43. Helen C. Loring to DLD, Sept. 27, 1836.
44. William Ellery Channing to DLD [Nov. 20, 1836].
45. DLD to Dorothy Dix, Sept. 28 [1836], Jan. 8, 1837; DLD to MTT, Feb. 8 [1837].
46. DLD to MTT, Oct. 1, 1836; DLD to Dorothy Dix, Nov. [?], 1836; DLD to AEH, Nov. 12, 1836.

47. DLD to Dorothy Dix, Sept. 28 [1836]; Nov. [?], 1836.

48. DLD to Dorothy Dix, Sept. 28 [1836]; DLD, MS. poem, "To Miss Rathbone, While She Was from Home," September 1836, DLD MSS., HLHU (bMS Am1838).

49. AEH to DLD, Oct. 14, 1836.

50. DLD to Dorothy Dix, Sept. 28 [1836].

51. Ibid., March 1, 1837; DLD, "To a *Very Kind Friend,*" October 1836, MS. notebook no. 2, DLD MSS. HLHU (bMS Am1838).

52. DLD to Dorothy Dix, Sept. 28 [1836].

53. Ibid., DLD to AEH, Nov. 12, 1836.

54. DLD to Dorothy Dix, Jan. 8, 1837.

55. DLD to Dorothy Dix, Nov. [?], 1836.

56. H. M. Rathbone to Elizabeth Joseph Fry, May 30, 1836.

57. John Hamilton Thom to DLD, n.d.

58. DLD to Dorothy Dix, Nov. [?], 1836.

59. Ibid.; DLD to Dorothy Dix, Oct. [?], 1836.

60. DLD to Dorothy Dix, Jan. 8, 1837.

61. DLD to AEH, Jan. 25, 1837.

62. DLD to Dorothy Dix, Sept. 28 [1836], Nov. [?], 1836; DLD to MTT, Oct. 1, 1836; DLD to AEH, Nov. 12, 1836.

63. DLD to MTT, April 23, 1837; E. G. Gair to DLD, n.d.

64. John Hamilton Thom to William Ellery Channing, April 19, 1837, Channing MSS., HLHU (bMS Am1428).

65. Ibid.

66. DLD to MTT, April 23, 1837.

67. DLD to MTT, Oct. 1, 1836.

68. DLD to MTT, April 23, 1837.

69. DLD to Dorothy Dix, March 1, 1837, May 16 [1837].

70. Helen C. Loring to DLD, n.d.; DLD to MTT, May 29, 1837.

71. John Hamilton Thom to DLD, n.d.

72. My account of Dix's experience in Liverpool contrasts sharply with the transformation described in Gollaher, *Voice for the Mad,* pp. 95–113. According to Gollaher, Dix painfully realized at Greenbank that her debility resulted from "something akin to what later ages have called depression"; for months after her arrival, she supposedly "teetered on the brink, beset by a fear that her mind had snapped and was slipping helplessly into madness" (p. 106). By enabling her to overcome this condition, the compassionate care she received in the Rathbone home prepared her to appreciate the similar principles underlying the treatment of insanity pioneered at the York Retreat. She then, according to Gollaher, experienced an Ericksonian "moratorium" (pp. 107, 112) in which she absorbed not only the premises of asylum therapy but also a new vision of government responsibility for social

welfare arising from the reform of the Poor Law. She accordingly returned to America with a blueprint for her future career as a champion of public mental hospitals.

While imaginatively encapsulating the valuable observation of Andrew Scull that influential American historiography has neglected the English origins of the asylum, Gollaher's story is utterly fanciful. Dix was dispirited before her voyage and at times in Liverpool, as she had good reason to be, but there is no evidence that she was "slipping helplessly into madness" or that she ever thought she was. To the contrary, she bitterly rejected the suggestion of her friends that her affliction was more elusive than a pulmonary condition. Her intellectual horizons as well as her self-understanding remained essentially unchanged in England. Although Gollaher juxtaposes his biographical narrative with developments at the York Retreat and in British welfare policy, Dix had no meaningful direct contact with either of these models in 1836–37. Instead, she rarely left Greenbank, rarely met English visitors, and rarely read anything new. She showed a casual familiarity with insanity and welfare policy at various times before she found her vocation, but as I discuss in Chapter 4 she returned from England with no clear views about how she would lead her life, and certainly with no sense of a mission on behalf of the insane. Although Dix's adaptation of British models is important to understanding several aspects of her life, her visit to Liverpool does not tidily epitomize that theme. See also David L. Gollaher, "Dorothea Dix and the English Origins of the American Asylum Movement," *Canadian Review of American Studies* 23 (Spring 1993): 149–175.

4. I Tell What I Have Seen!

1. Mary R. Harris to DLD, April 6 [1884].
2. Administration of Dorothy Dix Estate, Suffolk County Probate Records, File No. 31557; Richard Rathbone to DLD, Dec. 7, 1837; Hannah Reynolds to DLD, Jan. 5, 1838; DLD to AEH, Feb. 24, 1838.
3. John Howe, MS. account book, 1839–1840, Heath Family MSS., MHS.
4. Susan Heath, MS. diary, Oct. 31, 1837, Heath Family MSS.; AEH to DLD, Jan. 6, 1838.
5. Hannah Williams Howe, MS. diary, Heath Family MSS., MHS; AEH to DLD, Jan. 6, 1838; DLD to AEH, Feb. 24, 1838.
6. DLD to AEH, March 3, July 9, 1838.
7. DLD to AEH, Feb. 24, March 3, 30, 1838.
8. DLD to AEH, Nov. 4, 1838.
9. DLD to AEH, Oct. 14, 1839. Adrift though Dix was at this point, there is no basis for the claim in David Gollaher, *Voice for the Mad: The Life of Dorothea Dix* (New York: The Free Press, 1995), pp. 122–125, that at the age of thirty-seven she entered into an "affair" with twenty-one-year-old Roswell Dwight

Hitchcock that eventually "forced her to contemplate marriage." That sensational misreading of Hitchcock's letters distorts a relationship in which Dix sought to act as a mentor and supporter in his preparations to enter the ministry, as she did for many other young men throughout her adult life. Hitchcock did not intimate that he planned to propose to Dix, as Gollaher states; to the contrary, during their correspondence he was courting his future wife. The stretching of evidence in pursuit of scandal is typified by Gollaher's inference that the relationship with Hitchcock must have "occupied a special niche" in Dix's memory because she "felt his correspondence was too precious to destroy." In fact, she preserved the letters of almost 700 different correspondents in the main collection of her papers now at HLHU.

10. M. T. Torrey to DLD, March 6, June 5, 1838, Oct. 18, 1839; Margaret Fuller to Ralph Waldo Emerson, April 9, 18, 1842, in Robert N. Hudspeth, ed., *The Letters of Margaret Fuller* (Ithaca: Cornell University Press, 1983–), 3: 58, 60.

11. DLD to AEH, Dec. 6, 1839; Harold Kirker, *The Architecture of Charles Bulfinch* (Cambridge: Harvard University Press, 1969), pp. 158–60; Elizabeth Palmer Peabody, *Reminiscences of Rev. Wm. Ellery Channing, D.D.* (Boston: Roberts Brothers, 1880), pp. 332, 344.

12. DLD to AEH, Jan. 11, 1840, Jan. 22 [1840].

13. DLD to AEH, April 13 [1840].

14. Jurgen Herbst, *And Sadly Teach: Teacher Education and Professionalization in American Culture* (Madison: University of Wisconsin Press, 1989); Massachusetts State Normal School Papers, Widener Library, Harvard University.

15. Cyrus Peirce to HM, March 19, Aug. 7, 1841, HM MSS., MHS; Arthur O. Norton, ed., *The First State Normal School in America: The Journals of Cyrus Peirce and Mary Swift* (Cambridge: Harvard University Press, 1926), p. 78.

16. John Taylor Gilman Nichols to James Freeman Clarke, n.d., reprinted in James Freeman Clarke, "Dorothea L. Dix," in *The Disciples' Pulpit: The Sermons of James Freeman Clarke,* vol. 1, no. 9 (Boston: Geo. H. Ellis, 1887), p. 5n; John Taylor Gilman Nichols, "Tales of a Grandfather, 1897–1900," pp. 94–96, typescript, Andover-Harvard Theological Library.

17. Philanthropic Society in the Theological School of Harvard University, MS. minutes, March 31, 1841, Harvard University Archives; Gary L. Collison, " 'A True Toleration': Harvard Divinity School Students and Unitarianism, 1830–1859," in Conrad Edick Wright, ed., *American Unitarianism, 1805–1865* (Boston: Northeastern University Press, 1989), pp. 216–217.

18. John Taylor Gilman Nichols to James Freeman Clarke, n.d., reprinted in Clarke, *Dorothea L. Dix,* p. 5n; *Laws of the Commonwealth of Massachusetts,* chap. 223 (April 13, 1836), chap. 129 (April 7, 1835); *Massachusetts House of Representatives Document No. 47* (September 15, 1842), p. 4; Susan E. Maycock, *East Cambridge* (rev. ed.; Cambridge, Mass: M.I.T. Press, 1988), pp. 140–145; Gerald Grob, *The State and*

the *Mentally Ill: A History of the Worcester State Hospital in Massachusetts, 1830–1920* (Chapel Hill: University of North Carolina Press, 1966), pp. 95–102.

19. William Rathbone, Jr. to Bessie Rathbone, June 2, 1841, Rathbone Family MSS., University of Liverpool.

20. DLD to Nathan Appleton, July 28, Oct. 29 [1841]; Nathan Appleton to DLD, Aug. 9, 1841; John Clark to Nathan Appleton, Aug. 29, Sept. 7, 1841; all in Appleton Family MSS., MHS.

21. Cyrus Peirce to HM, Aug. 7, 1841, HM MSS., MHS.

22. Cyrus Peirce to HM, Sept. 14, 1841, HM MSS., MHS.

23. Cyrus Peirce to HM, Sept. 13, 14, 1841, HM MSS., MHS.

24. Harold Schwartz, *Samuel Gridley Howe: Social Reformer, 1801–1876* (Cambridge: Harvard University Press, 1956), pp. 39–113.

25. SGH to DLD [Sept. 23, 1841], Julia Ward Howe Family MSS., SLRC.

26. Ibid.; SGH to DLD [October 1841], Julia Ward Howe Family MSS., SLRC.

27. Joseph Henry Allen to Joseph Allen, Dec. 13, 1841, American Prose MSS., Historical Society of Pennsylvania, Philadelphia.

28. William O. Moseley to DLD, Dec. 30, 1841; AEH to DLD [Dec. 31, 1841].

29. Edward Jarvis, *Insanity and Insane Asylums* (Louisville, Ky.: Prentice and Weissinger, 1841).

30. Norman Dain, *Concepts of Insanity in the United States, 1789–1865* (New Brunswick, N.J.: Rutgers University Press, 1964), pp. 168–172, shows that Dix's understanding of insanity was typical of contemporary thinking about the subject.

31. Charles Capper, *Margaret Fuller, an American Romantic Life: The Private Years* (New York: Oxford University Press, 1992), p. 371n.27.

32. SGH to John G. Palfrey, June 15, 1842, Palfrey Family MSS., HLHU (bMS Am 1704).

33. DLD, MS. notes of visits to Worcester and Leicester, June 17, 1842, Miscellaneous MSS., HLHU (*43M-87). Robert C. Waterston, "The Insane of Massachusetts," *Christian Examiner* 33 (January 1843): 352, confirms that in June 1842 Dix began a systematic survey of the condition of the insane that was distinct from her previous occasional visits to institutions.

34. Boston *Courier,* Aug. 26, 1842; SGH to DLD, Aug. 29 [1842], Julia Ward Howe Family MSS., SLRC.

35. Boston *Daily Advertiser,* Sept. 8, 16, 27, 30, Oct. 3, 1842; Massachusetts House of Representatives Document no. 47, *Documents Printed by Order of the House of Representatives of the Commonwealth of Massachusetts, during the Sessions of the General Court, A.D. 1842* (Boston: Dutton and Wentworth, State Printers, 1842) (Sept. 15, 1842).

36. SGH to DLD [Sept. 18, 1842], Julia Ward Howe Family MSS., SLRC; SGH to John G. Palfrey, Oct. 24, 1842, Palfrey Family MSS., HLHU.

37. Susan Heath, MS. diary, Oct. 19, 1842, Heath Family MSS., MHS.

38. Ibid.

39. Boston *Evening Mercantile Journal,* Oct. 3, 1842.

40. DLD to AEH [November 1842]; SGH to DLD, n.d. [Sunday], Julia Ward Howe Family MSS., SLRC.

41. SGH to John Gorham Palfrey, Oct. 24, 1842, Palfrey Family MSS., HLHU.

42. SGH to DLD [December 1842], Julia Ward Howe Family MSS., SLRC.

43. SGH to DLD, n.d. [Jan. 16, 1843], Julia Ward Howe Family MSS., SLRC.

44. DLD, "Prisons and Alms-houses—the Insane and Idiotic; how provided for in this Christian country" [September 1842], DLD MSS., HLHU.

45. SGH to DLD, n.d., Julia Ward Howe Family MSS., SLRC; DLD, *Memorial to the Legislature of Massachusetts* (Boston: Munroe & Francis, 1843), pp. 3, 6–7.

46. DLD, *Massachusetts Memorial,* p. 3.

47. Ibid., pp. 4, 7–8, 16–17, 22–23.

48. Ibid., p. 4; SGH, "Insanity in Massachusetts," *North American Review* 56 (January 1843): 173.

49. DLD, *Massachusetts Memorial,* pp. 17–18, 20.

50. On the shift of religious discourse from the doctrinal to the imaginative, see David S. Reynolds, *Beneath the American Renaissance: The Subversive Imagination in the Age of Emerson and Melville* (New York: Alfred A. Knopf, 1988), pp. 15–53.

51. William Ellery Channing, "An Address Delivered at Lenox, on the First of August, 1842, being the Anniversary of Emancipation in the British West Indies," in *Works of William Ellery Channing* (Boston: American Unitarian Association, 1886), p. 922; DLD, *Massachusetts Memorial,* p. 10.

52. SGH, "Insanity in Massachusetts," p. 176.

53. DLD, *Massachusetts Memorial,* pp. 3–9, 14–15, 26.

54. Ibid., pp. 12–17.

55. On the importance of self-control in Unitarian doctrine, see Daniel Walker Howe, *The Unitarian Conscience: Harvard Moral Philosophy, 1805–1861* (Cambridge: Harvard University Press, 1970), pp. 60–64.

56. DLD, *Massachusetts Memorial,* pp. 8, 13, 27.

57. Lydia Maria Child, "The Missionary of Prisons," *The Present* 1 (Dec. 15, 1843): 212.

58. DLD, *Massachusetts Memorial,* p. 11.

59. Ibid., pp. 3, 25.

60. Ibid., pp. 17, 21–22.

61. Ibid., p. 24.

62. SGH, "Insanity in Massachusetts," pp. 179–180.

63. DLD, *Massachusetts Memorial,* pp. 24–25.

64. Charles Francis Adams, MS. diary, Feb. 25, 1843, Adams Family MSS., MHS (microfilm edition); Charles J. Bullock, *Historical Sketch of the Finances and Financial Policy of Massachusetts from 1780 to 1905* (New York: Macmillan Co., 1907), pp. 34–58, 140–141. On the legislation to expand the Worcester State Hospital, see generally Grob, *The State and the Mentally Ill,* pp. 102–116.

65. Danvers Overseers of the Poor, "A Memorial to the Legislature of Massachusetts" (Salem: Gazette Office, 1843); Salem *Gazette*, Jan. 27, 1843; Greenfield *Democrat*, Feb. 9, 1843.

66. Boston *Courier*, Feb. 2, 22, 1843.

67. William Bentley Fowle to DLD, Feb. 9, 1843; Boston *Evening Gazette*, Feb. 11, 1843.

68. Boston *Mercantile Journal*, Feb. 11, 21, 1843.

69. L. M. Sargent to DLD, Jan. 22, 1843; Daniel Sharp to DLD, Feb. 1, 1843.

70. Newburyport *Herald*, Feb. 6, 9, 1843; Thomas Bayley Fox to DLD, Feb. 17, 1843.

71. DLD to John W. Proctor, Feb. 13, 1843 (copy).

72. Anson Hooker to DLD, Jan. 12, 24, Feb. 3, 1843.

73. SGH to DLD [Jan. 19, 1843], reprinted in Laura E. Richards, *Letters and Journals of Samuel Gridley Howe*, 2 vols. (Boston: Dana Estes, 1906–1909), vol. 2: *The Servant of Humanity*, pp. 166–167.

74. Boston *Courier*, Feb. 2, 1843.

75. Boston *Courier*, Feb. 25, 1843.

76. DLD to Gentlemen of the Committee for Charitable Appropriations, Feb. 14 [1843]; Massachusetts House Document no. 38, *Documents Printed by Order of the Commonwealth of Massachusetts, during the Session of the General Court, 1843* (Boston: Dutton and Wentworth, State Printers, 1843) (February 1843); SGH to DLD [Feb. 22, 1843], Julia Ward Howe Family MSS., SLRC; Boston *Daily Advertiser*, Feb. 27, 1843.

77. J. H. Rockwell to DLD, Feb. 1, 1843; Luther V. Bell to DLD, Feb. 4, 1843; William Wilson to DLD, Feb. 11, 1843; Isaac Ray to DLD, Feb. 20, 1843.

78. SGH to DLD, n.d., Julia Ward Howe Family MSS., SLRC; DLD to John G. Palfrey, n.d., Palfrey Family MSS., HLHU; John G. Palfrey to DLD, Feb. 25 [1843].

79. DLD to Samuel C. Allen, March 9 [1843] (draft).

80. AEH to DLD, [Feb.] 23, 1843; Lydia Maria Child, "Treatment of the Insane," *National Anti-Slavery Standard*, March 9, 1843; HM to DLD, Jan. 27, 1843; DLD to HM, Feb. 1, 1843, HM MSS., MHS.

81. SGH to Charles Sumner, March 20, 1843, Howe Family MSS., HLHU (*44M-314); DLD to TSK, May 14 [1851], TSK MSS., PHA.

82. Julia Ward to Charles Sumner, Feb. 27, 1843, Howe Family MSS., HLHU; Deborah Pickman Clifford, *Mine Eyes Have Seen the Glory: A Biography of Julia Ward Howe* (Boston: Atlantic Monthly Press, 1978), pp. 60–66.

83. DLD to HM, Feb. 1, 1843, HM MSS., MHS.

5. *This Mighty Vortex of Labor*

1. Gerald Grob, *Mental Institutions in America: Social Policy to 1875* (New York: The Free Press, 1973), pp. 343–395; Nancy Tomes, *A Generous Confidence: Thomas Story*

Kirkbride and the Art of Asylum-Keeping, 1840–1883 (Cambridge: Cambridge University Press, 1984), p. 74. The private hospitals were the Friends' Asylum for the Insane at Frankford, Pennsylvania (opened 1817); Massachusetts General Hospital's McLean Asylum (1818); New York Hospital's Bloomingdale Asylum (1821); the (Hartford) Connecticut Retreat for the Insane (1824); and the Pennsylvania Hospital's Pennsylvania Hospital for the Insane (1841). The figure of twelve public asylums is slightly more subjective because several institutions founded long before 1843 as purely custodial facilities gradually adopted the goals of moral treatment during the period 1830–1850. Of these, I have counted as modern mental hospitals the Virginia Eastern Lunatic Asylum, the Virginia Western Lunatic Asylum, the South Carolina Lunatic Asylum, and the Maryland Hospital for the Insane, but I have not included the Kentucky Eastern Lunatic Asylum for reasons discussed in Chapter 6. Eight public asylums that clearly expressed the asylum ideology in 1843 were the Worcester State Lunatic Hospital (opened 1833); the Vermont Asylum for the Insane (1836); the Ohio Lunatic Asylum (1839); the Boston Lunatic Hospital (1839); the Maine Insane Asylum (1840); the Tennessee Hospital for the Insane (1840); the New Hampshire Asylum for the Insane (1842); and the New York State Lunatic Asylum (1843).

2. DLD to GBE [Sept. 28, 1843], DLD MSS., BPL.

3. William G. Goddard to DLD, Oct. 17, 1843.

4. Francis Tiffany, *Life of Dorothea Lynde Dix* (Boston: Houghton, Mifflin and Co., 1890), p. 96.

5. Louisa Jane Hall to Francis Tiffany, May 17, 1889.

6. DLD to Edward Brooks Hall, April 20 [1849], Edward Brooks Hall Autograph Collection, MHS; DLD to HCH, Feb. 15, 1850; William Rathbone, Jr., "Reminiscence of Dorothea Lynde Dix," DLD MSS., HLHU.

7. Ellen Dwyer, *Homes for the Mad* (New Brunswick, N.J.: Rutgers University Press, 1987), pp. 34–38; Stanley Burton Klein, "A Study of Social Legislation Affecting Prisons and Institutions for the Mentally Ill in New York State, 1822–1846," (Ph.D. diss., New York University, 1956), pp. 305–352.

8. DLD to GBE, Nov. 13, 1843, DLD MSS., BPL.

9. DLD to GBE [Sept. 28, 1843], DLD MSS., BPL.

10. DLD, *Memorial to the Honorable the Legislature of the State of New-York,* Assembly Doc. no. 21 (Jan. 12, 1844), pp. 7, 30, 34, 40, 45.

11. [Theodric Romeyn] Beck to DLD, n.d.; DLD to William H. Seward, Nov. 20, 1843, Seward MSS., University of Rochester, Rochester, New York; Lydia Maria Child to DLD, Dec. 1, 1843; Lydia Maria Child, "The Missionary of Prisons," *The Present* 1 (Dec. 15, 1843): 212.

12. DLD, *New York Memorial,* p. 4.

13. Ibid., p. 55.

14. Ibid., pp. 7, 40.

15. Ibid., p. 48.
16. Ibid., p. 56.
17. Grob, *Mental Institutions in America,* pp. 325–336; William Ll. Parry-Jones, "The Model of the Geel Lunatic Colony and Its Influence on the Nineteenth-Century Asylum System in Britain," in *Madhouses, Mad-Doctors, and Madmen: The Social History of Psychiatry in the Victorian Era,* ed. Andrew Scull (Philadelphia: University of Pennsylvania Press, 1981).
18. The relationship between the development of the moral treatment and the medical profession has recently been studied extensively by historians. I have relied particularly on Anne Digby, *Madness, Morality and Medicine: A Study of the York Retreat, 1796–1914* (New York: Cambridge University Press, 1985); Jan Goldstein, *Console and Classify: The French Psychiatric Profession in the Nineteenth Century* (New York: Cambridge University Press, 1987); Grob, *Mental Institutions in America;* Constance M. McGovern, *Masters of Madness: Social Origins of the American Psychiatric Profession* (Hanover, N.H.: University Press of New England, 1985); Andrew Scull, *Museums of Madness: The Social Organization of Insanity in Nineteenth-Century England* (London: Allen Lane, 1979); Andrew Scull, *Social Order / Mental Disorder: Anglo-American Psychiatry in Historical Perspective* (Berkeley: University of California Press, 1989); and Tomes, *A Generous Confidence: Thomas Story Kirkbride.*
19. DLD, *New York Memorial,* p. 54.
20. Isaac Ray to DLD, Feb. 20, 1843. On Ray's unusual attitude toward separate institutions, which he soon changed, see Grob, *Mental Institutions in America,* p. 306.
21. Amariah Brigham to DLD, Jan. 14, 1844; [Brigham,] "Asylums Exclusively for the Incurable Insane," *American Journal of Insanity* 1 (July 1844): 50–52.
22. Amariah Brigham to DLD, Jan. 14, 1844 (copy), William Bouck MSS., Cornell University Library, Ithaca, New York; "Asylums Exclusively for the Incurable Insane," p. 52.
23. Amariah Brigham to TSK, March 3, 1845, quoted in Dwyer, *Homes for the Mad,* p. 38.
24. DLD to Daniel S. Dickinson, Feb. 27, 1844, Dickinson MSS., Broome County Historical Society, Binghamton, New York.
25. New York *Tribune,* March 18, 1844; G. Brigham to DLD, April 14, 1844.
26. Tiffany, *Life of Dix,* pp. 96–98.
27. DLD to GBE, May 11, 1844, DLD MSS., BPL.
28. Luther V. Bell to TSK, June 3, 1844; DLD to TSK, Feb. 15, 1845, both in TSK MSS., PHA; DLD to GBE, Sept. 2, 1844, DLD MSS., BPL; DLD, *Memorial Soliciting a State Hospital for the Insane, Submitted to the Legislature of Pennsylvania* (Harrisburg: J. M. G. Lescure, 1845), pp. 25, 27–28, 30–31, 35–36.
29. DLD to GBE, July 1, Sept. 2, 1844, DLD MSS., BPL.
30. DLD to GBE, Sept. 2, Oct. 16, 1844, DLD MSS., BPL; DLD to N. Ewing, Aug. 18, 1844.

31. DLD to GBE, Sept. 2, 1844, DLD MSS., BPL.

32. DLD to Robert and HCH, Sept. 22, 1844.

33. DLD to GBE, July 1, Sept. 2, Oct. 16, 1844, DLD MSS., BPL; DLD to MTT [Jan. 23, 1845] (fragment).

34. Charlotte N. Freedland to DLD, Oct. 13, 1844; DLD to GBE, Oct. [?], 1844, DLD MSS., BPL; Frederick M. Herrmann, *Dorothea L. Dix and the Politics of Institutional Reform* (Trenton: New Jersey Historical Commission, 1981), pp. 14–18.

35. DLD to GBE, Oct. [?], 1844, DLD MSS., BPL.

36. DLD to GBE, Dec. 15, 1844, DLD MSS., BPL.

37. DLD, *Memorial Soliciting a State Hospital for the Insane, Submitted to the Legislature of New Jersey* (2d ed.; Trenton: Printed by order of the legislature of New Jersey, 1845), p. 4; DLD, *Pennsylvania Memorial*, p. 55.

38. DLD, *New Jersey Memorial,* pp. 4, 29, 33, 37.

39. Ibid., pp. 35, 42; DLD, *Pennsylvania Memorial*, p. 53.

40. DLD, *Memorial of D. L. Dix, Praying a Grant of Land for the Relief and Support of the Indigent Curable and Incurable Insane in the United States,* 30th Cong., 1st sess. (June 27, 1848), p. 2n; DLD, *Memorial Soliciting a State Hospital for the Protection and Cure of the Insane, Submitted to the General Assembly of North Carolina* (Raleigh: Seaton Gales, 1848), p. 41; DLD, *Memorial Soliciting Adequate Appropriations for the Construction of a State Hospital for the Insane in the State of Mississippi* (Jackson: Fall & Marshall, 1850), p. 12.

41. DLD, *New Jersey Memorial,* pp. 39–42.

42. Ibid., p. 5; see *Report in Relation to an Asylum for the Insane Poor* (Harrisburg: Boas and Coplan, Printers, 1839), and *Report of the Commissioners, Appointed by the Governor of New Jersey to Ascertain the Number of Lunatics and Idiots in the State* (Newark: M. S. Harrison and Co., 1840), both reprinted in *The Origins of the State Mental Hospital in America: Six Documentary Studies, 1837–1856,* ed. Gerald N. Grob (New York: Arno Press, 1973).

43. DLD, *Pennsylvania Memorial,* p. 22; Washington Co. Directors of Poor to Walter Craig, March 3, 1845; R. P. Lane to Walter Craig, March 3, 1845; "Veritas" to Editor, *Harrisburg Argus,* undated newspaper clipping. See also Joseph Henderson to DLD, Aug. 28, 1844. All in DLD MSS., HLHU (bMS Am1838).

44. DLD, *New York Memorial,* p. 55; SGH, "Insanity in Massachusetts," *North American Review* 56 (January 1843): 173.

45. DLD to GBE, Oct. 16, 1844, DLD MSS., BPL.

46. DLD, *Pennsylvania Memorial,* pp. 5, 52.

47. Eliza Cope Harrison, ed., *Philadelphia Merchant: The Diary of Thomas P. Cope, 1800–1851* (South Bend, Ind.: Gateway Editions, 1978), p. 460; Herrmann, *Dorothea L. Dix,* p. 28.

48. GBE to DLD, Sept. 16, 1844; DLD, *New Jersey Memorial,* p. 5.

49. DLD to TSK, Feb. 15, July 22, 1845, TSK MSS., PHA; Amariah Brigham to TSK, March 3, 1845, quoted in Dwyer, *Homes for the Mad,* p. 38.
50. Harrison, *Philadelphia Merchant,* pp. 461–462.
51. Theodore Frelinghuysen to DLD, Feb. 27, 1845.
52. DLD to HCH, Feb. 3 [1845].
53. Ibid.; Newark *Daily Advertiser,* March 9, 1846; Harrison, *Philadelphia Merchant,* p. 462.
54. James Lesley to DLD, April 17, 1845.
55. Newark *Daily Advertiser,* March 9, 1846.
56. DLD to GBE, April 4, 1845, DLD MSS., BPL; William M. Awl to DLD, April 4, 1845; SGH to DLD, June 15, 1845.
57. James Lesley to DLD, April 17, 1845.
58. Harrison, *Philadelphia Merchant,* pp. 465–466; DLD to GBE, Oct. 11, 1845, DLD MSS., BPL.
59. DLD to TSK, July 27, Sept. 25, 1845, TSK MSS., PHA; Frank Rives Millikan, "Wards of the Nation: The Making of St. Elizabeths Hospital, 1852–1920" (Ph.D. diss., George Washington University, 1990), p. 17.
60. DLD to GBE, June 24, July 6, Oct. 11, 1845, DLD MSS., BPL.
61. DLD to GBE, June 24, Oct. 11, 1845, DLD MSS., BPL.
62. DLD to GBE, July 6, Oct. 11, 1845, DLD MSS., BPL; DLD to HCH, Nov. 28, 1846; Tiffany, *Life of Dix,* p. 105.

6. A Happiness Which Goes with You

1. DLD to GBE, Oct. 16, 1844, DLD MSS., BPL; DLD, MS. memorandum, "Extract from a Letter—Answer to a Question," August 1845, DLD MSS., HLHU (bMS Am1838).
2. See the discussion of Dix in John L. Thomas's classic essay, "Romantic Reform in America, 1815–1865," *American Quarterly* 17 (Winter 1965): 663.
3. MTT to DLD, Jan. 22, 1849; DLD to Elizabeth Rathbone [March 1855]; Lydia Maria Child, "The Missionary of Prisons," *The Present* 1 (Dec. 15, 1843): 211.
4. Joseph Dix to DLD, Feb. 14, 1844.
5. DLD to MTT [Jan. 23, 1845] (fragment); DLD to Joseph Dix, June 17 [1849].
6. DLD to Joseph Dix, June 5, 1848.
7. DLD to MTT [Jan. 23, 1845] (fragment); DLD to AEH, March 3, 1860.
8. AEH to DLD, Nov. 8, 1845.
9. DLD to AEH, July 18 [1845], Nov. 18, [?].
10. George Hillard to DLD, April 3, 1846.
11. DLD to AEH, Nov. 18, [?].
12. AEH to DLD, Jan. 15, 1849; DLD to AEH, n.d. [1859?].
13. DLD to GBE, n.d. [1844], Oct. 16, Dec. 15, 1844, July 6, 1845, DLD MSS., BPL.

14. GBE to DLD, Sept. 16, Oct. 23, 1844; DLD to GBE, Oct. [?], 1844, May 19, 1845, DLD MSS., BPL.

15. DLD to GBE, n.d. [1844], July 6, 1845, DLD MSS., BPL.

16. DLD to GBE, May 19, Dec. 24, 1845, DLD MSS., BPL.

17. DLD to GBE, Sept. 2, 1844, DLD MSS., BPL.

18. Ibid.

19. DLD, *Memorial Soliciting a State Hospital for the Protection and Cure of the Insane, Submitted to the General Assembly of North Carolina* (Raleigh: Seaton Gales, 1848), p. 1.

20. DLD, *Memorial Soliciting a State Hospital for the Insane, Submitted to the Legislature of New Jersey* (2d ed.; Trenton: Printed by order of the legislature of New Jersey, 1845), pp. 23–24.

21. DLD to GBE, July 1, 1844, DLD MSS., BPL.

22. DLD, *An Address by a Recent Female Visiter to the Prisoners in the Eastern Penitentiary of Pennsylvania* (Philadelphia: Joseph and William Kite, 1844).

23. DLD, *Memorial Soliciting a State Hospital for the Insane, Submitted to the Legislature of Pennsylvania* (Harrisburg: J. M. G. Lescure, 1845), p. 24; DLD, *Remarks on Prisons and Prison Discipline in the United States* (Boston: Munroe & Francis, 1845), p. 56; DLD, *Memorial of Miss D. L. Dix in Relation to the Illinois Penitentiary,* Illinois Legislature, 15th Assembly, 1st sess. (Feb. 5, 1847), p. 14.

24. DLD, *Remarks on Prisons,* p. 9. In addition to the *Address by a Recent Visiter,* see [DLD], *Letter to Convicts in the Western State Penitentiary of Pennsylvania, in Alleghany City* (2d ed.; n.p., 1848), for her moral instruction of prisoners.

25. Charles Dickens, *American Notes* (New York: Harper & Brothers, 1842), pp. 38–44. For stimulating overviews, see David J. Rothman, *The Discovery of the Asylum: Social Order and Disorder in the New Republic* (Boston: Little, Brown and Co., 1971), pp. 78–108; Michael Ignatieff, *A Just Measure of Pain: The Penitentiary in the Industrial Revolution, 1750–1850* (New York: Pantheon Books, 1978), pp. 194–197.

26. DLD to GBE, July 1, 1844, DLD MSS., BPL.

27. GBE to DLD, July 8, Sept. 16, 1844.

28. DLD to GBE, July 1, 24, 1844, DLD MSS., BPL.

29. DLD to GBE, Oct. 16, 1844, DLD MSS., BPL.

30. DLD, *New Jersey Memorial,* p. 19; DLD, *Pennsylvania Memorial,* pp. 10, 37, 46–47.

31. David Herbert Donald, *Charles Sumner and the Coming of the Civil War* (New York: Alfred A. Knopf, 1961), pp. 121–122; GBE to DLD, May 27, 1845.

32. DLD to Charles Sumner, May 25 [1845], Sumner MSS., HLHU (bMS Am1).

33. George Hillard to DLD, June 30, 1846; GBE to DLD, Aug. 7, 1844; see also Louis P. Masur, *Rites of Execution: Capital Punishment and the Transformation of American Culture, 1776–1865* (New York: Oxford University Press, 1989), pp. 66–70, 137–138.

34. George Hillard to DLD, June 30, 1846; Samuel Gridley Howe to DLD, June 15, 1845; Donald, *Charles Sumner,* pp. 122–129; Webster quoted in Robert F. Dalzell,

Jr., *Enterprising Elite: The Boston Associates and the World They Made* (Cambridge: Harvard University Press, 1987), p. 207.

35. DLD to GBE, [Sept.] 15, 1845, DLD MSS., BPL.
36. DLD, *Remarks on Prisons,* pp. 7, 64.
37. Ibid., pp. 22, 25, 61, 73.
38. Ibid., pp. 22, 42, 67–68, 73–86.
39. Ibid., pp. 70, 72, 74.
40. Charles Sumner, "Prisons and Prison Discipline," *Christian Examiner* 40 (January 1846): 124; Samuel A. Eliot to Mary Eliot, Oct. 12, 1845, Eliot MSS., Pusey Library, Harvard University.
41. GBE to DLD, Jan. 16, 1846; James Dunlop to DLD, Sept. 24, 1845; DLD to GBE, Oct. 11, Dec. 24, 1845, DLD MSS., BPL; *The Harbinger,* Nov. 8, 1845; Newark *Daily Advertiser,* Sept. 17, 1845; Francis Lieber to DLD, Nov. 5, 1846; John S. Mollet to DLD, May 10, 1847.
42. Eliza Cope Harrison, ed., *Philadelphia Merchant: The Diary of Thomas P. Cope, 1800–1851* (South Bend, Ind.: Gateway Editions, 1978), p. 455; MTT to DLD, April 8, 1845; Sumner, "Prisons and Prison Discipline," p. 123.
43. L[ydia] Maria Child, *Letters from New York, Second Series* (New York: C. S. Francis & Co., 1845), p. 271.
44. James J. Barclay to Francis Lieber, Feb. 25, 1845; Francis Lieber, MS. memorandum, "Miss D. L. Dix After a Visit at Our House in April 1851," both in Francis Lieber MSS., Huntington Library, San Marino, California.
45. DLD to GBE, Dec. 10 [1845], DLD MSS., BPL; Gerald Grob, *Edward Jarvis and the Medical World of Nineteenth-Century America* (Knoxville: University of Tennessee Press, 1978), pp. 49–58; Ronald F. White, "John Rowan Allen, M.D., and the Early Years of the Psychiatric Profession in Kentucky, 1844–1854," *Filson Club History Quarterly* 62 (January 1989): 14–15.
46. DLD to GBE, Dec. 10 [1845], DLD MSS., BPL.
47. Francis Lieber, MS. memorandum, "Miss D.L. Dix—After a Visit at Our House in April 1851," Lieber MSS., Huntington Library.
48. DLD to HCH, Dec. 22, 1845.
49. Ibid.; DLD to GBE, Dec. 10 [1845], DLD MSS., BPL.
50. Ronald F. White, "Custodial Care for the Insane at Eastern State Hospital in Lexington, Kentucky, 1824–1844," *Filson Club History Quarterly* 62 (July 1988): 311.
51. Louisville *Journal,* n.d, clipping in DLD MSS., HLHU. DLD's letter to the newspaper is dated Jan. 21, 1846.
52. DLD, *A Review of the Present Condition of the State Penitentiary of Kentucky, with Brief Notices and Remarks upon the Jails and Poor-houses in Some of the Most Populous Counties* (Frankfort: A. G. Hodges, 1846), p. 5.
53. DLD to GBE, Dec. 10 [1845], Dec. 24, 1845, DLD MSS., BPL.
54. DLD, *Review of . . . State Penitentiary of Kentucky,* pp. 3, 5.

55. DLD, *Memorial Soliciting an Appropriation for the State Hospital for the Insane, at Lexington; and Also Urging the Necessity for Establishing a New Hospital in the Green River Country* (Frankfort: A. G. Hodges, 1846), pp. 9–10; DLD, *North Carolina Memorial,* p. 35.

56. DLD to HCH, March 14, 1846; Frankfort *Daily Commonwealth,* Feb. 12–25, 1846.

57. P. Butler to Dr. Mercer and Miss Young, March 6, 1846, DLD MSS., HLHU; *Congressional Globe,* 32nd Cong., 1st sess., p. 2467 (Aug. 30, 1852) (remarks of Sen. Joseph Underwood).

58. DLD to GBE, March 14 [1846], DLD MSS., BPL; DLD to [?], April 8, 1846.

59. J. O. King, "The Insane Hospital: Interesting Facts Concerning Its History," Jacksonville *Daily Journal,* May 8, 1886; Don Harrison Doyle, *The Social Order of a Frontier Community: Jacksonville, Illinois, 1825–1870* (Urbana: University of Illinois Press, 1978), pp. 18–71.

60. King, "The Insane Hospital"; DLD, "Memorial of Miss Dix," Illinois Legislature, 15th Assembly, 1st sess. (Jan. 11, 1847), p. 8. For full details of Dix's activities in the state, see David L. Lightner, "Ten Million Acres for the Insane: The Forgotten Collaboration of Dorothea L. Dix and William H. Bissell," *Illinois Historical Journal* 89 (Spring 1996): 19–24.

61. DLD to AEH, Nov. 16, 1846; DLD to Joseph Dix, Dec. [?], 1846.

62. Doyle, *Social Order of a Frontier Community,* pp. 70–71; King, "The Insane Hospital"; DLD, "Memorial of Miss Dix"; Sangamo *Journal* newspaper clippings, DLD MSS., HLHU; William Thomas to DLD, July 4, 1852. See also Carl E. Black, "Origin of Our State Charitable Institutions," *Journal of the Illinois State Historical Society* 18 (April 1925): 187–190.

63. DLD to HCH, March 10, [1847]; William Thomas to DLD, March 27, 1847.

64. DLD, *Memorial of Miss D. L. Dix, in Relation to the Illinois Penitentiary,* Illinois Legislature, 15th Assembly, 1st sess. (Feb. 5, 1847), p. 5; DLD to HCH, March 10 [1847]; Lightner, "Ten Million Acres," p. 24.

65. DLD to Francis Lieber, Oct. 28, 1846, Lieber MSS., Huntington Library; George W. Howe to DLD, Nov. 16, 1846.

66. King, "The Insane Hospital."

67. DLD to GBE, n.d. [1844], DLD MSS., BPL.

68. DLD to GBE, Dec. 24, 1845, DLD MSS., BPL.

69. DLD to Joseph Dix, Dec. [?], 1846.

70. AEH to DLD, July 30, 1847; DLD to AEH, n.d.

71. DLD to AEH, Aug. 17 [1847]; DLD, MS. memorandum, "Twenty-two months' routes, 1845, '46, '47" DLD-Heath MSS., HLHU.

72. DLD to HCH, June 5, 1847; AEH to DLD, July 30, 1847.

73. DLD to AEH, Oct. 27, 1847.

74. E. Bruce Thompson, "Reforms in the Care of the Insane in Tennessee, 1830–1850," *Tennessee Historical Quarterly* 3 (December 1944): 319–334.

75. DLD to HCH, Dec. 1, 1847.

76. DLD, *Memorial Soliciting Enlarged and Improved Accommodations for the Insane of the State of Tennessee, by the Establishment of a New Hospital* (Nashville: B. R. M'Kennie, 1847), pp. 3, 30–31.

77. Thompson, "Reforms in the Care of the Insane in Tennessee," pp. 330, 332; Harriet Campbell et al. to DLD, Jan. 26, 1848.

78. DLD to Mrs. Wheat et al., Jan. 29, 1848 (copy).

79. Thompson, "Reforms in the Care of the Insane in Tennessee," p. 332; Tennessee General Assembly, Resolution, Feb. 5, 1848, DLD MSS., HLHU.

80. DLD to TSK, March 26, 1848, TSK MSS., PHA; Sue Battle to Mrs. Clement Claiborne Clay, March 24, 1848, Clement Claiborne Clay MSS., Perkins Library, Duke University.

81. DLD to AEH, April 15 [1848].

7. The Property of the People

1. DLD to HCH, May 23 [1848]; Luther V. Bell to DLD, June 5, 1848.

2. Gerald N. Grob, *Mental Institutions in America: Social Policy to 1875* (New York: The Free Press, 1973), pp. 191–202.

3. *Report of the Commission of the General Land Office,* 30th Cong. 1st sess., Sen. Exec. Doc. no. 41 (April 11, 1848), p. 269; *DeBow's Commercial Review of the South and the West,* 6 (August 1848): 97.

4. A new synthesis of antebellum land politics comparable to Daniel Feller, *The Public Lands in Jacksonian Politics* (Madison: University of Wisconsin Press, 1984) is much needed. James W. Oberly, *Sixty Million Acres: American Veterans and the Public Lands Before the Civil War* (Kent, Ohio: Kent State University Press, 1990) supplies an important piece of the puzzle. Paul W. Gates, *History of Public Land Law Development* (Washington, D.C.: Government Printing Office, 1968), Roy M. Robbins, *Our Landed Heritage: The Public Domain, 1776–1936* (Princeton, N.J.: Princeton University Press, 1942), and George M. Stephenson, *The Political History of the Public Lands from 1840 to 1862* (Boston: Richard G. Badger, 1917) remain the most valuable general guides.

5. Oberly, *Sixty Million Acres,* p. 15; DLD to TSK, June 21, 1848, TSK MSS., PHA.

6. S. 328, 30th Cong., 1st sess. (1848). Dix clearly settled on these aspects of her proposal long before any bill was reported in Congress. DLD to HCH, May 23, 1848; DLD to TSK, June 21, 1848, TSK MSS., PHA. The bill identified the approved expenses somewhat ambiguously and might be interpreted either to bar application of the federal fund for any building costs or merely to prohibit spending for nontherapeutic facilities. The only direct contemporary comment on the clause indicated that it was understood to bar federal support for all construction and provide solely for operating expenses. *Congressional Globe,* 33rd Cong., 1st sess., app., p. 969 (statement of Sen. C. C. Clay).

7. DLD, *Memorial Praying a Grant of Land for the Relief and Support of the Indigent Curable and Incurable Insane in the United States,* S. Misc. Doc. no. 150, 30th Cong., 1st sess. (June 27, 1848), pp. 30–31.

8. *Congressional Globe,* 30th Cong., 1st sess., p. 696 (April 27, 1848).

9. DLD to HCH, May 23 [1848].

10. DLD to TSK, March 23, 1848, TSK MSS., PHA.

11. Feller, *Public Lands in Jacksonian Politics,* pp. 39–70, 111–119.

12. DLD to HCH, May 23 [1848].

13. Daniel Walker Howe, *The Political Culture of the American Whigs* (Chicago: University of Chicago Press, 1979), pp. 37, 300, identifies Dix's legislation as a prime example of Whig values for the restructuring of American society.

14. Feller, *Public Lands in Jacksonian Politics,* pp. 149–155.

15. DLD to HCH, May 23 [1848].

16. DLD to HCH, July 5, 1848.

17. DLD, *Memorial Praying a Grant of Land,* pp. 1–4. David Rothman, *The Discovery of the Asylum* (Boston: Little, Brown, and Co., 1971), pp. 110–119, shows that by 1848 this analysis was "as much a cliché as an insight."

18. DLD, *Memorial Praying a Grant of Land,* pp. 4, 24, 32.

19. Ibid., pp. 4, 7, 31.

20. DLD to HCH, July 5, July 21, 1848; DLD to L. A. Smith, July 5, 1848, Gratz Collection, Historical Society of Pennsylvania, Philadelphia.

21. DLD to Joseph Dix, June 5, 1848, Jan. 30, 1849; DLD to HCH, July 5, 1848; John Adams Dix to DLD, May 1, 1849; *Congressional Globe,* 30th Cong., 1st sess., pp. 873–874 (June 26, 1848); New York *Tribune,* June 28, 1848; Richard H. Sewell, *Ballots for Freedom: Antislavery Politics in the United States, 1837–1860* (New York: Oxford University Press, 1976), pp. 142–151.

22. *Congressional Globe,* 30th Cong., 1st sess., p. 875 (June 27, 1848); DLD to HCH, July 5, 1848. The presentation of Whitney's proposal after the acquisition of California marked a new phase in the transcontinental railroad campaign that he had launched in Congress in 1845. See Margaret L. Brown, "Asa Whitney and His Pacific Railroad Publicity Campaign," *Mississippi Valley Historical Review* 20 (September 1933): 209–224.

23. DLD to HCH, July 5, 1848.

24. DLD to L. A. and Mrs. Smith, July 5, 1848, Gratz Collection, Historical Society of Pennsylvania, Philadelphia; Charles Sumner to DLD, July 6, 1848; *Commercial Review of the South and the West* 6 (September 1848): 234–235.

25. S. 328, 30th Cong., 1st sess. (1848); DLD to HCH, July 21, 1848.

26. DLD to HCH, July 21, 1848.

27. Charles M. Wiltse, *John C. Calhoun: Sectionalist, 1840–1850* (New York: Russell & Russell, 1951), pp. 345–348; *Congressional Globe,* 30th Cong., 1st sess., app., pp. 868–873 (June 27, 1848).

28. DLD to HCH, July 31, 1848.

29. DLD to TSK, Aug. 8, 1848, TSK MSS., PHA; Joseph Henry to Harriet Henry, Aug. 8, 1848, Joseph Henry MSS., Smithsonian Institution, Washington, D.C.

30. DLD, *Memorial to the Honorable the Legislature of the State of New-York* (Assembly Doc. no. 21, Jan. 12, 1844), p. 49.

31. DLD to Joseph Dix, Sept. 21, 1848.

32. Margaret Callender McCulloch, "Founding the North Carolina Asylum for the Insane," *North Carolina Historical Review* 13 (July 1936): 190; Clark R. Cahow, *People, Patients and Politics: The History of North Carolina Mental Hospitals 1848–1960* (New York: Arno Press, 1980), pp. 22–24.

33. DLD to HCH, Nov. 27, 1848; McCulloch, "Founding the North Carolina Asylum," p. 190.

34. *North Carolina Standard,* Dec. 27, 1848, quoted in McCulloch, "Founding the North Carolina Asylum," pp. 191–192.

35. DLD to AEH, Jan. 29 [1849]; *Congressional Globe,* 30th Cong., 2d sess., pp. 490–491 (Feb. 9, 1849).

36. DLD to TSK, March 6, 1848, TSK MSS., PHA; HM to DLD, n.d.; C. P. Sengstack to DLD, Jan. 16, 1849.

37. DLD to Joseph Dix, Feb. 23 [1849]; DLD to HCH, Feb. 26/March 1, 1849.

38. Robert O. Mellown, "The Construction of the Alabama Insane Hospital, 1852–1861," *Alabama Review* 38 (April 1985): 84–85; DLD to HCH, Nov. 15, 1849; DLD to HM, Nov. 22, 1849, HM MSS., MHS; undated newspaper clipping, DLD MSS., HLHU; Alabama *Journal,* Dec. 14, 1849.

39. DLD to AEH, Jan. 15, 1850; DLD, *Memorial Soliciting Adequate Appropriations for the Construction of a State Hospital for the Insane in the State of Mississippi* (Feb. 6, 1850); Jackson *Weekly Southron,* March 15, 1850; DLD to HCH, March 15, 1850.

40. DLD to AEH, Nov. 22, 1849, Feb. 18, 1850; DLD to HM, Dec. 8, 24, 1849, HM MSS., MHS; HM to DLD, Dec. 15, 18, 1849; DLD to HCH, Jan. 17, 1850.

41. DLD to AEH, Feb. 18, 1850.

42. DLD to Joseph Henry, May 1, 1850, Henry MSS., Smithsonian Institution, Washington, D.C.; Joseph Henry to DLD, May 10, 1850; HM to DLD, May 14, 1850.

43. DLD to AEH, May 25, 1850.

44. DLD to [Elizabeth?] Rathbone, June 9 [1850].

45. DLD to TSK, May 21, 1850, TSK MSS., PHA; Paul Wallace Gates, *The Illinois Central Railroad and Its Colonization Work* (Cambridge: Harvard University Press, 1934), pp. 33–34.

46. DLD to HM, n.d., no. 21 [June 24, 1850?], June 28, 1850, July 5 [1850], n.d., no. 14 [August 1850?], HM MSS., MHS; *Congressional Globe,* 31st Cong., 1st sess., pp. 1546–1547 (Aug. 8, 1850), 1805 (Sept. 12, 1850).

47. Hugh Campbell to DLD, Jan. 15, 1849; DLD to Joseph Dix, Jan. 30, 1849; William E. Dodd, "The Principle of Instructing United States Senators," *South*

Atlantic Quarterly 1 (October 1902): 326–332; Holman Hamilton, *Prologue to Conflict: The Crisis and Compromise of 1850* (Lexington: University of Kentucky Press, 1964), pp. 75–76, 114.

48. DLD to Samuel Finley Patterson et al., Jan. 5 [1849], Samuel Finley Patterson MSS., Perkins Library, Duke University.

49. DLD to HM, n.d., no. 17 [January 1849?], HM MSS., MHS; *AJI* 5 (January 1849): 286–287; DLD to TSK, June 7, 1850, TSK MSS., PHA; DLD to Benjamin Silliman, June 12 [1850], Silliman Family MSS., Sterling Memorial Library, Yale University; DLD to Francis Lieber, June 23 [1850], Francis Lieber MSS., South Caroliniana Library, University of South Carolina; TSK to DLD, July 8, 1850, TSK MSS., PHA.

50. HM to Mary Peabody Mann, Sept. 16, 1850, HM MSS., MHS.

51. Donald Fred Tingley, "The Jefferson Davis–William H. Bissell Duel," *Mid-America* 38 (July 1956): 146–155; James A. Pearce to Joseph Henry, June 17, 1850, Henry MSS., Smithsonian Institution, Washington, D.C.; Salmon P. Chase to DLD, June 29, 1850.

52. HM to DLD, Jan. 28, 1850; DLD to HM, n.d., no. 22, HM MSS., MHS.

53. *Congressional Globe,* 31st Cong., 1st sess., pp. 1290 (June 25, 1850), 1331 (July 3), Senate Misc. Doc. no. 118 (June 25, 1850), House Misc. Doc. no. 487 (Aug. 8, 1850).

54. DLD to Benjamin Silliman [June 30, 1850], Silliman MSS., Sterling Memorial Library, Yale University; DLD to HM, July 28, 1850, HM MSS., MHS; DLD to AEH, Aug. 5 [1850]; HM to Mary Peabody Mann, Sept. 16, 1850, HM MSS., MHS.

55. Charles M. Snyder, ed., *The Lady and the President: The Letters of Dorothea Dix and Millard Fillmore* (Lexington: The University Press of Kentucky, 1975) (hereafter cited as *Dix-Fillmore Letters*), p. 16; Robert J. Rayback, *Millard Fillmore: Biography of a President* (Buffalo, N.Y.: Buffalo Historical Society, 1959), pp. 13, 45–46.

56. Rayback, *Millard Fillmore,* pp. 124–132, 185–186; [DLD] to MF, Aug. 30 [1850], in *Dix-Fillmore Letters,* pp. 82–84; MF to DLD, Sept. 6 [1850], ibid., p. 87.

57. DLD to AEH, Sept. 6, 1850; Thomas Donaldson, *The Public Domain: Its History, with Statistics* (Washington, D.C.: Government Printing Office, 1880), pp. 219–221; Gates, *The Illinois Central Railroad,* pp. 21–43; Oberly, *Sixty Million Acres,* pp. 1–53; James M. Bergquist, "The Oregon Donation Act and the National Land Policy," *Oregon Historical Quarterly* 58 (March 1957): 17–35; Robert W. Johannsen, *Stephen A. Douglas* (New York: Oxford University Press, 1973), pp. 306–317.

58. *Congressional Globe,* 31st Cong., 1st sess., p. 1839 (Sept. 17, 1850); 31st Cong., 1st sess., S. 349 (Sept. 17, 1849); see also H.R. 383 (Aug. 8, 1850).

59. DLD to MF [Sept. 21, 1850], *Dix-Fillmore Letters;* MF to DLD, Sept. 22, 1850, ibid. This collection follows the microfilm edition of the Fillmore Papers in suggesting a date of January 1851 for Dix's letter. The date I have indicated is

supported by the context of events and by Fillmore's quotation of Dix's note in his dated reply.

60. *Congressional Globe,* 31st Cong., 1st sess., pp. 1957–1959 (Sept. 24, 1850), 1961 (Sept. 25, 1850), 2005 (Sept. 26, 1850).

61. Ibid., pp. 2005–2006 (Sept. 26); see generally Arthur Bestor, "State Sovereignty and Slavery: A Reinterpretation of the Proslavery Constitutional Doctrine, 1846–1860," *Journal of the Illinois State Historical Society* 54 (Summer 1961): 117–180; Don E. Fehrenbacher, *The Dred Scott Case: Its Significance in American Law and Politics* (New York: Oxford University, 1978), pp. 128–177.

62. *Congressional Globe,* 31st Cong., 1st sess., pp. 2006–2008 (Sept. 26, 1850).

63. Ibid.

64. DLD to AEH and Lydia Greene, Sept. 27 [1850].

65. MF to DLD, Sept. 27, 1850, *Dix-Fillmore Letters,* p. 91; Francis Lieber to DLD, Oct. 30, 1850, Lieber MSS., Huntington Library, San Marino, California; Benjamin Silliman to DLD, Nov. 4, 1850.

66. See generally Paula Baker, "The Domestication of Politics: Women and American Political Society, 1780–1920," *American Historical Review* 89 (June 1984): 620–647; Anne M. Boylan, "Women and Politics in the Era before Seneca Falls," *Journal of the Early Republic* 10 (Fall 1990): 363–382; Lori D. Ginzberg, *Women and the Work of Benevolence: Morality, Politics, and Class in the Nineteenth-Century United States* (New Haven: Yale University Press, 1990), pp. 67–97; Linda K. Kerber, "Separate Spheres, Female Worlds, Woman's Place: The Rhetoric of Women's History," *Journal of American History* 75 (June 1988): 9–39; Mary P. Ryan, *Women in Public: Between Banners and Ballots, 1825–1880* (Baltimore: Johns Hopkins University Press, 1990); Elizabeth R. Varon, "Tippecanoe and the Ladies, Too: White Women and Party Politics in Antebellum Virginia," *Journal of American History* 82 (September 1995): 494–521.

67. DLD to GBE, Dec. 10 [1845], DLD MSS., BPL.

68. DLD to AEH, March 3, 1838, Jan. 21 [1851]; DLD to GBE, Dec. 10 [1845], DLD MSS., BPL; DLD to HM, n.d., no. 1, HM MSS., MHS; DLD to HCH, Jan. 17, 1850.

69. DLD, *Memorial Praying a Grant of Land,* p. 31; DLD to AEH, Jan. 21 [1851]; DLD to HM, n.d., no. 18, HM MSS., MHS.

70. HM to Mary Peabody Mann, Sept. 16, 1850, HM MSS., MHS; DLD to Miss Foster, Oct. 2, 1867, DLD MSS., Huntington Library, San Marino, California.

71. DLD to HCH, March 15, 1850.

72. Mary Kelley, *Private Woman, Public Stage: Literary Domesticity in Nineteenth-Century America* (New York: Oxford University Press, 1984) describes the anxieties that celebrity placed on popular women authors.

73. DLD to Mrs. Wheat et al., Jan. 29, 1848 (copy).

74. DLD to William Bentley Fowle, June 26, 1849, Fowle MSS., MHS; DLD to AEH,

Jan. 9, 1850; DLD to HM, n.d., no. 13, 18, HM MSS., MHS; HM to Mary Peabody Mann, May 21, 1850, HM MSS., MHS.

75. DLD to AEH, March 31, Nov. 16, Dec. 22, 1846, Jan. 9 [1850]; AEH to DLD, Jan. 9, 1860.

76. Fredrika Bremer to Marcus and Rebecca Spring, July 13, 1850, reprinted in Signe Alice Rooth, *Seeress of the Northland: Fredrika Bremer's American Journey, 1849–1851* (Philadelphia: American Swedish Historical Foundation, 1955), pp. 175–176; Adolph B. Benson, ed., *America of the Fifties: Letters of Fredrika Bremer* (New York: American Scandanavian Foundation, 1924), p. 188; Fredrika Bremer to DLD [August 1850]; Samuel Gilman to DLD, June 26, 1851; Fredrika Bremer, *The Homes of the New World,* 3 vols. (London: Arthur Hall, Virtue & Co., 1853), 2: 106–109.

77. DLD to Sarah J. Hale, Jan. 1, 7, 1851 (copies). For an analysis of Harriet Beecher Stowe's similarly ambivalent but much less vitriolic answer to the same invitation from Hale, see Kelley, *Private Woman, Public Stage,* pp. 185–186.

78. George Hillard to DLD, Jan. 9, 1851; John Adams Dix to DLD, Jan. 14, 1851; MTT to DLD, Jan. 14, 1851; DLD to AEH, Jan. 21 [1851].

79. Sarah Josepha Hale, *Women's Record; or Sketches of All Distinguished Women from "The Beginning" until A.D. 1850* (New York: Harper & Brothers, 1852), pp. 862–864; Ruth E. Finley, *The Lady of Godey's* (Philadelphia: J. B. Lippincott & Co., 1931), pp. 232–236.

80. DLD to William A. Graham, Dec. 11 [1850], J. G. de Roulhac Hamilton, Max R. Williams, and Mary Reynolds Peacock, eds., *The Papers of William A. Graham* (Raleigh: North Carolina Department of Archives and History, 1957–1992), 3: 489; Francis Lieber to DLD, Feb. 11, 1851, Lieber MSS., Huntington Library, San Marino, California. On the difficulties of passing legislation in the short session, see *Congressional Globe,* 33rd Cong. 1st sess., p. 1337 (May 30, 1854) (remarks of Sen. Albert G. Brown).

81. *Congressional Globe,* 31st Cong., 2d sess., pp. 506–511 (Feb. 11, 1851).

82. *Senate Journal,* 31st Cong., 2d sess., p. 169 (Feb. 11, 1851); *Congressional Globe,* 31st Cong., 2d sess., pp. 506–511, 522 (Feb. 11–12, 1851); DLD to [Elizabeth Rathbone?], Feb. 11, 1851.

83. Francis Lieber to DLD, Feb. 16, 1851, Lieber MSS., Huntington Library, San Marino, California; *National Intelligencer,* Feb. 12, 1851; New York *Tribune,* Feb. 12, 1851.

84. *Congressional Globe,* 31st Cong., 2d sess., pp. 753–54 (Feb. 28, 1851).

85. Ibid.; *Congressional Globe,* 31st Cong., 2d sess., pp. 777–78 (March 3, 1851).

86. DLD to AEH and Lydia Greene, March 6 [1851].

87. Francis Lieber to DLD, March 1, 1851, Lieber MSS., Huntington Library, San Marino, California; DLD to MF [March 7, 1851], *Dix-Fillmore Letters,* p. 102; DLD to HM, March 12 [1851], HM MSS., MHS.

8. A National Work

1. DLD to TSK, March 12 [1851], TSK MSS., PHA; DLD to AEH, April 2 [1851].

2. Richard La Tease to DLD, March 2, 1851, HM MSS., MHS.

3. DLD to MF, March 23 [1851], April 8, 1851, *Dix-Fillmore Letters,* pp. 104–113.

4. DLD to MF, March 23 [1851], April 8, 1851, *Dix-Fillmore Letters,* pp. 104–113.

5. DLD to AEH, April 2 [1851].

6. DLD to MF, April 8, 1851, *Dix-Fillmore Letters,* p. 111.

7. Ibid., p. 109; DLD to Francis Lieber, April 27 [1851], Lieber MSS., Huntington Library, San Marino, California.

8. DLD to Harriet Henry, April 28 [1851], Joseph Henry MSS., Smithsonian Institution, Washington, D.C.

9. DLD to Francis Lieber, April 27 [1851], Lieber MSS., Huntington Library, San Marino, California; DLD to William E. Hacker, April 26, 1851, DLD MSS., New York Public Library.

10. Francis Lieber to DLD, May 17, 27, 1851, Lieber MSS., Huntington Library, San Marino, California.

11. DLD to AEH, June 23, 1851.

12. DLD to Nathaniel I. Bowditch, May 22, 1851, Bowditch MSS., Boston Athenæum; DLD to Thomas and Henry Lee, n.d. (copy).

13. DLD to AEH, June 23, 1851.

14. William Logie Russell, *The New York Hospital: A History of the Psychiatric Service, 1771–1936* (New York: Columbia University Press, 1945) (reprint ed., New York: Arno Press, 1973), pp. 138, 247.

15. Nichols quoted in Constance McGovern, *Masters of Madness: Social Origins of the American Psychiatric Profession* (Hanover, N.H.: University Press of New England, 1985), p. 121; Nancy Tomes, *A Generous Confidence: Thomas Story Kirkbride and the Art of Asylum-Keeping, 1840–1883* (Cambridge: Cambridge University Press, 1984), p. 268; Isaac Ray to DLD, Dec. 8, 1851.

16. Isaac Ray to DLD, Sept. 15, 1851.

17. D. S. Kennedy to DLD, Sept. 29, 1851; DLD to D. S. Kennedy, Oct. 6, 1851; DLD, "General and Concise Summary," Oct. 7, 1851, reprinted in Russell, *The New York Hospital,* pp. 516–517.

18. DLD, "General and Concise Summary," pp. 517–518; DLD to George Trimble, Dec. 2 [1851]; Pliny Earle to DLD, Nov. 22, 1851; Charles H. Nichols to DLD, Nov. 27, 1851; Isaac Ray to DLD, Dec. 8, 1851. See also Tomes, *A Generous Confidence,* pp. 84–85, 268.

19. DLD to Edward D. Morgan, Oct. 6, 1851; DLD to Benjamin Swan, n.d.; DLD to Augustus Fleming, Oct. 13, 1851.

20. DLD to TSK [Oct. 30, 1851], n.d. [1851], TSK MSS., PHA; Pliny Earle to DLD,

Nov. 22, 1851; Charles H. Nichols to DLD, Nov. 27, 1851; M. H. Ranney to DLD, Nov. 27, 1851; Isaac Ray to DLD, Dec. 8, 1851.

21. "Report by the Bloomingdale Asylum Committee on the Subject of Miss Dix's Report," reprinted in Russell, *The New York Hospital,* pp. 519–521; George T. Trimble to DLD, Dec. 11, 1851; D. S. Kennedy to DLD, Dec. 15, 1851; James Gore King to DLD, Dec. 26, 1851.

22. Russell, *The New York Hospital,* pp. 203, 243; Lydia Prime to DLD, Oct. 29, 1851; Charles H. Nichols to DLD, Feb. 7, 23, May 9, 1852; George T. Trimble to DLD, June 2, 1852.

23. James Gore King to DLD, Dec. 26, 1851.

24. Joel Silbey, *The Shrine of Party: Congressional Voting Behavior, 1841–1852* (Pittsburgh: University of Pittsburgh Press, 1967), pp. 201–212, identifies the party affiliations of the members of Congress.

25. DLD to MF, Dec. 11, 1851, *Dix-Fillmore Letters,* pp. 114–116; MF to DLD, Dec. 13, 1851, ibid., pp. 116–117; *Congressional Globe,* 32nd Cong., 1st sess., pp. 224–225 (Jan. 7, 1852), 461 (Feb. 4), 469 (Feb. 5).

26. DLD to Henry Clay Yeatman, Dec. 16 [1850], Yeatman-Polk MSS., Tennessee State Library and Archives, Nashville; DLD to AEH, Jan. 21 [1851].

27. DLD to AEH, Jan. 21 [1851].

28. DLD to MF, Jan. 31, March 11, 1852, *Dix-Fillmore Letters,* pp. 120–123; MF to DLD, March 9, 1852, ibid., p. 122.

29. DLD to MF [March 6, 1851], March 23, 1851, Dec. 24 [1851], March 24, 1852, April 5 [1852], April 26 [1852], *Dix-Fillmore Letters,* pp. 100, 104–108, 118–119, 124–125, 129–131, 131–132.

30. DLD to William H. Seward, Feb. 19, March 4, 1852, Seward MSS., Rush Rhees Library, University of Rochester.

31. DLD to Charles Sumner, Dec. 15 [1851], [Feb. 5, 1852?], Sumner MSS., HLHU (bMS Am1).

32. Francis Lieber to DLD, April 10, 1852, Lieber MSS., Huntington Library, San Marino, California; DLD to Francis Lieber, April 29, 1852, ibid.

33. Charles Sumner to DLD, n.d. (Saturday), n.d. (Sunday), n.d. (Monday); DLD to Charles Sumner, n.d., June 2 [1852], Sumner MSS., HLHU; MF to DLD, Aug. 13, 1852, *Dix-Fillmore Letters,* p. 136.

34. DLD to HM, March 12 [1851], Feb. 25, 1852, HM MSS., MHS.

35. Thomas Wyse to R. S. Stewart, Feb. 19, 1852; DLD, *Memorial of Miss D. L. Dix, to the Honorable the General Assembly in Behalf of the Insane of Maryland,* Sen. Doc. C (Feb. 25, 1852), pp. 10–18 (quotation p. 10).

36. *State Capitol Gazette,* May 29, 1852; DLD to William E. Hacker, May 27 [1852], DLD MSS., New York Public Library; George T. Trimble to DLD, June 2, 1852.

37. *Congressional Globe,* 32d Cong., 1st sess., pp. 1455–1456 (May 24, 1852), 1527 (June 7, 1852); DLD to HM, n.d., no. 16, HM MSS., MHS.

38. *Congressional Globe,* 32nd Cong., 1st sess., pp. 1527–1529 (June 7, 1852), 1926 (July 26), 2048–2049 (Aug. 2), 2228–2230 (Aug. 16), 2235–2236 (Aug. 17); Edward Stanly to DLD [Aug. 17, 1852].

39. MF to DLD, August 17, 1852, *Dix-Fillmore Letters,* pp. 136–37.

40. Philadelphia *North American,* Aug. 25, 1852.

41. DLD to William H. Seward, Aug. 18 [1852], Seward MSS., Rush Rhees Library, University of Rochester.

42. DLD to Charles Sumner [August 1852], Sumner MSS., HLHU; *Congressional Globe,* 32d Cong., 2d sess., pp. 2239 (Aug. 18) (remarks of Sen. Hunter).

43. *Congressional Globe,* 32nd Cong., 1st sess., pp. 2465–69 (Aug. 30, 1852); quotation p. 2468 (Sen. Underwood).

44. Ibid., pp. 2467, 2469.

45. Frank Rives Millikan, "Wards of the Nation: The Making of St. Elizabeths Hospital, 1852–1920," Ph.D. diss., George Washington University, 1990, pp. 19–28. I am very grateful to Dr. Millikan for sharing with me his knowledge about St. Elizabeths. See also unidentified newspaper clipping [Nov. 8?, 1852], DLD MSS., HLHU; HM to Mary Peabody Mann, Aug. 17, 1852, HM MSS., MHS; James G. King to DLD, Aug. 20, 27, 1852; DLD to AEH, Aug. 28 [1852].

46. R. S. Stewart to DLD, Sept. 4, 1852.

47. Quoted in Millikan, "Wards of the Nation," p. 28.

48. McGovern, *Masters of Madness,* pp. 107–109.

49. Alexander H. H. Stuart to David R. Atchison, Dec. 28, 1852, reprinted in "Asylum for the Insane of the Army and Navy and the District of Columbia," *AJI* 9 (April 1853): 387.

50. Millikan, "Wards of the Nation," p. 39.

51. Charles H. Nichols to DLD, Sept. 11, 1852.

52. Charles H. Nichols to DLD, June 22, 1852.

53. Charles H. Nichols to DLD, Sept. 11, 18, 1852.

54. MF to DLD, Oct. 1, 1852, *Dix-Fillmore Letters,* pp. 137–138; DLD to Charles H. Nichols, Oct. 2, 1852 (draft?).

55. Jane Erwin Yeatman Bell to Henry Clay Yeatman, Oct. 18, Nov. 11, 1852, Yeatman-Polk MSS., Tennessee State Library and Archives, Nashville.

56. MF to DLD, Oct. 21, 1852, *Dix-Fillmore Letters,* p. 140; TSK to DLD, Oct. 26, 1852, TSK MSS., PHA; Isaac Ray to DLD, Nov. 3, 1852.

57. DLD to Charles Sumner [Nov. 12, 1852], Sumner MSS., HLHU.

58. Millikan, "Wards of the Nation," pp. 35–40.

59. Alexander H. H. Stuart to DLD, Oct. 1, 1852.

60. Alexander H. H. Stuart to David R. Atchison, Dec. 28, 1852, reprinted in "Asylum for the Insane of the Army and Navy," pp. 388–389.

61. DLD to Charles Sumner [Nov. 12, 1852], Sumner MSS., HLHU. The legislation of August 1852 stipulated that the total expenditures for asylum construction were

not to exceed the $100,000 appropriation. P.L. 53, *Congressional Globe,* 32d Cong., 1st sess., p. xvii (Aug. 31, 1852). The eventual cost of the Government Hospital was approximately $500,000. See Millikan, "Wards of the Nation," p. 50.

62. Charles H. Nichols to DLD, Nov. 13 [1852]; Thomas Blagden to DLD, Nov. 13, 1852.

63. Charles H. Nichols to DLD, Dec. 9 [1852?].

64. Charles H. Nichols to DLD, Jan. 1, July 24, 1853.

65. Charles H. Nichols to DLD, March 28, 1853; Tomes, *A Generous Confidence,* p. 372 n.19, similarly notes that "some of their letters border on the romantic."

66. Charles H. Nichols to DLD, n.d. (Tuesday), March 19, 28, July 24, Nov. 28, Dec. 29, 1853; DLD to Joseph Dix, June 28 [1853].

67. DLD to Pupils in Illinois Institution for Deaf Mutes, April 6, 1852 (copy). U.S. Manuscript Census for 1850, roll 56, p. 165, lists Dix as thirty-seven, presumably either on the basis of her report or on the estimate of Joseph Henry, in whose house she then lived. Francis Lieber, "Miss D. L. Dix—After a Visit at our House in April 1851," Lieber MSS., Huntington Library, San Marino, California, guesses that she is thirty-six to thirty-eight years old or younger.

68. DLD to AEH, Jan. 4, 1853; R. S. Stewart to DLD, Jan. 4, 28, 1853; Thomas Donaldson to DLD, Jan. 31, Feb. 4, 1853; Alexander H. H. Stuart to DLD, Feb. 8, 1853; DLD to William E. Hacker, Feb. 17 [1853], DLD MSS., New York Public Library (quotation); HM to Mary Peabody Mann, Feb. 24, 1853, HM MSS., MHS.

69. DLD to Charles Sumner, Feb. 18 [1853], Sumner MSS., HLHU; Jane Erwin Yeatman Bell to Henry Clay Yeatman, Feb. 3, 1853, Yeatman-Polk MSS., Tennessee State Library and Archives, Nashville.

70. *Congressional Globe,* 32d Cong., 2d sess., pp. 529 (Feb. 8, 1853), 760 (Feb. 22).

71. James Gore King to DLD, March 1, 1853; MTT to DLD, March 5, 1853.

72. *Congressional Globe,* 32nd Cong., 2nd sess., pp. 1091 (Butler) (March 3, 1853).

73. Ibid., pp. 1093 (Sen. Augustus C. Dodge), 1094 (Chase) (March 3, 1853).

74. Jane Erwin Yeatman Bell to Henry Clay Yeatman, March 4, 1853, Yeatman-Polk MSS., Tennessee State Library and Archives, Nashville.

75. Francis Lieber to DLD, March 13, 1853, Lieber MSS., Huntington Library, San Marino, California.

76. James Gore King to DLD, March 7, 15, 1853.

77. DLD to MF, April 2, 1853, *Dix-Fillmore Letters,* pp. 147–148.

9. *The Moral Horizon of a Unitarian Minister*

1. M. R. Almon to DLD, Feb. 28, 1853; Henry Bell to DLD, April 5, 1853; *The British Colonial,* June 14, 1853; DLD to Joseph Dix, June 16, 1853, June 28 [1853]; DLD to AEH and Lydia Greene, June 17 [1853], June 28, 1853; Eben Merriam to [potential subscribers], Sept. 10, 1853.

2. DLD to Eben Merriam, n.d., DLD MSS., Menninger Foundation; DLD to AEH, Nov. 28 [1853]; Boston *Daily Advertiser,* Dec. 4, 1853; DLD to New York *Journal of Commerce,* Dec. 14, 1853 (draft); DLD to MF [Dec. 29, 1853], *Dix-Fillmore Letters,* p. 166; Henry Bell to DLD, Jan. 16, 1854; DLD to [Eben Merriam?], Oct. 3, 1854, DLD MSS., Menninger Foundation.

3. Roy Franklin Nichols, *Franklin Pierce: Young Hickory of the Granite Hills,* 2d ed. (Philadelphia: University of Pennsylvania Press, 1958), p. 538. On the significance of Dix's land bill in national politics at this juncture, see Thomas J. Brown, "Franklin Pierce's Land Grant Veto and the Kansas-Nebraska Session of Congress," *Civil War History* 42 (June 1996): 95–115.

4. John Adams Dix to DLD, March 18, 1853.

5. DLD to AEH, Nov. 8, 1853; DLD to MF, Nov. 25, Dec. 8, 1853, *Dix-Fillmore Letters,* pp. 158–159, 162–164; DLD to Charles Sumner, Dec. 9 [1853], Sumner MSS., HLHU (bMS Am1); *Congressional Globe,* 33rd Cong., 1st sess., pp. 45, 67, 73 (Dec. 14, 20–21, 1853). Unless otherwise indicated, all references to the *Congressional Globe* in this chapter are to the first session of the Thirty-third Congress and all legislative dates cited are in 1854.

6. DLD to MF, Dec. 8, 1853, Jan. 3 [1854], *Dix-Fillmore Letters,* pp. 162–164, 167; MF to DLD, Dec. 20, 1853, ibid., p. 165.

7. On the origins of the Kansas-Nebraska bill, see William W. Freehling, *The Road to Disunion: Secessionists at Bay, 1776–1854* (New York: Oxford University Press, 1990), pp. 536–565; Robert W. Johannsen, *Stephen A. Douglas* (New York: Oxford University Press, 1973), pp. 401–434; Roy F. Nichols, "The Kansas-Nebraska Act: A Century of Historiography," *Mississippi Valley Historical Review* 43 (September 1956): 187–212; Robert R. Russel, "The Issues in the Congressional Struggle over the Kansas-Nebraska Bill, 1854," *Journal of Southern History* 29 (May 1963): 187–210.

8. DLD to MF, Dec. 8, 1853, Jan. 3, 18, Feb. 11 [1854], *Dix-Fillmore Letters,* pp. 162–164, 167, 169–170, 175–176.

9. For Pierce's attitudes toward railroad grants, see James D. Richardson, comp., *Messages and Papers of the Presidents* (Washington, D.C.: Bureau of National Literature and Art, 1907), 5: 216–217, 220–222; Paul W. Gates, *History of Public Land Law Development* (Washington, D.C.: Public Land Law Review Commission, 1968), pp. 360–362.

10. The perceived connection between the Kansas-Nebraska bill and the homestead bill is articulated in the Richmond *Enquirer,* March 3, 1854; the New York *Journal of Commerce,* March 10, 1854; Johannsen, *Stephen A. Douglas,* pp. 435–437; Nichols, *Franklin Pierce,* p. 335; George M. Stephenson, *The Political History of the Public Lands from 1840 to 1862* (Boston: Richard G. Badger, 1917); Gerald W. Wolff, *The Kansas-Nebraska Bill: Party, Section, and the Coming of the Civil War* (New York: Revisionist Press, 1977), pp. 183–194.

11. DLD to MF, Jan. 18 [1854], *Dix-Fillmore Letters,* pp. 169–170.

12. Solomon Foot to DLD, Feb. 3, 1854; MF to DLD, Feb. 9, 1854, *Dix-Fillmore Letters,* pp. 173–174.

13. *Congressional Globe,* pp. 389–390 (Feb. 9); DLD to MF, Feb. 9 [1854], *Dix-Fillmore Letters,* pp. 171–172; MF to DLD, Feb. 18, 1854, ibid., pp. 181–182.

14. *Congressional Globe,* pp. 455–456 (Feb. 21).

15. Ibid., pp. 494–495 (Feb. 28).

16. Ibid., app., p. 550 (May 3)(statement of Sen. Foot).

17. Brown, "Franklin Pierce's Land Grant Veto," p. 104. Compare with David Gollaher, *Voice for the Mad: The Life of Dorothea Dix* (New York: The Free Press, 1995), p. 321, which naively endorses Dix's hope that "she could, if need be, beat Franklin Pierce at his own game," despite her frustrations during the Fillmore administration.

18. *Congressional Globe,* p. 507 (March 1).

19. Ibid. (Mason); ibid., app., pp. 232–240 (Feb. 24–25) (Butler).

20. *Congressional Globe,* pp. 507–509 (March 1) (Hunter, Isaac Walker, Charles Stuart), 517–519 (March 2) (Butler, A. G. Brown), 556–561 (March 7) (Stephen Adams, James Bayard, A. G. Brown).

21. *Congressional Globe,* p. 572 (March 8).

22. DLD to AEH, March 9, 1854.

23. DLD to AEH, April 7 [1854], *Congressional Globe,* pp. 787–788 (March 29).

24. *Congressional Globe,* pp. 952–954 (April 19).

25. *National Intelligencer,* April 19, 1854; Baltimore *American,* quoted in *National Intelligencer,* April 25, 1854; Baltimore *Sun,* April 20, 1854; Richmond *Enquirer,* April 25, 1854.

26. AEH to DLD, April 22, 1854, DLD-Heath Letters, HLHU; New York *Times,* April 20, 23, 24, 25, 1854; Baltimore *Sun,* April 20, 25, 28, 1854; Richmond *Enquirer,* April 25, 1854; New York *Herald,* April 24, 1854; New York *Tribune,* April 29, 1854; Pennsylvania *Inquirer,* undated clipping, DLD MSS., HLHU.

27. Baltimore *Sun,* April 25, 1854; New York *Times,* April 24, May 3, 1854; New York *Herald,* April 28, 1854; unidentified newspaper clipping, DLD MSS., HLHU.

28. Charles H. Nichols to TSK, May 2, 1854, TSK MSS., PHA (photocopy).

29. DLD to AEH, April 28 [1854].

30. *Congressional Globe,* pp. 1061–1063 (May 3).

31. Ibid.

32. DLD to MF, May 20 [1854], *Dix-Fillmore Letters,* pp. 195–196; Ida Russell to Caleb Cushing, May 5, 1854, Cushing MSS., Library of Congress.

33. Ida Russell to Caleb Cushing, May 5, 1854, Cushing MSS., Library of Congress; New York *Herald,* May 5, 1854; DLD to Robert Hare, n.d. (written on *National Intelligencer,* May 11, 1854, clipping file, DLD MSS., HLHU).

34. DLD to AEH, May 18 [1854].

35. Francis R. Valeo and Richard D. Hupman, comps., *Presidential Vetoes* (Washington, D.C.: U.S. Government Printing Office, 1969), pp. 1–12.

36. Surveying the reaction, Pierce's biographer called the veto "a low point in political imperceptiveness." Nichols, *Franklin Pierce,* p. 541. See New York *Times,* May 3, 1854; New York *Tribune,* May 5, 1854; Boston *Advertiser,* May 6, 9, 1854; Boston *Atlas,* May 6, 1854; Nashville *Union & American,* May 10, 1854; *National Intelligencer,* May 10, 1854.

37. New York *Tribune,* May 4, 1854; "Proceedings of the Association," *American Journal of Insanity* 11 (July 1854): 55. See also Baltimore *Sun,* May 4, 5, 1854; Washington *Evening Star,* May 4, 1854, reprinted in *Richmond Enquirer,* May 9, 1854; New York *Journal of Commerce,* May 5, 1854; New York *Herald,* May 4, 5, 1854.

38. *Congressional Globe,* pp. 1063–1070 (May 3).

39. Charleston *Courier,* May 6, 1854; Richmond *Enquirer,* May 9, 1854.

40. Baltimore *Sun,* May 4, 1854; New York *Journal of Commerce,* May 5, 6, 1854; New York *Tribune,* May 5, 1854; Richmond *Enquirer,* May 5, 1854; *National Intelligencer,* May 6, 9, 1854; Washington *Sentinel,* May 7, 1854; Nashville *Union and American,* May 10, 1854. The New York *Times,* May 8, 1854, anticipated the backlash view that the veto did not cover the homestead bill. See also New York *Journal of Commerce,* May 13, 1854; Richmond *Enquirer,* May 13, 1854; Stephenson, *Political History of the Public Lands,* pp. 179–180.

41. *Congressional Globe,* pp. 1086, 1088 (May 4) (William Gwin, John Weller, Stephen Mallory), p. 1348 (May 31) (Charles Stuart), p. 1460 (June 20) (Isaac Walker).

42. Ibid., pp. 1083–1089 (May 4), pp. 1123–1128 (May 8).

43. *Congressional Globe,* p. 1460 (June 20).

44. Ibid., app., p. 959 (June 19) (William Seward), p. 991 (June 21) (Isaac Toucey).

45. Ibid., app., p. 1000 (June 15).

46. DLD to MF, May 20 [1854], *Dix-Fillmore Letters,* pp. 195–196; MF to DLD, May 26, 1854, ibid., pp. 196–198; DLD to AEH, May 18, June 18 [1854].

47. *Congressional Globe,* p. 1621 (July 6) (vote). This analysis of the vote includes all senators who paired or asked a proxy to announce their position at the roll call.

48. Henry James, *The Portrait of a Lady,* Chap. 42.

49. DLD to Charles Sumner, July 27 [1854], Sumner MSS., HLHU.

50. DLD to MF, July 22 [1854]; *Dix-Fillmore Letters,* pp. 199–200; Charles H. Nichols to DLD, July 26 [1854].

51. DLD to AEH, July 17, 29 [1854].

52. Robert J. Rayback, *Millard Fillmore: Biography of a President* (Buffalo, N.Y.: Buffalo Historical Society, 1959), p. 395; DLD to MF, July 27, 30, Aug. 2, 6, 7, 8, 12, 13, 20, 26, 1854, *Dix-Fillmore Letters,* pp. 201–214. The quotations in this paragraph are from DLD's letters of July 30, Aug. 6, and Aug. 12.

53. DLD to MF, Aug. 13 [1854], [Aug. 20, 1854], *Dix-Fillmore Letters,* pp. 211–213.

Fillmore sent Dix a copy of his daughter's obituary notice on Aug. 2 and other printed material on Aug. 10, but no letters until his farewell note of Aug. 29, 1854. See *Dix-Fillmore Letters,* pp. 201–214.

54. Susan Heath, MS. diary, Aug. 24, 1854, Heath Family MSS., MHS; DLD to MF, Aug. 26 [1854], *Dix-Fillmore Letters,* p. 214; Charles H. Nichols to DLD, Aug. 31, 1854; M. T. Torrey to DLD, Oct. 22, 1854; Morgan Dix, *Memoirs of John Adams Dix,* 2 vols. (New York: Harper & Brothers, 1883), 1: 287.

55. Nancy W. Burnap to DLD, Aug. 9, 1850; Fredrika Bremer to DLD, Nov. 23, 1850; Daniel Webster to Abbott Lawrence, Aug. 28, 1852, Dix MSS., HLHU; DLD to Elizabeth Rathbone, July 21, 1853.

56. DLD to [Elizabeth Rathbone], Aug. 27, 1854.

10. The American Invader

1. New York *Tribune,* Sept. 11, 1854; DLD to AEH, Sept. 11, 1854; DLD to MF, Sept. 16 [1854], *Dix-Fillmore Letters,* pp. 222–223; DLD to AEH and Lydia Greene, Nov. 16 [1854].

2. DLD to AEH, Sept. 11, 1854.

3. DLD to AEH, Dec. 8 [1854].

4. DLD to AEH and Lydia Greene, Nov. 16 [1854].

5. Abbott Lawrence to George Hayward, Sept. 9, 1854, DLD MSS., HLHU.

6. Lord Shaftesbury to Matthew D. Hill, Sept. 29, 1854, DLD MSS., HLHU; Lord Shaftesbury to DLD, Sept., 29, 1854; R. W. S. Lutwidge to DLD, Oct. 2, 1854; Geoffrey B. A. M. Finlayson, *The Seventh Earl of Shaftesbury, 1801–1885* (London: Eyre Methuen, 1981), pp. 228–233.

7. DLD to Maria Buttolph, n.d.; DLD to AEH, Dec. 8, 1854; DLD to AEH and Lydia Greene, Nov. 16, 1854. On the conditions Dix observed, see generally Mark Finnane, *Insanity and the Insane in Post-Famine Ireland* (London: Croom Helm, 1981), pp. 13–52.

8. [DLD to Horace Buttolph], Feb. 1, 1855.

9. DLD to [Maria Buttolph], n.d.; DLD to [Horace Buttolph], June 15, 1855. On the nonrestraint controversy, see Andrew Scull, "John Conolly: A Victorian Psychiatric Career," in his *Social Order/Mental Disorder: Anglo-American Psychiatry in Historical Perspective* (Berkeley: University of California Press, 1989), pp. 188–193; Gerald Grob, *Mental Institutions in America: Social Policy to 1875* (New York: The Free Press, 1973), pp. 206–210.

10. William Ll. Parry-Jones, *The Trade in Lunacy: A Study of Private Madhouses in England in the Eighteenth and Nineteenth Centuries* (London: Routledge & Kegan Paul, 1972), p. 6; Olive Checkland, *Philanthropy in Victorian Scotland: Social Welfare and the Voluntary Principle* (Edinburgh: John Donald Publishers, 1980), pp. 165–177.

11. DLD to [Horace Buttolph, Thomas Kirkbride, and Charles Nichols?], Feb. 19, 1855; DLD to James Moncrieff, n.d. (draft).

12. DLD to AEH, Feb. 24, 1855; Van Wyck Brooks, *The Flowering of New England* (New York: E. P. Dutton & Co., 1936), pp. 7–8.

13. William Rathbone to DLD, Jan. 20, 30, 1855; David Skae to DLD, Feb. 15, 1855; W. A. F. Browne to DLD, April 10, 1855.

14. DLD to Elizabeth Rathbone, Feb. 20, 1855.

15. David Skae to DLD, Feb. 15, 1855; W. A. F. Browne to DLD, April 10, 1855; DLD to James Moncrieff, n.d. (draft).

16. Daniel Hack Tuke to Francis Tiffany, August 1888, reprinted in Francis Tiffany, *Life of Dorothea Lynde Dix* (Boston: Houghton, Mifflin and Co., 1890), pp. 242–243; Thomas Stewart Traill to DLD, Feb. 26, 1855.

17. DLD to MTT, March 8, 1855 (copy).

18. DLD to [Horace Buttolph], March 8, 1855.

19. Ibid.

20. DLD to Elizabeth Rathbone, March 18 [1855].

21. DLD to Elizabeth Rathbone, April 10, 1855.

22. Sir James Clark to DLD, June 19, 1855.

23. DLD to AEH, June 1, 1855.

24. *Dix-Fillmore Letters,* pp. 229–239.

25. DLD to Horace Buttolph, July 18 [1855].

26. Elizabeth Rathbone to DLD, n.d. (Thursday).

27. DLD to [Elizabeth Rathbone], n.d.

28. Charles Nichols to DLD, Oct. 29, 1855.

29. DLD to Elizabeth Rathbone, July 27 [1855]; William Rathbone to DLD, July 28, 1855; D. H. van Leeuwen to DLD, Aug. 4 [1855].

30. William Rathbone to DLD, July 28, 1855; Elizabeth Rathbone, pocket diary, Aug. 7–Oct. 9, 1855, Rathbone Family MSS., University of Liverpool.

31. DLD to Horace Buttolph, Oct. 1, 1855; DLD to Elizabeth Rathbone, July 5, 1857; DLD to Elizabeth Rathbone, May 14 [1857], May 2, 1860, Rathbone Family MSS., University of Liverpool.

32. DLD to Horace Buttolph, Oct. 1, 1855; John Adams Dix to DLD, Dec. 16, 1855; DLD to AEH and Lydia Greene, May 4, 1856.

33. DLD to AEH [Oct. 28, 1855].

34. DLD to MF, n.d. [Nov. 9, 1855?], *Dix-Fillmore Letters,* pp. 244–245; DLD to [Elizabeth Rathbone], n.d. [Nov. 1855], Nov. 10, 1855; DLD to Horace Buttolph, Dec. 3, 1855; DLD to MTT, Dec. 8, 1855.

35. GBE to Lucy Emerson Lowell, Nov. 14, 19, 27, Dec. 4, 11, 18, 25, 30, 1855, GBE MSS., MHS; DLD to MTT, Dec. 8, 1855.

36. DLD to Maria Buttolph [Nov. 17, 1855]; DLD to [Elizabeth Rathbone?], n.d.

37. DLD to MTT, Dec. 8, 1855.

38. Ibid.

39. GBE, MS. diary, Jan. 4, 1856, GBE MSS., MHS.

40. DLD to AEH, Dec. 8, 1854.

41. DLD to AEH and Lydia Greene, Nov. 16 [1854].

42. Frank J. Coppa, *Pope Pius IX: Crusader in a Secular Age* (Boston: Twayne Publishers, 1979), pp. 122, 162–168.

43. DLD to Robert Dale Owen, Feb. 5 [1856], Miscellaneous MSS., Sterling Memorial Library, Yale University; DLD to Horace and Maria Buttolph, Feb. 28, 1856. For a contemporary view, see John Francis Maguire, *Rome: Its Ruler and Its Institutions* (New York: D & J Sadlier, 1858), pp. 204–207.

44. Francis Tiffany, *Life of Dorothea Lynde Dix* (Boston: Houghton, Mifflin and Co., 1890), pp. 286–293; James Freeman Clarke, "Dorothea L. Dix," *The Disciples' Pulpit: The Sermons of James Freeman Clarke,* vol. 1, no. 9 (October 1887), pp. 6–7; J. P. Bancroft to DLD, Feb. 7, 1876.

45. DLD to [William Rathbone], March 7, 1856.

46. DLD to Horace and Maria Buttolph, Feb. 28, 1856. GBE to Lucy Emerson Lowell, Feb. 17, 1856, GBE MSS.; DLD to MTT, March 6, 1856; DLD to [William Rathbone], March 7, 1856.

47. DLD to Horace and Maria Buttolph, Feb. 28, 1856; DLD to Elizabeth Rathbone, March 3, 1856; DLD to MTT, March 6, 1856.

48. DLD to [William Rathbone], March 7, 1856.

49. DLD to Robert Dale Owen, Feb. 5 [1856], Miscellaneous MSS., Sterling Memorial Library, Yale University; DLD to Horace and Maria Buttolph, Feb. 28, 1856; DLD to [William Rathbone], March 7, 1856; DLD to AEH, March 7, 1856.

50. DLD to MTT, March 6, 1856.

51. Matilda Lieber to Frances Appleton Longfellow, May 28 [1856], Francis Lieber MSS., Huntington Library, San Marino, California.

52. F. B. Sanborn, *Memoirs of Pliny Earle, M.D.* (Boston: Damrell & Upham, 1898), p. 308.

53. DLD to [Horace Buttolph], Nov. 13, Dec. 20, 1854.

54. DLD to AEH, Nov. 16 [1854], Feb. 24 [1855]; DLD to MF, Dec. 26, 1854, *Dix-Fillmore Letters,* pp. 226–229.

55. DLD to [Horace Buttolph], Dec. 20, 1854; DLD to Horace Buttolph and TSK, April 12 [1855].

56. Francis Lieber to DLD, May 25, 1856, Lieber MSS., Huntington Library, San Marino, California.

57. DLD to [Horace Buttolph], March 27, 1856.

58. DLD to William Rathbone, April 2 [1856].

59. DLD to Elizabeth Rathbone, April 10, 1856, reprinted in Tiffany, *Life of Dix,* pp. 298–299.

60. DLD to Elizabeth Rathbone, [April] 16, 1856; DLD to [?], April 29, 1856; DLD to [Horace Buttolph and TSK], May 1, 1856; Cyrus Hamlin to Francis Tiffany, Aug. 7, 1889, reprinted in Tiffany, *Life of Dix,* pp. 300–302.

61. DLD to [Horace Buttolph], March 27, 1856; DLD to [Horace Buttolph?], April 25 [1856]; DLD to AEH and Lydia E. Greene, May 4, 1856.

62. DLD to [Horace Buttolph?], April 25, 1856; DLD to [?], April 29, 1856.

63. DLD to AEH and Lydia Greene, May 4, 1856.

64. Ibid.; DLD to [Horace Buttolph and TSK], May 1, 1856.

65. DLD to [William Rathbone], May 22/25, 1856.

66. Ibid.

67. DLD to [Horace and Maria Buttolph], June 26, 1856.

68. DLD to [Horace Buttolph and TSK], May 1, 1856.

69. DLD to [Horace and Maria Buttolph], June 26, 1856; DLD to [Horace Buttolph and TSK?], July 7, 1856.

70. DLD to Elizabeth Rathbone, Aug. 5, 1856; DLD to AEH and Lydia Greene, Aug. 14, 1856.

71. John M. Galt, "The Farm of St. Anne," *AJI* 11 (April 1855): 352–357.

72. TSK to DLD, July 22, 1855, quoted in Nancy Tomes, *A Generous Confidence: Thomas Story Kirkbride and the Art of Asylum-Keeping, 1840–1883* (Cambridge: Cambridge University Press, 1984), p. 373 n.33; "Proceedings of the Association of Medical Superintendents of American Institutions for the Insane," *AJI* 12 (July 1855): 39–49, 61, 97–98; DLD to [Horace Buttolph], Aug. 15, 1856.

73. DLD to [Sir Walter and Lady Calverly Trevelyan], Aug. 25, 1856; DLD to AEH, Jan. 30 [1857?]; see also Caroline Healey Dall to DLD, May 3, 1858. On Anna Jameson, see Clara Thomas, *Love and Work Enough: The Life of Anna Jameson* (Toronto: University of Toronto Press, 1967).

74. Charles Bracebridge to DLD, Aug. 22, 1856; Elizabeth Rathbone to DLD, [Aug.] 25, [1856]; DLD to Elizabeth Rathbone [Aug. 29, 1856].

75. Mary Carpenter to DLD, Aug. 26, 1856.

76. DLD to William Rathbone, Sept. 3, 1856.

77. Charles W. Bracebridge to DLD, Sept. 10, 14, 1856.

78. DLD to MTT, Dec. 8, 1855; DLD to William Rathbone, Sept. 3, 1856; DLD to [Elizabeth Rathbone], Jan. 25 [1857]; DLD to Elizabeth Rathbone, Dec. 12 [1859]; Helen Hay Carnegy to DLD, Aug. 4, 1857; DLD to William Rathbone, April 20, 1858, Rathbone Family MSS., University of Liverpool.

11. *Our People Need to Suffer*

1. DLD to [Elizabeth Rathbone], Jan. 25 [1857].

2. DLD to [?], Nov. 20 [1854]; DLD to MF, Dec. 26, 1854, *Dix-Fillmore Letters,* pp. 226–229; DLD to AEH, Feb. 24, 1855; DLD to [Horace Buttolph], June 15, 1855.

3. DLD to MF, Dec. 26, 1854, *Dix-Fillmore Letters,* pp. 226–229; DLD to Charles Sumner, March 2 [1855], Sumner MSS., HLHU (bMS Am1).

4. DLD to [Horace Buttolph], Aug. 15, 1856; DLD to MF, Nov. 8, 1856, *Dix-Fillmore Letters,* pp. 264–266; Jessie Benton Frémont to DLD, July 18 [188–].

5. MF to DLD, Oct. 9, Oct. 30, 1856; DLD to MF, Oct. 8, 19, 22, Nov. 3, 1856, *Dix-Fillmore Letters,* 249–260.

6. DLD to MF, Nov. 8, 1856, *Dix-Fillmore Letters,* p. 265.

7. DLD to MF, Nov. 26, 1856, *Dix-Fillmore Letters,* pp. 264–268.

8. See David J. Rothman, *The Discovery of the Asylum* (Boston: Little, Brown, 1971), pp. 264–287, on the deterioration of mental hospitals.

9. *Report and Memorial of the County Superintendents of the Poor of this State on Lunacy and its Relation to Pauperism,* New York State Legislature, Senate Doc. no. 17, Jan. 23, 1856, and *Report of the Select Committee on Report and Memorial of County Superintendents of the Poor, on Lunacy and Its Relation to Pauperism,* New York State Legislature, Senate Doc. no. 71, March 5, 1856, both reprinted in Gerald N. Grob, advisory ed., *The Origins of the State Mental Hospital in America* (New York: Arno Press, 1973); "New Asylum Proposed in the State of New York," *AJI* 11 (April 1855): 392; John B. Chapin, "Insanity in the State of New York," *AJI* 13 (July 1856): 39–50; Ellen Dwyer, *Homes for the Mad: Life inside Two Nineteenth-Century Asylums* (New Brunswick, N.J.: Rutgers University Press, 1987), 40–43; D. T. Brown to DLD, Oct. 2, 1856, Feb. 9, March 9, 1857.

10. DLD to AEH, Dec. 30, 1856.

11. DLD to MF, Jan. 4/19 [1857], *Dix-Fillmore Letters,* pp. 274–275; DLD to [William Rathbone], Jan. 18 [1857].

12. James W. Trent, Jr., *Inventing the Feeble Mind: A History of Mental Retardation in the United States* (Berkeley: University of California Press, 1994), pp. 10–59; Peter L. Tyor and Leland V. Bell, *Caring for the Retarded in America: A History* (Westport, Conn.: Greenwood Press, 1984), pp. 3–19.

13. *Fifth Annual Report of the Board of Directors of the Pennsylvania Training School for Feeble-Minded Children* (Philadelphia: Henry B. Ashmead, Book and Job Printer, 1858), pp. 6–8; DLD, *Massachusetts Memorial,* p. 12; DLD, *New Jersey Memorial,* p. 1; DLD, *Pennsylvania Memorial,* p. 1; DLD, *Kentucky Memorial,* p. 9; DLD, *North Carolina Memorial,* p. 4; DLD, *Federal Memorial,* p. 4; DLD, *Maryland Memorial,* p. 5; "A Bill Making a Grant of Public Lands to the Several States of the Union for Certain Purposes," S. 328, 30th Cong., 1st sess; DLD to [William Rathbone], Jan. 18 [1857]; DLD to William Rathbone, March 3 [1857], Rathbone Family MSS., University of Liverpool.

14. DLD to Alonzo Potter, Feb. 7 [1857], Charles Roberts Autograph Collection, Haverford College, Haverford, Pennsylvania; Pennsylvania Training School, Board Minutes, Feb. 13, March 6, 1857, Elwyn Archives, Elwyn, Pennsylvania; Joseph Parrish to DLD, Feb. 26, 1857; DLD to [Alonzo Potter], March 16 [1857], American Prose MSS., Historical Society of Pennsylvania, Philadelphia.

15. D. T. Brown to DLD, March 9, 1857; DLD to AEH, March 13 [1857].

16. DLD to [Alonzo Potter], March 16 [1857], American Prose MSS., Historical Society of Pennsylvania, Philadelphia.

17. DLD to MF, April 21 [1857], *Dix-Fillmore Letters,* pp. 280–281, 283–284.

18. DLD to MF, April [27], 1857, *Dix-Fillmore Letters,* pp. 284–285.

19. DLD to Editor, Edinburgh *Daily Scotsman,* June 22, 1857.

20. DLD to AEH, May 25 [1857]; DLD to MF, June 3, 1857, *Dix-Fillmore Letters,* pp. 288–289; Joseph Parrish to DLD, June 7, 9, 23, 1857; Board Minutes, Pennsylvania Training School for Feeble-Minded Children, May 5, 1857, Elwyn Archives, Elwyn, Pennsylvnia; *Fifth Annual Report of the Pennsylvania Training School,* pp. 7–9.

21. DLD to MF, April 27 [1857], June 3, 1857, *Dix-Fillmore Letters,* pp. 285, 288.

22. DLD to MF, March 11 [1857], *Dix-Fillmore Letters,* pp. 279–280; DLD to AEH, March 13 [1857]; AEH to DLD, March 17, 1857; DLD to Elizabeth Rathbone, March 30 [1857], Rathbone Family MSS., University of Liverpool.

23. Edinburgh *Daily Scotsman,* May 18, 27–28, June 22, 1857; London *Times,* May 30, 1857; London *Evening Post,* June 1, 1857; Glasgow *Herald,* June 3, 1857; Edinburgh *Daily Express,* June 6, 13, 1857; James Coxe to DLD, June 4, 20, 1857; DLD to Elizabeth Rathbone, July 5, 1857; W. A. F. Browne to DLD, Sept. 23, 1857; David Skae to DLD, July 7, 1858; Olive Checkland, *Philanthropy in Victorian Scotland* (Edinburgh: John Donald Publishers, 1980), pp. 174–176.

24. New York *Journal of Commerce,* June 20, 1857.

25. John Harper to DLD, July 25, 1857; Marion Hathway, "Dorothea Dix and Social Reform in Western Pennsylvania, 1845–1875," *Western Pennsylvania Historical Magazine* 17 (December 1934): 251–252; [unidentified city] *Evening Chronicle,* July 16, 1857.

26. W. A. Cheatham to DLD, Jan. 14, 1859.

27. DLD to AEH, Aug. 12 [1857]; DLD to William Rathbone, Sept. 6 [1857].

28. DLD to MF, Oct. 4/16, 1857, *Dix-Fillmore Letters,* pp. 293–294; DLD to AEH, Nov. 23 [1857]; Kenneth Stampp, *America in 1857: A Nation on the Brink* (New York: Oxford University Press, 1990), pp. 213–234.

29. DLD to TSK, Jan. 17 [1858], March 8, 1858, TSK MSS., PHA; Thomas Donaldson to DLD, Feb. 8, 1858; Baltimore *Sun,* March 8, 1858; DLD to [William Rathbone], March 27, 1858.

30. MTT to DLD, March 16, 1858; DLD to [William Rathbone], March 27, 1858; Franklin Taylor to DLD, May 7, 1858.

31. DLD to AEH, Sept. 24, 1858; DLD to William Rathbone, Sept. 9, 1858, Rathbone Family MSS., University of Liverpool.

32. DLD to William Rathbone, April 20, 1858, Rathbone Family MSS., University of Liverpool; Stampp, *America in 1857,* pp. 234–238.

33. DLD to William Rathbone, April 20, 1858, Rathbone Family MSS., University of Liverpool.

34. DLD to AEH, Oct. 2, 10, 1858; Susan Heath, MS. diary, Sept. 19—December 1, 1858, Heath Family MSS., MHS.
35. AEH to DLD, Sept. 3, 1850.
36. Grace Heath to AEH, n.d., Heath Family MSS., MHS.
37. DLD to AEH, n.d. [November? 1859].
38. DLD to AEH, March 3, 1860.
39. HM to DLD, March 7, 1859.
40. Mary Peabody Mann to DLD, March 5, 1859.
41. Mary Peabody Mann to DLD, April 22, 1859.

12. Downright Madness

1. DLD to MF, Sept. 24, 1858, Nov. 15 [1858], March 16, 1859, *Dix-Fillmore Letters,* pp. 306, 310, 316.
2. DLD to MF, March 16, 1859, *Dix-Fillmore Letters,* p. 316.
3. MTT to DLD, Jan. 25, 1859; DLD to MF, Feb. 9, 1859, *Dix-Fillmore Letters,* p. 313.
4. DLD to MF, Feb. 9, 1859, *Dix-Fillmore Letters,* p. 313.
5. J. R. Young to John Hamilton Cornish, Feb. 5, 1859, John Hamilton Cornish MSS., South Caroliniana Library, University of South Carolina.
6. Thomas F. Green to DLD, Jan. 25, 1859; MF to DLD, May 19, 1859.
7. DLD to TSK, May 17, 25 [1858?], TSK MSS., PHA; Patrick W. Bryce to DLD, Dec. 19, 28, 31, 1859; Jan. 20, 28, March 11, April 25, 30, July 13, 1860, May 8, 1868; Reuben Searcy to DLD, July 11, 1860.
8. DLD to MF, March 16, 1859; DLD to AEH, Nov. 19 [1859].
9. DLD to [?], March 28, 1859; AEH to DLD, April 3, 1859.
10. DLD to [?], March 28, 1859; DLD to AEH, April 11, 1859; DLD to [MTT], April 13, 1859.
11. DLD, MS. pocket diary, 1859, DLD MSS., HLHU; DLD to [?], March 28, 1859; DLD to AEH, April 11, May 12, 1859.
12. Charlotte C. Eliot, *William Greenleaf Eliot: Minister, Educator, Philanthropist* (Boston: Houghton, Mifflin and Co., 1904), pp. 65, 134.
13. DLD to William Greenleaf Eliot and Abigail Adams Eliot, June 2, 1859; William Greenleaf Eliot to DLD [June 1859], both in Abigail Adams Eliot MSS., SLRC; DLD to Rose Lamb, May 17, 1881.
14. DLD to William Greenleaf Eliot and Abigail Adams Eliot, June 2, 1859, Abigail Adams Eliot MSS., SLRC.
15. M. W. Phillips to DLD, Sept. 21, 1859.
16. DLD to MF, Nov. 21 [1859], *Dix-Fillmore Letters,* pp. 323–324.
17. J. J. Williams to DLD, Nov. 19, 1859.
18. DLD to MF, Nov. 21 [1859], *Dix-Fillmore Letters,* pp. 323–324; DLD to AEH, Nov. 25 [1859], Dec. 8, 1859; DLD to [MTT?], Jan. 17, 1860.

19. DLD to [William Rathbone], Nov. 29/Dec. 6/Dec. 19, [1859]; Benjamin Franklin Perry to [?], Dec. 8, 1859, Benjamin Franklin Perry MSS., South Caroliniana Library, University of South Carolina; DLD to AEH, Dec. 8, 1859. Steven A. Channing, *Crisis of Fear: Secession in South Carolina* (New York: Simon & Schuster, 1970) describes this legislative session thoroughly.

20. J. W. Parker to DLD, Nov. 12, 1859; Charleston *Mercury*, Dec. 8, 10, 19, 21, 23, 24, 1859; Patrick Bryce to DLD, Dec. 28, 1859; AEH to DLD, Jan. 9, 1860.

21. DLD to [MTT?], Jan. 17, 1860.

22. W. S. Chipley to DLD, Feb. 3, 1860; DLD to William Rathbone, Feb. 22, 1860.

23. DLD to William Rathbone, Feb. 22, 1860.

24. Ibid.; Franklin Taylor to DLD, Dec. 23, 1859; J. A. Reed to DLD, April 11, 1860.

25. DLD to AEH, March 3, 1860; DLD to William Rathbone, March 26, 1860, Rathbone Family MSS., University of Liverpool.

26. Ibid.

27. J. A. Reed to DLD, Feb. 27, April 11, 15, 1860; DLD to MF, April 10 [1860], *Dix-Fillmore Letters,* pp. 327–328.

28. DLD to AEH, March [1860].

29. DLD to William Rathbone, Feb. 22, 1860; DLD to Elizabeth Rathbone, March 3, 1860; DLD to William Rathbone, March 26, 1860, Rathbone Family MSS., University of Liverpool; DLD to MF, April 10 [1860], *Dix-Fillmore Letters,* pp. 327–328.

30. Jane Erwin Yeatman Bell to [Mary Yeatman?], n.d., Yeatman-Polk MSS., Tennessee State Library and Archives, Nashville.

31. DLD to MF, April 10 [1860], *Dix-Fillmore Letters,* p. 328.

32. DLD to Elizabeth Rathbone, May 2, 1860, Rathbone Family MSS., University of Liverpool.

33. DLD to Elizabeth Rathbone, May 18, 1860, Rathbone Family MSS., University of Liverpool.

34. DLD to Elizabeth Rathbone, May 2, 1860, Rathbone Family MSS., University of Liverpool; MF to DLD, July 31, 1860, *Dix-Fillmore Letters,* pp. 329–330; DLD to MF, Sept. 18, 1860, ibid., pp. 330–331.

35. DLD to [William Rathbone], Aug. 27, 1860.

36. Ibid.; DLD to MF, Feb. 9, 1859, *Dix-Fillmore Letters,* p. 313; DLD to MF, Oct. 5, 1860, ibid., p. 335.

37. DLD to MF, Nov. 10, 1860, *Dix-Fillmore Letters,* pp. 338–339; W. S. Chipley to DLD, Dec. 19, 1860.

38. DLD to AEH, Dec. 23 [1860].

39. Ibid.

40. DLD to Charles Sumner [Dec. 21, 1860], Jan. 16, 1861, Sumner MSS., HLHU

(bMS Am1); Charles Sumner to DLD, Jan. 14, 1861, Jane Gay Dodge MSS., SLRC.

41. Charles H. Nichols to TSK, April 6, 1861, in Clifford B. Farr, ed., "The Civil War Correspondence of Dr. Thomas S. Kirkbride," *Pennsylvania Magazine of History and Biography* 83 (January 1959): 77–78.

42. DLD to AEH, Jan. 12, 1861.

43. DLD to Charles Nichols, Jan. 11, 1861 (typescript); DLD to MF, Jan. 12, 1861, *Dix-Fillmore Letters,* pp. 341–342.

44. Samuel M. Felton quoted in William Schouler, *A History of Massachusetts in the Civil War,* 2 vols. (Boston: E. P. Dutton & Co., 1868), 1: 59–60.

45. DLD to AEH, Jan. 26, 1861.

46. DLD to Joseph Henry, Jan. 24, 1861, Joseph Henry MSS., Smithsonian Institution; DLD to MF, Jan. 26, 1861, *Dix-Fillmore Letters,* pp. 345–346; L. N. Andrews and Samuel Haycraft to DLD, Feb. 8, 1861.

47. DLD to Charles Sumner, Feb. 18, 1861, Sumner MSS., HLHU; DLD to AEH, Feb. 21, 1861; DLD to MF, Feb. 21, 1861, *Dix-Fillmore Letters,* pp. 347–348.

48. DLD to William H. Seward, April 6, 1861, Seward MSS., Rush Rhees Library, University of Rochester.

49. Maria R. Buttolph to Francis Tiffany, Dec. 25, 1889, DLD MSS., HLHU; John G. Nicolay to [?], April 19, 1861, quoted in Helen Nicolay, *Our Capital on the Potomac* (New York: The Century Co., 1924), pp. 363–364.

50. DLD to Elizabeth Rathbone, Jan. 13, 1860, Rathbone Family MSS., University of Liverpool. Daniel W. Crofts, *Reluctant Confederates: Upper South Unionists and the Secession Crisis* (Chapel Hill: University of North Carolina Press, 1989), pp. 114–117, presents many examples of this imagery.

51. Florence Nightingale, *Notes on Nursing: What It Is and What It Is Not* (New York: Dover Publications, 1969; first published 1860), p. 32; Edward Cook, *The Life of Florence Nightingale,* 2 vols. (London: Macmillan and Co., 1913), 1: 106. On Nightingale's ideas about nursing and hospitals, see Susan M. Reverby, *Ordered to Care: The Dilemma of American Nursing, 1850–1945* (New York: Cambridge University Press, 1987), pp. 39–43, and Charles E. Rosenberg, *The Care of Strangers: The Rise of America's Hospital System* (New York: Basic Books, 1987), pp. 124–135.

52. DLD, *Memorial Soliciting Enlarged and Improved Accommodations for the Insane of the State of Tennessee* (Nashville: B. R. M'Kennie, 1847), p. 11.

53. DLD to William Rathbone, March 26, 1860, Rathbone Family MSS., University of Liverpool; see also DLD, *Memorial Soliciting an Appropriation for the State Hospital for the Insane* (Frankfort, Ky.: A. G. Hodges, 1846), p. 4.

54. Nightingale, *Notes on Nursing,* p. 3.

55. DLD to Elizabeth Rathbone, March 3, 1860; William Greenleaf Eliot to DLD, May 6, 1860, Abigail Adams Eliot MSS., SLRC.

56. Horace Lamb, DLD estate inventory, n.d., Lamb Family MSS., Boston Athenæum.

57. Francis Lieber to DLD, Jan. 1, 1858, Francis Lieber MSS., Huntington Library, San Marino, California.

58. Sarah J. Hale, "Editor's Table," *Godey's Lady's Book* 62 (January 1861): 77–78; DLD to AEH, Jan. 26, 1861.

59. DLD to AEH, April 20, 1861; John G. Nicolay to [?], April 19, 1861, quoted in Nicolay, *Our Capital on the Potomac*, pp. 363–364; *Letters of John Hay and Extracts from Diary,* 3 vols. (New York: Gordian Press, [1908] 1969), 1: 13.

60. DLD to AEH, April 20 [1861].

61. DLD to Simon Cameron, April 22 [1861], Letters Received, Office of the Surgeon General, National Archives.

62. *The War of the Rebellion: A Compilation of the Official Records of the Union and Confederate Armies,* 128 vols. (Washington. D.C.: Government Printing Office, 1880–1901), ser. 3, 1: 107.

13. A Huge Wild Beast Has Consumed My Life

1. DLD to TSK, April 26, 1861, TSK MSS., PHA; George Worthington Adams, *Doctors in Blue: The Medical History of the Union Army in the Civil War* (New York: Henry Schuman, 1952), pp. 4, 26.

2. DLD to TSK, April 29, 1861, TSK MSS., PHA; DLD to Robert C. Wood, April 25, 1861, Letters Received, Office of the Surgeon General, National Archives.

3. DLD to TSK, n.d. [1861], TSK MSS., PHA.

4. *The War of the Rebellion: A Compilation of the Official Records of the Union and Confederate Armies* (128 vols.; Washington, D.C.: Government Printing Office, 1880–1901), Ser. 3, 1: 139–140.

5. Jane Grey Swisshelm, *Half a Century* (New York: Source Book Press, 1970; reprint of 2d ed., Chicago: Jansen, McClurg & Company, 1880), p. 354.

6. DLD to Louisa Lee Schuyler, April 29, 1861, reprinted in Sylvia G. L. Dannett, ed., *Noble Women of the North* (New York: Thomas Yoseloff, 1959), pp. 62–63.

7. Ibid.

8. Reprinted in Agatha Young, *The Women and the Crisis: Women of the North in the Civil War* (New York: McDowell, Obolensky, 1959), pp. 99–100.

9. On the early lack of publicity for nursing opportunities, see Elizabeth D. Leonard, *Yankee Women: Gender Battles in the Civil War* (New York: W. W. Norton & Co., 1994), p. 6.

10. On the founding of the Sanitary Commission, see Walter Donald Kring, *Henry Whitney Bellows* (Boston: Skinner House, 1979), pp. 224–235; William Quentin Maxwell, *Lincoln's Fifth Wheel: The Political History of the United States Sanitary Commission* (New York: Longmans, Green & Co., 1956), pp. 2–8.

11. Kring, *Bellows,* p. 194; George Fredrickson, *The Inner Civil War* (New York: Harper & Row, 1965), p. 27.

12. Charles J. Stillé, *History of the United States Sanitary Commission* (New York: Hurd and Houghton, 1868), p. 70.

13. AEH to DLD, Aug. 13, 1847.

14. DLD to Reverend [Bishop Potter?], May 18, 1861, American Literary Duplicates, Historical Society of Pennsylvania, Philadelphia.

15. *Official Records,* Ser. 3, 1: 217.

16. Maxwell, *Lincoln's Fifth Wheel,* p. 50.

17. Charles H. Nichols to DLD, May 9, 1861.

18. See Charles E. Rosenberg, *The Care of Strangers: The Rise of America's Hospital System* (New York: Basic Books, 1987), pp. 124–135; Charles E. Rosenberg, "Florence Nightingale on Contagion: The Hospital as Moral Universe," in *Healing and History,* ed. Charles Rosenberg (New York: Science History Publications, 1979), pp. 116–135.

19. Boston *Evening Transcript,* May 30, 1861.

20. Charles H. Nichols to TSK, June 12, 1861, in Clifford B. Farr, ed., "The Civil War Correspondence of Dr. Thomas S. Kirkbride," *Pennsylvania Magazine of History and Biography* 83 (January 1959): 81–82. See generally Ann Douglas Wood, "The War within a War: Women Nurses in the Union Army," *Civil War History* 18 (September 1972): 197–212.

21. Florence Nightingale, *Notes on Hospitals,* ed. Charles E. Rosenberg (New York: Garland Publishing, 1989, 3d ed. first published in 1863), pp. 181–187.

22. James M. McPherson, *Battle Cry of Freedom* (New York: Oxford University Press, 1988), p. 487. Adams, *Doctors in Blue,* p. 3, reports that the ratio was ten to one.

23. DLD to AEH, May 26, 31, 1861; Boston *Evening Transcript,* June 6, 1861.

24. DLD to AEH, May 31, 1861, June 24 [1861]; Maxwell, *Lincoln's Fifth Wheel,* pp. 78–79; Philadelphia *Evening Bulletin,* June 13, 1861.

25. DLD to Esther Hare, n.d., Hare-Willing Family MSS., American Philosophical Society, Philadelphia, Pennsylvania.

26. Simon Cameron to the Surgeon General, June 10, 1861, Letters Received by the Adjutant General's Office, National Archives; General Orders no. 31, *Official Records,* Ser. 3, 1: 263.

27. Simon Cameron to the Surgeon General, June 10, 1861.

28. Stillé, *History of the Sanitary Commission,* p. 532, lists the commissioners.

29. William Rathbone to DLD, June 14, 1861; *Official Records,* Ser. 3, 1: 308.

30. Elizabeth Blackwell to Barbara Smith Bodichon, June 5, 1861, quoted in Nancy Ann Sahli, "Elizabeth Blackwell, M.D. (1821–1910): A Biography," Ph.D. diss., University of Pennsylvania, 1974, p. 151.

31. On the generational dynamics of the Woman's Central Association, see Lori Ginz-

berg, *Women and the Work of Benevolence* (New Haven, Conn.: Yale University Press, 1990), pp. 140–143.

32. Anne L. Austin, *The Woolsey Sisters of New York: A Family's Involvement in the Civil War and a New Profession* (Philadelphia: American Philosophical Society, 1971), p. 43.

33. Quoted in Dannett, *Noble Women of the North*, pp. 89–91.

34. Ibid., p. 91.

35. Anna L. Boyden, *Echoes from Hospital and White House: A Record of Mrs. Rebecca R. Pomroy's Experience in War-Times* (Boston: D. Lothrop & Co., 1884), pp. 161–162.

36. Rebecca R. Pomroy to Sister H., Oct. 12, 1861, in Boyden, *Echoes from Hospital and White House,* pp. 25–26.

37. Boyden, *Echoes from Hospital and White House,* p. 176; Linus P. Brockett and Mary C. Vaughan, *Woman's Work in the Civil War: A Record of Heroism, Patriotism, and Patience* (Philadelphia: Zeigler, McCurdy & Co., 1867), p. 107; Sophronia E. Bucklin, *In Hospital and Camp: A Woman's Record of Thrilling Incidents among the Wounded in the Late War* (Philadelphia: John E. Potter & Co., 1869), pp. 61, 72–74, 111–118, 198–199, 228–229, 244, 306; Mary A. Gardner Holland, *Our Army Nurses* (Boston: B. Wilkins & Co., 1895), pp. 212, 263, 299, 474; James Phinney Munroe, ed., *Adventures of an Army Nurse in Two Wars* (Boston: Little, Brown, and Co., 1903), pp. 33, 35–36, 64, 121; Caroline A. Burghardt to DLD, May 26, 1885; Harriet Douglas Whetten to Kate [?], May 8, 1862, in Paul H. Hass, ed., "A Volunteer Nurse in the Civil War: The Letters of Harriet Douglas Whetten," *Wisconsin Magazine of History* 48 (Winter 1964–65): 135.

38. Sarah Low to Aunt [?], Sept. [?], 1862, Sarah Low MSS., New Hampshire Historical Society, Concord; Mary Everingham to Horrie S. Ward, July 31, 1887, DLD MSS., HLHU. A. T. Perry to Alfred S. Roe, April 27, 1888, reprinted in Roe, *Dorothea Lynde Dix: A Paper Read before the Worcester Society of Antiquity, November 20th, 1888* (Worcester: Franklin P. Rice, 1889), pp. 14–16, is one of the most vivid of the numerous nurses' recollections of Dix.

39. Catherine S. Lawrence, *Autobiography* (Albany: Amasa J. Parker, 1893), pp. 66–67.

40. Ibid. See generally Mary Denis Maher, *To Bind Up the Wounds: Catholic Sister Nurses in the U.S. Civil War* (New York: Greenwood Press, 1989), pp. 128–132.

41. Lawrence, *Autobiography,* pp. 70–74.

42. Allan Nevins and Milton Halsey Thomas, eds., *The Diary of George Templeton Strong: The Civil War, 1860–1865* (New York: Macmillan, 1952), p. 164.

43. Ibid., pp. 165, 173–174.

44. Laura Wood Roper, *FLO: A Biography of Frederick Law Olmsted* (Baltimore: Johns Hopkins University Press, 1973) is the standard biography. See also Charles Caper McLaughlin, *The Papers of Frederick Law Olmsted,* vol. 4: *Defending the Union,* ed. Jane Turner Censer (Baltimore: Johns Hopkins University Press, 1986).

45. Dannett, *Noble Women of the North,* p. 92.

46. Elizabeth Blackwell to DLD, July 21, Aug. 24 [1861], Jane Gay Dodge MSS., SLRC; Ginzberg, *Women and the Work of Benevolence,* p. 160; Kirstie Ross, "Arranging a Doll's House: Refined Women as Union Nurses," in *Divided Houses,* ed. Catherine Clinton and Nina Silber (New York: Oxford University Press, 1992), p. 99.

47. Frederick Law Olmsted to Henry Whitney Bellows, Oct. 3, 1861, in Censer, ed., *Defending the Union,* p. 211.

48. Abraham Lincoln, Military Pass for DLD, DLD MSS., HLHU.

49. *Official Records,* Ser. 3, 1: 398.

50. See DLD to Miss Wilcox, Aug. 3, 1861, Edward McPherson MSS., Library of Congress.

51. John C. Frémont to DLD, Aug. 21, 1861 (telegraph), Military Pass for DLD, Sept. 2, 1861; William E. Parrish, "The Western Sanitary Commission," *Civil War History* 36 (March 1990): 17–35.

52. Maxwell, *Lincoln's Fifth Wheel,* pp. 97–106.

53. Nevins and Thomas, *Diary of George Templeton Strong,* p. 182. The strained interpretations in Fredrickson, *Inner Civil War,* p. 110, and Ann Douglas, *The Feminization of American Culture* (New York: Alfred Knopf, 1977), pp. 186–187, fail to take into account the context of this diary entry in Dix's evolving relations with the Sanitary Commission.

54. Frederick Law Olmsted to Henry Whitney Bellows, Sept. 25, 1863, in Censer, *Defending the Union,* pp. 202–203.

55. Ibid., p. 206 n. 16.

56. Olmsted to Bellows, Sept. 25, 1863, in Censer, *Defending the Union,* pp. 202–203; Ross, "Arranging a Doll's House," p. 99.

57. Bucklin, *In Hospital and Camp,* p. 94; see also Swisshelm, *Half a Century,* p. 241.

58. DLD to [William Rathbone], Nov. 28 [1861].

59. DLD to William Rathbone, n.d. [January 1862?], Rathbone Family MSS., University of Liverpool.

60. DLD to William Rathbone, Oct. 26, 1862.

61. DLD to [William Rathbone], Nov. 28 [1861]; DLD to AEH, Sept. 15, 1863, Aug. 17, 1864.

62. DLD to AEH, Aug. 26, Sept. 15, 22, 30, 1863.

63. DLD to AEH, Oct. 8, 1861; DLD to [William Rathbone], Nov. 28 [1861].

64. DLD to Elizabeth Rathbone, June 20, 1862, Rathbone Family MSS., University of Liverpool.

65. Ibid.

66. DLD to [William Rathbone], Nov. 28 [1861].

67. DLD to Esther Hare, Oct. 24, 1864, Hare-Willing Family MSS., American Philosophical Society, Philadelphia, Pennsylvania.

68. DLD to Esther Hare, May 24, 1864, Hare-Willing Family MSS., American Philosophical Society, Philadelphia, Pennsylvania.

69. John W. Ward to Frances Willard, n.d., in Willard, "Dorothea Dix," *The Chautauquan* 10 (October 1889): 64. Compare with Fredrickson, *Inner Civil War,* p. 110, which argues that "that pathetic sympathy with human suffering which had been the mainspring of her long and wonderful philanthropic career, now, when she was brought face to face with such massive suffering she could not relieve, served only to unnerve her."

70. Roe, *Dorothea Lynde Dix,* p. 13. On the tendency of many women nurses to write about individual patients, see Jane E. Schultz, "The Inhospitable Hospital: Gender and Professionalism in Civil War Medicine," *Signs* 17 (Winter 1992): 378–379.

71. L. H. Hiester to Hudson Taylor, Oct. 13, 1861, Miscellaneous MSS., Huntington Library, San Marino, California.

72. *Official Records,* Ser. 1, 5: 103.

73. New York *Times,* Dec. 4, 1861.

74. Maria Lydig Daly, *Diary of a Union Lady,* ed. Harold Earl Hammond (New York: Funk and Wagnalls, 1962), p. 76.

75. Quoted in Holland, *Our Army Nurses,* p. 19.

76. Mary A. Livermore, *My Story of the War* (Hartford, Conn.: A. D. Worthington & Co., 1889), p. 246.

77. Boyden, *Echoes from Hospital and White House,* p. 141.

78. Frederick Law Olmsted to Henry Whitney Bellows, Sept. 25, 1861, in Censer, *Defending the Union,* pp. 202–203; Bucklin, *In Hospital and Camp,* pp. 241–244; Swisshelm, *Half a Century,* pp. 324–325.

79. Gerald Schwartz, ed., *A Woman Doctor's Civil War: Esther Hill Hawks' Diary* (Columbia: University of South Carolina Press, 1984), pp. 3–11, 15.

80. For waivers of the age restriction, see Bucklin, *In Hospital and Camp,* pp. 39–40; Holland, *Our Army Nurses,* pp. 171–172, 324, 467–469; William Howell Reed, ed., *War Papers of Frank B. Fay* (Boston: privately printed, 1911), p. 25. On the dress code, see Dannett, *Noble Women of the North,* p. 63; Holland, *Our Army Nurses,* pp. 289–290. Jane E. Schultz, "Race, Gender, and Bureaucracy: Civil War Army Nurses and the Pension Bureau," *Journal of Women's History* 6 (Summer 1994): 64 n. 12, suggests that "applicants rejected by Dix were frequently told that they were too young to serve, although social status was more likely the decisive issue." This speculation is consistent with views that Dix outlined in her teaching and asylum careers, and there is no doubt that she wanted her nurses to conform to ideals of respectability that were related to the construction of social class. It should be noted, however, that she resisted the unsanctioned voluntarism of women who enjoyed considerable social status, as her encounter with Georgeanna Wolsey illustrates. She also rejected the application of Anna Lowell, an impeccable representative of the Brahmin elite of Boston, on the basis of age. The role of class in the composition of Dix's corps became even more complex after her break with the Sanitary Commission and its allies eliminated her ready source for the recruitment of middle-class

women. Lowell's friend Sarah Low observed that "women that no one would be willing to receive into his house, they are women that Miss Dix employed." Sarah Low to Matty, Oct. 2, 1862, Anna Lowell to Sarah Low, Nov. 6, 1862, both in Sarah Low MSS., New Hampshire Historical Society, Concord.

81. DLD to Charles Steedman, Jan. 15 [1862], Charles Steedman MSS., Perkins Library, Duke University.

82. Joseph Henry to Simon Cameron, Dec. 5, 1861, Henry MSS., Smithsonian Institution; DLD to Simon Cameron, Jan. 12, 1862, Cameron MSS., Library of Congress.

83. Patricia Carley Johnson, ed., "Sensitivity and Civil War: The Selected Diaries and Papers, 1858–1866, of Frances Adeline [Fanny] Seward," Ph.D diss., University of Rochester, 1963, pp. 444–446; Abraham Lincoln to DLD, Feb. 19, 1862, Robert W. Woodruff Library, Emory University; Abraham Lincoln to DLD, May 4, 1862; DLD to Abraham Lincoln [May 5, 1862], Duke Medical Center Library; Rebecca R. Pomeroy to Mary [?], Feb. 21, 1862 (typescript), Miscellaneous MSS., SLRC. See also Boyden, *Echoes from Hospital and White House.*

84. Katharine Prescott Wormeley to "Dear Friend," May 16, 1862, in Wormeley, *The Other Side of War* (Boston: Ticknor and Co., 1889), p. 44.

85. Harriet Douglas Whetten to Sister Kate, May 8, 1862, in Hass, "A Volunteer Nurse in the Civil War," pp. 133–136.

86. Robert Ware to [?] Adams, April 28, 1862, Robert Ware MSS., Countway Medical Library, Harvard University.

87. DLD to Elizabeth Rathbone, June 20, 1862, Rathbone Family MSS., University of Liverpool.

88. Surgeon General's Office, Circular Orders no. 7–8, July 14, 1862, DLD MSS., HLHU. See also George Hayward to Edward Jarvis, Aug. 30, 1862, Jarvis MSS., Countway Medical Library, Harvard University.

89. Simon Cameron to the Surgeon General [June 10, 1861], Letters Received by the Office of the Surgeon General, National Archives. Dix estimated the number of nurses under her direct supervision as 250 in February 1862 and 150 in March 1863. See Boyden, *Echoes from Hospital and White House,* p. 54; DLD to AEH, March 16, 1863. Hammond reported a total patient population of 11,062 in the general hospitals at Washington, Falls Church, Alexandria, Fortress Monroe, Harrison's Landing, and for the Army of Virginia on August 1, 1862. See *Official Records,* Ser. 3, 2: 389. Adams, *Doctors in Blue,* p. 178, estimated that women represented about one-fifth of the Army nursing force during the war. A government clerk analyzing a proposed pension for veteran women nurses in 1890 estimated that 3,214 women appeared on the nurses' payroll during the war. This estimate included women appointed by Dix, her agents outside of Washington, and the Surgeon General. See Julia C. Stimson and Ethel C. Thompson, "Women Nurses with the Union Forces during the Civil War," Part 2, *Military Surgeon* 62 (February 1928): 222. Schultz, "Race, Gender, and Bureaucracy," points out that

women classified as cooks or laundresses often performed nursing duties and estimates that approximately 18,000 women worked in Union hospitals.

90. DLD to William A. Hammond, June 9, 1862, Letters Received by the Surgeon General, National Archives, Washington, D.C.; Sarah Low to Aunt [?], Sept. [?], 1862, Sarah Low MSS., New Hampshire Historical Society, Concord; Elizabeth D. Leonard, "Civil War Nurse, Civil War Nursing: Rebecca Usher of Maine," *Civil War History* 41 (September 1995): 192.

91. Surgeon General's Office, Circular no. 7, DLD MSS., HLHU (bMS Am1838); Bonnie Ellen Blustein, *Preserve Your Love for Science: Life of William A. Hammond, American Neurologist* (New York: Cambridge University Press, 1991), p. 67.

92. Munroe, *Adventures of an Army Nurse,* pp. 32–37.

93. Anna Lowell to Sarah Low, Nov. 6 [1862]; Sarah Low to Aunt [?], Feb. 5, 1863, both in Sarah Low MSS., New Hampshire Historical Society, Concord.

94. Sarah Low to Aunt [?], Sept. [?], 1862; Anna Lowell to Sarah Low, Nov. 6 [1862]; both in Sarah Low MSS., New Hampshire Historical Society, Concord. On Dix's view of Bickerdyke, see Munroe, *Adventures of an Army Nurse,* p. 188; Mary Ann Bickerdyke to DLD, April 29, 1874; James E. Yeatman to DLD, March 17, May 12, 30 [1874].

95. George Worthington Adams, "Health and Medicine in the Union Army: 1861–1865," Ph.D diss., Harvard University, 1946, p. 551, quoting Surgeon General's Circular Letter, Oct. 28, 1862; Sarah Low to Aunt [?], September 1862, Sarah Low MSS., New Hampshire Historical Society.

96. DLD to Simon Cameron, April 10, 1863, Simon Cameron MSS., Dauphin County Historical Society, Harrisburg, Pennsylvania. On Stanton and Hammond, see Maxwell, *Lincoln's Fifth Wheel,* pp. 139–143; Benjamin P. Thomas and Harold M. Hyman, *Stanton: The Life and Times of Lincoln's Secretary of War* (New York: Alfred A. Knopf, 1962), pp. 366–368.

97. DLD to William Rathbone, Oct. 26, 1862.

98. Ellen Wright to Laura Stratton, Jan. 31, 1863, quoted in Mary Elizabeth Massey, *Bonnet Brigades* (New York: Alfred A. Knopf, 1966), p. 47. The currency of the nickname is indicated by the refutation in Munroe, *Adventures of an Army Nurse,* p. 36.

99. Mary A. Newcomb, *Four Years of Personal Reminiscences of the War* (Chicago: H. S. Mills & Co., 1893), p. 14.

100. Constant C. Hanks to Mary Rose, Feb. 15 [1863?], Constant C. Hanks MSS., Perkins Library, Duke University.

101. Roe, *Dorothea Lynde Dix,* pp. 16–17.

102. Woman's Central Association of Relief, *How Can We Best Help Our Camps and Hospitals?* (New York: William C. Bryant, 1863); United States Sanitary Commission, *Hospital Transports* (Boston: Ticknor and Fields, 1863).

103. Katharine Prescott Wormeley, *The United States Sanitary Commission* (Boston: Lit-

tle, Brown and Co., 1863), pp. 246–247. See also *The Sanitary Commission Bulletin* 1 (March 15, 1864): 295–296.

104. Swisshelm, *Half a Century,* p. 239; New York *Tribune,* May 13, 1863.

105. Quoted in Cornelia Hancock to Sarah [?], June 7, 1864, in Hancock, *South after Gettysburg,* ed. Henrietta Stratton Jacquette (New York: Thomas Y. Crowell, 1937), pp. 130–131.

106. Frederick Law Olmsted to Henry Whitney Bellows, July 4, 1863, in Censer, *Defending the Union,* pp. 639–640.

107. Quoted in Martha Saxton, *Louisa May* (Boston: Houghton Mifflin Co., 1977), p. 256.

108. Louisa May Alcott, *Hospital Sketches,* ed. Bessie Z. Jones (Cambridge: John Harvard Library, 1960; first published 1863), p. 69.

109. Joseph K. Barnes to E. D. Townsend, Oct. 13, 22, 1863, Letters Received by the Adjutant General's Office, National Archives.

110. DLD to AEH, April 24, 1863.

111. DLD to Ezra Stiles Gannett, Oct. 27, 1863, Gannett Family MSS., HLHU (bMS Am1888.4).

112. *Official Records,* Ser. 3, 3: 943–944.

113. Jane Stuart Woolsey, *Hospital Days* (New York: D. Van Nostrand, 1870), p. 42.

114. Cornelia Hancock to "Sister," Nov. 17, 1863, in Hancock, *South after Gettysburg,* pp. 35–36; Bucklin, *In Hospital and Camp,* pp. 91–92, presents the view of Dix's partisans.

115. New York *Times,* Dec. 13, 1863.

116. Adams, "Health and Medicine in the Union Army," p. 553 n. 62.

117. Mary Peabody Mann to DLD, Jan. 18, 1864 (typescript), Mary Peabody Mann MSS., Library of Congress.

118. Woolsey quoted in Dannett, *Noble Women of the North,* p. 305. See also DLD to Mrs. Gird, June 4, 1864, Dorothea Dix MSS., Menninger Foundation, Topeka, Kansas; DLD to [?], Nov. 24, 1864, Huntington-Bright Collection, Jervis Public Library, Rome, New York; Holland, *Our Army Nurses,* pp. 289–290, 467–469, 505.

119. DLD to [William Rathbone], Jan. 10 [1864].

120. DLD to AEH, March 16, 1863.

121. McPherson, *Battle Cry of Freedom,* pp. 791–802; William Best Hesseltine, *Civil War Prisons: A Study in War Psychology* (New York: Frederick Ungar, 1930), pp. 114–209.

122. Hesseltine, *Civil War Prisons,* pp. 210–211; Hans Trefousse, *Ben Butler* (New York: Twayne Publishers, 1957), pp. 140–142.

123. DLD to Esther Hare, Jan. 5 [1864], Hare-Willing Family MSS., American Philosophical Society, Philadelphia, Pennsylvania; Pliny Earle, diary, Feb. 21, 1864, quoted in Franklin B. Sanborn, *Memoirs of Pliny Earle, M.D.* (Boston: Damrell &

Upham, 1898), p. 258; Benjamin F. Butler to DLD, March 1, 1864, Benjamin F. Butler MSS., Library of Congress.

124. DLD to Benjamin F. Butler, March 12, 1864, in *Private and Official Correspondence of General Benjamin F. Butler,* 5 vols. (Norwood, Mass.: Plimpton Press, 1917), 3: 516.

125. Trefousse, *Ben Butler,* pp. 135–145; DLD to Benjamin F. Butler, March 14, 18, 1864, Benjamin F. Butler to DLD [March 12, 1864], in *Butler Correspondence,* 3: 516–517, 538, 551; DLD to Benjamin F. Butler, April 9, 1864, in *Butler Correspondence,* 4: 43–44; DLD to Benjamin F. Butler, April 6, 1864, Benjamin F. Butler MSS., Library of Congress.

126. DLD to Esther Hare, n.d. [June 1864], n.d. [Dec. 1864?], Jan. 3 [1865], March 24, 1865, Hare-Willing Family MSS., American Philosophical Society, Philadelphia, Pennsylvania; DLD to AEH, April 24 [1864]; Boyden, *Echoes from Hospital and White House,* pp. 198–199.

127. DLD to Esther Hare, May 24, 1864, n.d. [June 1864], n.d. [Sept. 9, 1864]; DLD to Esther and Clark Hare, March 24, 1865, all in Hare-Willing Family MSS., American Philosophical Society, Philadelphia, Pennsylvania; undated newspaper clipping, Haverford College Library, Haverford, Pennsylvania.

128. Benjamin F. Butler to DLD [March 12, 1864], DLD to Benjamin F. Butler, March 14, 1864, *Butler Correspondence,* 3: 516–517.

129. DLD to Ethan Allen Hitchcock, Nov. 8, 1864, with Hitchcock's endorsements, Nov. 11, 12, 1864, DLD MSS., HLHU; McPherson, *Battle Cry of Freedom,* p. 796 n. 48; Hesseltine, *Civil War Prisons,* p. 203; DLD to Ethan Allen Hitchcock, Nov. 25, 1864, in *Official Records,* ser. 2, 7: 1159.

130. Edwin Greble to Susan V. Greble, Dec. 11, 1864, Edwin Greble MSS., Library of Congress.

131. DLD to Horace Binney, Jr., May 25, May 28, 1864, Hare-Willing Family MSS., American Philosophical Society, Philadelphia, Pennsylvania; United States Sanitary Commission, *Narrative of the Privations and Sufferings of United States Officers and Soldiers while Prisoners of War in the Hands of the Rebel Authorities* (Philadelphia: King and Baird, 1864); Maxwell, *Lincoln's Fifth Wheel,* 307–308; Hesseltine, *Civil War Prisons,* pp. 198–200.

132. DLD to Esther Hare, Aug. 31, 1864, Hare-Willing MSS., American Philosophical Society, Philadelphia, Pennsylvania; Robert J. Rayback, *Millard Fillmore: Biography of a President* (Buffalo, N.Y.: Buffalo Historical Society, 1959), p. 428.

133. DLD to AEH, Oct. 14, 1864.

134. DLD to AEH, Sept. 30 [1863], March 29 [1864], Oct. 14, 1864; DLD to AEH, Jan. 6, 1864, DLD MSS., HLHU.

135. DLD to Elizabeth Rathbone, October 17, 1864, Rathbone Family MSS., University of Liverpool.

136. Fanny Seward to DLD, April 20, 1865.

137. DLD to AEH, Nov. 7 [1870].
138. Clara Barton to DLD, May 26, 1865; Stephen B. Oates, *A Woman of Valor: Clara Barton and the Civil War* (New York: The Free Press, 1994), p. 297; DLD to Esther Hare, May 31 [1865], Hare-Willing Family MSS., American Philosophical Society, Philadelphia, Pennsylvania; DLD to AEH, Sept. 11, 1865.
139. Francis Tiffany, *Life of Dorothea Lynde Dix* (Boston: Houghton, Mifflin and Co., 1890), p. 339.
140. Josephine E. Dayton to DLD, Nov. 16, 1864; Linus Pierpont Brockett to DLD, Aug. 20, 1867.
141. DLD to Elizabeth Rathbone, Jan. 6, 1869, Rathbone Family MSS., University of Liverpool; DLD to AEH, Feb. 3, 21, 1869.
142. Horatio A. Lamb, memorandum re conversation with DLD, Oct. 27, 1881, DLD MSS., HLHU.
143. DLD to Elizabeth Rathbone, Sept. 24, 1867, Rathbone Family MSS., University of Liverpool.
144. Caroline A. Burgardt to DLD, Oct. 19, 28, 1875, April 3, 1877, Sept. 11, 1878.
145. DLD to Miss Foster, Oct. 2, 1867, DLD MSS., Huntington Library, San Marino, California; Caroline A. Burghardt to DLD, Feb. 8, 1875, May 3, [?], Oct. 13, 1881, July 4, 1882; Harriet Dame to DLD, June 19, 1882; Jane Gay to DLD, June 28, [?].
146. Charles H. Nichols to DLD, Jan. 19, 1866; Edwin M. Stanton, "Order in Relation to the Services of Miss Dix," December 3, 1866, DLD MSS., HLHU; Robert C. Winthrop to DLD, Dec. 26, 1873, Nov. 10, 1876; Horatio A. Lamb, memorandum re meeting with DLD, March 14, 1886, DLD MSS., HLHU; Jerome D. Greene to Christopher R. Eliot, Jan. 29, 1943, Abigail Adams Eliot MSS., SLRC.
147. James Curry to DLD, May 1, 1866; DLD to Elizabeth Rathbone, May 5, Aug. 18, 1866.
148. DLD to Charles G. Loring, June 17, 1866; DLD to Elizabeth Rathbone, Aug. 18, 1866; DLD, List of Subscribers to Monument Fund, May 1866, DLD MSS., HLHU.
149. DLD to [MTT], Dec. 11, 1867; DLD to AEH, n.d. [1867?].
150. Edwin M. Stanton to DLD, May 12, 1868; U. S. Grant to DLD, Oct. 20, 1869; Jane Stuart Woolsey to DLD, Sept. 26, 1871, Silliman Family MSS., Sterling Library, Yale University; Marianna Davenport Trott to Francis Tiffany, Feb. 19, 1890, DLD MSS., HLHU.
151. DLD to Elizabeth Rathbone, Aug. 18, 1866.

14. At Last

1. DLD to AEH, August 2 [1863?], Sept. 11, 1865.

2. DLD to W. J. Mullen, Jan. 19, 1862, Dreer MSS., Historical Society of Pennsylvania, Philadelphia.

3. DLD to MTT, n.d. [1868], quoted in Francis Tiffany, *Life of Dorothea Lynde Dix* (Boston: Houghton, Mifflin and Co., 1890), p. 353.

4. Susan Heath, MS. diary, Nov. 27–Dec. 6, 1865, Heath Family MSS., MHS; AEH to DLD, June 26, 1867.

5. Gerald N. Grob, *Mental Institutions in America: Social Policy to 1875* (New York: The Free Press, 1973), pp. 308–309; DLD to AEH, Dec. 20 [1865].

6. Ellen Dwyer, *Homes for the Mad: Life inside Two Nineteenth-Century Asylums* (New Brunswick, N.J.: Rutgers University Press, 1987), pp. 43–46.

7. [John P. Gray], "The Willard Asylum, and Provision for the Insane," *AJI* 22 (October 1865): 193–212; "Summary," *AJI* 22 (October 1865): 246–252; Dwyer, *Homes for the Mad*, pp. 46–49; Grob, *Mental Institutions in America*, pp. 309–319.

8. DLD to TSK, Feb. 15 [1866], TSK MSS., PHA; DLD to AEH, Feb. 23, 1866; Charles H. Nichols to DLD, March 29, 1866; D. T. Brown to DLD, March 31, April 7, 1866.

9. George Cook to DLD, March 15, 1866; [Gray], "The Willard Asylum, and Provision for the Insane," p. 208; [John P. Gray], "Proceedings of the Association: Provision for the Chronic Insane," *AJI* 24 (January 1868): 321–322.

10. Chapin quoted in Grob, *Mental Institutions in America*, p. 315; John B. Chapin, "On Provision for the Chronic Insane Poor," *AJI* 24 (July 1867): 29–42; Bonnie Ellen Blustein, *Preserve Your Love for Science: Life of William A. Hammond, American Neurologist* (New York: Cambridge University Press, 1991), pp. 164–200.

11. Chapin, "On Provision for the Chronic Insane Poor," p. 35.

12. [Gray], "The Willard Asylum, and Provision for the Insane," pp. 199–201; Grob, *Mental Institutions in America*, pp. 270–302; Robert H. Bremner, *The Public Good: Philanthropy and Welfare in the Civil War Era* (New York: Alfred A. Knopf, 1980), pp. 152–158.

13. Franklin Benjamin Sanborn, *Memoirs of Pliny Earle, M.D.* (Boston: Damrell & Upham, 1898), pp. 305–306; Mary O. Furner, *Advocacy and Objectivity: A Crisis in the Professionalization of American Social Science, 1865–1905* (Lexington: University of Kentucky Press, 1975), pp. 19–22.

14. New York *Tribune*, April 9, 1866; [Gray], "The Willard Asylum, and Provision for the Insane," p. 199n.

15. *Hartford Courant*, May 3, June 15, 23, 1866; DLD to Charles G. Loring, June 17, 1866; Abram Marvin Shew, "History and Description of the Connecticut Hospital for the Insane," *AJI* 33 (July 1876): 2–3.

16. Shew, "History and Description of the Connecticut Hospital for the Insane," p. 1;

DLD to Joseph Henry, June 7, 1866; Benjamin Silliman, Jr., to Joseph Henry, June 30, 1866; Joseph Henry to Benjamin Silliman, Jr., July 3, 1866; Joseph R. Hawley to DLD, July 14, 1866, all in Joseph Henry MSS., Smithsonian Institution; "Connecticut State Hospital for the Insane," *AJI* 24 (July 1867): 99.

17. Samuel G. Willard to DLD, Oct. 23, 1866; D. T. Woodruff to DLD, Oct. 24, 1866; Richard S. Fellowes to DLD, Nov. 12, 1866, June 21, 1867.

18. John B. Chapin to DLD, Feb. 11, 23, 1867.

19. Joseph M. Cleaveland to DLD, Jan. 1, Feb. 14 [1867], March 5, 30, 1867; "The New Hudson River Hospital," *AJI* 26 (January 1870): 379; Grob, *Mental Institutions in America,* p. 277.

20. DLD to Elizabeth Rathbone, June 2, 1868, Rathbone Family MSS., University of Liverpool.

21. DLD, MS. travelog [1869], DLD MSS., HLHU; Marguerite L. Sinclair to Christopher Rhodes Eliot, Oct. 31, Dec. 3, 1942, Abigail Adams Eliot MSS., SLRC. Christopher Rhodes Eliot reported that Dix and the Eliots attended the driving of the golden spike on May 10, 1869; I have not been able to confirm or disprove that claim. Dix's travel journal does not indicate their itinerary in the week after they left Omaha on May 4, and her vivid description of Promontory does not refer to the railroad or any ceremonies. The occasion has inspired many detailed narratives, but I have found no account that mentions Dix or the Eliots.

22. DLD to Elizabeth Rathbone, Sept. 18, 1869, Rathbone Family MSS., University of Liverpool.

23. DLD to Thomas Lamb Eliot, July 23, Sept. 8, Oct. 16, 1869, DLD-Eliot MSS., HLHU (*45M-339f).

24. Charles H. Nichols to DLD, July 17, Aug. 7, Nov. 26, Dec. 12, 21, 1869; DLD to AEH, Sept. 28, 1869. Nichols's assistant testified that other guests used the room when Dix was absent and even occasionally when she was in Washington. W. W. Godding to DLD, Dec. 12, 1869.

25. DLD to AEH, Jan. 20, 1870.

26. Ibid.; GBE to DLD, Feb. 13, 1870.

27. DLD to AEH, Jan. 20, April 16, 1870; DLD to Henrietta Eliot, April 6, 1870, DLD-Eliot MSS., HLHU; William L. Peck to Charles H. Nichols, May 27, 1870 (typescript), DLD MSS., HLHU.

28. DLD to Henrietta Eliot, May 19, 1870, DLD-Eliot MSS., HLHU; DLD to AEH, Jan. 24, 1876.

29. Charles H. Nichols to DLD, Aug. 30, 1870.

30. DLD to Thomas Lamb Eliot, Jan. 26 1872, n.d. [1873], DLD-Eliot MSS., HLHU.

31. MTT to DLD, Feb. 22, 1868; DLD to Henrietta Eliot, April 6, 1870, DLD-Eliot MSS., HLHU; DLD to Elizabeth Rathbone, Nov. 24, 1870, Rathbone Family MSS., University of Liverpool.

32. Bellows quoted in Walter Donald Kring, *Henry Whitney Bellows* (Boston: Skinner

House, 1979), pp. 309–310; DLD to Thomas Lamb Eliot and Henrietta Eliot, April 14, 1871, DLD-Eliot MSS., HLHU; DLD to Rose Lamb, May 17, 1881.

33. DLD to William Rathbone, Jr., April 20, 1868; DLD to Elizabeth Rathbone, April 4, 1872, Rathbone Family MSS., University of Liverpool; DLD to Mrs. Atkinson, Dec. 16, 1872; DLD to Abby Heath Barnett, Jan. 4 [1873], both in DLD-Heath MSS., HLHU.

34. DLD to Elizabeth Rathbone, Nov. 24, 1870, March 18, 1871, Rathbone Family MSS., University of Liverpool.

35. DLD to AEH, Dec. 8, 27, 1873.

36. DLD to Alexander Randall, May 2, 1874, Brune-Randall Family MSS., Maryland Historical Society, Baltimore; Nancy Tomes, *A Generous Confidence: Thomas Story Kirkbride and the Art of Asylum-Keeping, 1840–1883* (New York: Cambridge University Press, 1984), pp. 301–303.

37. DLD to Alexander Randall, May 2, 1874, Brune-Randall Family MSS., Maryland Historical Society, Baltimore.

38. Charles F. Folsom, *Diseases of the Mind* (Boston: Albert J. Wright, 1877), p. 23; Tiffany, *Life of DLD,* pp. 356–357; Daniel Roberts Brower to DLD, Jan. 25, 1876, April 23, 1877; J. E. Bowers to DLD, Oct. 27, 1880.

39. John Harper to DLD, April 13, 1867, July 6, 1876.

40. On Packard, see Myra Samuels Himelhoch and Arthur H. Shaffer, "Elizabeth Packard: Nineteenth-Century Crusader for the Rights of Mental Patients," *Journal of American Studies* 13 (December 1979): 343–375, and Barbara Sapinsley, *The Private War of Mrs. Packard* (New York: Paragon House, 1991).

41. "Summary," *AJI* 27 (October 1870): 260; DLD to Thomas Lamb Eliot, Jan. 21, 1875, DLD-Eliot MSS., HLHU; *Congressional Globe,* 43d Cong., 2d sess., pp. 238, 258, 831 (Jan. 5, 28, 1875); Isaac Ray to John W. Sawyer, Feb. 21, 1875, quoted in Grob, *Mental Institutions in America,* pp. 268–269.

42. See Ellen Carol DuBois, *Feminism and Suffrage: The Emergence of an Independent Women's Movement in America, 1848–1869* (Ithaca: Cornell University Press, 1978).

43. Himelhoch and Shaffer, "Elizabeth Packard," p. 365.

44. DLD to Miss Foster, Oct. 2, 1867, DLD MSS., Huntington Library, San Marino, California; DLD to Henrietta Eliot, April 6, 1870, and DLD to Henrietta and Thomas Lamb Eliot, June 20, 1874, both in DLD-Eliot MSS., HLHU; DLD to Maria Mitchell, Aug. 28, Sept. 28, 1871, Maria Mitchell Library, Nantucket Maria Mitchell Association, Nantucket, Massachusetts; Maria Mitchell to DLD, Sept. 20, 1871.

45. Sapinsley, *Private War of Mrs. Packard,* pp. 188–190; Himelhoch and Shaffer, "Elizabeth Packard," p. 371; H. F. Carriel to DLD, Feb. 22, 1875; John W. Sawyer to DLD, March 20, 1875; Mark Ranney to DLD, April 7, 1875; "Proceedings of the Association—May 1875," *AJI* 32 (January 1876): 322–323.

46. DLD to D. W. Voorhees, May 22, 1876, reprinted in *Congressional Globe,* 44th

Cong., 1st sess., House Rep. no. 793, pp. 367–368; New York *Tribune,* Aug. 1, 1876; W. W. Godding to DLD, May 21, 1876; Sapinsley, *Private War of Mrs. Packard,* pp. 189–192.

47. DLD to Henry Wadsworth Longfellow, May 8, 1876, Longfellow MSS., HLHU (bMS Am1340.2); DLD to TSK, Nov. 19, 1879, Jan. [?], 1881, TSK MSS., PHA.

48. Horace A. Lamb, MS. memoranda re conversations with DLD, Oct 27–28, Nov. 11, 1881, DLD MSS., HLHU.

49. DLD to Rose Lamb, Nov. 25, 1881; Sarah D. Peck to DLD, Jan. 18, 1883.

50. Lydia H. Prime to Horatio A. Lamb, Aug. 11, 1882, DLD MSS., HLHU; DLD to Rose Lamb, Oct. 3, 1882.

51. DLD to Horace A. Lamb, Aug. 3, 1882; William Greenleaf Eliot to Horatio Appleton Lamb, Aug. 6, 1882, DLD MSS., HLHU.

52. DLD to Horace A. Lamb, March 17, 1883; DLD to Elizabeth Randall [?], Feb. 23, 1883, Brune-Randall Family MSS., Maryland Historical Society, Baltimore; DLD to Abby Heath Barnett, n.d., DLD-Heath MSS., HLHU.

53. John W. Ward to Frances E. Willard, n.d., reprinted in Frances E. Willard, "Dorothea Dix," *The Chautauquan* 10 (October 1889): 62–64; William Greenleaf Eliot to DLD, March 27, 1883, Abigail Adams Eliot MSS., SLRC; Horatio A. Lamb, memorandum re conversation with DLD, n.d., DLD MSS., HLHU.

54. John Greenleaf Whittier to [?], Oct. 19, 1890, quoted in Samuel T. Pickard, *Life and Letters of John Greenleaf Whittier,* 2 vols. (Boston: Houghton, Mifflin, and Co., 1894), 2: 458; John Greenleaf Whittier to Francis Fisher Browne, Nov. 15, 1885, *The Letters of John Greenleaf Whittier,* ed. John B. Pickard, 3 vols. (Cambridge: Harvard University Press, 1975), 3: 513–514.

55. DLD to John Greenleaf Whittier, May 5, 1884, John Greenleaf Whittier MSS., HLHU (bMS Am1844); Christopher Rhodes Eliot, MS. sermon, July 24, 1887, Abigail Adams Eliot MSS., SLRC; John Greenleaf Whittier to Horatio A. Lamb, Sept. 26, 1889, DLD MSS., HLHU.

56. DLD to Horace A. Lamb, March 31, 1886.

57. Horace A. Lamb, inventory of DLD's drawers, n.d., Lamb Family MSS., Boston Athenæum.

58. DLD to William Greenleaf Eliot and Abigail Adams Eliot, n.d.; William Greenleaf Eliot to DLD, March 4, 1886, both in Abigail Adams Eliot MSS., SLRC; Caroline A. Burghardt to DLD, Sept. 21, 1886.

59. Lucy E. A. Kebler to Henrietta Eliot, Jan. 25, 1887, DLD-Eliot MSS., HLHU; Eric Sigg, *The American T. S. Eliot* (New York: Cambridge University Press, 1989), pp. 1–35.

60. Christopher Rhodes Eliot, untitled MS. sermon, July 24, 1887; Christopher Rhodes Eliot, "Memories and a Memorial," MS. sermon, Jan. 4, 1943, both in Abigail Adams Eliot MSS., SLRC.

Acknowledgments

Like Dix's career, the writing of her life has depended on aid from many directions that belies an appearance of independent achievement. I am grateful to all of the people and organizations that have contributed to this book. My wife, Josie, has shared in the burdens of the project from the outset. Although the undertaking at times seemed quixotic, my parents never wavered in their conviction that I should do what I wanted or in their confidence that I would do it well. My sisters and brother similarly offered a sustaining respect that it has been a pleasure to try to deserve, and Mary Beth provided valuable counsel on numerous particulars. Among many helpful friends, Ted Phillips has distinguished himself as a wonderful source of encouragement.

From the beginning of my research, the staff of the Houghton Library at Harvard University helped to make my extended residence in that archive a delight. I benefited from the expert and gracious assistance of too many other repositories to list individually, but I cannot fail to thank the staff of the Massachusetts Historical Society for the friendly attention I received during many visits. At various stages the Mrs. Giles M. Whiting Foundation, the Littleton-Griswold Fund of the American Historical Association, and the Department of History at Harvard University provided support that was welcome financially and as an expression of confidence. The History Department and the Committee on Degrees in History and Literature offered teaching opportunities that enriched my research rather than competed with it, and the tutorial office of the History Department was extremely accommodating in setting aside space for me in Robinson Hall. Walter B. Edgar and Peter Becker kindly facilitated the final revision of the manuscript after I came to the University of South Carolina.

The critical insight demonstrated by the people who read part or all of the manuscript during its preparation was matched only by their goodwill. David Hall, in reading two different versions of the entire work, provided perceptive advice at every stage and pinpointed the thorniest issues. William Gienapp devoted time and careful thought to his multiple readings with the same generosity that he has extended to me in other ways. I was fortunate to be writing at Harvard alongside Michael Vorenberg, Bob Allison, Fred Dalzell, and Jeff Pasley, all of whom helped me to rethink early formulations while providing an unwarranted encouragement that I deeply appreciate. I learned a great deal from a discussion of the project in a colloquium of the History of American Civilization program, one of the many opportunities afforded me by Alan Heimert and his predecessor as chair of the program, Stephan Thernstrom. The participation of Lawrence Buell did much to make that occasion memorable, as did the comments of Lyde Cullen Sizer, who went on to read the entire manuscript and share with me her superb understanding of the women of Dix's era. Aïda DiPace Donald, Elizabeth Suttell, and Donna Bouvier of Harvard University Press were sympathetic readers and expert guides to the editorial process; it has been a pleasure to work with them. For additional sensitive scrutiny of various parts and versions of the manuscript, I am grateful to Mary Elizabeth Brown, Jane Garrett, Leston Havens, Daniel Walker Howe, Louis Masur, and Donald Yacovone. I would also like to thank Bernard Bailyn, who has not read any of this work but whose example has fundamentally shaped my approach to Dix and the study of history.

By far my greatest scholarly debt is to David Herbert Donald. Begun as the last doctoral dissertation prepared under his supervision, this book can have no higher aspiration than to serve as a satisfactory conclusion to the inspiring career as a teacher that he combined with the writing of his own brilliant biographies. Although he nominally retired shortly after I began my research, he devoted to the project the same meticulous attention and legendary editorial judgment that have been acknowledged by other authors for the past fifty years. From the conceptualization of the subject to the practical problems of mechanics, through countless drafts, letters, and meetings, he patiently took time to aid my efforts in any way possible. His unsurpassed devotion to students took many forms other than the direction of graduate work, but this context highlighted the personal depth of his commitment because he made such careful efforts to limit his influence. He prefaced almost every piece of advice with a reminder that I was writing my book, not his, and he reserved opinions with the same wisdom that he demonstrated in offering suggestions. He has accordingly earned a right to absolution for the many flaws that remain in the text, and I cheerfully release him and the other readers from responsibility for what I have written.

Index